The Oryx Holocaust Sourcebook

William R. Fernekes

Oryx Holocaust Series

Oryx Press
Westport, Connecticut • London

The rare Arabian Oryx is believed to have inspired the myth of the unicorn. This desert antelope became virtually extinct in the early 1960s. At that time, several groups of international conservationists arranged to have nine animals sent to the Phoenix Zoo to be the nucleus of a captive breeding herd. Today, the Oryx population is over 1,000, and over 500 have been returned to the Middle East.

Library of Congress Cataloging-in-Publication Data

Fernekes, William R.
    The Oryx Holocaust sourcebook / William R. Fernekes
        p. cm.—(Oryx Holocaust series)
    ISBN 1-57356-295-5 (alk. paper)
    1. Holocaust, Jewish (1939–1945)—Bibliography. 2. Holocaust, Jewish (1939–1945)—Audio-visual aids—Catalogs. 3. Holocaust, Jewish (1939–1945), in literature—Bibliography. 4. Holocaust, Jewish (1939–1945)—Personal narratives—Bibliography. 5. Holocaust, Jewish (1939–1945)—Study and teaching—Bibliography. I. Title. II. Series.
Z6374.H6F
[D804.3]
016.94053'18—dc21   2001058030

British Library Cataloguing in Publication Data is available.

Library of Congress Catalog Card Number: 2001058030
ISBN: 1-57356-295-5

First published in 2002

Oryx Press, 88 Post Road West, Westport, CT 06881
An imprint of Greenwood Publishing Group, Inc.
www.oryxpress.com

Printed in the United States of America

∞™

The paper used in this book complies with the Permanent Paper Standard issued by the National Information Standards Organization (Z39.48–1984).

10 9 8 7 6 5 4 3 2 1

CONTENTS

PREFACE

The Holocaust, also termed the "Shoah," refers to the planned, systematic efforts undertaken by the Nazi government of Germany between 1933 and 1945 to commit genocide against Jews, Sinti/Roma (Gypsies), and the disabled. In the process, Nazi Germany, its allies, and collaborators in Occupied Europe also engaged in murder, expropriation of property and wealth, and acts of terror that led to the destruction of millions of Poles, Soviet prisoners of war, and other civilians in Germany and Occupied Europe.

Few topics in the late twentieth century have engaged such widespread public and scholarly interest and study as the Holocaust. The continuing publication of books, articles, computer software, motion pictures, and online resources, combined with the development of public history museums in North America, Europe, and Israel, has demonstrated the vitality of Holocaust scholarship along with the unflagging public interest in this dark period of human history. This proliferation of materials can be a daunting challenge for the interested layperson, the student, or the scholar who seeks to investigate the topic and locate key resources for study and teaching about the Holocaust. *The Oryx Holocaust Sourcebook* addresses this important challenge by providing guidance in the selection of resources for a broad audience seeking understanding about this complex historical era and its contemporary legacies.

The *Sourcebook*'s seventeen chapters provide a comprehensive selection of high-quality resources in the field of Holocaust studies. Drawn from a wide array of scholarly disciplines ranging across the humanities and social sciences, the items included in each chapter were selected using the following criteria: (1) current availability for use or purchase from publishers; (2) availability in English, unless an item in a language other than English was so significant that its exclusion would hamper inquiry in the field; (3) scholarly legitimacy, meaning it is recognized as a work of authentic scholarship that contributes to advancement of knowledge in the field; (4) relationship to topical categories for study of the Holocaust as noted in the Curriculum Guidelines of the Association of Holocaust Organizations, listed in major bibliographic works, and included as topics in the contents of *Holocaust and Genocide Studies*, the leading journal in the field; and (5) in the case of online resources (Internet sites), adherence to standards of scholarly documentation established by learned societies or recognized and reputable scholarly institutions, as well as the display of accurate and credible content about the Holocaust drawn from reputable scholarship.

The emphasis of this book is primarily on the Holocaust, not on the history of Nazi Germany, although some resource entries focus on the integration of the Holocaust within the structure and practices of the Nazi state. While the selection of materials included in *The Oryx Holocaust Sourcebook* emphasizes those published from 1990 to the present, major works with an earlier publication date have been included. Additionally, a conscious effort was made to avoid placing inordinate emphasis on the life history of Adolf Hitler, a decision that reflects the multicausal emphasis of most current scholarship regarding the Holocaust.

Each chapter begins with a concise overview essay that discusses the content of entries in that chapter, as well as the criteria employed to select resources for inclusion. The individual resource entries contain complete bibliographic information (where available), followed by descriptions of the resource and, in selected chapters, recommendations regarding appropriate user audiences. Listings of vendors and distributors of resources for selected categories of resources are placed at the end of specific chapters, while the Appendix contains a list of general distributors and vendors.

Clearly, the dynamic nature of Holocaust scholarship demands that students and teachers remain current with the outpouring of resources in the field. *The Oryx Holocaust Sourcebook* will serve as a comprehensive entry point for their investigations and spur them to deeper, more intensive study of the complex history and multifaceted legacy of the Holocaust.

ACKNOWLEDGMENTS

The evolution of this book was informed by the contributions of many individuals. Colleagues at Hunterdon Central Regional High School include Jennifer Peck and Mary Elizabeth Azukas, who taught the Holocaust and Human Behavior social studies elective with me; Ken Kuhn, a dedicated German language educator who has many times shared with me his insights on contemporary Germany and the Holocaust's legacy; Harlene Rosenberg and her staff in the Zuegner Memorial Library, as fine an instructional media center as can be found in any high school; and, of course, the students in the Holocaust and Human Behavior classes, who have inspired me for many years in my study of the Holocaust and continue to do so on a daily basis.

I have benefited from the advice and suggestions offered through participation on the USHMM-T Listserve and the H-HOLOCAUS Listserve, two fine examples of online collegiality. Colleagues at the U.S. Holocaust Memorial Museum, particularly William S. Parsons, David Klevan, Warren Marcus, Dawn Marie Warfle, Bret Werb, and Shari Werb, have shared their ideas freely and comprehensively over the years I've worked with them. Dr. William Shulman, Director of the Association of Holocaust Organizations, has been generous with his support and advice during the development of this book, while Dr. Paul Winkler, Executive Director of the New Jersey Commission on Holocaust Education, has been a strong supporter of my work for many years.

Special thanks are reserved for Dr. Samuel Totten of the University of Arkansas, Karin Cooper of Montgomery Township (NJ) Public Schools,

Dr. John Roth of Claremont McKenna College, and Dr. Paul Levine of the University of Uppsala in Sweden, who made important suggestions for inclusion of resources in this volume, and who have been valued colleagues and friends for many years. Similarly, I owe many thanks to Margit Feldman and Sol Urbach, two survivors whose contributions to my understanding of the Holocaust have been exceptional, and whose friendship and support over the years have been essential for my development as an educator in this field.

Finally, and most importantly, my wife, Sheila Fernekes, has been my strongest supporter and soulmate for the many educational projects I've undertaken during the past three decades, and this book is no exception. Her love and devotion are the foundation for all my educational endeavors.

PART I

GENERAL PRINT RESOURCES

1

GENERAL REFERENCE WORKS

OVERVIEW

Studying the Holocaust is a daunting task given the vast scope of available information on this topic. The works included in Chapter 1 are valuable because they provide direction in the design and pursuit of inquiry about the Holocaust and related topics. Atlases offer a variety of historical and geographic information about both Nazi Germany and the Holocaust, often organized and presented thematically. The bibliographies and resource guides include annotated entries and, in some cases, essays that direct the reader to core and supplementary sources in the field. Dictionaries and encyclopedias are ready references with entries designed as concise summaries of people, events, concepts, locations, and related items. The collections of sources and historical articles present essays and facsimile reproductions of documents, introduced by experts who discuss the scope and significance of these volumes' contents for users. In contrast to the anthologies included in Chapter 7, where a more specific topical emphasis is evident, the collections of articles and historical sources in Chapter 1 contain a broad cross-section of print documents and scholarly interpretations of Holocaust history. The enterprising reader who begins a journey through the Holocaust with the materials in this chapter will be well informed and capable of defining the path for research and inquiry with confidence.

ATLASES

Freeman, Michael. *Atlas of Nazi Germany: A Political, Economic and Social Anatomy of the Third Reich.* Second Edition. New York: Longman Publishing, 1995. ISBN 0–582–23924–9. 217 pages. Paperback.

This comprehensive atlas of the Third Reich is organized into seven sections: "Prelude," "Rise of the Nazi Party," "Administrative and Political Structure of the Third Reich," "Society," "Population and Economy," "The Third Reich at War," and "The War Machine." The Holocaust is given a separate chapter in "The War Machine" section, relatively brief in comparison to the content of the other forty-four chapters in the work. Tables, charts, and graphs are employed in addition to maps to display visually the many topics included in the work, and all visual representations are accompanied by lengthy text explanations. The preface to the first edition by British scholar Tim Mason is retained, as well as the author's Introduction, both of which set forth major themes in the work. The goal of the *Atlas* is to set forth in visual images the changes wrought by Nazism in Germany and Occupied Europe, along with the consequences of Nazi policies for diverse nations and groups in both peace and war. A comprehensive list of sources for the book's visual representations is provided, as well as a select bibliography organized topically and coordinated with the text sections. A glossary and detailed index are included.

Gilbert, Martin. *Atlas of the Holocaust.* New York: William Morrow, 1993. ISBN 0–688–12364–3. 282 pages. Paperback.

Containing over 300 maps prepared by the author, this atlas is a standard reference in the field. Beginning with the pre–World War II period, Gilbert includes over twenty maps on the conditions affecting European Jews and their population distribution. The continent-wide scope of the *Atlas* is a major asset, as is the broad range of Nazi camps included, encompassing both slave labor and death camps. Resistance also receives special emphasis, with over 200 resistance acts displayed on a variety of maps. Liberation of survivors by Allied forces and postwar refugee movements also are visually represented. Each map is accompanied by a thorough text description. A comprehensive bibliography of sources used to inform map contents is provided, as well as an index of camps located in the *Atlas*'s many maps. Selected photos are integrated within the *Atlas* to supplement map content.

United States Holocaust Memorial Museum. *Historical Atlas of the Holocaust.* New York: Macmillan, 1996. ISBN 0–02–897451–4. 252 pages. Hardcover.

This atlas contains 222 newly designed maps, a glossary, bibliography, and gazetteer. Following a brief overview history of the Holocaust, the volume is divided by the Holocaust in European regions (Eastern Europe, Western Europe, Central Europe, and Southern Europe) and topics about the Holocaust (Europe

Before the War, Nazi Extermination Camps, Rescue and Jewish Armed Resistance, Death Marches and Liberation, and Postwar Europe, 1945–1950). Explanatory text accompanies each map, with broader scale maps of countries and European regions combined with micro views of cities, camps, and sections of countries. All maps are multicolored, with well-designed keys that make the maps easily decipherable. The book includes a European-wide reference map of European Regions and Administrative Units, which assists in understanding how Nazi Germany and its allies sought to reconfigure European boundaries during World War II. In comparison to Martin Gilbert's revised *Atlas of the Holocaust*, this atlas places less emphasis on the historical development of Jewish culture in Europe, but is more detailed and comprehensive in its portrayal of the Holocaust as a continent-wide phenomenon, reflecting the benefits of scholarship in newly opened archives in the former Soviet Union and Eastern Europe. An enhanced version of this book is available as an interactive CD-ROM with a teacher's guide in Windows format. See Chapter 10 for a discussion of the CD-ROM version of this valuable atlas. A gazetteer is included as a finding aid for locations and topics included in the work.

BIBLIOGRAPHIES

Bloomberg, Marty, and Buckley Barry Barrett. *The Jewish Holocaust: An Annotated Guide to Books in English*. San Bernardino: The Borgo Press, 1995. ISBN 0–8095–1406–0. 312 pages. Paperback.

This very extensive bibliographic work includes ten chapters with paragraph-length entries on books deemed critical to the development of a comprehensive Holocaust collection for libraries. Each entry contains a bibliographic citation (no ISBN, however) as well as a brief annotation that provides a content description, a recommendation for primary users, and a capsule evaluation of the work's overall merit. The book's content addresses both reference materials and specific content themes on the Holocaust, such as European Anti-Semitism, The Holocaust Years, Jewish Resistance, Concentration and Death Camps, War Crimes Trials, and Art and Literature. Teaching resources receive minimal attention, as do works for juveniles and young adults. The book concludes with a helpful list of core title recommendations for university and college libraries, public libraries, and high school libraries, along with a detailed index of authors and titles.

Sable, Martin H. *Holocaust Studies: A Directory and Bibliography of Bibliographies*. Greenwood, FL: Penkevill Publishing Co., 1987. ISBN 0–913283–20–7. 115 pages. Hardcover.

This compilation of bibliographies is combined with a directory of associations, institutions, organizations for research/study centers, museums, memorials, and educational programs to provide the reader with a starting point for inquiries about the Holocaust. The bibliographies are listed by their language of publication: English, Hebrew, European (continental), multilingual, and Yiddish. Addresses are provided but phone and fax numbers are omitted. Two indexes are included: an author index for the bibliography chapters and a geographic index for all other chapters.

The Vidal Sassoon International Center for the Study of Antisemitism at the Hebrew University of Jerusalem, http://sicsa.huji.ac.il.

This Web site contains a searchable, online bibliographic database of over 30,000 entries regarding anti-Semitism. The on-line version is divided into two major sections: the Annotated Bibliography, which includes publications from 1984 to the present; and the Retrospective Bibliography, which comprises books and articles published between 1965 and 1983. Each component of this bibliographic database, which is regularly updated with new material, is divided into three subsections: bibliographies and reference works, anti-Semitism through the ages, and anti-Semitism in literature and in the arts. Also available on the Web site is a separate bibliography, "The 'Jewish Question' in German Speaking Countries, 1848–1914." This is a separate bibliographic database that can also be examined online. Book versions also are available from KG Saur Ortlerstrasse 8 D-81373, Munchen, Germany, and complete publication information is provided on the Sassoon Center Web site. For specific inquiries about the publications by KG Saur, their Web site address is http://www.saur.de. Inquiries about the Center can be directed to the Vidal Sassoon International Center for the Study of Antisemitism, The Hebrew University of Jerusalem, Mount Scopus, 91905 Jerusalem, Israel. Phone: 972-2-5882492.

For additional bibliographies, please consult the "Resource Guides" section of Chapter 1, as well as the topical bibliographies in Chapters 4, 5, and 8. Additionally, the works listed under "Publications on Holocaust Study and Teaching" in Chapter 16 contain extensive lists of recommended works for study of the Holocaust.

CHRONOLOGIES AND DICTIONARIES

Comay, Joan. *Who's Who in Jewish History after the Period of the Old Testament.* Revised edition by Lavinia Cohn-Sherbok. London: Routledge, 1995. ISBN 0–19–521079–4. 407 pages. Paperback.

This broad-based biographical reference work includes over 1,000 entries concerning twenty centuries of Jewish history, from the period of the Old Testament to the present. The entries vary in length, and include both Jews and non-Jews depending upon the significance of their influence on Jewish life. Regarding the Holocaust, entries are provided on Adolf Hitler and many Jewish leaders of the period 1933–1945, such as Leo Baeck, Janusz Korczak, and others. The Holocaust is viewed as one tragic period within the long span of Jewish history, rather than as the major emphasis of the work. A chronology beginning in 134 B.C. and continuing to the early 1990s is provided, divided into geographic categories and linking names of key biographical entries to major events and eras in Jewish history. A detailed glossary and selected maps are provided as well, along with a thematic index.

Edelheit, Abraham J., and Hershel Edelheit. *History of the Holocaust: A Handbook and Dictionary.* Boulder, CO: Westview Press, 1994. ISBN 0–8133–2240–5. 524 pages. Paperback.

The authors have created a dual purpose book. Part I is a history of the Holocaust, thematically organized but following a general chronological sequence from sections entitled "Antecedents" of the Holocaust to "Aftermath and Recovery." Separate chapters on "Jewish Responses to Persecution," "Jewish-Gentile Relations," and "International Responses" are emblematic of the authors' broad scope of content. Photographs and illustrations are liberally used to complement the text narrative. Part II is a "Dictionary of Holocaust Terms," again employing not only photos but many tables and graphic aids to highlight key issues in the dictionary entries. A very comprehensive bibliography of books, archives, press/periodicals, journal articles, and anthologies is provided. Name, place, and subject indexes conclude the book.

Epstein, Eric J., and Philip Rosen. *Dictionary of the Holocaust: Biography, Geography and Terminology.* Foreword by Henry R. Huttenbach. Westport, CT: Greenwood Press, 1997. ISBN 0–313–30355–X. 440 pages. Hardcover.

This comprehensive dictionary includes entries about countries, cities, people, terms, significant events, and key statistical data on the Holocaust. Biographical entries discuss the historical background of the individuals and examine their importance within the historical context of the Holocaust. Geographic entries include ample statistical information about the prewar Jewish population and the impact of the Holocaust on Jewish life. Terminology is drawn not only from English, German, and Yiddish, but from French, Polish, and a dozen other languages. In contrast to other dictionaries on the same topic, the 2,000 entries in this volume reflect recent trends in Holocaust historiography which place greater emphasis on the broad participation of many German social institutions in the Holocaust, such as industrialists, the medical community, and the German military. The work also includes entries on postwar trials and the impact of the Holocaust on other victim groups, such as Sinti and Roma (Gypsies) and the disabled. The work contains an extensive bibliography to encourage further study of Holocaust content and it concludes with a detailed index.

Michael, Robert A. *The Holocaust: A Chronology and Documentary.* Northvale, NJ: Jason Aronson Inc., 1998. ISBN 0–7657–5984–5. 341 pages. Hardcover.

Robert Michael's book presents the Holocaust as a chronology of events and historical trends from 1933 to 1946. The presentation of events in chronological order includes entries on specific dates, beginning with January 30, 1933 (Hitler's assumption of the chancellorship in Germany) and concluding with July 4, 1946 (the date of the Kielce pogrom against Jews in postwar Poland). Descriptions of specific events are mixed with excerpts from a wide range of documentary sources, also referenced by specific dates in the chronology. Included among the documentary sources are eyewitness accounts, testimony from postwar trials, excerpts from government documents, excerpts from diaries and memoirs, newspaper headlines, and many others. Entries vary in length according to the topic's scope, and selected entries address a span of time when a series or pattern of events occurred, such as spring through summer 1944 (BBC broadcasts to the Hungarian government warning them not to deport Jews). The work includes a preface, which explains the organizational structure of the book, and a brief introduction, where key historical themes about the Holocaust are concisely presented in narrative form. The work also contains a list of references and detailed index. For teachers and students, this book is a useful work to place events and trends about Holocaust history within a chronological perspective that is easily accessible.

Taylor, James, and Warren Shaw. *Dictionary of the Third Reich.* New York: Penguin Putnam Inc., 1997. ISBN 0–140–51389–2. 341 pages. Paperback.

This concise dictionary offers readers a useful reference tool for study of the emergency of Nazism and Germany's role in World War II. A detailed chronology of the years 1933–1945 is presented initially, followed by alphabetical entries, many of which are cross-referenced to related entries in the work. Six appendices are included, all of them chronologies of specific military campaigns initiated by the Third Reich or the Allies during World War II. A brief listing of quotations concerning Nazism, organized by chronological periods (1923–1928; 1929–1932; 1937–1939; 1940–1945) is provided, along with a selected list of works for further reading. No index.

Wistrich, Robert S. *Who's Who in Nazi Germany.* London: Routledge, 1995. ISBN 0–415–11888–3. 296 pages. Paperback.

Organized alphabetically as a reference work, Wistrich's book includes detailed biographical entries on both well-known and lesser-known figures during the period 1933–1945 in Germany. The major figures of the Nazi regime are included, as well as both advocates and opponents of Nazism. The scope of the volume is broad, encompassing key figures from the fields of politics, science, business, entertainment and the arts, intellectual life, the military, and many others. Each entry includes the biographee's name and date of birth, or dates of birth and death. The book includes a detailed glossary, a table of comparative military ranks

(German Army, SS, British Army, and U.S. Army), and an extensive bibliography. Indexed.

ENCYCLOPEDIAS

Benz, Wolfgang, and Walter H. Pehle, editors. *Encyclopedia of German Resistance to the Nazi Movement.* New York: Continuum Publishing, 1997. ISBN 0–8264–0945–8. 354 pages. Hardcover.

This very significant book combines authoritative essays on various aspects of German resistance to Nazism with a series of encyclopedia entries and brief biographical sketches of key individuals involved in resistance to Nazism. The essays address often-neglected topics in the field, such as the role of exiles and women in the resistance movement, as well as resistance efforts by persecuted groups in Germany. A separate section of the book lists key subjects with cross-references to essay and encyclopedia entries. Lists of abbreviations used in the text and of contributors are provided. No index.

Charny, Israel W., editor-in-chief. *Encyclopedia of Genocide.* Forewords by Archbishop Desmond M. Tutu and Simon Wiesenthal. Volumes 1 and 2. Santa Barbara: ABC-CLIO Press, 1999. ISBN 0–87436–928–2. 718 pages. Hardcover.

This landmark two-volume work contains entries ranging across the entire field of genocide studies. Compiled by an international team of editors, the *Encyclopedia*'s contents include traditional encyclopedia summaries in core fields and topics; feature entries about basic conceptual issues in the field; features that present material in a journalistic style to supplement the traditional encyclopedia entries; and critical source documents on specific issues and topics. The Holocaust receives the greatest amount of attention, given its centrality in the study of genocides during the twentieth century and its role as a transformative event in the history of Western societies. All entries provide suggested references for further study and many are cross-referenced to other entries in the work. An extensive permissions and credits section is included, organized by author's name. The comprehensive index incorporates subtopic categories for authors (Entries, Features) to identify the specific locations of their contributions to the work.

Gutman, Israel, editor-in-chief. *Encyclopedia of the Holocaust.* Foreword by Elie Wiesel. 4-volume set. New York: Macmillan, 1990. ISBN 0–02–896090–4. 2-volume edition published in 1995. ISBN 0–02–864528–6 (Volume 1 of 2). ISBN 0–02–864529–4 (Volume 2 of 2). 1,905 pages. Hardcover.

This is the standard encyclopedia reference work on the Holocaust, prepared and edited by a distinguished team of scholars under the leadership of Israel Gutman.

The entries, while authoritative and comprehensive, are written in a style accessible to a general audience. Each topical entry includes bibliographic references considered to be central works by the contributing author, and all entries are cross-referenced to related topics in the four-volume set. Maps, graphics, and photos are used extensively to complement the narrative text, and four appendices are included: major Jewish organizations in Germany 1893–1943; structure of the Einsatzgruppen from June 22, 1941; trials of war criminals (Nuremberg Trials and British Trials); and estimated Jewish losses in the Holocaust. Although the work has not been revised substantially since its initial publication, it remains the central reference work in the field for general users and an excellent starting point for research by students and specialists. Indexed.

Laqueur, Walter, editor. Judith Tydor Baumel, associate editor. *The Holocaust Encyclopedia*. New Haven: Yale University Press, 2001. ISBN 0–300–08432–3. 765 pages. Hardcover.

Reflecting the fruits of recent scholarship, this one-volume encyclopedia of the Holocaust begins with an essay by Walter Laqueur that addresses issues of terminology (Shoah vs. Holocaust), the expansion of data and sources on the topic, and ongoing debates regarding interpretation of the Holocaust in the post–World War II era. In particular, Laqueur emphasizes the need for empathy and imagination in studying the topic as we move further away from its place in historical time. Organized alphabetically, the work contains an extensive chronology beginning in January 1933 and concluding in May 1945. All entries are cross-referenced to other articles in the text, and the encyclopedia incorporates 276 photographs and nineteen maps to supplement the detailed articles. The editors have assembled a distinguished set of contributors whose work reflects the most recent scholarship in the field, drawing upon recently opened archives in the former Soviet Union and Eastern European countries, and the expansion of survivor memoirs, film, and electronic resources. An excellent bibliographic essay by Robert Rozett is included, which offers direction for more in-depth research on many topics included in the encyclopedia. Indexed.

Roth, Cecil, and Geoffrey Wigoder, editors. *Encyclopedia Judaica*. Jerusalem: Keter, 1972–1991. ISBN 0–685–36253–1. Sixteen-volume set.

This is a definitive work about Jewish culture, history, and society in sixteen volumes. Volume 1 provides information on the development of the work, as well as a comprehensive index to the remaining fifteen volumes. Thousands of articles on numerous aspects of Jewish life are provided, with special emphasis on the Hebrew scriptures. Articles on the Holocaust figure prominently within the *Encyclopedia Judaica*, ranging from an historical overview on how the Holocaust affected Jews in specific European countries, to issues of protest and resistance, and the aftermath of the Holocaust, among others. Content on the Holocaust is integrated within many articles of the *Encyclopedia Judaica*, based upon related subject entries within the text (individuals, geographic locations, historical events, and others). The comprehensive index in Volume 1 provides a very useful entry point for locating the many articles with Holocaust content in the remaining fifteen volumes of this comprehensive work. An updated CD-ROM version of the *Encyclopedia Judaica* was released in 1997 and is included within Chapter Ten of this resource book.

Rozett, Robert, and Shmuel Spector, editors. *Encyclopedia of the Holocaust*. New York: Facts on File, 2000. ISBN 0–8160–4333–7. 528 pages. Hardcover.

This one-volume encyclopedia contains eight thematic essays that examine major issues about the Holocaust, ranging across topics as diverse as "Nazi Ideology and Its Roots," "The Destruction of the Jews," "On Being a Jew in the Holocaust," and "The Aftermath of the Holocaust and Its Influence on Present-Day Society," among others. More than 650 alphabetically organized entries follow these introductory essays, including people, places, events, organizations, significant historical topics, and dimensions of the Holocaust's legacy for contemporary society, such as museums and memorials. Integrated within the text are over 300 photographs from the Yad Vashem archives. A chronology, extensive bibliography, and comprehensive index are included.

Snyder, Louis L. *Encyclopedia of the Third Reich*. New York: McGraw-Hill, Inc., 1976. Reprint edition by Marlowe & Company. ISBN 1–56924–917–2. 410 pages. Paperback.

This classic work by the distinguished European historian Louis Snyder first appeared in 1976, and is written for a general audience. Beginning with a comprehensive chronology of the Nazi era, the work contains detailed entries that are thoroughly cross-referenced to other entries in the text. Combining standard encyclopedia entries with extended essays on topics such as art, architecture, theater, music, and education in the Third Reich, this is a critical reference work for the beginning or experienced student of Nazi Germany. A very comprehensive bibliography of articles and books is included, although no works after 1976 are incorporated into this reprint edition. Over 200 photos and drawings are interspersed to illustrate topical entries. No index.

Zentner, Christian, and Friedmann Bedurftig. *Encyclopedia of the Third Reich*. Translated by Amy Hackett. ISBN 0–306–80793–9. New York: Da Capo, 1991. Reprint of original edition. 1,150 pages. Paperback.

In more than 3,000 entries, this comprehensive encyclopedia contains entries by thirty-six of Germany's leading historians on the history of the Third Reich. Including more than 1,200 photographs, posters, and drawings, the *Encyclopedia of the Third Reich* addresses a broad scope of topics about life in Nazi Germany:

sports, politics, culture, religion, education, ideology, and military affairs. In addition to standard encyclopedia entries, selected major articles and overview essays are incorporated in the *Encyclopedia* on topics ranging from concentration camps to women in the Third Reich. More comprehensive than Louis Snyder's earlier work, this book is a standard reference source on Germany during the Nazi period. A comprehensive bibliography is included along with a detailed Index.

RESOURCE GUIDES

Charny, Israel, editor. *Genocide: A Critical Bibliographic Review.* Volume 1. New York: Facts on File, 1991. ISBN 0–7201–1876–X. 273 pages. Hardcover.

This first volume of the three-volume series contains thirteen topical essays by leading scholars in the field of genocide studies, with each essay accompanied by detailed annotated bibliographies. Following two introductory essays by Israel Charny concerning the study of genocide and efforts to intervene and prevent genocide, specific essays are devoted to the history and sociology of genocide, psychological and philosophical issues concerning genocide, the Holocaust, the genocide of the Armenians in the Ottoman Empire, the forced famine in the Ukraine under Soviet rule, and the Cambodian genocide of the 1970s. Three essays by Sam Totten of the University of Arkansas address the literature, art, and film of the Holocaust, genocide, and nuclear and other futuristic forms of destruction. Indexed.

———, editor. *Genocide: A Critical Bibliographic Review.* Volume 2. With a foreword by Leo Kuper. New York: Facts on File, 1991. ISBN 0–8160–2642–4. 432 pages. Hardcover.

The second of three volumes in the series, this volume contains detailed essays about topics with accompanying annotated bibliographies. Of the fifteen essays in this volume, those specifically about the Holocaust include Erich Kulka on "Denial of the Holocaust," Jan Darsa on "Educating about the Holocaust: A Case Study in the Teaching of Genocide," Samuel Totten on "Educating about Genocide: Curricula and Inservice Training," Sybil Milton on "The Memorialization of the Holocaust: Museums, Memorials and Centers," and Pearl M. Oliner and Samuel P. Oliner on "Righteous People in the Holocaust." Indexed.

———. *The Widening Circle of Genocide. Genocide: A Critical Bibliographic Review,* Volume 3. Foreword by Irving Louis Horowitz. New Brunswick: Transaction Publishers, 1994. ISBN 1–56000–172–0. 375 pages. Hardcover.

The third and final volume in this series is organized thematically, with sections on "Democracy and the Prevention of Genocide," "Religion and Genocide," "Compelling Confirmations of the Armenian Genocide in German and Austrian Sources," "Case Histories" (including the genocide of the Gypsies in the Holocaust), "The Widening Circle of Destruction and Trauma," and "Professional Study of Genocide and its Prevention." Similar to the other volumes in the series, the essays by scholars are accompanied by detailed annotated bibliographies of resources on their topics. Indexed.

Feldman, George. *Understanding the Holocaust: Volumes 1 and 2*. Detroit: UXL, 1998. ISBN 0–7876–174–07. 408 pages. Hardcover.

This two-volume set provides an historical overview of the Holocaust ranging across fourteen topical chapters. Volume 1 begins with the prewar period in Germany, and continues through Chapter 7, which discusses the beginning of mass murder during the invasion of the Soviet Union. Volume 2 includes chapters on the death camps, Auschwitz, case studies of life in Occupied Europe focusing on Denmark, the Netherlands, and France, relationships between Germany's allies (Italy and Hungary) and the Jews, and two concluding chapters entitled "Judgments" and "Remembering the Holocaust" focusing on efforts to hold perpetrators responsible for their crimes and issues of memory and legacy, respectively. Each volume in the two-volume set contains recommendations for further study and credits for the photos included within the text. A cumulative subject index is included in each volume.

Fischel, J.R. *The Holocaust*. Westport, CT: Greenwood Press, 1998. ISBN 0–313–29879–3. 196 pages. Hardcover.

As one volume in the Greenwood Guides to Historic Events of the Twentieth Century, this book offers a starting point for in-depth research by students of the Holocaust. "The Holocaust Explained" is a concise five-section history of the Holocaust, which includes a brief photo essay. The chapter "Conclusion" discusses the legacy of the Holocaust, including the development of efforts to bring war criminals to justice at Nuremberg and in later trials. The author includes a series of brief biographies of major participants, selected primary documents, a glossary of selected terms, and two appendixes (number of victims killed in concentration and extermination camps and estimated Jewish losses in the Holocaust). An annotated bibliography is provided. Indexed.

Friedman, Saul S. *Holocaust Literature: A Handbook of Critical, Historical, and Literary Writings*. Foreword by Dennis Klein. Westport, CT: Greenwood Press, 1993. ISBN 03–132622–17. Hardcover.

Divided into three major sections, this comprehensive guide to Holocaust study contains thirty-two chapters by a wide range of contributors, detailed author/title and subject indexes, and brief contributor biographies. Part I, "Conceptual Approaches to the Holocaust," focuses on the major historical and social science themes in Holocaust studies, such as the Nazi camp system, the rise of Nazism in Germany, pre-war Jewish philosophy and life, the role of the Church during the Holocaust, righteous Gentiles, Jewish women in the Holocaust, and the relationship between genocide studies and Holocaust studies. Part II, "Holocaust Area Studies," includes thirteen chapters on how the Holocaust was experienced by specific countries and regions, including the United States, countries in Occupied Europe, Allied countries such as Great Britain, and neutral states such as Switzerland and Spain. The final component of the book deals with "The Holocaust in Education and the Arts," and includes essays on poetry, fiction, music, art, museums and memorials, film, first-person accounts, and school textbooks, concluding with a chapter on "Resources for Holocaust Study" by editor Saul Friedman. Each chapter includes a select bibliography for further study.

Marrus, Michael R. *The Holocaust in History*. New York: Penguin, 1987. ISBN 0–452–00953–7. 267 pages. Paperback.

This historiographical review of Holocaust historical literature is the most comprehensive one available, although its publication date excludes literature published from 1986 to 2000. Providing an analytical discussion of nine topics following a brief introduction, Marrus ranges widely across the available literature in English, as well as selected sources in German. The major debates in Holocaust historiography are addressed: the uniqueness and universality of the Holocaust (Chapter 2, "The Holocaust in Perspective"), intentionalists versus functionalists (Chapter 3, "The Final Solution"), Jewish ghetto and camp life, particularly the role of the Judenrat (Chapter 6, "The Victims"), the extent of Jewish resistance (Chapter 7, "Jewish Resistance"), the role(s) of other world societies in responding to the Holocaust (Chapter 8, "Bystanders"), and the role of the Catholic Church during the Holocaust (Chapter 8, "Bystanders"). The organization of the volume gives credence to changing emphases in Holocaust historiography, such as the inclusion of a chapter on Jewish resistance, which has become more prominent as a subtopic of research and scholarship since the early-mid 1970s. The volume gives little attention to literature on the postwar trials of Nazi war criminals, nor does it include effective maps coordinated with chapter topics. Additionally, there is little evidence analysis of Holocaust historiography dealing with museums, monuments and other forms of Holocaust representation that have historical dimensions or portray Holocaust history in different contexts (i.e., film, art, and historical fiction). Indexed.

Niewyk, Donald, and Francis Nicosia. *The Columbia Guide to the Holocaust*. New York: Columbia University Press, 2000. ISBN 0–231–11200–0. 473 pages. Hardcover.

This five-part resource guide combines a general history of the Holocaust with detailed examination of eight major issues in the interpretation of the Holocaust, ranging from issues of definition to the behavior of perpetrators, bystanders, victims, and rescuers, along with the lasting impact of the Holocaust on contemporary life. The remaining three sections encompass a chronology of events, a selective encyclopedia that addresses more than 200 people, places, terms, and organizations, and a detailed resource listing that includes not only printed reference works, primary and secondary sources and films, but electronic resources and major Holocaust organizations, museums, and memorials. Two appendixes provide statistical tables and maps, while the work concludes with a detailed index. Throughout the work, cross-references are provided to related articles and entries.

Schmittroth, Linda, and Mary Kay Rosteck. *People of the Holocaust.* Two volumes: A-J and K-Z. Detroit: UXL, 1998. ISBN 0–7876–1743–1. 508 pages. Hardcover.

This two-volume set complements the publisher's title *Understanding the Holocaust* by presenting biographies of sixty individuals (men and women) who were participants in or influenced by the Holocaust. Text and photos are integrated in each biographical chapter, and each volume is organized alphabetically (Volume 1 includes A–J biographies, while Volume 2 includes K–Z biographies). A timeline, list of words to know, photo credits, and a reader's guide are included in each volume, along with biographies that include perpetrators, victims, rescuers, members of the resistance, major world figures of the period 1933–1945, and others. Each volume contains a cumulative subject index.

COLLECTIONS OF SOURCES AND HISTORICAL ARTICLES

Friedlander, Henry, and Sybil Milton, general editors. *Archives of the Holocaust: An International Collection of Selected Documents.* New York: Garland Publishing, Inc., 1995. 22 volumes. ISBN 0–8240–5492–X. Hardcover.

Drawing upon documents from North America, Israel, and Europe, this twenty-two volume series presents facsimiles of Holocaust sources drawn from a range of archives located in Europe, Israel, and the United States. Some of the major archives represented in the series are those of nongovernmental organizations (American Joint Distribution Committee, American Friends Service Committee), government (Bundesarchiv of the Federal Republic of Germany, Koblenz and Frieburg, Israel State Archives, and National Archives of Canada), private organizations (American Jewish Archives), and educational institutions (Columbia University Library and Robert F. Wagner Labor Archives of New York University), among others. The series introduction establishes the content scope and organizational framework for the series, while each volume in the series contains its own introduction to its specific contents. In each volume, a glossary of key people, organizations, and persons encountered is provided. Sources are presented as facsimiles of the originals without accompanying editorial commentary. No index.

Marrus, Michael, editor. *The Nazi Holocaust: Historical Articles on the Destruction of European Jews.* Westport, CT: Meckler, 1989. Series ISBN 0–88736–266–4. Hardcover.

In a series of fifteen volumes organized under nine distinct themes in the historical literature of the Holocaust, Michael Marrus has assembled major articles on a wide-ranging set of topics. "Perspectives on the Holocaust" gives overview essays on major historiographical debates, followed in order by these thematically organized volumes: origins of the Holocaust, the "Final Solution" within and outside of Germany, public opinion and relations to the Jews in Occupied Europe, the victims of the Holocaust, Jewish resistance, bystanders, and the end of the Holocaust. Each volume contains an introduction by the editor, which discusses major ideas encompassed in the volume's contents. A cumulative index of authors and titles is included in each volume.

Mendelson, John, editor. *The Holocaust: Selected Documents in Eighteen Volumes.* New York: Garland Publishing, Inc., 1982. 18 volumes. ISBN 0–8240–4875–X. Hardcover.

In a topically organized series of eighteen volumes, editor John Mendelson collected major documents on the Holocaust from German sources and from the U.S. State Department along with records from the Nuremberg Trial prosecutions, other U.S. agencies, and the National Archives. The opening volume contains an introduction to the series, and a list of all eighteen volumes and their contents. Documents are presented as facsimiles of the originals, without editorial commentary. Each volume in the series includes a concise introduction by the editor. The series begins with two volumes on "Legalizing the Holocaust" in Germany, continuing through efforts at Jewish emigration, aryanization, the implementation of deportations and mass killing programs, efforts to secure relief and rescue of targeted victim groups, and the prosecution of war criminals in postwar trials. No index.

Wyman, David S., editor. *America and the Holocaust: A Thirteen Volume Set Documenting the Editor's Book* The Abandonment of the Jews. New York: Garland Publishing, Inc., 1990. (ISBNs vary with each volume.) 13 volumes. Hardcover.

This thirteen-volume set provides facsimile reproductions of documents regarding the U.S. response to the Holocaust, correlated with the content themes of the editor's book *The Abandonment of the Jews.* A brief introduction introduces each volume, which discusses key aspects of the contents and outlines major themes evident in the sources. Topics encompassed in the series include U.S. immigration policies concerning Jewish refugees, efforts to develop strategies for rescue (War Refugee Board), the 1943 Bermuda Conference, the controversy concerning the bombing of Auschwitz, and assessing responsibility for U.S. policies and their impact during the Holocaust. No index.

2

NARRATIVE HISTORIES

OVERVIEW

A wide variety of interpretive perspectives is reflected in this chapter, demonstrating the vitality of scholarship about the history of the Holocaust. Examples range from Lucy Dawidowicz' strong intentionalist position, which argues that the "final solution" of the Jewish question was defined early by Adolf Hitler with little deviation during the Nazi regime, to functionalist works such as that by Karl Schluenes, which view the Holocaust as following a "twisted roal" that resulted more from trial and error and structural causes than the long-term goals of Hitler and the Nazi leadership. The scholarly one-volume histories discussed in this chapter are rewarding not only for their concise presentations of a very complex topic, but also for their excellent bibliographies, which point the reader to many other important works for further investigation. The section of narrative histories of Nazi Germany places the study of the Holocaust within the broader outlines of German history, offering a valuable perspective on the central role the Holocaust played in the operations of the Nazi state. Also included within this chapter are selected central historical studies about the Holocaust that are cited repeatedly as major sources by the authors of narrative histories of the Holocaust. Among these are Raul Hilberg's *The Destruction of the European Jews* and Leon Poliakov's *Harvest of Hate: The Nazi Program for the Destruction of the Jews of Europe*. Because the history of anti-Semitism is central to an understanding of the emergence of the Holocaust, selected major works on that topic are included.

NARRATIVE HISTORIES OF ANTI-SEMITISM

Poliakov, Leon. *The History of Anti-Semitism. Volume I: From the Time of Christ to the Court Jews*. Translated from the French by Richard Howard. New York: The Vanguard Press, 1965. No ISBN. 340 pages. Hardcover.

————. *The History of Anti-Semitism. Volume II: From Mohammed to the Marranos*. Translated from the French by Natalie Gerardi. New York: The Vanguard Press, 1973. ISBN 0–8149–0701–6. 399 pages. Hardcover.

————. *The History of Anti-Semitism. Volume III: From Voltaire to Wagner*. New York: The Vanguard Press, 1975. ISBN 0–8149–0762–8. 582 pages. Hardcover.

————. *The History of Anti-Semitism. Volume IV: Suicidal Europe, 1870–1933*. New York: Oxford University Press, 1985. ISBN 0–8149–0872–1. 528 pages. Hardcover.

These four works comprise a standard, comprehensive study of the history of anti-Semitism, beginning in the ancient world and continuing to the emergence of the Third Reich in 1933. Poliakov draws upon philosophy, religion, psychology, history, anthropology, and other fields to paint a detailed picture of how the Jews, particularly after their dispersion by the Romans following the destruction of the temple in Jerusalem, suffered as outcasts in Christian societies, while being tolerated but still functioning as second-class citizens in societies dominated by Islam. Throughout the four-volume work, the author discusses the relationship between persecution of Jews by the majority, and how such persecution contributed to the definition of Jewish identity in various historical eras. Each volume begins with an essay that defines the key themes that contributed to Poliakov's interpretation for that historical period. All four volumes contain extensive notes and are thoroughly indexed.

Wistrich, Robert. *Antisemitism: The Longest Hatred*. New York: Schocken Books, 1994. ISBN 0–8052–1014–8. 341 pages. Paperback.

Robert Wistrich's one-volume history explores the historical origins of anti-Semitism, and then traces its emergence primarily within Christian societies as the foundation of Jewish persecution. Wistrich's narrative continues by placing emphasis in the nineteenth century on the development of racial anti-Semitism, which was heavily influenced by Darwinian biology and its application as a bulwark of racist ideology in Europe and the Americas. The work views anti-Semitism as fundamental regarding the origins of the Holocaust, and discusses patterns of anti-Semitism after World War II in Europe and the Middle East. The book contains an extensive bibliography and a detailed index.

NARRATIVE HISTORIES OF THE HOLOCAUST

Bauer, Yehuda. *A History of the Holocaust.* New York: Franklin Watts, 1982. ISBN 0–531–09862–1. 398 pages. Paperback.

Centrally locating the study of the Holocaust within the long history of the Jewish people, Bauer emphasizes the role(s) of Jews in defining a place for themselves following the Diaspora in predominantly Christian societies where anti-Semitic hostility toward them was the rule, rather than the exception. Bauer examines the relationship of Jewish communities in Europe to historical developments during the nineteenth century (Chapter 2, "Liberalism, Emancipation, and Antisemitism"), in the early twentieth century (Chapter 3, "World War I and Its Aftermath"), and throughout the period of Nazi rule in Germany and Occupied Europe (Chapter 6, "German Jewry in the Prewar Era, 1933–1938"; Chapters 7 and 8, "Poland—The Siege Begins" and "Life in the Ghettoes"; and Chapter 10, "West European Jewry, 1940–44"). Bauer places much greater emphasis on Jewish resistance and rescue attempts concerning Jews during the Holocaust than do many other Holocaust historians, devoting separate chapters to each of these topics, and including in his final chapter ("The Last Years of the Holocaust, 1943–45") a discussion of rescue negotiations for Jews in Eastern Europe not yet decimated by the "final solution." Weaknesses of Bauer's interpretation are his virtual exclusion of any other victims of the Holocaust (for example, Gypsies are mentioned only twice, the handicapped only in relation to Christian protests against euthanasia in Germany, and homosexuals not at all); his downplaying of the origins of Nazi genocide in the T-4 euthanasia program; and his selective discussion of resistance in Western Europe to the Holocaust, where he addresses the Danish rescue of Jews but ignores Italian rescue efforts. Clearly at odds with Hilberg's interpretation of Jewish resistance, Bauer emphasizes the complexity of decision making in the Judenrat, analyzing four separate Jewish Councils (Lodz, Vilna, Warsaw, and Minsk) and suggesting that the Judenrat was not the compliant extension of Nazi policy presented by Hilberg and Hannah Arendt. Indexed.

Benz, Wolfgang. *The Holocaust: A German Historian Examines the Genocide.* New York: Columbia University Press, 1999. ISBN 0–231–11214–9. 186 pages. Hardcover.

Translated from the German, this slim volume is a concise introduction to the Holocaust that presents the chronological development of Nazi anti-Jewish policies from 1933 to 1945. Beginning with a brief chapter describing the Wannsee Villa conference in 1942, the author uses this administrative meeting as his point of departure and then interprets the steps that had led to the Wannsee Conference, where the planned annihilation of 11,000,000 people had been discussed over lunch. Benz then describes the patterns of persecution faced by Jews in Germany, their exclusion from the mainstream of German society, and patterns of German Jewish emigration in response to Nazi policies. The processes of ghettoization, aryanization, deportation of German Jews, and massacres in the East flank the most critical chapter in the book, "From Antisemitism to Genocide." In this chapter, Benz interprets the consistency of Nazi claims that Jews were the historic enemy of the German people in the context of the radicalization of German anti-Jewish policy after 1938, when he asserts that the idea of a "comprehensive solution" became a central feature of Nazi policy and planning. Drawing upon evidence concerning the Madagascar plan, which was seriously considered as an option for removing the entire Jewish population of Europe to a remote location for their eventual destruction, Benz sees the blueprint for genocide already in place prior to the June 1941 invasion of the USSR. What remained was simply the possibility of carrying it out, which after the Madagascar plan was no longer deemed feasible, and which became a project that could be realized in Eastern Europe itself. The remainder of the book includes chapters on Theresienstadt, industrialized mass murder in the extermination camps, and the genocide of the Sinti and Roma. A select bibliography is provided for further study. Indexed.

Berenbaum, Michael. *The World Must Know*. Boston: Little, Brown & Company, 1993. ISBN 0–316–09134–0. 240 pages. Paperback.

This illustrated narrative history of the Holocaust is organized to parallel the presentation of the permanent exhibit at the U.S. Holocaust Memorial Museum. The great strengths of the work are its clear and concise narrative and the many photographs and graphics that are integrated throughout the text, drawn from the permanent exhibit of the U.S. Holocaust Memorial Museum. While giving primacy to Jews as the major victim group of Nazi genocidal policies, Berenbaum's work reflects more recent scholarship by incorporating sections on Nazi mass murder of Sinti and Roma, the disabled, and Soviet prisoners of war. He also provides substantial sections on various phases of the "final solution," utilizing eyewitness accounts and photographic evidence to address the broad geographic scope of Nazi genocide. Concluding chapters concern the readjustment of Holocaust survivors after World War II, the creation of Israel, and efforts to hold perpetrators responsible via war crimes trials. Indexed.

Bruchfeld. Stephane, and Paul A. Levine. *Tell Ye Your Children...A Book about the Holocaust in Europe, 1933–1945*. Stockholm: Swedish Government Offices Living History Project, 1998. ISBN 91–630–6486–9. 84 pages. Paperback.

Written in response to a commission from the Swedish government for the Swedish "Living History Project," this slim volume provides a concise and clearly structured introduction to the key dimensions of the Holocaust. Literary excerpts, photographs, timelines, primary source documents, and maps are integrated within the narrative to highlight key historical themes: Jewish Life before the War, Persecution of Targeted Victim Groups, Ghettoization, Deportations, Policies of

Genocide, Resistance and Rescue, The Bystanders, and The Holocaust: Lessons to be Learnt? The authors have incorporated recent research findings throughout the text, highlighted by their inclusion of Sinti/Roma and the disabled as important victim groups during the genocide, as well as content on both armed and bureaucratic resistance to Nazi genocidal policies. The book's language is accessible to students and the general public, and a select bibliography is provided for further study, along with descriptive material on the Swedish Living History Project. No index.

Dawidowicz, Lucy. *The War against the Jews*. New York: Bantam Books, 1986. ISBN 0–553–34302–5. 466 pages. Paperback.

Dawidowicz' work is a classic example of the intentionalist school of Holocaust historiography, placing special emphasis on Adolf Hitler's obsessive hatred of the Jews, and his consistent focus on their annihilation as a central goal of Nazi policy. The book is organized in three sections. Part I begins with an analysis of how Hitler envisioned the Jews and carries through to the development and implementation of the "final solution," all tied together by Hitler's obsession for annihilating the Jews using a variety of methods, but focusing on war as the ultimate weapon to achieve his goals. Part II is a comprehensive discussion of the Jewish response to Nazi policies, both within Germany and in Occupied Europe. In contrast to many other narrative histories of the Holocaust, Dawidowicz devotes even more space to the Jewish response than to the narrative history of the perpetrators' planning and implementation of genocide. Part III encompasses a country-by-country description of how European societies responded to Nazi genocide, followed by a brief statistical appendix of Jewish losses in each country presented as total number killed and the percentage lost of the prewar Jewish population. This edition of Dawidowicz' work includes an important introduction that places the author's interpretation within the context of the ongoing historical debate between intentionalist and structuralist historians. Dawidowicz also addresses the efforts of some scholars and commentators to engage in revisionism and denial of the Holocaust, which she systematically critiques and discredits. Indexed.

Friedlander, Saul. *Nazi Germany and the Jews, Volume 1: The Years of Persecution, 1933–1939*. New York: HarperCollins, 1997. ISBN 0–06–019042–6. 436 pages. Hardcover.

The first in a two-volume work, *Nazi Germany and the Jews* integrates perpetrator policies, the attitudes of the society in which the policies were implemented, and the impact of those policies on the culture of German Jews. Relying heavily on the voices of the victims, the author places considerable importance on how German Jews responded to Nazi policies of oppression, utilizing first-person accounts, documentary sources, and materials from German Jewish organizations, the German Jewish press, and related groups. Friedlander recognizes the complexity of factors that contributed to the Holocaust, such as extreme German nationalism, anti-Bolshevism, the use of technology for mass industrial killing, and the bureaucratic and technical control evident in modern societies, all of which have been enriched by much recent scholarship. However, the author contends that Adolf Hitler's role was essential in the attempt to annihilate European Jews, notably his critical role in all major policy decisions of the Nazi state and his consistent desire to advance the ideology of Nazism, which at its core was a virulent brand of racial anti-Semitism. In contrast to scholars who believe that the project of the "final solution" was fully developed prior to the Nazi assumption of power, Friedlander places considerable emphasis on a blend of ideological consistency in Hitler's worldview and tactical decisions that were influenced by emerging events, the response of the German population and outside forces to Nazi policies, and other contingencies. The potential for radicalization of Nazi policies, rooted in racial anti-Semitism, was either facilitated or stemmed by these factors, but Friedlander argues that the consistency of this ideological vision had much to do with the commitment of Nazi leaders to the achievement of the "final solution." Indexed.

Gilbert, Martin. *The Holocaust: A History of the Jews of Europe during the Second World War.* New York: Henry Holt & Company, 1985. ISBN 0–8050–0348–7. 959 pages. Paperback.

Gilbert's work draws heavily upon firsthand accounts to develop a comprehensive history of the Jews in Europe during World War II. Of the book's forty-one chapters, the first six deal with the historic oppression of Jews in Europe, the rise of Nazism, and the development of Nazi policies of oppression in Germany and selected areas of Central Europe prior to the outbreak of World War II in September 1939. With the exception of Chapter 41 and the epilogue, the remainder of the book is a series of topical chapters detailing the Jewish response to Nazi policies. Chapter 16, "Eye-witness to Mass Murder," contains the notes of a Jew who had witnessed mass murder in the Chelmno death camp, prefaced by a brief introduction and a short concluding section that links the eyewitness excerpts to efforts to inform Jews in Polish ghettos such as Lodz about the reality of the Nazi's "final solution" for European Jews. The incorporation of many eyewitness accounts constitutes the bulk of Chapters 7–40 in Gilbert's book, making it primarily a study of Jewish responses to genocide rather than a systematic study of perpetrator policies and victim responses. There is no discussion of the systematic murder of the disabled in Germany and little discussion of the mass murder of Sinti and Roma. The book has a very thorough and detailed index.

Goldhagen, Daniel Jonah. *Hitler's Willing Executioners: Ordinary Germans and the Holocaust.* New York: Alfred A. Knopf, 1996. 0–679–44695–8. 622 pages. Hardcover.

Goldhagen argues that the fundamental cause of the Holocaust was the historical eliminationist anti-Semitism of the German population. Adolf Hitler's genocidal project found "willing executioners" among the German population because the participants chose to kill their victims. These were individuals who were not primarily placed in their executioner roles by chance or circumstance; rather, the deeply-rooted anti-Semitism in German culture influenced the perpetrators to believe they were doing the right thing for Germany and for their race in killing Jews. Drawing from a broad range of primary and secondary sources, including postwar trial transcripts of perpetrators, the author contends that along the continuum of anti-Semitism in Germany (extending from the idea that Jews were vaguely different to the idea that Jews were demonic), the tendency among Germans was to adopt an eliminationist mind-set, which had the propensity to sanction extermination of the Jews. Since its publication, *Hitler's Willing Executioners* has engendered heated scholarly and public debate about the motivations of perpetrator behavior, as well as the centrality of anti-Semitism in the development of Nazi genocidal policies. Indexed.

Hilberg, Raul. *The Destruction of the European Jews*. 3 volumes, revised edition. New York: Holmes & Meier, 1985. ISBN 0–8419–0832–X. 1,274 pages. Hardcover.

This meticulous, comprehensive study of how Nazi Germany sought to eliminate the Jews of Europe is considered by Michael Marrus to be "the most important work ever to be written on the subject" (Marrus, *The Holocaust in History*, 48). First published in 1961, Hilberg's study describes in fastidious detail the complex processes employed by Nazi Germany to identify, deport, concentrate, and liquidate the Jews of Europe. Throughout all three volumes, Hilberg examines the roles of perpetrators, victims, and bystanders, although his sources are predominantly those of the perpetrators. Hilberg places little emphasis on resistance by targeted groups to the genocidal policies of Nazi Germany, and is critical of the role played by Jewish councils (Judenrat) as they confronted Nazi policies of concentration and liquidation, notably in Eastern Europe. Hilberg gives little voice to the victims of the Holocaust, preferring to explain how the perpetrators (Nazi Germany, its allies, and collaborators in Occupied Europe) developed and implemented their policies. Despite its shortcomings, it remains the single most comprehensive work detailing the Nazi processes of destruction directed primarily against European Jewry between 1933 and 1945. Indexed.

Landau, Ronnie S. *The Nazi Holocaust*. Chicago: Ivan R. Dee, 1994. ISBN 1–56663–054–1. 356 pages. Hardcover.

Written primarily for students of history, but including content applicable to the fields of psychology, sociology, religious studies, and literature, *The Nazi Holocaust* is a narrative history that places the Holocaust within broad themes of Jewish history, German history, and the escalating problem of genocide in the twentieth century. Beginning with an introduction that sets forth the author's main premises concerning historical, educational, and moral dimensions of the topic, the remainder of the text is divided into three sections. In Part I, the author includes chapters on Jewish history from the ancient world to 1700 and the role of the European Jew in the modern world, which precede the study of Nazism's emergence and the rise of Hitler to power. Part II includes a tripartite division of the Holocaust's history, organized chronologically: Anti-Jewish Policy and Legislation (1933–1938); From Kristallnacht to Ghettoization in the East (1939–1941); and From Dehumanization to Annihilation (1941–1945). Part III addresses "Themes, Issues and Protagonists," with an entire chapter devoted to public opinion in Germany during the Nazi period, and concluding with a discussion of the Holocaust's aftermath and subsequent impact. In this final chapter, the author discusses creation of the state of Israel, war crimes trials, and genocides that have occurred after 1945. Throughout the book, the author is attentive to the ongoing tension between advocates of the uniqueness of the Holocaust and those who emphasize its universal implications for human behavior. A chronology of the Holocaust, a glossary of basic terms, a listing with brief descriptions of principal characters involved in the Holocaust, and a series of appendixes are provided, the latter encompassing selected primary documents and statistical data on the history of the Holocaust. No photographs or illustrations are included. Indexed.

Levin, Nora. *The Holocaust: The Destruction of European Jewry, 1933–1945*. Melbourne, FL: Krieger, 1990. ISBN 0–89464–223–5. 384 pages. Paperback.

This narrative history emphasizes the efforts of Nazi Germany to annihilate the Jewish population of Europe, along with a detailed discussion of various forms of Jewish resistance. Regularly incorporated into the text are excerpts from documents that give voice to how individuals were affected by Nazi policies. Part I, entitled "The Preparation," is a chronological survey of the rise of Nazism and Adolf Hitler, continuing through eighteen chapters that conclude with Jewish resistance in the Warsaw Ghetto and by partisan groups in the ghettos and forests of Occupied Eastern Europe. The second section of the book, entitled "The Deportations," is a survey organized by specific countries and regions in Europe of how Nazi genocidal policies were resisted, supported, and endured between 1938 and 1945. The final four chapters of this section address policies of attempted rescue, the liberation of the camps, rescuers and bystanders, and the return of Jews to their former homes in Europe and emigration to Israel. A key omission in the second section, based upon the initial date of publication, is a chapter on the Holocaust in the Soviet Union, given the limited access to sources by Western scholars during the Cold War. Two compilations of photographs are provided that highlight Nazi policies of oppression and the Jewish response. An appendix drawing upon earlier scholarly works provides three different statistical estimates of Jewish losses during the Holocaust.

Neville, Peter. *The Holocaust*. Cambridge, UK: Cambridge University Press, 1999. ISBN 0–521–59501–0. 103 pages. Paperback.

Written primarily for upper-level secondary school students and undergraduates, this slim volume focuses its attention on the genocidal policies of Nazi Germany and their primary target, the Jews of Europe. Recognizing the importance of integrating primary source study within classroom instruction about the Holocaust, each of the book's eight chapters on the experience of the Holocaust includes document case studies that highlight important themes of each chapter. Questions for document study are provided by the author. The author is comprehensive in addressing not only the design of the perpetrators, but the response of victim groups, neutral countries, and the Allies to Nazi genocide. Also included are chapters on the issue of efforts at Holocaust denial in Europe and the United States, as well as the legacy of the Holocaust, which addresses not only war crimes trials and the creation of the state of Israel, but the issue of the Holocaust in memory and compensation for victims of Nazi acts. A select bibliography and a chronology of the period 1933–1945 (also including Adolf Eichmann's execution in 1962) concludes the book. Indexed.

Poliakov, Leon. *Harvest of Hate: The Nazi Program for the Destruction of the Jews of Europe.* New York: The Holocaust Library, 1986. ISBN 0–89604–006–2. 350 pages. Paperback.

Originally published in France in 1951, this updated edition of one of the first major efforts to detail the Nazi program for the destruction of European Jews begins with a brief chapter (thirty pages) where Poliakov establishes the historical minority status of Jews in Germany, and describes the Nazi anti-Jewish ideology, quoting liberally from Nazi speeches and documents. Viewing Kristallnacht and the onset of World War II as critical junctures for the intensification of Nazi anti-Jewish policies, the author argues that two alternative solutions were put forth by Hitler for the Jews in 1939: mass deportation to an isolated location or mass murder and annihilation. The remainder of the book details how the Nazis sought to achieve the second alternative, notably after the invasion of the USSR in 1941. Drawing heavily upon captured Nazi documents and accounts from victim groups, the latter most often illuminating the very difficult situations faced by Jews in ghettos and campus, Poliakov describes in great detail the systematic processes used by the Nazi state to achieve the "final solution of the Jewish question.'" The author includes a chapter on "Nazi Plans for the 'Inferior Peoples,'" which addresses policies of slave labor, kidnapping of children, exploitation and starvation of prisoners, and other policies directed against Gypsies, Poles and Czechs, Soviet peoples, and others in Occupied Europe. The final chapter, "Genocide and the Peoples of Europe," attempts to assess the reasons for collaboration, bystander behavior, and the many dimensions of the Jewish response in Europe during the Holocaust. An appendix in this edition includes sections on the "Total Number of Jewish Victims" and the Nazi document "Statistical Report Prepared by Korherr—The Final Solution of the Jewish Problem in Europe" from 1943. Indexed.

Schluenes, Karl A. *The Twisted Road to Auschwitz: Nazi Policy toward German Jews 1933–1939.* Revised edition. Urbana: University of Illinois Press, 1990. ISBN 0–252–06147–0. 284 pages. Paperback.

One of the most important advocates of a "functionalist" interpretation of how the Holocaust emerged, Schluenes argues that there was no predetermined plan for the annihilation of European Jews within the Nazi state. Rather, the evolution of the "final solution" was unplanned, more a response to conflicts about the nature of the Jewish problem within the Nazi hierarchy. The author asserts that the Nazi regime responded to expanded opportunities for addressing the status of Jews by improvising new alternatives when, for example, many more Jews came under their control following the conquest of Eastern European countries with large Jewish populations (Poland, parts of the Soviet Union). Additionally, Schluenes contends that even though Hitler never deviated from his obsessive anti-Semitism, a core element of Nazi ideology, the extent to which his followers shared this obsession and agreed on how to solve the "Jewish problem" is problematic. The numerous conflicts within the Nazi bureaucracy and leadership hierarchy about how to deal with Jews demonstrates, according to Schluenes, that the Nazi state resembled a feudal fiefdom more than a monolithic state responding to Hitler's absolute rule. The eventual design for mass murder, epitomized in the death camp system, was the result of successive failure of Nazi policy according to Schluenes, and was a logical option that only emerged after earlier solutions, such as boycotts, emigration, and forced labor, had proved ineffective. Indexed.

Soumerai, Eve Nussbaum, and Carol D. Schulz. *Daily Life during the Holocaust.* Westport, CT: Greenwood Press, 1998. ISBN 0–313–30202–2. 312 pages. Hardcover.

Organized chronologically, this narrative history of the Holocaust places substantial emphasis on the experiences of ordinary people, drawing heavily on first-person accounts. Relying upon a broad range of eyewitness accounts, some never before published, the authors discuss the impact of Nazi policies and practices on Jews, Gypsies, homosexuals, Jehovah's Witnesses, and political dissidents. The work contains photographs that illustrate key points in the narrative, and each chapter concludes with a works-cited page. A glossary, epilogue, and selected bibliography and videography conclude the book. Indexed.

Weiss, John. *Ideology of Death: Why the Holocaust Happened in Germany.* Chicago: Ivan R. Dee, 1996. ISBN 1–56663–088–6. 427 pages. Hardcover.

John Weiss argues that the roots of the Holocaust rest in historical anti-Semitism in Germany, which set the stage for the rise of Nazism. Such anti-Semitism was historically prominent in nineteenth century Germany and Austria, became a central element of political platforms and popular debate, and provided a ready pool of followers for Nazism after the defeat in World War I and the resulting discontent arising from the collapse of the German and Austro-Hungarian Empires in 1918. The racial anti-Semitism at the center of Nazi ideology was, in the author's view, a rallying point for disaffected groups in both Germany and Austria, particularly members of the lower middle class. However, disagreeing with theories of collective guilt, the author argues that approximately one-half of all Germans, mostly but not exclusively political progressives and leftists, rejected calls for Jewish persecution, even at the height of Hitler's popularity. These opponents of Nazi anti-Jewish policies, despite their efforts, were unable to stem the power of a racist ideology, which, once holding political power in Germany, received the voluntary support of major political, economic, and military elites. Weiss systematically demonstrates that the creation of a racial empire in the East, which was a central war aim of Nazi Germany, had the voluntary support of many public and private institutions, as well as the large numbers of personnel who carried out this genocidal project, in the process killing millions of Jews and other subject peoples. In the final three of the book's twenty-five chapters, the author addresses questions of responsibility, resistance, and aftermath, establishing that the virulence of racist anti-Semitism was indeed the critical factor underlying support for Nazi Germany's genocidal policies. Indexed.

Yahil, Leni. *The Holocaust.* New York: Oxford University Press, 1991. ISBN 0–19–504522–X. 808 pages. Paperback.

Introducing her work with an essay locating it within the evolving debate about the nature of the Holocaust in Israel itself, Leni Yahil's history of the Holocaust strikes a middle ground between the Judeocentrism of Bauer and the perpetrator emphasis of Hilberg. Dividing the text into three parts: 1932–September 1939 ("The Jews of Germany during the Rise and under the Rule of the National Socialists"), 1939–1941 ("Prologue to the 'Final Solution': The First Phase of World War II"), and 1941–1945 ("Holocaust"), Yahil presents a very comprehensive narrative history of the Holocaust throughout all of Europe, drawing upon wide-ranging sources, including many authored by survivors, as well as a large body of scholarship in Hebrew by Israeli scholars. Yahil includes four chapters on resistance and rescue, with the armed resistance chapter authored by the historian Yisrael Gutman, a survivor of the Warsaw Ghetto and Jewish resistance movement in World War II. Unlike Bauer, Yahil does address the persecution of Gypsies in detail, and explains the linkages between the euthanasia program implemented in German institutions to kill the handicapped and the development of killing technology and procedures for the extermination camps in Poland. One weakness of the study is its failure to address the trials of war criminals (Nazis and collaborators), although interspersed throughout the text are references from testimony at the Nuremberg trials and other postwar proceedings. Indexed.

NARRATIVE HISTORIES OF NAZI GERMANY AND THE HOLOCAUST

Burleigh, Michael. *The Third Reich: A New History*. New York: Hill & Wang, 2000. ISBN 0–8090–9325–1. 965 pages. Hardcover.

This one-volume history of the Third Reich is a comprehensive effort that draws upon much recent research about the "microhistory" of Nazi Germany, specifically how the ordinary German reacted to and was involved in the emergence and triumph of Nazism. Burleigh emphasizes the criminality of the Nazi regime, not only during the Holocaust but during the consolidation of power in the early years of the Third Reich. He places considerable emphasis on the scale and scope of Nazism's grand design to reshape the population, labor, and economic landscape of Europe, which contributed to the genocidal project carried out by Germany and its allies against European Jews. Throughout the book, moral considerations are often integrated into the analysis, concentrating on the decisions that both German elites and average citizens made to support, with little overt opposition, a regime that engaged in massive crimes against its own people and millions of others in Europe. The book concludes with an extensive section of notes, a comprehensive bibliographic essay, and a detailed index. This book is an important contribution to the field of German history, and has particular value in the author's mastery of a very broad literature on the subject.

Collotti, Enzo. *Hitler and Nazism*. New York: Interlink Books, 1999. ISBN 1–56656–238–4. 157 pages. Paperback.

Part of the Interlink Illustrated History series, this volume by Enzo Collotti places the emergence of Nazi Germany in the context of unresolved tensions within Germany about the role of the political system and the rise of totalitarian regimes in Europe following the end of World War I. The author examines the problems facing Germany after the Versailles Settlement in 1919, which contributed to the difficulties faced by the Weimar Republic and facilitated the rise of authoritarian responses such as the Nazi party. He also places substantial importance on the central role of racism in Nazi ideology, which was critical in setting the foundations for policies of oppression and genocide. The design of the book incorporates a large number of photographs and graphics (posters, cartoons, charts) that are integral to the narrative, providing visual evidence with detailed captions for the author's argument. A select bibliography and chronology conclude the book. Indexed.

Dulffer, Jost. *Nazi Germany 1933–1945: Faith and Annihilation*. New York: St. Martin's Press, 1996. ISBN 0–340–65265–9. 242 pages. Hardcover.

Translated from the German original, this history of the Nazi regime addresses the Holocaust as the outgrowth of policies of "ostracization" (the exclusion of persons deemed unfit for membership in the national community) and racial war, the latter focused on developing a racially acceptable Europe and the annihilation of groups deemed unfit to live. Dulffer views German aggression in World War II as the logical outgrowth of Hitler's ideological worldview, where conflict against racially inferior groups was an inevitable struggle. The persecution of Jews in Germany prior to 1939 set the stage for what was to follow the invasion of Poland on September 1 of that year, particularly the mass forced migration of European populations to achieve the "reordering" of Europe envisioned in Nazi policies, such as the SS General Plan East (Ostplan). Slavs, ethnic Germans, Jews, and other populations in Occupied Europe were affected by forced migration policies, but in the author's view, the fate of the Jews was not only influenced by their potential economic value. Rather, the annihilation of European Jews was a central goal of Nazi ideology, which Dulffer argues was made more urgent by the failure of the German army to achieve a total victory in the Soviet Union, thus leading to mass industrial murder in the death camps. This combination of ideological consistency originating with Hitler and mass participation in the killing process, including participants ranging from high-ranking SS and Nazi leaders to low-level bureaucrats and officials, were the two critical factors that characterized the genocidal policies of Nazi Germany, primarily directed against Jews but also impacting millions of other Poles, Soviets, and other victims. The author draws upon perpetrator sources most often, giving little voice to victim groups, since his purpose overall is to interpret the rise, development, and eventual collapse of the Nazi regime. A select bibliography is provided for further reading, organized by topical categories. Indexed.

Fischer, Klaus P. *Nazi Germany: A New History.* New York: Continuum, 1995. ISBN 0–8264–0797–8. 734 pages. Hardcover.

A comprehensive single-volume history of the Third Reich, Fischer views the Holocaust as a central component of Nazi government policy, emerging from four cultural patterns in German society, which made mass extermination of targeted groups not only possible, but a reality. These four critical patterns are: (1) a virulent form of anti-Semitism with strong biological and religious components, (2) a powerful tradition of institutionalized authoritarianism in family, school, and everyday life, (3) belligerent nationalism based on lack of identity, insecurity, and the trauma of defeat in war, and (4) rule by a criminal leadership (pp. 512–513). Fischer's interpretation of Nazi German responsibility for the Holocaust provides no apologies for the policies of extermination, and he provides a useful analysis of the legacy of the Nazi period in postwar Germany, with particular emphasis on the need for contemporary Germany to address this legacy on its own terms. His discussion of the 1980s historians' debate in Germany highlights the difficulties that contemporary German society has in facing the burden of guilt still evident from the Nazi period, as well as the compelling need for today's Germans to establish a national identity rooted in "humane statehood" (p. 576) that is devoid of the cultural patterns that produced the Nazi regime. Indexed.

McDonough, Frank. *Hitler and Nazi Germany*. Cambridge: Cambridge University Press, 1999. ISBN 0–521–59502–9. 152 pages. Paperback.

Written for secondary level students and undergraduates, this book provides a thorough introduction to the rise of Adolf Hitler and the twelve-year regime he ruled in Nazi Germany. The book is organized topically, with each chapter containing a document case study section that provides brief excerpts from sources on that chapter's contents and a series of analysis questions for use with the documents. Chapter 7, "Mass Murder under Nazi Rule," and part of Chapter 8, "The Verdict of Historians," address the Holocaust specifically. Reflecting recent scholarship, the contents of Chapter 7 include discussions of the Nazi euthanasia program, as well as "the broader dimensions of Nazi genocide," which encompasses the broader range of Nazi victims, including Soviet prisoners of war, non-Jewish Poles, Sinti and Roma, and others. At the same time, the author recognizes the "singular fate" of the Jews given the size and scope of the Nazi genocidal project designed to annihilate all European Jews. The discussion in Chapter 8 of historians' disputes about the origins, development, and consequences of the Holocaust is valuable because McDonough provides a useful summary of contemporary scholarly conflicts in the field, such as the notion of "national responsibility" advanced in Goldhagen's *Hitler's Willing Executioners* and the criticisms of that position by other scholars. The book concludes with a select bibliography, a glossary with brief descriptions of key terms, and a chronology beginning with Hitler's birth in 1889 and concluding with his death in Berlin in May 1945. Indexed.

3

PERSPECTIVES FROM THE SOCIAL
SCIENCES AND OTHER FIELDS

OVERVIEW

As the twenty-first century begins, the multidisciplinary nature of Holocaust scholarship is increasingly prominent. The selections included in this chapter represent important works in their respective fields, chosen based upon their contributions to furthering inquiry about the Holocaust from their disciplinary or professional perspectives, as well as their recognized scholarly merit. These works enrich understanding of the Holocaust by presenting their findings from the unique disciplinary perspectives of history, journalism, law, mass communications, philosophy, political science, psychology, sociology, and theology. In the process, readers gain insight from these works by examining behavior using different frames of reference—psychologists emphasize the study of individuals, sociologists focus on group behavior, and philosophers study how humans construct meaning about their world. In each case, understanding of the Holocaust is deepened as readers learn new insights about human behavior while becoming more knowledgeable about the methods and sources used by scholars in these disciplines. The final section, "Specialized Historical Studies," presents important works about a range of primarily historical topics that are more specialized than those encountered in the narrative histories presented in Chapter 2. The entries included in this section of the chapter include anthologies of articles on major issues in Holocaust histo-riography and related topics. Within the brief introductions to each per-spective, those topics about the Holocaust discussed in the works that follow are noted.

JOURNALISM AND THE MASS MEDIA

The books included in this subsection discuss the place of Adolf Hitler in the popular imagination, the images of concentration and death camps, the role of television in presenting the Holocaust to mass audiences, and how topics such as the liberation of the camps by Allied forces became pervasive as a metaphor for the public's encounter with genocide during the late twentieth century.

Rosenbaum, Ronald. *Explaining Hitler.* New York: Random House, 1998. ISBN 0–679–43151–9. 444 pages. Hardcover.

This book analyzes scholarly controversies about Adolf Hitler and the policies and practices he oversaw as leader of the Third Reich. Topics examined include the origins of Hitler's family and his early rise to political prominence during the Weimar Republic; debate over the role of Hitler's sexual practices and their influence on his behavior; whether Hitler's war aims and genocidal plans evolved from his experiences prior to 1920 or were a result of political and strategic decisions made once he was installed in power after 1932; and the extent to which Hitler's life represents a singular, unique phenomenon in the history of the twentieth century, or a more general set of behavioral and personality characteris-tics evident in humankind. Rosenbaum does not discuss in detail recent German scholarship on Hitler's life and leadership of the Third Reich, preferring to study opposing points of view evident in two major Hitler biographers from Britain (Alan Bullock and Hugh Trever-Roper) and the positions of selected scholars, theologians, and artists (filmmaker Claude Lanzmann and writer George Steiner) on the topic of Hitler's explainability. Indexed.

Shandler, Jeffrey. *While America Watches: Televising the Holocaust.* New York: Oxford University Press, 1999. ISBN 0–19–511935–5. 316 pages. Hardcover.

The author discusses television in the United States as the most prominent form of Holocaust "mediation," defined as a path to understanding using a particular form of representation—in this case television. Both positive and negative conse-quences of such mediation are discussed in the book, as Shandler interprets the major historical events in the representation of the Holocaust since the end of World War II. Beginning with the newsreels created about the liberation of Nazi camps, continuing through programs during the 1950s ("This Is Your Life") and "big events" such as the television miniseries "Holocaust," and carrying his narrative through to the recent past (reporting on the opening of the U.S. Holocaust Memorial Museum and the human rights atrocities in the former Yugoslavia), the author views television as part of a larger Holocaust memory culture. This culture can facilitate historic remembrance within a broader humanistic commitment to education, particularly because television can encourage the development of collective memory and an openness of approach to Holocaust studies. However, because television presents its messages in a routine, intimate, and ubiquitous manner, there is dissonance between how the Holocaust is portrayed on television and the substance and scale of the events themselves. Additionally, even though televised representations of the Holocaust are becoming more extensive, this does not guarantee the prevention of ongoing human rights violations or genocides such as those that occurred in Bosnia and Rwanda. This challenging and provocative book has extensive notes to each chapter and is fully indexed.

Zelizer, Barbie. *Remembering to Forget: Holocaust Memory through the Camera's Eye*. Chicago: University of Chicago Press, 1998. ISBN 0–226–97972–5. 292 pages. Hardcover.

The author addresses how World War II atrocity photographs serve to link the past and present, focusing on the definition of collective memory as a process that reconfigures the past by making it conform to configurations of the present. Collective memory can facilitate fabrication, rearrangement, elaboration, and omission of details about the past, and in the process potentially shortchange accuracy and authenticity to accommodate broader contemporary concerns about identity formation, power and authority, and political affiliation. The photographs of the Holocaust, particularly those taken when the Nazi camps were liberated in 1944 and 1945, serve as a vessel of memory, connecting the unimaginable with the imaginable. Because these images are pervasive in Holocaust recollections, they also serve as a background context for interpreting more recent examples of barbarity and genocide. Zelizer provides a detailed analysis of the camp liberation photos, how they were created and disseminated, their function as a form of collective memory, and the implications today of using Nazi atrocity photos as a metaphor or paradigm of brutality when presenting contemporary forms of human rights violation and genocidal acts. Many photographs are included within the text to illustrate the author's interpretation. A selected bibliography and extensive notes are included for each chapter. Indexed.

LAW

The development of international law following World War II was directly influenced by the events and aftermath of the Holocaust. Postwar trials of war criminals, beginning at Nuremberg and continuing to the present, efforts to develop international treaties for punishment of genocidal acts, and the growth of human rights standards are central topics encountered here. Additionally, the roles of education and art in presenting aspects of the Holocaust, as well as in preventing future genocides and human rights violations, are explored.

Ball, Howard. *Prosecuting War Crimes and Genocide: The Twentieth Century Experience.* Lawrence: University Press of Kansas, 1999. ISBN 0–7006–0977–6. 288 pages. Hardcover.

This book examines the history of how war crimes have been addressed during the twentieth century, and suggests that the formation of the International Criminal Court offers the best prospect for systematically holding individuals and states accountable for war crimes and crimes against humanity in the twenty-first century. The book's eight chapters include analysis of the legacy of the Nuremberg Tribunal, developments in international law that emerged from Nuremberg, the world's failure to respond to the Cambodian genocide in the 1970s, the formation of recent war crimes tribunals to address the mass murders and genocidal acts committed in Rwanda and the former Yugoslavia, and the creation of the International Criminal Court statute, despite the reluctance of the United States to support this landmark development. Despite the recent events in Kosovo, the author is optimistic about the forward momentum in establishing standards and procedures for accountability when violations of human rights and humanitarian law occur. Extensive notes are provided, along with a select bibliography and detailed index.

Decoste, F.C., and Bernard Schwartz, editors. *The Holocaust's Ghost: Writings on Art, Politics, Law and Education.* Edmonton: University of Alberta Press, 2000. ISBN 0–88864–358–6. 568 pages. Hardcover.

Containing the papers from a conference entitled "Holocaust: Art/Politics/Law" held at the University of Alberta in 1997, as well as newly commissioned essays, this interdisciplinary anthology presents multiple perspectives on Holocaust study. Contributions in Part I include essays on visual arts, poetry, drama and memorials, along with the history of the Holocaust, specifically chapters on the Roma Holocaust, artistic policies of the Third Reich, and the role of terror organizations in Nazi Germany. Part II ("Law and Education") includes essays on the impact of Nazi ideology and practices on German law, philosophical dimensions of German legal practice before and during the Third Reich, and contemporary issues of Holocaust denial, with particular attention paid to hate propaganda and Canadian law. The education selections address issues of content selection, the role of Holocaust education within an antiracist and multicultural curriculum in Canada, and the relationship of Holocaust studies to education for social responsibility and human rights education. An appendix containing excerpts from a panel discussion on the contemporary significance and implications of Holocaust study from the October 1997 University of Alberta conference concludes the volume. Indexed.

Gutman, Roy, and David Rieff. *Crimes of War: What the Public Should Know*. New York: W.W. Norton, 1999. ISBN 0–393–31914–8. 399 pages. Paperback.

Structured similar to a dictionary, this book presents articles written by journalists and legal experts on issues of humanitarian law, building upon the historic precedents set at Nuremberg and in other twentieth century contexts. Combining text with dramatic photographs taken in many regions of the world where humanitarian law violations have occurred, *Crimes of War: What the Public Should Know* is written in a direct, yet powerful style accessible to the general public. Articles within the book range from "Act of War" (A) to "Willfulness" (W) with all key aspects of humanitarian law addressed at some point in the book. The foreword to the book is by Richard Goldstone, former director of the South African Truth Commission and a highly respected international jurist. Contributor biographies, notes on the law and legal terms, a listing of major international humanitarian laws, a select bibliography, and a listing of selected legal resources online conclude the book. No index.

Neier, Aryeh. *War Crimes: Brutality, Genocide, Terror and the Struggle for Justice*. New York: Random House, 1998. ISBN 0–8129–2381–2. 286 pages. Hardcover.

Former director of Human Rights Watch and Holocaust survivor Aryeh Neier presents a forceful case in this book for the creation of a permanent international criminal court to address war crimes and crimes against humanity in the contemporary world. Surveying recent cases of mass murder and genocide in Bosnia-Herzegovinia and Rwanda, Neier asks fundamental questions that continue to haunt the world community since the landmark precedents established at Nuremberg in 1945–1946: why does the world stand by and watch massive crimes be committed, and what should be done to hold perpetrators accountable for their actions? Among the topics discussed by Neier in this book are the issue of how individual countries can address the legacy of crimes against civilians (truth commissions, amnesty, and other measures), the role of the United Nations in forging a more humane world community and prosecuting war criminals, and the role of governments in engendering a social climate where the incitement to genocide and mass murder would become less likely than was the case in Nazi Germany or more recent cases, such as the former Yugoslavia. Chapter notes are provided, but there is no bibliography for further study. Indexed.

PHILOSOPHY AND RELIGION

Philosophers and religious scholars have grappled with many aspects of the Holocaust since 1945, and the works included here are no exception. Given that the Holocaust occurred in a continent where Christianity was the dominant faith, many works in both philosophy and theology have examined the complex issues of Christian-Jewish relations before, during, and after the Shoah. The uniqueness of the Holocaust, the role of religious faith during the Shoah, experiences in the death camps, and Jewish-Christian relations in the post-Holocaust era are major topics encompassed in the works of this subsection.

Amery, Jean. *At the Mind's Limits: Contemplations by a Survivor on Auschwitz and Its Realities*. Translated by Sidney Rosenfeld and Stella P. Rosenfeld. Bloomington: Indiana University Press, 1980. ISBN 0–253–21173–5. 111 pages. Paperback.

Written by a survivor of Auschwitz, this work consists of five autobiographical essays that seek answers to how one human being comes to understand the reality of horror inflicted by humans against one another. First issued in 1966, this edition contains the preface to the first edition and a new preface written by the author in 1977. In the book, Amery discusses how he responded to torture, with a resulting loss of faith in the world; how he responded to the land of his perpetrators when he returned to his hometown of Vienna; and how he regained his sense of self and human dignity by embracing his Jewish identity, despite the fact that during his early life Judaism was a marginal aspect of his daily life. This edition includes an afterword by Sidney Rosenfeld, which places this work of Jean Amery's within the context of his lifelong intellectual journey, and which also discusses the role Amery played in the ongoing discussions within German society about the legacy of the Holocaust and the continuing need to hold individuals responsible for their actions. No index.

Barnett, Victoria J. *Bystanders: Conscience and Complicity during the Holocaust*. Westport, CT: Praeger, 1999. ISBN 0–275–97045–0. 185 pages. Paperback.

This book is an attempt to analyze the factors that shaped the behavior of ordinary citizens during the Holocaust, exploring the factors that fostered passivity and complicity in Germany and Occupied Europe as genocide was implemented. Rather than seeking to exonerate bystanders, the work attempts to grasp why they remained passive and inactive in the face of suffering, when a minority of others did not. The author also challenges the reader to consider a framework for understanding that enables people to prevent the inaction of the 1930s as the world faces new challenges, including not only human rights violations, but mass murder and genocide. The work includes a select bibliography and a detailed index.

Fackenheim, Emil. *To Mend the World: Foundations of Post-Holocaust Jewish Thought.* Second edition. New York: Schocken Books, 1989. ISBN 0–8052–0938–7. 358 pages. Paperback.

The esteemed Jewish philosopher Emil Fackenheim argues that the Holocaust was a "rupture," not only of Jewish faith and life but of everything considered "human," and in this book he presents an argument that the continuity of Western philosophical thought presents no easy answers to the tragedy of the Holocaust and its powerful influences on modern life. Instead, Fackenheim finds inspiration in the actions and behaviors of common persons who resisted Nazi oppression, seeking models to construct a theology of faith for the future. A list of source abbreviations is provided, along with chapter notes and a detailed index.

Lang, Berel. *Act and Idea in the Nazi Genocide.* Chicago: University of Chicago Press, 1990. ISBN 0–226–46869–0. 258 pages. Paperback.

This rigorous philosophical study forces the reader to reconsider the definitions of individual and group responsibility, how knowledge plays a role in ethical decisions, and the relationship between guilt and forgiveness, all in relationship to the genocidal policies and practices of Nazi Germany. The author challenges commentators, authors, and teachers to rethink their purposes and forms of representation when dealing with Holocaust content, precisely because of the ethical and moral dimensions that are always present in this subject. No chapter notes are provided. Indexed.

Levi, Primo. *The Drowned and the Saved.* Translated by Raymond Rosenthal. New York: Summit Books, 1988. ISBN 0–679–72186-X. 203 pages. Paperback.

Levi's final major work, this book contains reflections on the meaning of the Holocaust, often cast in "gray" shades rather than black or white. Written relatively close to his untimely death, the essays emphasize the personal burden of remembrance that every Holocaust survivor carries within him- or herself, a set of memories that Levi believes never depart and that permeate much of the survivor's approach to contemporary life. Levi's essays do not cast the perpetrators as demons or madmen. Instead, he describes them, as well as his fellow victims, as human beings who made choices and acted upon those decisions. Unlike many other authors of Holocaust memoirs, Levi effectively juxtaposes thick description of his experiences with philosophical judgments about the motivations and consequences of human behavior. Readers who have studied his earlier work *Survival in Auschwitz* will find continuities of style and tone in *The Drowned and the Saved,* but also a more pessimistic, stoic perspective on the meaning of the Holocaust, which could only have emerged after many years of continuing reflection. No index.

Rittner, Carol, Stephen D. Smith, and Irena Steinfeldt, editors. *The Holocaust and the Christian World*. London: Kuperard, 2000. ISBN 1–85733–277–6. 278 pages. Paperback.

This anthology addresses critical issues about the Holocaust and the response by Christians in Germany, Europe, and other world regions. Contributions by a range of authors address historic anti-Semitism, the response of Christian institutions to Nazi oppression, and issues of legacy such as Christian-Jewish relations after the Holocaust, among others. Each section of the anthology contains sidebar questions to provoke thought about the content, suggestions for further reading, and biographical sketches of chapter authors. Also included within the anthology are selected eyewitness accounts that further illustrate the content of chapter essays. In addition to the suggested readings, a list of films and selected online resources is provided. Indexed.

Rosenbaum, Alan S., editor. *Is the Holocaust Unique?* Boulder, CO: Westview Press, 1998. ISBN 0–8133–2542–7. 222 pages. Paperback.

This collection of essays provides competing perspectives on the study of genocide. Included are essays arguing for the uniqueness of the Holocaust among other genocides, as well as contributions that place the Holocaust in a comparative perspective. Other genocides discussed in the volume are the genocide of the Armenians in the Ottoman Empire, the forced famine in the Ukraine, and the Atlantic slave trade. Additionally, an essay by Ian Hancock examines the Holocaust of the Roma (Gypsies), while Robert Melson's contribution views the Armenian genocide as a precursor to the Holocaust. The foreword by Israel W. Charny, editor-in-chief of the *Encyclopedia of Genocide*, challenges the reader to examine the works in the volume carefully, as there are directly opposing views evident on important questions about genocide studies in its contents. He also provides a series of questions for consideration by the reader to analyze the essays. Biographical sketches of each contributor are included. Indexed.

Rosenberg, Alan, and Gerald E. Myers, editors. *Echoes from the Holocaust: Philosophical Reflections on a Dark Time*. Philadelphia: Temple University Press, 1988. ISBN 0–87722–539–7. 453 pages. Hardcover.

This anthology includes twenty-three contributions organized into four separate sections: "The Historical Impact," "Assault on Morality," "Echoes from the Death Camps," and "Challenges to the Understanding." Among the esteemed authors included in the collection are Lawrence Langer, John Roth, George Kren, Hans Jonas, Berel Lang, Steven Katz, Hannah Arendt, and Alice and A. Roy Eckardt. The editors present an overview of the volume's contents in the preface, with emphasis placed on the field of philosophy's commitment to self-examination about how it did or did not contribute to the rise of Nazism and its impact on the modern world. Chapter notes are provided, along with brief contributor biographies. Indexed.

Roth, John K., editor. *Ethics after the Holocaust: Perspectives, Critiques, and Responses.* St. Paul, MN: Paragon House, 1999. ISBN 1–55778–771–9. 363 pages. Paperback.

This collection of essays by noted philosophers presents varied perspectives on the study of ethics, focusing on the Holocaust's impact on this branch of philosophical inquiry since 1945. Among the topics addressed in the anthology are the relationship of science to the determination of the good, Martin Heidegger's philosophical works and their relationship to Nazi ideology, and a discussion of diverse interpretive paradigms in the study of ethics following the Holocaust. Each chapter begins with an essay by a specific philosopher, followed by critiques from other contributors to the anthology and a response by the essay author. Editor John Roth introduces the major themes of the essays, and offers a postscript with commentary by the anthology contributors that suggests future paths for inquiry. A selected bibliography and detailed index are included.

Roth, John K., and Michael Berenbaum, editors. *Holocaust: Religious and Philosophical Implications.* New York: Paragon House, 1989. ISBN 1–55778–212–1. 390 pages. Paperback.

Assembling an eclectic group of authors, the editors present essays by historians, philosophers, theologians, survivors, literary scholars, and psychologists to address three key questions: "What if the Holocaust Is Unique?," "Is It True What One Hears of Selections, of Gas, of Crematoriums?," and "Where Is God Now?" The editors present a brief overview of the history of the Holocaust in the prologue, followed by a selective chronology of major events in the Holocaust, They also introduce each section, providing a foreshadowing of the major themes addressed by section authors, and then offer brief introductions to each author's contribution. Each section concludes with suggestions for further reading. The quality of the contributors and the essays included in this volume make it an excellent starting point for consideration of the religious and philosophical issues posed by the editors, and readers will no doubt pursue other works by the authors included in the anthology. Indexed.

Roth, John K., and Richard Rubenstein. *Approaches to Auschwitz: The Holocaust and Its Legacy.* Atlanta: John Knox Press, 1987. ISBN 0–8042–0778–X. 422 pages. Hardcover.

Drawing upon theological, philosophical, and historical perspectives, the authors examine the early historical roots of anti-Judaism in Christian societies, the policies and practices of Nazism and how genocide became integral to the Nazi vision of the future, the impact of the Holocaust on victims and survivors, and responses to the Holocaust, particularly in the areas of Jewish-Christian relations, literature, and philosophical and religious reflection. They conclude the work with a section on "The Legacy of the Holocaust" and an epilogue entitled "Some

Concluding Reflections on a Century of Progress," both of which challenge the reader to reassess the capacity of Western civilization to overcome barbarism, given the fact that the Holocaust not only occurred, but has cast such a shadow on the twentieth century. A very extensive bibliography is provided, along with detailed chapter notes and both subject and name indexes. The combination of perspectives employed in this book makes it an important contribution to a broad, interdisciplinary understanding of the Holocaust.

Rubenstein, Richard L. *The Cunning of History*. Introduction by William Styron. New York: Harper & Row, 1987. ISBN 0–06–132068–4. 112 pages. Paperback.

This lengthy essay, divided into six chapters, addresses the propensity of twentieth century societies to develop surplus populations who are economically deprived, and then condemn those same populations to outcast status or exterminate them. Drawing upon a broad literature encompassing the history of slavery, the sociology of Max Weber, the political theory of Hannah Arendt, and works about the Holocaust such as Raul Hilberg's *The Destruction of the European Jews,* Richard Rubenstein examines the Holocaust as a more recent example of destructive forces in the long-term development of Western society. Slavery and other patterns of domination, with Auschwitz as the most glaring example in recent history, are central issues for Rubenstein in the six interrelated chapters of the book. Chapter notes are provided. No index.

Todorov, Tzvetan. *Facing the Extreme: Moral Life in the Concentration Camps*. New York: Henry Holt, 1996. ISBN 0–8050–4263–6. 307 pages. Hardcover.

Drawing upon a vast literature including eyewitness accounts, secondary sources, political theory, and philosophy, the author examines the nature of moral life in the Nazi camp system and the Soviet gulag. He concludes that moral life did not vanish, and that despite extreme circumstances, ordinary examples of dignity, care, compassion, and solidarity were displayed, which permitted inmates to sustain their moral universe. The final chapter, "Notes on Morality," presents observations on how the lessons of the past can inform our understanding of human behavior, with emphasis placed on the analysis of social forces (the fragmentation of daily life and a related depersonalization of human relations) and our potential to encourage good rather than evil in ordinary, daily behavior. A list of sources consulted is provided, along with a detailed index. This work raises important questions about how moral life can be sustained under very difficult circumstances, and offers the reader hope that insights from the Holocaust can positively influence future social experience.

PSYCHOLOGY

The application of psychological theory and methodologies within Holocaust studies has a distinguished history, ranging from memoirs such as Viktor Frankl's *Man's Search for Meaning* to studies of how the children of Holocaust survivors come to terms with the legacy of their parents' experiences. The works included here address diverse topics, ranging from how Israelis and Germans seek to reconcile their conflicting views of a common past, to psychiatric analyses of Adolf Hitler's actions and beliefs, to studies of collective violence informed by social psychology.

Bar-On, Daniel, editor. *Bridging the Gap: Storytelling as a Way to Work Through Political and Collective Hostilities.* Hamburg: Korber Stiftung, 2000. ISBN 3–89684–030–4. 213 pages. Paperback.

Drawing upon his work with encounters between descendants of Holocaust survivors and Nazi perpetrators, Daniel Bar-On has compiled a volume that details the storytelling method employed to help descendants come to terms with their past, and how that method has been applied in more recent contexts of regional and collective violence. The first section of the book presents the dialogue-based approach entitled "To Reflect and Trust" that Bar-On and his associates employed with Israelis and Germans. The second section describes how this approach was applied in new contexts: the Israeli-Palestine conflict, Northern Ireland, and South Africa. Section 3 offers participant perspectives from the various meetings, and the final section offers evaluation and discussion of the approach in each context, with suggestions for future research and investigation. The appendix provides a detailed bibliography, brief biographies of the project leaders in each location, and contact information for the dialogue group projects in the United States, Germany, Israel-Palestine, South Africa, and Northern Ireland. No index.

Epstein, Helen. *Children of the Holocaust: Conversations with Sons and Daughters of Survivors.* New York: Penguin, 1988. ISBN 0–14–011284–7. 351 pages. Paperback.

Building upon her own memories and life experiences as the daughter of Holocaust survivors, the author interviewed scores of men and women who also were sons and daughters of survivors. Integrating reflections on her own life with the stories of her informants, Epstein explores the nightmares, fears, hopes, and struggles that both the parents (survivors) and their children encountered. Noting that a growing literature is emerging about the psychosocial impact of the survivor experience on families, and particularly survivors' children, Epstein includes insights from that literature in her discussions of individuals' family experiences, as well as an extensive bibliography on the topic prepared by Eva Fogelman. No index.

Kren, George M., and Leon Rappaport. *The Holocaust and the Crisis in Human Behavior*. Revised Edition. New York: Holmes & Meier, 1994. ISBN 0–8419–1305–6. 228 pages. Paperback.

Co-authored by a psychologist and a historian, this book argues that the Holocaust is the major historical crisis of the twentieth century, because it "has discredited the basic social institutions that were supposed to protect our civilization from such horrors as Auschwitz" (p. 11). Placing the study of the Holocaust within a context that contains unremitting use of the Holocaust as a metaphor in popular culture, the authors examine the history of the Holocaust using a wide range of sources, with special emphasis on historical and psychological studies. As an example, examination of Adolf Hitler's central role in the chapter "Why Germany?" relies heavily on psychological analyses of Hitler's life. A psychosocial perspective is employed in the chapter on "The SS: A Unique Institution," where the authors rely heavily on personality theory to interpret the motivations of SS personnel to their mission and social psychology to explain the commitment of the SS to completing terrible deeds. Overall, the authors conclude that the Holocaust was an exceptional, totally unique phenomenon in the history of the twentieth century, with a level and type of violence that sets it apart from other forms of mass killing. Primarily, this was the result of a process of mass dehumanization, which they claim was unprecedented in both its scale and the use of technological, industrial means to achieve its goals. The book concludes with an extensive bibliographic essay, chapter notes, and a detailed index.

Redlich, Fritz. *Hitler: Diagnosis of a Destructive Prophet*. New York: Oxford University Press, 1998. ISBN 0–19–505782–1. 448 pages. Hardcover.

Dr. Fritz Redlich, a practicing medical doctor and psychiatrist, presents in this book the first major study of Adolf Hitler drawing upon Hitler's medical records. The purpose of the study is to shed light on Hitler's physical and mental health and, in the process, determine whether evidence about his physical and mental health offered insights about Hitler's behavior. Based upon his analysis, the author develops a medical review and psychopathological profile of Hitler, highlighting the blend of denial, projection, paranoia, sexual repression, and narcissism that heavily influenced his behavior. Lengthy appendixes providing information on Hitler's extended family, a chronology of Hitler's illnesses and treatments, a glossary of medical terms, a list of significant medications and laboratory reports, electrocardiographic reports and recommendations, eye examinations, and an autopsy report are included. Extensive notes and a detailed index conclude the book.

Staub, Ervin. *The Roots of Evil: The Origins of Genocide and Other Group Violence*. New York: Cambridge University Press, 1989. ISBN 0–521–42214–0. 336 pages. Paperback.

Presenting a comprehensive psychosocial interpretation of the origins of genocide and group violence, Ervin Staub addresses four cases in this work: the Holocaust, the genocide of the Armenians in the Ottoman Empire, the genocide in Cambodia, and disappearances in Argentina during the 1970s and early 1980s. The first part of the book introduces key concepts and explores issues of motivation, obedience to authority, the relationship of the individual to the state, cultural and individual characteristics, the psychology of perpetrators, and the involvement of perpetrators and bystanders in what Staub labels the "continuum of destruction." In Parts II and III of the book, he applies the core concepts and theoretical constructs introduced in Part I to the four cases noted previously, and in Part IV, analyzes the cultural and psychological origins of war and how caring and nonaggressive persons and societies can be created. Staub draws from a vast literature in psychology, history, social theory, and other fields, and presents a compelling analysis that offers much important insight for shaping human behavior toward more humane ends. Extensive chapter notes and a detailed index conclude this important work.

POLITICS AND SOCIOLOGY

This section includes works that inform our study of the Holocaust by examining patterns of group conflict, drawing primarily from concepts emerging from politics and sociology such as power, social structure, socialization, and others. A decided emphasis is placed by these authors on patterns of group behavior, as manifested in the camp system, by rescuers in Occupied Europe, and by children within ghettos and camps or in other contexts. In contrast to works of a purely psychological focus, these studies place less focus on individual motivation and the influence of personality, and more on how social institutions influenced behavior during the Holocaust.

Arendt, Hannah. *Eichmann in Jerusalem: A Report on the Banality of Evil*. Revised and enlarged edition. New York: Penguin, 1977. ISBN 0–14–004450–7. 312 pages. Paperback.

This book, originally a series of articles published in *The New Yorker* in 1963, was based upon Hannah Arendt's coverage of the Eichmann trial in Jerusalem. The expanded and revised edition includes additional material that came to light after the trial, as well as a postscript where Arendt comments on the controversy regarding her main ideas in the book. As one of the most significant works on the legacy of the Holocaust and its implications for understanding human behavior,

Arendt's *Eichmann in Jerusalem* introduced the phrase "the banality of evil" into cultural discourse, inspiring other scholars to investigate how individuals such as Adolf Eichmann could have become perpetrators. Although Arendt quite effectively describes Eichmann as an ordinary and banal man who had little difficulty participating in genocide, she does not engage in detailed analysis of the psychological, cultural, or sociological explanations for his behavior. Trained as a political philosopher, Arendt raises important issues about the rationale for the Eichmann trial and its relationship to international legal standards that evolved after World War II, as well as how human society can address the crimes committed by a bureaucratic apparatus when the legal system primarily addresses the crimes of individuals. Challenging and provocative, *Eichmann in Jerusalem* is a central work on the legacy of the Holocaust and is recommended to all students of the topic. A selected bibliography is provided, along with a detailed index.

Eisen, George. *Children and Play in the Holocaust: Games among the Shadows*. Amherst: University of Massachusetts Press, 1990. ISBN 0–87023–708–X. 153 pages. Paperback.

George Eisen examines children's play during the Holocaust using psychological, historical, and anthropological concepts, producing a study that helps the reader understand how children's play and games functioned to help children accommodate to their changed circumstances during the Holocaust. Play emerges in this book as a means by which children negotiated the requirements for survival, in this case under extreme circumstances. The author draws upon a broad literature, including survivor accounts, children's poetry and drawings, and secondary sources, in his analysis of the adaptation of children during the Holocaust. He addresses not only the impact on children during the Holocaust, but the implications for child survivors of their experiences, including both children who survived the camps and ghettos and those who were hidden to prevent their oppression by the Nazis and their allies. The book includes two appendices: a list of ghettos and camps identified in the text, and a list of persons mentioned in the text. Chapter notes and a select bibliography precede the detailed index.

Feig, Konnilyn G. *Hitler's Death Camps: The Sanity of Madness*. New York: Holmes & Meier, 1981. ISBN 0–8419–0676–9. 547 pages. Paperback.

This work benefits from an interdisciplinary set of sources, drawing upon insights from literature, survivor accounts, music, drama, interviews, the social sciences, medicine, science, philosophy, and religion. As a study of the major camps in the Nazi system, this work begins with an historical overview of how the Holocaust originated and was implemented, followed by examination of the camps in Germany, Poland, and Czechoslovakia. Separate chapters address the process of liberation and the legacy of the Holocaust in Poland, which the author labels "the graveyard of the thousand-year kingdom of Judaism." The final section of the book addresses the role of bystanders, perpetrators, and resistance movements, concluding with commentary on the "madness of the Holocaust" and "lessons the Holocaust taught us." The appendices include directions to the camps discussed in the book, the dates the camps were in existence and who commanded them, and the fate of the commandants during and after World War II. Extensive chapter notes, a listing of sources, and a select bibliography are provided, along with a detailed index. Throughout the book, diagrams of the camps are provided for easy reference along with selected photographs of camp memorial sculptures.

Friedrich, Otto. *The Kingdom of Auschwitz*. New York: HarperCollins Publishers, 1994. ISBN 0–06–097640–3. 103 pages. Paperback.

Otto Friedrich's essay about Auschwitz provides a concise, yet powerful description of the most notorious death camp during the Holocaust. Drawing upon eyewitness accounts by survivors and perpetrators, as well as a broad secondary literature, Friedrich discusses the origins of the camp, its function within the overall project of Nazi genocide, the daily activities of the perpetrators and victims who existed at Auschwitz, and the implications for human behavior of what occurred in Auschwitz between 1939 and 1945. He also discusses more recent issues concerning Auschwitz, such as the controversy concerning the placement of a convent at the death camp in the late 1980s and early 1990s, and the efforts to restore the camp, which is a state museum under the authority of the Polish government. A brief essay on sources concludes the book. Indexed.

Katz, Fred E. *Ordinary People and Extraordinary Evil: A Report on the Beguilings of Evil*. Albany: State University of New York Press, 1993. ISBN 0–7914–1442–6. 154 pages. Paperback.

This book examines the issue of how ordinary people can commit evil acts, using the theory proposed by Hannah Arendt in *Eichmann in Jerusalem* that ordinary people can commit evil acts, and pursuing this idea within a sociological framework. The author examines the behavior of perpetrators, primarily during the Holocaust, but also in more recent contexts, such as the My Lai massacre. Using sociological categories, Katz examines (1) impediments to accepting the insight that average people can engage in evil acts and (2) the attributes of ordinary human behavior that contribute to producing evil. The final chapter describes five paradoxes that individuals may encounter where the potential to do evil is present, but that coexist with opportunities to act humanely and blunt the development of evil behaviors. Essentially, Katz argues that humans engage in a complex balancing act between the potential to engage in evil and the propensity to act humanely, and his analysis offers pathways for deeper understanding of the factors that influence this precarious balance. Chapter notes and a select bibliography are provided, along with a detailed index.

Oliner, Samuel, and Pearl Oliner. *The Altruistic Personality: Rescuers of Jews in Nazi Europe.* New York: The Free Press, 1992. ISBN 0–02–923829–3. 419 pages. Paperback.

Basing their findings upon a detailed study of over 680 rescuers of Jews during the Holocaust, the authors examined the sociopsychological factors contributing to altruistic behavior. They focused primarily on two questions: was rescue the result of opportunity (the consequence of particular external circumstances) and was rescue a matter of personal qualities, such as particular values, attitudes, and personality characteristics? This book presents their findings as well as a detailed appendix that describes the study's methodology, the data employed as the basis for the analysis, and the questionnaire employed with the sample of rescuers involved in the study. The authors found that individuals who engaged in rescue were primarily people who had extensive associations in their communities, who did not believe they were engaged in rescue for any "special reasons," who predominantly had a sense of caring and responsibility for others beyond their own family, and who were socialized at home or in other settings where these qualities were reinforced. The implications for contemporary human behavior of this study are important, and the authors discuss them in their chapter entitled "Moral Heroism and Extensivity." This book is strongly recommended as a model of social science analysis that provides insight into how the legacy of the Holocaust can inform both current and future patterns of behavior and public policy. Extensive chapter notes and a select bibliography are included, along with a detailed index.

Oliner, Pearl, Samuel P. Oliner, Lawrence Baron, Lawrence A. Blum, Dennis L. Krebs, and M. Zuzanna Smolenska, editors. *Embracing the Other: Philosophical, Psychological, and Historical Perspectives on Altruism.* New York: New York University Press, 1992. ISBN 0–8147–6190–9. 460 pages. Paperback.

This anthology of essays contains diverse perspectives on altruism, drawing upon an interdisciplinary set of authors from the fields of anthropology, education, history, philosophy, psychology, and sociology. The book contains six sections, ranging across topics as varied as defining altruism, the relationship between sociobiology and moral altruism, how altruism develops and is manifested, the embracing of the "other," and strategies for promoting altruistic bonds. Essays about the Holocaust include case studies on rescuers in Poland and the Netherlands, as well as how research on altruistic bonds drawn from studies of Holocaust rescuers can influence contemporary social policy and practice. Brief contributor biographies are provided, along with chapter notes. Indexed.

Sofsky, Wolfgang. *The Order of Terror: The Concentration Camp.* Translated by William Templer. Princeton: Princeton University Press, 1997. ISBN 0–691–04354–X. 356 pages. Hardcover.

This study's purpose is to examine the nature of power within the concentration camp system, which the author claims was unique and different from traditional patterns of power and domination. Terror, organization, and excessive violence dominated the concentration camp's power system, which Sofsky claims was a closed social system. Although influenced by historical forces outside of the camp, the concentration camp was a "colony of terror" far removed from other social institutions and normal patterns of social interaction. Relying heavily on prisoner testimonies and other forms of "thick description" of camp life, the work is organized in five sections: an introduction, space and time, social structures, work, and violence and death. By placing the concentration camp system within a framework of sociological analysis, Sofsky lays bare the dominant patterns of behavior that reinforced the structures of power and domination initially established by the SS, and were later continually renegotiated in each camp by the guards and prisoners. A selected glossary and list of abbreviations is included, along with extensive chapter notes and a very detailed bibliography. Not indexed.

WOMEN'S STUDIES

Female voices are given priority in these works, which examine dimensions of the Holocaust using gender as a key category of social analysis. The use of a feminist perspective raises important questions about aspects of the Holocaust that have not been sufficiently emphasized, such as the experiences of "mischlinge" survivors, the role of gender within the concentration camp system, how power and gender intersected in the Holocaust, and many others. Particularly in the anthologies of articles and essays included here, new paths for research are suggested that can challenge traditional perspectives in Holocaust scholarship.

Crane, Cynthia. *Divided Lives: The Untold Stories of Jewish-Christian Women in Nazi Germany*. New York: St. Martin's Press, 2000. ISBN 0–312–21953–9. 372 pages. Hardcover.

The two introductory chapters in this book establish the context within which "mischlinge," or women in mixed marriages (Jewish-Christian unions), lived during the Nazi regime. The author's own family was mischlinge, with her father being a Jew and her mother raised as a Christian, thus giving the author a special insight into the life histories presented of ten women of similar status who lived through the Nazi period. The impact of the Nazi racial laws on families with mixed marriages is explored in each of the ten life histories, along with the legacy of the victims' suffering on their lives after the end of World War II. A common theme evident in the life histories is the ostracism and pain inflicted on these survivors by other Germans in the years of the Third Reich. Each life history is introduced by the author, who sets a context for the edited interview excerpts that comprise each survivor's story. Chapter notes are provided, along with a list of works consulted by the author. Indexed.

Morrison, Jack G. *Ravensbruck: Everyday Life in a Women's Concentration Camp, 1939–1945*. Princeton: Markus Wiener, 2000. ISBN 1–55876–218–3. 367 pages. Paperback.

This is a comprehensive study of the only camp in Germany expressly designed as a women's concentration camp. Morrison begins with an overview of how the Nazi regime decided to incarcerate women within the concentration camp system, eventually deciding to create the Ravensbruck camp in 1934. He examines the SS administration, the role of female overseers, and the manner in which arriving prisoners were processed by the camp guards. Part II is subdivided into chapters about each prisoner group: criminals, asocials, and Gypsies; Jehovah's Witnesses; Jews; political prisoners; prisoners from specific national groups (French, Poles); and the prisoner administration. Part III explores daily life in Ravensbruck, including such topics as friendships, work, the subcamp system, sickness and health, punishments, and children, among others. The final section deals with Ravensbruck's demise and liberation, as well as the changing nature of Ravensbruck's role during 1944–1945, when it moved gradually from being solely a concentration camp to an extermination center. Throughout the text, photographs taken by the SS are used (with qualifying statements about their deceptive purposes) along with drawings by prisoners to illustrate key points made in the text. Extensive notes, a detailed bibliography, and a glossary and abbreviations list are included.

Ofer, Dalia, and Lenore J. Wietzman, editors. *Women in the Holocaust*. New Haven: Yale University Press, 1998. ISBN 0–300–08080–8. 402 pages. Paperback.

This anthology consists of twenty-one essays, divided into four sections: "Before the War," "Life in the Ghettos," "Resistance and Rescue," and "Labor Camps and Concentration Camps." The editors provide an introduction that sets forth key themes present in the essays: structural sources of gender difference, prewar roles and responsibilities, anticipatory reactions by women, German policy and treatment of men and women, responses of Jewish men and women, and issues of resistance to research on gender in the Holocaust. The contributors address one or more of these themes in their essays, and the contributors represent a diverse set of perspectives on the subject. Some are survivors, while others are historians, sociologists, and literary scholars. This work breaks new scholarly ground by providing original contributions to the study of the Holocaust from women's perspectives, and furthering the analysis of what has to this point been a field dominated by the experience of men. Extensive chapter notes are provided, along with contributor biographies. Indexed.

Rittner, Carol, and John K. Roth, editors. *Different Voices: Women and the Holocaust*. New York: Paragon House, 1993. ISBN 1–55778–504–X. 435 pages. Paperback.

This twenty-six chapter anthology presents the experiences, interpretations, and reflections of women on the Holocaust. Including selections by survivors, rescuers, poets, scholars, and others, the anthology begins with an introductory essay by editors Carol Rittner and John Roth where issues of gender are analyzed and placed at the center of Holocaust study, rather than on the periphery. The three sections of the anthology—Voices of Experience, Voices of Interpretation, and Voices of Reflection—begin with brief introductions by the editors, and each chapter is briefly introduced in a similar manner. Voices of Experience emphasizes first-person accounts, while Voices of Interpretation engages scholarship by women about gender issues in the Holocaust. Voices of Reflection retrospectively examines women's experiences in the Holocaust, including a revealing essay by Joan Ringelheim concerning how Holocaust research can be reconsidered from a feminist perspective. The book contains a chronology where the impact of the Holocaust on women's experience is highlighted. There are many suggestions for additional reading, an extensive glossary, and a thorough index.

SPECIALIZED HISTORICAL STUDIES

Bartov, Omer, editor. *The Holocaust: Origins, Implementation, Aftermath.* New York: Routledge, 2000. ISBN 0–415–15036–1. 300 pages. Paperback.

As part of Routledge's "Rewriting Histories" series, Omer Bartov's edited volume on the Holocaust includes an introductory essay by Bartov analyzing both historical and contemporary scholarship in three areas: the Holocaust's origins, implementation of genocidal policies, and the aftermath of the Holocaust. These three key themes form the structure of the book's contents, which encompass essays about "Origins," "Implementation," and "Aftermath." Major scholars in the field, among them Raul Hilberg, Michael Burleigh, and Henry Friedlander, provide contributions to the "Origins" section. The "Implementation" section focuses on the intentionalist-functionalist debate that emerged in the 1970s, and notes that both poles of interpretation have become less distant based upon recent scholarship, which tends to emphasize studies of the "average" person's involvement as a perpetrator, bystander, or victim. The "Aftermath" section includes contributions by Primo Levi, Lawrence Langer, and Alain Finkelkraut, as well as an important discussion by Bartov regarding the difference between legitimate scholarly revisionism and the negationism engaged in by Holocaust deniers and "revisionists." Each section contains a brief introduction to the major literature and controversies in the field, and this work is particularly useful for teachers and students who want a concise but scholarly entry point for the major historiographic issues in the field of Holocaust studies. Indexed.

Bauer, Yehuda. *Rethinking the Holocaust.* New Haven: Yale University Press, 2000. ISBN 0–300–08256–8. 336 pages. Hardcover.

Providing a concise but compelling synthesis of major themes in Holocaust historiography, Yehuda Bauer revisits major issues in the field within this series of essays. Bauer argues for the uniqueness of the Holocaust, while simultaneously decrying one-dimensional interpretations of the emergence of the "final solution." He places substantial emphasis on the voices of the victims, and discusses in detail issues such as Jewish resistance, the complex role of the Jewish councils, rescue plans for Jews, and the relationship between the Holocaust and the establishment of the state of Israel. The final chapter in this provocative book contains the text of Bauer's speech to the German Bundestag in January 1998. Summarizing the major themes of the work, he concludes with a deeply felt call to teach and study about the Holocaust as a joint responsibility of both Germans and Jews—and, by extension, of all humans if we are to avoid being passive onlookers to mass murder and genocide in the future. The work is a very helpful discussion of major topics in Holocaust history, written in an accessible style that refrains from exaggeration and overstatement. The work contains an extensive bibliography, comprehensive chapter notes, and a detailed index.

Berenbaum, Michael, editor. *A Mosaic of Victims: Non-Jews Persecuted and Murdered by the Nazis*. New York: New York University Press, 1990. ISBN 0–8147–1175–8. Hardcover.

This anthology of essays addresses the broad scope of victimization during the Holocaust, when approximately 11,000,000 people were killed by the Nazis. The twenty-three chapters in this book encompass programs of mass killing (Gypsies, Soviet prisoners of war), slave labor, victimization of homosexuals, policies of sterilization and euthanasia, and others. Among the fields represented by the international set of contributors are history, psychology, sociology, and theology. Brief contributor biographies are provided, along with chapter notes. Indexed.

Berenbaum, Michael, and Abraham J. Peck, editors. *The Holocaust and History: The Unknown, the Disputed and the Reexamined.* Bloomington: Indiana University Press, 1998. ISBN 0–253–33384–1. 836 pages. Hardcover.

This comprehensive anthology of essays is an effort to assess the current state of research and study about the Holocaust, and to suggest paths for further inquiry. The fifty-four chapters are divided into eleven sections: "Probing the Holocaust: Where We Are, Where We Need to Go," "Antisemitism and Racism in Nazi Ideology," "The Politics of Racial Health and Science," "The Nazi State: Leaders and Bureaucracy," "Ordinary Men: The Sociopolitical Background," "Multiple Voices: Ideology, Exclusion and Coercion," "Concentration Camps: Their Task and Environment," "The Axis, the Allies and the Neutrals," "Jewish Leadership, Jewish Resistance," "The Rescuers," and "The Survivor Experience." The contributors represent a broad cross-section of major Holocaust scholars, and their essays reflect both their own scholarship and a consideration of current controversies in the field. Each section is introduced with a brief essay by the editors that sets the contributions in context, and points to major disputes and trends in that area of inquiry. For readers interested in the current state of Holocaust scholarship and the continuing debates in the field, this is an essential volume. Contributor biographies are provided, and chapter notes are included. Indexed.

Boonstra, Janrense, Hans Jansen, and Joke Kniesmeyer. *Antisemitism: A History Portrayed.* 2nd revised edition. Amsterdam: Anne Frank Foundation, 1993. ISBN 90–12–08032–0. 131 pages. Paperback.

Based upon an exhibition mounted at the Anne Frank House in Amsterdam, this book presents a thorough discussion of the history of anti-Semitism, with many historic black-and-white photographs, black-and-white graphics and full-color illustrations. The authors have drawn upon the very extensive record of anti-Semitic visual material available in Europe from theological sources, the mass media, historic publications, and sources in popular culture. Beginning with anti-Semitism in the Roman world and early Christianity, the book proceeds chronologically and continues to the early 1990s, with substantial emphasis on the emergence of racial anti-Semitism in the late nineteenth century and its connections to the growth of Nazism. The book also presents more recent controversies concerning the legacy of the Holocaust, such as myths of Holocaust deniers, Soviet anti-Semitism, developments in the Middle East, and the emergence of neo-Nazism in Europe and other world regions. A bibliography for further study is included, along with a source listing of all illustrations used in the book. Indexed.

Browning, Christopher. *Ordinary Men: Reserve Police Battalion 101 and the Final Solution in Poland.* New York: HarperCollins Publishers, 1992. ISBN 0–06–019013–2. 231 pages. Hardcover.

Browning's case study of one German reserve police battalion's participation in genocide employs as its major source the trial records of selected members of the battalion who were indicted and put on trial in Germany during the period 1962–1972. Using the interrogation records of 125 members of the approximately 500 man battalion, Browning reconstructs the daily life of these "ordinary men," who were responsible for the killing of approximately 38,000 Jews in Poland from July 1942 through November 1943, and for the deportation of over 45,000 Jews in Poland to death camps during eight months in the same time span. Browning rejects the "demonization" of the perpetrators, and recognizes the importance of explaining their actions as those of human beings who made individual decisions every day to participate in these mass killings. His overall interpretation emphasizes the twin influences of careerism for certain members of the battalion's officers and rank and file, combined with peer pressure placed on many battalion members to follow the lead of more aggressive, determined personnel who were enthusiastic killers. Browning's analysis clearly rejects the suggestion by some scholars that the Reserve Police were "self-selected" killers, as has been posed for the SS. Rather, these were individuals who had no consistent ideological orientation in favor of Nazism, and who were more or less the "dregs" of the conscription pool in German society. Ideological indoctrination during the war, which was heavily oriented to supporting the destruction of Jews by all segments of the German military, SS, and support groups (such as Reserve Police Battalion 101), had some effect in this case, but pales in comparison to the powerful effects of conformity to group norms. Overall, Browning's book is the most detailed study of how a group of "ordinary men" became capable of participating in mass killing through direct means (actual shootings) or as a smaller segment of a larger process (organizing deportations, moving Jews out of villages and onto trains) where their face-to-face participation in extermination was limited, but their significance in the overall outcome remained critical for the completion of the process. Indexed.

Burleigh, Michael, and Wolfgang Wippermann. *The Racial State: Germany 1933–1945*. Cambridge: Cambridge University Press, 1991. ISBN 0–521–39802–9. 386 pages. Paperback.

The authors present a comprehensive examination of the racial ideology that permeated Nazi Germany, linking it to prevalent theories of racial biology and eugenics throughout Europe in the late nineteenth and early twentieth centuries. The book contains extensive use of documents and photographs that highlight the pervasive influence of biological racism on Nazi policy development. Following a thorough description of the historic roots of Nazi racial ideology, the book contains separate chapters on the persecution of Jews, Sinti and Roma (Gypsies), and others deemed to be "life unworthy of life" (the "hereditarily ill," "asocials," and homosexuals). The final section analyzes how Nazi racial ideology, translated into state policies, sought to create a racially pure national community. Separate chapters on youth, women, and men in the Third Reich discuss how the creation of what the authors contend was a "barbaric utopia" affected virtually every aspect of German culture, from education to the mass media to private family life. Rejecting the argument that Hitler's vision of a future Germany was primarily anachronistic, emphasizing a return to a medieval past, the authors argue persuasively that the future of the Reich was to be based upon a more "modern" conception of racial hierarchy, not divisions between social classes. Through the elimination of population groups who did not meet the Nazi criteria for a racially pure society, this ideal utopian vision could be realized and a "pure" national community created. The book concludes with an extensive bibliographic essay that highlights key works for further research. Indexed.

Dobroszycki, Lucjan, editor. *The Chronicle of the Lodz Ghetto, 1941–1944*. New Haven: Yale University Press, 1984. ISBN 0–300–03208–0. 551 pages. Hardcover.

Written by a small group of workers in the Department of Archives of the Lodz Ghetto, this unique work represents a chronicle of the daily activities in the ghetto from January 12, 1941 through July 30, 1944. Detailed and powerful in its direct and stark portrayal of ghetto life, its value as a record of the systematic destruction of Jewish life is unrivaled. The in-depth introduction to the *Chronicle* written by Holocaust survivor and historian Lucjan Dobroszycki places the *Chronicle* in historical context by evaluating the role of the ghetto in the German war economy and discussing the significance of the *Chronicle* as a source about ghettos under Nazi occupation. An appendix of Polish and German street names is provided, along with selected maps of Lodz. Indexed.

Fritzche, Peter. *Germans into Nazis*. Cambridge: Harvard University Press, 1998. ISBN 0–674–35091–X. 269 pages. Hardcover.

In this work, Peter Fritzche argues that Nazism owed much of its political success to the development of popular nationalism in the period 1914–1933, an historical trend that contained the seeds of destruction for the Weimar Republic and fueled the rise of Nazism as a popular movement. Fritzche's argument focuses on how the Nazi party effectively combined elements from the ideologies of the Left and the Right, blending nationalism with social reform programs, and a harkening to the past with a utopian social vision. Downplaying the emphasis traditionally placed on economic crisis and military defeat by historians, the author contends that the attraction of ideas proposed by the Nazis, rooted in loyalties to the nation and focusing on popular mobilization, was the key in garnering support for the rise and eventual success of the Nazis in the early 1930s. Chapter notes are provided, along with a detailed index.

Gellatelly, Robert. *The Gestapo and German Society: Enforcing Racial Policy, 1933–1945*. Oxford: Oxford University Press, 1991. ISBN 0–19–820297–0. 297 pages. Paperback.

This very fine example of "microhistorical analysis" presents the results of an investigation into the operations of the Gestapo in the area of Wurzburg and Lower Franconia during the Nazi period. Gellatelly initially presents an overview of the role of the Gestapo in the Nazi state, and how they were organized in local areas as part of the German police network. The book's major focus is on how the Gestapo could so effectively enforce compliance with Nazi policies and practices. The author concludes that the support of the local population, particularly through denunciations of individuals, made the work of the Gestapo in identifying suspected "criminals" that much easier. In particular, the author presents substantial evidence of how the cooperation of the local population helped the Gestapo identify "criminals" who were not compliant in the private spheres of daily life— family, sexual behavior, and other forms of daily social interaction. This same conclusion applies to the enforcement of anti-Semitic policies, and Gellatelly argues convincingly that without citizen support of such policies through denunciations, it would have been a much harder effort to enforce compliance within the Third Reich. Another important conclusion emerging from this work is that the local police who became part of the expanded Nazi internal security apparatus after the 1933 takeover of power more often than not simply adjusted to their new status, and did not have to become ideological zealots to comply with directives that would have been anathema prior to Hitler's assumption of the chancellorship. They "adjusted" relatively easily, and found the new environment conducive to upward mobility within the police hierarchy. The book concludes with an extensive bibliography of sources and a detailed index.

Gutman, Yisrael, and Michael Berenbaum, editors. *Anatomy of the Auschwitz Death Camp*. Bloomington: Indiana University Press, 1994. ISBN 0–253–32684–2. 638 pages. Hardcover.

This anthology of essays about the Auschwitz camp complex is divided into six sections: "A History of the Camp," "Dimensions of Genocide," "The Perpetrators," "The Inmates," "The Resistance," and "Auschwitz and the Outside World." Drawing upon an international set of contributors, the essays reflect an interdisciplinary approach to the topic, including perspectives drawn from architecture, literature, sociology, psychology, and history. The preface sets out the key themes for the anthology, while each section has a brief overview written by the editors outlining the major issues addressed by the section authors. For individuals desiring a comprehensive introduction to the topic of the Auschwitz camp complex, this is the best book available. Chapter notes are provided, but there is no select bibliography. A detailed index is included.

Hackett, David A., editor and translator. *The Buchenwald Report*. With a foreword by Frederick A. Praeger. Boulder: Westview Press, 1995. ISBN 0–8133–1777–0. 397 pages. Hardcover.

Originally prepared in German by a special intelligence team from the Psychological Warfare Team of SHAEF, assisted by a committee of Buchenwald prisoners in April–May 1945, *The Buchenwald Report* was prepared to document the experiences of inmates in this notorious Nazi concentration camp. Later used as evidence in war crimes trials, *The Buchenwald Report* provides firsthand accounts by prisoners about the daily life, organization, and operations of a major Nazi concentration camp. Part I, the "Main Report," presents the findings of the SHAEF interview team, which employs evidence from interviews with inmates as well as Nazi files and records held in the camp itself. Part II, the "Individual Reports," are categorized by subtopic and include eyewitness testimonies by the inmates about specific aspects of camp life, such as "daily life," "work details," "punishments, "sanitary and health question," and many others. Editor David Hackett's introduction places *The Buchenwald Report* within an historical context as a major source on the Holocaust, describing how it was used by German author and Buchenwald prisoner Eugen Kogon as a key source for his work *The SS State* (published in German in 1946). Ironically, *The Buchenwald Report* was never published until the appearance of this edition, even though selections from it were introduced as evidence at the Nuremberg Trials. A glossary of terms, notes to the introduction by the editor, a selected bibliography, and detailed index are included. As a major source on the crimes committed by Nazism within the concentration camp system, *The Buchenwald Report* is essential reading for students of both Nazism and the Holocaust.

Johnson, Eric. *Nazi Terror: The Gestapo, Jews and Ordinary Germans.* New York: Basic Books, 1999. ISBN 0–465–04906–0. 636 pages. Hardcover.

Drawing upon the earlier work by Robert Gellatelly and other scholars, Eric Johnson spent five years researching how the Nazi terror apparatus worked, focusing primarily on three German communities in the Rhineland: Cologne, Krefeld, and Bergheim. Using documentary sources from the Gestapo and special court files, along with survey data and interviews with perpetrators, Jewish victims, and bystanders, Johnson concluded that the Nazi terror apparatus relied for its effectiveness on cooperation and support of the local population. The small numbers of the Gestapo could not have succeeded in their use of selective terror were it not for the support of ordinary Germans, who typically were not affected directly by the use of terror during the Nazi era. Relying heavily on firsthand accounts of how the selective use of terror functioned in the Nazi state, the author discusses how a range of groups—Jews, Communists, Jehovah's Witnesses, clergy, the disabled, and others—suffered while most Germans did not intervene or protest. Johnson also concludes that with the selective use of terror by the Gestapo, it was apparent that many ordinary Germans knew about some or many aspects of the Nazi mass murder campaign against the Jews. He argues that despite this knowledge, most ordinary Germans did not act on the victims' behalf due to a lack of moral concern about individuals and groups labeled as social outcasts and as a result of Nazi reinforcement of the traditional German deference to authority. The book has extensive notes, a very comprehensive bibliography for further study, and a detailed index.

Neufeld, Michael U., and Michael Berenbaum, editors. *The Bombing of Auschwitz: Should the Allies Have Attempted It?* New York: St. Martin's Press, 2000. ISBN 0–312–19838–8. 350 pages. Hardcover.

Drawing upon an eclectic mixture of scholars, the editors have fashioned a diverse set of essays on the topic of whether the Allies in 1944 should have bombed the Auschwitz death camp complex. The essays, some reprinted from earlier publications and others emerging from a conference on the topic held at the U.S. Holocaust Memorial Museum, provide perspectives on the diplomatic, military, and historiographic dimensions of the debate. Included among the contributors are photographic experts, participants who lived through the Nazi era (Gerhardt Riegner), historians, military analysts, and others. An extensive set of documents about the controversy, encompassing appeals to the United States and British regarding the possibility of bombing Auschwitz and related documents on the conditions in Auschwitz in spring 1944, are provided. The preface by Michael Berenbaum and the introduction by Michael Neufeld place the origins of the book and the evolution of the debate in context, as do each of the four section introductions. Extensive use of photos in the text provides important evidence to supplement the essays, particularly those addressing feasibility questions regarding bombing of the Auschwitz camp. A select bibliography and brief biographies of the editors and contributors are included. Indexed.

Novick, Peter. *The Holocaust in American Life.* New York: Houghton Mifflin, 1999. ISBN 0–395–84009–0. 373 pages. Hardcover.

Peter Novick's book discusses how the Holocaust has come to play a major role in American societal discourse. The author seeks to answer two questions: Why has the Holocaust become a central element of discussion and concern in U.S. society some fifty years after the end of World War II, and why has the Holocaust become so prominent a topic of examination in the United States of America, since the United States is not the central location where it occurred, nor is its population heavily constituted by survivors or their descendants? Novick's analysis relies upon the use of the concept of "collective memory," drawn from the French sociologist Maurice Halbwachs, which refers to how present-day concerns "determine what of the past we remember and how we remember it" (p. 3). Throughout his analysis of the historical development of Holocaust as collective memory in American life, Novick examines how collective memory works against a historicized perspective by simplifying interpretations, engaging in reductivist thinking about events, and limiting tolerance of ambiguities. Novick argues that while the Holocaust was initially marginalized in American culture following World War II, political, social, and cultural changes among the American Jewish community have led the Holocaust to assume a more central role in defining Jewish identity within the United States. At the same time, Novick contends that the Holocaust's increased prominence in defining Jewish identity within the United States has been problematic, since while it provides a symbol around which Jews can rally, it also presents an image of "victimhood" based upon the assertion that the Holocaust was a "unique" phenomenon. Novick also challenges the use of the Holocaust for educational purposes, specifically whether the "lessons of the Holocaust" can be instructive for guiding future behavior and public policy. He argues that the Holocaust, if deemed to be a unique historical phenomenon, may have less power to promote moral and historical responsibility because it can lead to evasion within American society of other moral failures and crimes. In short, this approach to encountering the Holocaust may lead to a devaluing of historical responsibility by Americans. Clearly controversial, *The Holocaust in American Life* challenges basic assumptions about the function of the Holocaust within American culture and this alone makes it an important work for serious examination. Extensive chapter notes. No bibliography. Indexed.

Persico, Joseph E. *Nuremberg: Infamy on Trial.* New York: Viking Penguin, 1994. ISBN 0–670–84276–1. 520 pages. Hardcover.

This account of the Nuremberg Trials draws upon the scholarship of the period from 1945 to the early 1990s, highlighting the intense drama of the proceedings and providing the important background planning and deliberation that led to the creation of the International Military Tribunal and the "trial of the century." In addition to telling the story of the Nuremberg Trials, Persico includes an epilogue where he comments on the long-term influence of the trials, and their increasing influence in a world where the precedents established at Nuremberg are being cited as the basis for new war crimes tribunals dealing with crimes in the former Yugoslavia and Rwanda. An appendix dealing with unanswered questions about the Goring suicide, a listing of the post-trial activities of the major figures in the Nuremberg Trials, detailed source notes, and an index conclude the book. For readers desiring a thorough understanding of the Nuremberg Trials written in plain language, this is the best book available.

Rittner, Carol, RSM, and Sondra Myers, editors. *The Courage to Care: Rescuers of Jews during the Holocaust.* New York: New York University Press, 1986. ISBN 0–8147–7406–7. 157 pages. Paperback.

Including stories of rescuers from throughout Occupied Europe, this volume contains the accounts of individuals and groups who risked their lives to save Jews from the Nazis and their collaborators. The accounts are told by both rescuers and those who were rescued, and the text is liberally illustrated with photographs of the locations and the individuals involved in each act of rescue. Concluding the book is a set of reflections on the acts of rescue by five individuals: three survivors, including Elie Wiesel, one theologian, and a filmmaker (Pierre Sauvage, creator of a film about the rescue of Jews in the southern French town of Sur le Chambon). This concluding section examines why the rescuers profiled in the book acted in specific ways, along with raising questions about why most of Occupied Europe did little to assist Jews targeted for extermination by the Nazi regime.

Shermer, Michael, and Alex Grobman. *Denying History.* Berkeley: University of California Press, 2000. ISBN 0–520–21612–1. 312 pages. Hardcover.

This comprehensive analysis of the origins and contemporary status of efforts to deny the Holocaust clearly establishes the flaws and fallacies of denier claims, while providing thorough refutations of central denial claims, such as the assertion that Jews were not systematically gassed and murdered in camps. The authors establish a solid basis for their analysis in Part I, where they discuss the relationship of the issue of Holocaust denial to First Amendment freedoms. More importantly, they offer a detailed set of definitions and discussion of how historians reconstruct the past. These chapters provide a foundation for the remainder of the book, where the processes of historical reconstruction and tests of evidence/arguments are applied to denier claims. The concluding chapter, "The Rape of History," provides suggestions on how to detect denier claims and how to distinguish legitimate historical revision from the distortions and fallacies of Holocaust deniers. Detailed notes to each chapter and an extensive bibliography are included. Indexed.

Wyman, David S., editor. *The World Reacts to the Holocaust.* Baltimore: Johns Hopkins University Press, 1996. ISBN 0–8018–4969–1. 981 pages. Hardcover.

This wide-ranging work examines the world's reaction to the Holocaust since 1945, with emphasis placed on how individual societies in North America, Europe, the Middle East, and Africa have engaged the legacy of the Holocaust within institutions (government, religion, education, voluntary associations), in the mass media, and in scholarship, literature, and film. Following editor David Wyman's introduction, which discusses the continuing tension in the study of the Holocaust between the unique and the universal as well as a typology of reactions to the Holocaust (denial, denationalization, trivialization, rationalization, and universalization), each chapter presents one or more world societies and how they have responded to the Holocaust since the end of World War II. These chapters provide a concise history of Jewish culture in that society, examine the reactions of that society to the Holocaust, and, where applicable, offer a brief history of the Holocaust in that society. A valuable contribution to how the Holocaust has become an important part of the world's consciousness during the second half of the twentieth century, this book includes contributor biographies and a detailed index.

4

DRAMA, FICTION, AND POETRY

OVERVIEW

The vast landscape of Holocaust literature is dominated by works of drama, fiction, and poetry. Although some scholars define first-person accounts (diaries, memoirs, and autobiographies) as literature, for the purposes of this chapter only drama, fiction, and poetry are included. Chapter 8 should be consulted for selected resources in the area of first-person accounts. Primacy of place in this chapter has been given to anthologies of drama, fiction, and poetry, as these represent important starting points for further investigation of each genre. In virtually every anthology, editors have included comprehensive introductions that discuss major themes in the study of Holocaust drama, fiction, and poetry, and many of these works contain detailed bibliographies or chapter notes that facilitate more extended investigation by the reader. Also included in this chapter are works of literary criticism, as well as bibliographic works that assist the reader in identifying works of literary merit and how they relate to specific content themes about the Holocaust. Where individual works of drama, fiction, and poetry have been included as entries, they were selected based upon their recognized literary merit and their inclusion in bibliographies and listings of key works of Holocaust literature. Drawn from a vast collection of Holocaust fiction, these works represent a cross-section of high quality fiction that addresses both the history of the Holocaust and its legacy for contemporary life. They also include diverse settings of time and place and reflect a variety of literary styles addressing the experiences of Holocaust survivors and their descendants.

DRAMA

Fuchs, Elinor, editor. *Plays of the Holocaust: An International Anthology.* New York: Theatre Communications Group, 1987. ISBN 0–93–0452–63–1. 310 pages. Paperback.

This anthology begins with an introduction by Elinor Fuchs that discusses two types of drama about the Holocaust: (1) those depicting catastrophic events as private experience and (2) those depicting catastrophic events as collective experience (community catastrophe). Each of the six plays in the anthology is described, with background information provided on the playwrights, a brief summary of the play, and some key ideas and themes to emphasize during reading or performance. The six plays represented in this anthology are *Eli: A Mystery Play of the Sufferings of Israel* by Nelly Sachs (Germany/Sweden); *Mister Fugue or Earth Sick* by Liliane Atlan (France); *Auschwitz* by Peter Barnes (Great Britain); *Replika* by Jozef Szajna (Poland); *Ghetto* by Joshua Sobol (Israel); and *Cathedral of Ice* by James Schevill (United States). The work concludes with an annotated bibliography of Holocaust plays by Alvin Goldfarb. No index.

Isser, Edward R. *Stages of Annihilation: Theatrical Representations of the Holocaust.* Madison, NJ: Fairleigh Dickinson University Press, 1997. ISBN 0–8386–3674–8. 209 pages. Hardcover.

This series of essays examines Holocaust drama from multiple perspectives: as representations of particular national traditions in drama (American British, French, German); as the response of specific playwrights to the Holocaust and Nazism (Arthur Miller); as a form of theatrical exploitation, as an entry point for study of "closed" topics about the Shoah; and as a metaphor for inquiries into contemporary issues such as homosexuality and AIDS. The extensive introduction provides a brief history of Holocaust drama as a subgenre in the broader field of Holocaust literature, and continues with a presentation of the critical parameters in the field. Isser juxtaposes Robert Skloot's emphasis on the uniqueness of the Holocaust with other interpretations that view the Holocaust as a tragedy with significant implications for contemporary society, but that see the uniqueness claim as a constraint on the artistic imagination. The book has detailed chapter notes, a very comprehensive bibliography, and a thorough index.

Schumacher, Claude, editor. *Staging the Holocaust: The Shoah in Drama and Performance.* Cambridge: Cambridge University Press, 1998. ISBN 0–521–62415–0. 353 pages. Hardcover.

This comprehensive anthology of articles on Holocaust drama brings together an international collection of contributors, including scholars, playwrights, and directors from the United States, Israel, Germany, and France. The introduction by Claude Schumacher clarifies the key themes in the volume and discusses the role of imaginative art (poetry, theatre, and other genres) in portraying the Holocaust, a role complementary to, but different from, that served by historians. The book contains a useful annotated list of Holocaust plays created between 1933 and 1997, as well as a select bibliography and a detailed index.

Skloot, Robert. *The Darkness We Carry: The Drama of the Holocaust.* Madison: University of Wisconsin Press, 1988. ISBN 0–299–11660–3. 147 pages. Hardcover.

This book provides a thorough introduction to Holocaust drama, discussing representative works in six categories: Choice and/or Survival, Tragedy and the Holocaust, The "Tragic" Comic Vision, Revisions and Reversals, Some German Voices, and Responses and Responsibilities. The twenty-five plays discussed in the book sometimes are examined in more than one chapter based upon their dramatic purpose and content. Skloot analyzes each work from two perspectives: as moral texts and as theatrical events. The brief introduction establishes the author's rationale for the book, explains his analytical framework, and discusses the role of the Holocaust in the evolution of his scholarly interests and activities. Indexed.

———. *The Theatre of the Holocaust, Volume 1.* Madison: University of Wisconsin Press, 1982. ISBN 0–299–09074–4. 333 pages. Paperback.

This anthology includes an introduction that presents a brief historical overview of the Holocaust, and then discusses theatre of the Holocaust in a context of addressing five specific purposes: paying homage to the victims; educating audiences to the facts of history; producing an emotional response to the historical facts; raising moral questions for audiences to discuss and reflect upon; and drawing lessons from the recreated events. Skloot discusses the role of Holocaust literature and the tensions evident when artistic representations of history interact with the Holocaust as historical fact. By rejecting "silence," artists must address questions of the Holocaust's uniqueness, along with the danger of metaphorical/analogical discussion and the problematic use of realism in Holocaust plays. The author examines the works in the anthology and offers directions that the plays point toward for the future, noting questions about moral choices and how the viewer can connect with distant times and places to make good choices in contemporary contexts. The plays included in Volume I are *Resort 76* by Shimon Wincelberg, *Throne of Straw* by Harold and Edith Lieberman, *The Cannibals* by George Tabori, and *Who Will Carry the Word?* by Charlotte Delbo. A selected bibliography and playwright/ author biographical sketches are included. No index.

————. *The Theatre of the Holocaust, Volume 2*. Madison: University of Wisconsin Press, 1999. ISBN 0–299–16274–5. 407 pages. Paperback.

The second volume of Robert Skloot's *Theatre of the Holocaust* contains six plays, all different from the four plays included in Volume 1. The introduction carries forward ideas introduced in the first volume, updating the reader regarding the proliferation of both historical and imaginative works on the Holocaust since the early 1980s. Skloot discusses the expansion of voices about the Holocaust: second- and third-generation authors, women/feminist perspectives, and use of new forms of representation (as discussed in other works by Lawrence Langer and Saul Friedlander). Each play's contents and performance characteristics are summarized, and in contrast to Volume 1, the playwrights have contributed brief introductions to their works. The six plays in this volume are *Camp Comedy* by Roy Kift, *The Survivor and the Translator* by Lenny Sack, *Dreams of Anne Frank* by Bernard Krops, *The Model Apartment* by Donald Margulies, *The Portage to San Cristobal* by George Steiner, adapted by Christopher Hampton, and *H.I.D. (Hess Is Dead)* by Howard Brenton. A selected bibliography and brief contributor biographies are included. No index.

FICTION: BIBLIOGRAPHIES AND HANDBOOKS

Edelheit, Abraham J., and Hershel Edelheit, editors. *Bibliography of Holocaust Literature*. Boulder, CO: Westview Press, 1986. ISBN 0–8133–7233–X. 842 pages. Hardcover.

————. *Bibliography of Holocaust Literature*. Supplement. Boulder, CO: Westview Press, 1986. ISBN 0–8133–0896–8. 684 pages. Hardcover.

These two works include exhaustive listings of literature on the Holocaust, including original works, collections and anthologies, and critical essays and literary criticism. Indexed.

Simon, Ralph R. *A Selected Annotated Bibliography of Literature on the Holocaust for Juvenile and Young Adult Collections*. Revised edition. New York: Association of Jewish Libraries, 1992. ISBN 0–929262–29–8. 44 pages. Paperback.

This bibliography includes recommended reference works, nonfiction books for juvenile and young adult readers, fictional works for juvenile and young adult readers, works about the impact of the Holocaust in the United States, and nonfiction books for high school and adult collections.

WORKS OF LITERARY CRITICISM

Hartmann, Geoffrey, editor. *Holocaust Remembrance: The Shapes of Memory.* Oxford: Blackwell Publishers, 1994. ISBN 1–55786–367–9. 306 pages. Paperback.

This collection of essays addresses the concept of memory and how it shapes contemporary understanding of the Holocaust. Contributors include literary scholars, sociologists, philosophers, film scholars, poets and writers of fiction, historians, architects, and scholars of Jewish studies. In each essay, the emphasis is on how memory is shaped and transmitted through specific works, whether they be testimonies, memorials, film, historical structures, fiction, poetry, and other forms. Editor Geoffrey Hartman's introduction presents major themes encompassed in the anthology's contents, and he discusses the essays briefly in relation to how the shaping of memory takes place in the range of media examined in the work. Chapter notes are provided. Indexed.

Lang, Berel, editor. *Writing and the Holocaust.* New York: Holmes & Meier, 1988. ISBN 0–8419–1184–3. 301 pages. Hardcover.

The central theme of this essay collection is the relationship between the moral implications of the Holocaust and how it is rendered through literary means. Key questions addressed by the contributors are: how does the past enter or shape representations in the present, how can evil be conceptualized or embodied in art, and how do writers of imaginative literature incorporate historical discourse in their works? Drawing primarily from presentations made at a conference entitled "Writing and the Holocaust" held at SUNY Albany in 1987, the book contains essays by Raul Hilberg, Lawrence Langer, Terrence Des Pres, Saul Friedlander, George Steiner, Aharon Appelfeld, and others. A roundtable discussion regarding the meaning of the conference is also included, showcasing the ideas of Raul Hilberg, Cynthia Ozick, Aharon Appelfeld, and Saul Friedlander. Along with a detailed index, brief biographies of contributors are included.

Langer, Lawrence. *Admitting the Holocaust: Collected Essays.* New York: Oxford University Press, 1995. ISBN 0–19–509357–7. 202 pages. Hardcover.

This collection of essays, many previously published, offers insights by Lawrence Langer into the meaning of the Holocaust and its legacy in literature, film, theology, history, and videotaped testimonies. The main emphasis in the essays is the author's focus on the manner in which modern society confronts the reality of the Holocaust and its impact on contemporary consciousness. Among the topics included in this collection are essays on the use of history in Holocaust literature, the language of Aharon Appelfeld, the works of Cynthia Ozick, how the Holocaust has been Americanized in drama and film, and the relationship between history and memory in Holocaust testimonies. This collection serves as a good starting point for the consideration of Langer's important work as a literary scholar on the Holocaust, since it addresses a broad range of issues and reflects many years of scholarship. Chapter notes are provided along with a detailed index.

―――. *The Holocaust and the Literary Imagination.* New Haven: Yale University Press, 1975. ISBN 0–300–02121–6. 300 pages. Paperback.

Lawrence Langer's pioneering work on study of the "literature of atrocity" notes that many writers have perceived the Holocaust as unqiue, and have therefore sought to render the "unspeakable" in art, clearly a daunting task. Arguing that the existence of the death and concentration camps was not only an historical phenomenon, but also a transformative influence on how modern society understands the nature of reality, Langer discusses five interrelated themes: the replacement of life consciousness with the power and presence of death; the violation of childhood innocence; the assault on physical reality; the crumbling of rationality; and the disruption of chronological time. In the seven chapters of the book, a range of selected works is used to illustrate these five themes, with Langer preferring in-depth study of fewer works to an encyclopedic survey. Indexed.

Young, James E. *Writing and Rewriting the Holocaust: Narrative and the Consequences of Interpretation.* Bloomington: Indiana University Press, 1990. ISBN 0–253–36716–6. 243 pages. Paperback.

James Young's work challenges the reader to consider the power of narrative as a central theme in the study of the Holocaust. Rejecting hard and fast distinctions between history, literature, and memoirs/testimonies, Young argues that how we hear what is passed down from the past to current generations constitutes an important dimension of how we understand. Covering drama, documentary fiction, diaries, memoirs, poetry, memorials, and video and film testimony, the author advocates a critical reading of such works to develop a deeper understanding of how the narratives in these texts can influence contemporary life. Chapter notes and a very comprehensive bibliography are included. Indexed.

ANTHOLOGIES

Brown, Jean F., Elaine C. Stephens, and Janet E. Rubin, editors. *Images from the Holocaust: A Literature Anthology.* Lincolnwood, IL: National Textbook Company, 1997. ISBN 0–8442–5920–9. 579 pages. Paperback. Instructor's edition available.

This broad-based anthology includes essays, excerpts from historical works and literature, first-person accounts, poetry, drama, and selections from memoirs and personal testimony. The editors have organized the contents into ten chapters, which are roughly chronological in design: "Rumblings of Danger," "In Hiding," "Fleeing for Their Lives," "Surrounded by Ghetto Walls," "Imprisoned in the Camps," "Resisting Evil," "Liberation," "The Days After," "A Mosaic of Courage," and "Echoing Reflections." Brief introductions describing the major themes of each section are provided by the editors, who also introduce each selection with a capsule biography of the author and selected details about their work. A detailed set of source acknowledgments is provided, as well as an index of authors and titles. The instructor's edition includes background information for teaching, as well as suggestions for responding through writing and discussion for each selection presented in the anthology.

Eliach, Yaffa. *Hasidic Tales of the Holocaust.* New York: Vintage, 1988. ISBN 0–679–72043–X. 267 pages. Paperback.

Drawn from oral histories and interviews, the eighty-nine original Hasidic tales in this anthology offer witness to the suffering endured by Hasidic Jews. The collection is divided into four sections: "Ancestors and Faith," "Friendship," "Spirit Alone," and "At the Gates of Freedom." The editor's foreword describes how the interviews and oral histories were collected, and the tales extracted from those original testimonies. It also discusses the thematic division of the eighty-nine stories in the anthology, at all times emphasizing the spiritual struggle for survival that dominates the content of the tales. A glossary, name and subject indexes, and notes to selected tales are included. Indexed.

Friedlander, Albert H., editor. *Out of the Whirlwind: A Reader of Holocaust Literature.* Revised and expanded edition. New York: UAHC Press, 1999. ISBN 0–8074–0703–8. 594 pages. Paperback.

This revised and expanded edition of the classic anthology first published in 1968 incorporates an entire new section entitled "Looking Back," which includes excerpts from sources as diverse as Daniel Goldhagen's *Hitler's Willing Executioners,* Bernard Schlink's novel *The Reader,* and Theo Richmond's *Konin.* This new section includes material not only by scholars and survivors, but from the second generation—descendants of both perpetrators and victims. Each section of the anthology has a brief introductory essay on section themes, plus a black and white illustration by Jacob Landau. The selections in the seven sections of the anthology begin with headnotes by the editor that describe the selection's content and provide some background information on the author. A general introduction to the anthology follows a new preface to this edition where the editor offers his rationale for the expanded version and describes the significance of its contents. No index or contributor biographies.

Glatstein, Jacob, Israel Knox, and Samuel Margoshes, editors; Mordecai Bernstein and Adah B. Fogel, associate editors. *Anthology of Holocaust Literature.* New York: Atheneum, 1968. ISBN 0–689–70343–0. 412 pages. Paperback.

An eclectic selection of eyewitness accounts, all by survivors or victims of the Holocaust, this volume contains excerpts from memoirs, diaries, journals, histories of specific towns and events, and autobiographical accounts. The selections are overwhelmingly focused on Eastern Europe, with scant attention paid to Western and Southern Europe, and little material offered about the Soviet Union. Recognizing this geographic orientation, the selections are effective in depicting ghetto life, conditions affecting children, the concentration and death camps, resistance efforts by Jews, and rescue efforts of Poles on behalf of Jews. While a useful starting point to enter the world of Jewish persecution as interpreted by the victims themselves, the volume needs to be supplemented with accounts of Jews and non-Jews who suffered at the hands of the Nazis and their collaborators throughout all of Occupied Europe. A glossary of terms, set of author biographies, and listing of source acknowledgments are included. No index.

Langer, Lawrence. *Art from the Ashes: A Holocaust Anthology*. New York: Oxford University Press, 1995. ISBN 0–19–507559–5. 693 pages. Hardcover.

This very comprehensive anthology, introduced and edited by one of the world's leading literary scholars on the Holocaust, contains a diverse collection of historical essays, poetry, prose, documents, diaries, eyewitness accounts, drama, and a visual presentation of selected works by Terezin artists. The six sections of the anthology are: "The Way it Was," "Journals and Diaries," "Fiction," "Drama," "Poetry," and "Painters of Terezin." As valuable as the contributions are by the authors whom Langer has selected, the editor's essays introducing the work and each section are equally valuable for their insights into themes about the Holocaust and literary style that permeate this collection. Despite lacking an index and set of author biographies, this anthology is highly recommended as an introduction to the broad range of Holocaust literature that students of the topic will encounter.

Lorenz, Dagmar G.G., editor. *Contemporary Jewish Writing in Austria: An Anthology*. Lincoln: University of Nebraska Press, 1999. ISBN 0–8032–2923–2. 362 pages. Hardcover.

This collection encompasses a broad selection of twentieth-century Jewish writing from Austria, including authors born before World War I and those from the very recent past. Among the contributors are Jean Amery, Ruth Kluger Angress, Jakov Lind, Paul Celan, and Ilse Aichinger. The genres represented are essays, poetry, and fiction, and a common theme underlying the contributions is the degree to which Jews are viewed as the "other" and discriminated against within predominantly Christian Austrian society. The opening critical essay by Dagmar G.G. Lorenz provides an historical analysis of the key themes evident in the works included in the collection. Brief biographical sketches are included before each author's contribution to the collection. Source acknowledgments are provided, but there is no index.

Ramras-Rauch, Gilas, and Joseph Michman-Melkman, editors. *Facing the Holocaust: Selected Israeli Fiction*. Afterword by Gershon Shaked. Philadelphia: Jewish Publication Society, 1985. ISBN 0–8276–0253–7. 292 pages. Hardcover.

This anthology of twelve selections from Israeli authors brings together both the realistic and symbolic/fantastic themes that have dominated the Israeli Holocaust literature since the end of World War II. Authors well known in Europe and North America such as Aharon Appelfeld and Uri Orlev are included in this collection, along with other distinguished Israeli writers. The introduction by Gilas Ramras-Rauch provides a thematic context for the works encompassed in the anthology, and the book concludes with a brief set of author biographies. No index.

Raphael, Linda Schermer, and Marc Lee Raphael, editors. *When Night Fell: An Anthology of Holocaust Short Stories*. New Brunswick: Rutgers University Press, 1999. ISBN 0–8135–2663–9. 300 pages. Paperback.

Short stories by nineteen authors are included in this anthology. The introduction explores the rational for creating this anthology, and provides an historical and literary analysis of the contents. Among the works included in the anthology are selections by Aharon Appelfeld, Hans Peter Richter, Ida Fink, and sixteen others representing Europe, Israel, and North America. Works by Jews and non-Jews, survivors, authors who lived through World War II, and more contemporary authors demonstrate the eclectic nature of the contributors. This collection is one of the few anthologies of short stories dealing with Holocaust themes and content available for interested readers. No index.

SELECTED WORKS OF FICTION

Becker, Jurek. *Jacob the Liar*. Translated by Leila Vennewitz. New York: Arcade Publishing, 1990. ISBN 1–55970–315–6. 244 pages. Hardcover.

This story tells how Jacob Heym, a young Jew in a Polish ghetto, creates the illustion that he has a radio that provides news from the outside world, the purpose being to sustain morale for the ghetto inhabitants during their desperate struggle for survival. Becker himself was a camp survivor, and *Jacob the Liar* puts into perspective the complex emotions of ghetto inhabitants who had limited contact with the outside world, and whose daily lives were beset by uncertainty, human suffering, and death.

Bellow, Saul. *Mr. Sammler's Planet*. Introduction by Stanley Crouch. New York: Penguin, 1996. New edition of the work first published in 1972. ISBN 0–14–01–8936–X. 313 pages. Paperback.

Using a Holocaust survivor as the central figure and set in New York City, Saul Bellow creates a plot that interweaves themes of moral decay and the complexity of human relationships. Mr. Sammler's journey through the urban landscape brings him from an austere distance to a compassionate embrace of other humans, and the rejection of impersonal science and technology. Mr. Sammler's empathy is hard-won, but is a triumph because he rejects the attractions of indifference and apathy toward other human beings, despite their imperfections and failings.

Borowski, Tadeusz. *This Way for the Gas, Ladies and Gentlemen.* Selected and translated by Barbara Vedder. Introduction by Jan Kott. Introduction translated by Michael Kandel. New York: Penguin, 1976. ISBN 0–1401–8624–7. 180 pages. Paperback.

This set of short stories by Tadeusz Borowski, an Auschwitz and Dachau survivor, presents reflections about his concentration camp experiences. Written within a year of his liberation, these stories illuminate the daily routine of atrocities encountered in the camp universe. As individuals struggle to survive, their compassion for their fellow human beings is challenged by self-interest, with the competition between humanity and inhumanity as an omnipresent element.

Doctorow, E.L. *City of God.* New York: Penguin, 2000. ISBN 0–452–28209–8. 272 pages. Paperback.

This novel emphasizes the search for spiritual renewal within a secular civilization at the close of the twentieth century. Set in New York City, the story is about how an Episcopal priest and a female Jewish rabbi, the daughter of a Holocaust survivor, search for a lost cross. As the tale unfolds, the two key characters encounter a diverse group of New York residents, among them war veterans, clerics, Holocaust survivors, theologians, crooners, and moviemakers. Memories of Holocaust experiences are embedded within the text as Doctorow paints a complex picture of how people attempt to construct meaning in their search for spiritual renewal.

Fink, Ida. *The Journey.* Translated by Joanna Wechsler and Francine Prose. New York: Penguin, 1993. ISBN 0–452–27015–4. 250 pages. Paperback.

Drawing upon the author's own experiences as a Jew in hiding during World War II, this novel details the story of how two sisters seeking to survive used forged identities to hide in Germany. The sisters survive a ghetto deportation action, and later engage in a series of desperate efforts to escape the Nazis, eventually reuniting with their family after the defeat of Nazi Germany.

Friedman, Carl. *Nightfather.* Translated from the Dutch by Arnold and Erica Pomerans. New York: Persea Books, 1994. ISBN 0–89255–210–7. 136 pages. Paperback.

This fictional account, told in the voice of a female child of a Holocaust survivor, illustrates how survivor experiences are transmitted to the second generation, then becoming the property of the younger generation. The young female narrator lives in two worlds, the everyday world of school, play, and friends and the world of camp memories shared by her father at home. In the "Afterword" to the story, author Carl Friedman discusses the details of her father's life, which formed the basis for *Nightfather,* and explains the importance of using literature to promote kindness and tolerance, particularly in light of the suffering her father and many others endured in World War II at the hands of Nazi Germany.

Hackl, Eric. *Farewell Sidonia.* Translated by Edna McCown. New York: Fromm International, 1991. ISBN 0–88064–124–X. 135 pages. Paperback.

This novel relates the story of how an orphaned Gypsy girl in Austria is taken in by the Breirather family. Set in Styr, Austria, home of the author, the novel is rooted in historical research and describes how the Gypsy girl Sidonia faces discrimination, segregation, deportation, and ultimately death at the hands of Nazi racism. Issues of responsibility, bureaucratic cruelty, and the town's indifference to racism permeate the novel, because the young girl's "difference" was the cause of her persecution and provided an excuse for the townspeople to sacrifice her.

Hersey, John. *The Wall.* New York: Vintage, 1988. Original edition published in 1950. ISBN 0–394–75696–7. 632 pages. Paperback.

Drawing upon the events and documents detailing the life and eventual destruction of the Warsaw Ghetto, John Hersey's novel focuses on the efforts of forty Jews to escape and resist the German occupation of Poland. Written in the style of a diary, the novel relies on the use of many references to actual events, locations, and historical individuals during World War II in Poland. Given its original publication date of less than a decade after the events its describes, *The Wall* communicates the tragic fate of Polish Jews under Nazi rule with an immediacy that is only surpassed by the original sources themselves.

Karmel, Ilona. *An Estate of Memory.* Afterword by Ruth K. Angress. New York: Feminist Press, 1986. ISBN 0–935312–64–1. 457 pages. Paperback.

This novel about the experiences of four women in a concentration camp is marked by their gradual degradation and loss of the will to live, until the birth of a baby poses them with a daunting challenge: how can they help the baby survive, while keeping its birth and existence a secret from the camp guards. The dependence upon one another of the four women and the intensity of their daily struggle to survive are key themes of the novel, which emphasizes the strength and commitment of the female community in a camp system created by men. In contrast to many other works of Holocaust fiction, this novel places men at the periphery of the story, giving the central roles and decisions to women.

Keneally, Thomas. *Schindler's List.* New York: Touchstone, 1992. ISBN 0–671–44972–9. 398 pages. Paperback.

This work of historical fiction is based upon extensive research in documentary sources and with survivors who were saved through the efforts of Oskar Schindler. Originally a Nazi party member who sought to maximize his financial standing as a war profiteer, Oskar Schindler became a savior for over 1,000 Jews who worked in his factories, first in Poland and later in Czechoslovakia. Thomas Keneally's story necessarily focuses on the dominant figure of Schindler, but the reader receives a detailed portrait of the sadistic commandant of the Plaszow concentration camp, Amon Goeth, as well as indelible portraits of prisoners who worked closely with Schindler or whose lives illustrated the key elements of survival as part of Schindler's workforce. Keneally's work became the basis for one of the most widely viewed Holocaust films of all time, Steven Spielberg's *Schindler's List.*

Kolitz, Zvi. *Yosl Rakover Talks to God.* Translated by Carol Brown Janeway. Originally published in German in 1996. New York: Vintage, 1999. ISBN 0–375–40451–1. 99 pages. Paperback.

This short story was originally written by Zvi Kolitz for a Yiddish newspaper in Buenos Aires in 1946. This edition contains a second element, the story of German journalist Paul Badde's search for the author in the late 1990s. The basic meaning of the story is that God should not be abandoned by human beings, even in the midst of widespread suffering and death, such as occurred in the Warsaw Ghetto. For this edition, a meditation on Kolitz' short story by the distinguished French philosopher Emanuel Levinas and additional commentary on the religious meanings of the story by Leon Wieseltier are included. No index.

Kuznetzov, A. Anatoli. *Babi Yar: A Document in the Form of a Novel.* Translated by David Floyd. New York: Farrar, Straus & Giroux, 1970. ISBN 037–4–5281–79. 478 pages. Paperback.

Originally published in censored form in the Soviet magazine *Yunost* in 1966, *Babi Yar* was smuggled out of the USSR and published in its uncensored form in 1970. The work is told through the eyes of a young Soviet boy, and depicts the oppression faced by Soviet Jews and Ukrainians under both Soviet and German rule. The chapter entitled "Babi Yar" is a harrowing account of the survival of D.M. Pronicheva, who endured the massacre of over 33,000 Jews in two days during September 1941 in Kiev. Pronicheva's account, based upon an interview done by the author with this survivor in the 1960s, is one of a number of documents included within this work of fiction that lend it authority as a work on the Holocaust.

Lind, Yakov. *Soul of Wood.* Translation by the author of the German original, published in 1962. New York: Hill & Wang, 1964. ISBN 0–8090–1526–9. 186 pages. Hardcover.

This collection of seven stories about the Holocaust includes "Soul of Wood," a novella that deals with efforts to shield a young disabled Jewish boy from the oppression of the Nazis. Lind's writing emphasizes irony, satire, and twists of fate, along with rich, detailed character portraits of individuals including aristocratic supporters of Hitler, members of the SS, and Jews seeking refuge. Themes of exploitation, evil, and the abuse of power dominate many of his stories, suggesting that humans have made little progress since the end of World War II in mitigating the factors that produced the Holocaust.

Oz, Amos. *Touch the Water, Touch the Wind.* Translated from the Hebrew by Nicholas de Lange in collaboration with the author. New York: Harcourt Brace Jovanovich, 1974. ISBN 0–15–690772–X. 179 pages. Paperback.

Relating the tale of a journey from Poland to Israel by Elisha Pomeranz, a watchmaker, mathematician, and musician, this novel links the horror of the Holocaust to an effort at seeking immortality in Israel during the 1967 Arab-Israeli war. Intertwining imagery of the past and present, the author successfully establishes connections that forge a complex identity for Elisha and Stefa Pomeranz, the main characters of the story.

Ozick, Cynthia. *The Shawl.* New York: Vintage, 1990. ISBN 0–679–72926–7. 70 pages. Paperback.

Actually two works, a short story and a novella, *The Shawl*'s first section (short story) is set in a concentration camp, where Rosa's daughter Magda is killed by a guard after being held by Rosa in her shawl. Later, in the novella ("Rosa"), Rosa is an indigent single woman living in a Miami hotel whose main contact with her family is her niece Stella. Although Rosa no longer is employed, she lives in a world symbolized by the shawl that reminds her of her daughter. Functioning both as a remembrance of her daughter and as a symbol of the emptiness felt by Rosa for all the years since her daughter's murder, the shawl symbolizes how Rosa's life is inextricably linked to the Holocaust, despite the intervening years.

Remarque, Erich Maria. *Spark of Life: A Novel of Resistance.* New York: Ballantine Books, 1998. Originally published in 1952. ISBN 0–449–91251–5. 365 pages. Paperback.

This novel presents the response of concentration camp inmates to the end of World War II, describing camp operations, the role of the SS, and efforts by prisoners to survive as SS terror escalates with the impending end of the war. The extreme difficulties encountered by Jewish prisoners relocated to Germany at the end of the war are detailed, while the resistance of prisoners to the ongoing efforts at dehumanization by the SS are a central theme of the work.

Schlink, Bernard. *The Reader.* Translated by Carol Brown Janeway. London: Phoenix, 1997. ISBN 0–75380–470–0. 216 pages. Paperback.

This contemporary novel about the Holocaust's legacy in Germany focuses on the relationship between a young man (the narrator) and an older woman, which serves as the vehicle for examination of connections between Germany during the Third Reich and modern-day German life.

Uris, Leon. *Mila 18.* New York: Bantam, 1962. ISBN 0–553–24160–5. 563 pages. Paperback.

Based upon extensive historical research, this novel relates the story of the 1943 Warsaw Ghetto uprising and the subsequent destruction of the ghetto. The book's title is taken from the location of the ghetto fighter headquarters in Warsaw during the uprising. Author Leon Uris integrates journal entries by key character Alexander Brandel within the novel, thus emphasizing the interplay between the private and the public as the ghetto uprising unfolds. The relationship between actual events and the contents of the novel is very close, and readers interested in Jewish resistance to Nazi oppression will find it a worthy introduction to study of this important aspect of the Holocaust.

————. *QB VII.* New York: Bantam, 1972. ISBN 0–553–27094–X. 426 pages. Paperback.

Leon Uris' fictional courtroom novel is based upon post–World War II efforts to hold perpetrators accountable for war crimes and crimes against humanity. The story focuses on efforts in Great Britain to prosecute a Polish medical doctor who allegedly functioned as a sadistic doctor in a concentration camp under Nazi control. Themes of Polish anti-Semitism, post–World War II political intrigue, and Cold War politics are intertwined with the war crimes prosecution that forms the core of the novel.

POETRY

Anthologies

Fishman, Charles, editor. *Blood to Remember: American Poets on the Holocaust.* Lubbock: Texas Tech University Press, 1991. ISBN 0–89672–215–5. 426 pages. Paperback.

Including selected works on the Holocaust by 185 American poets, the contents of this anthology are divided into five thematic categories: After the Holocaust—No Poetry?, The Terrified Meadows, Crystal Night, Without Jews, and The Late Train: Memory. A number of the poets represented in the anthology are survivors of the Holocaust, but many are not. The editor does not provide a narrative introduction to the work's contents, but offers extensive notes on the poems in two chapters following the listing of source acknowledgments. Separate indexes of poets, translators, and titles are included to help the reader locate specific works in the anthology.

Schiff, Hilda, compiler. *Holocaust Poetry*. New York: St. Martin's, 1995. ISBN 0–312–13086–4. 234 pages. Hardcover.

This eclectic anthology includes 119 poems by fifty-nine different poets, all united by their focus on the Holocaust. Following an introduction where the compiler discusses her rationale for choosing the work's contents, as well as how it is organized, the book is divided into eight thematic sections: "Alienation," "Persecution," "Destruction," "Rescuers, Bystanders, Perpetrators," "Afterwards," "Second Generation," "Lessons," and "God." The broad range of authors encompassed in the anthology includes poets from Europe, Israel, and North America, as well as works by survivors and poets who confronted the Holocaust after World War II ended. Biographical sketches of the contributors are provided, along with four indexes (poets, translators, titles, and first lines). For the reader desiring an effective entry point for the range of Holocaust poetry available today, this is an excellent place to begin.

Teichman, Milton, and Sharon Ledes, editors. *Truth and Lamentation: Stories and Poems on the Holocaust*. Urbana: University of Illinois Press, 1994. ISBN 0–252–06335–X. 526 pages. Paperback.

Dividing the contents into "Truth" and "Lamentations," the editors have included works by a broad cross-section of authors, including Jews and non-Jews, survivors, writers from the post–World War II era who have made the Holocaust a central theme of their writing, and others. Truly international in scope, the collection encompasses contributions from Europe, Israel and the Western Hemisphere. The anthology's introduction is comprehensive, explaining the rationale for the selections in the book, as well as describing the anthology's thematic organization and how its contents illustrate varied dimensions of the Holocaust experience. An extensive bibliography is provided, along with brief biographies of the contributors and a detailed listing of source acknowledgments. No index.

Works by Individual Poets

Abse, Dannie. *White Coat, Purple Coat: Collected Poems, 1948–1988*. Foreword by M. L. Rosenthal. New York: Persea Books, 1991. ISBN 0–89255–153–4. 274 pages. Hardcover.

A practicing physician of Jewish heritage in Great Britain, Dannie Abse's collected works include a number of poems on Holocaust themes. Works such as "No More Mozart" and "Uncle Isidore" employ Holocaust imagery and content to express the poet's discontent with humanity's inability to put an end to cruelty and barbarity. No index.

Aichinger, Ilse. *Selected Poetry and Prose.* Edited and translated by Allen H. Chappel. With an introduction by Lawrence L. Langer. Durango, CO: Logbridge-Rhodes, 1983. No ISBN given. 143 pages. Paperback.

This collection of Ilse Aichinger's works includes poems (in German and English translation) as well as essays, prose dialogues, and the radio play "The Jouet Sisters." Aichinger's works often deal with the persecution of Austrian Jews during the Holocaust, and are informed by her personal history as the daughter of a female Jewish physician and a non-Jewish father. No index.

Delbo, Charlotte. *Auschwitz and After.* Translated by Rosette C. Lamont. New Haven: Yale University Press, 1995. ISBN 0–300–07057–8. 355 pages. Paperback.

This trilogy of poems, prose poems, and vignettes represents the major work of Charlotte Delbo, a non-Jew imprisoned by the Nazis in Auschwitz and Ravensbruck. Introduced by the eminent literary scholar Lawrence Langer, this edition presents Delbo's three major works on the Holocaust: "None of Us Will Return," "Useless Knowledge," and "The Measure of Our Days." Similar to Primo Levi, Delbo viewed as one of her critical missions to render "the inexplicable" to readers so that the experiences of Auschwitz and other camps would not be forgotten or thrust into the recesses of modern consciousness. This trilogy is an essential volume for readers who seek an encounter with a survivor whose gifts as a poet and essayist help contemporary society to grapple with the horror and heroism that existed in the Nazi camp system. No index.

Levi, Primo. *Collected Poems.* Translated from the Italian by Ruth Feldman & Brian Swann. London: Faber and Faber, 1992. ISBN 0–571–16539–7. 104 pages. Paperback.

This book includes two collections of Primo Levi's poetry, "Shema," "At an Uncertain Hour," and a set of previously unpublished poems. Notes are included along with an index of titles and a brief biography of the author. The works range from those created during World War II to 1987, the year of Levi's death, and they deal with the Holocaust as well as issues of memory, friendship, and perennial moral and ethical issues. For readers familiar with Levi's prose works, his poetry yields valuable insights about the human condition based upon his reflection on the survivor experience over a time span of more than forty years.

Pagis, Dan. *Selected Poems*. Translated from the Hebrew by Stephen Mitchell. Oxford: Carcanet Press Ltd., 1972. No ISBN. 63 pages. Hardcover.

Holocaust survivor Dan Pagis is one of Israel's most esteemed poets. In this collection, works such as "Written in Pencil in the Sealed Railway-Car," "The Roll Call," and others powerfully illuminate the experience of the Holocaust. No index.

Sachs, Nelly. *O the Chimneys. Selected Poems, including the verse play, ELI*. Translated from the German by Michael Hamburger, Christopher Holme, Ruth and Matthew Mead, and Michael Roloff. New York: Farrar, Straus & Giroux, 1967. No ISBN. 387 pages. Hardcover.

This selection of Nelly Sachs' works, introduced by the contemporary German writer Hans Magnus Enzensberger, includes nine collections of her poetry, as well as the verse play *ELI*. Having fled Germany for Sweden in 1940, Sachs wrote poetry about the destruction of Jewish culture in Germany and Europe, and this collection establishes her stature as the leading German Jewish female poet of her generation. No index.

————. *The Seeker and Other Poems*. Translated from the German by Ruth and Matthew Mead and Michael Hamburger. New York: Farrar, Straus & Giroux, 1970. No ISBN. 399 pages. Hardcover.

Nelly Sachs' works, provided in both German and English in this edition, address the legacy of the Holocaust and the impact on Jewish identity and culture of life under Nazi rule. No index.

Volavkova, Hana, editor. . . . *I Never Saw Another Butterfly. Children's Drawings and Poems from Terezin Concentraton Camp, 1942–1944*. Expanded second edition by the United States Holocaust Memorial Museum. Foreword by Chaim Potok. Afterword by Vaclav Havel. ISBN 0–8052–1015–6. 106 pages. Paperback.

This expanded edition of the children's drawings and poems from Terezin is the best available edition of this classic work dealing with children's life experiences in the Terezin ghetto. Comprised of a selection of sixty-five drawings from the over 4,000 catalogued in the archives of the State Jewish Museum in Prague, and thirty-seven poems from the same archive, they are presented in the book without commentary, with only their creators' names listed. The visual presentation of the drawings is of a very high quality, and the book includes a descriptive catalogue of all the drawings and poems that provides information about their origins. The foreword, epilogue, and afterword place the children's work in literary, historical, and contemporary contexts, respectively, highlighting the power of the children's visual and poetic imaginations.

5

BOOKS FOR CHILDREN AND YOUNG ADULTS

OVERVIEW

The expansion of Holocaust study to new audiences has characterized the period 1975–2000. School curricula have proliferated that either mandate or recommend the study of the Holocaust at the upper elementary and secondary school age levels. With the growth in public awareness of Holocaust history through formal instruction, presentations on television, and through films, as well as the annual commemorations of the Holocaust by many municipalities, states, and national governments, young people have expressed substantial interest in learning more about the Holocaust. The vitality of work about the Holocaust published for young people is reflected in the wide-ranging set of genres available (atlases, narrative histories, historical series, collections of primary sources, first-person accounts, and others), which provides considerable flexibility to librarians and classroom teachers who integrate Holocaust instruction within school curricula. The books included in this chapter were chosen based upon their recognized literary or scholarly merit, and the appropriateness of their content for young people nine to fifteen years of age. They are also referenced in bibliographies and reading lists prepared for Holocaust instruction by members of the Association of Holocaust Organizations.

Those works deemed appropriate for ages 8–10 (corresponding with grades 3–5) are designated for elementary grades, while those appropriate for ages 11–15 (corresponding with grades 6–10) are designated as works for young adults.

ATLASES

Gilbert, Martin. *The Holocaust: Maps and Photographs*. Third edition. New York: Braun Holocaust Institute of the Anti-Defamation League, 1994. ISBN 0–88464–141–4. 59 pages. Paperback.

This much briefer version of the author's *Atlas of the Holocaust* is designed for student use, and is appropriate for use in middle grades through high school. It includes a reading list for further study. Young adult.

BIBLIOGRAPHIES

Simon, Ralph R. *A Selected Annotated Bibliography of Literature on the Holocaust for Juvenile and Young Adult Collections*. Revised edition. New York: Association of Jewish Libraries, 1992. ISBN 0–929262–29–8. 44 pages. Paperback.

This bibliography includes recommended reference works, nonfiction books for juvenile and young adult readers, fictional works for juvenile and young adult readers, works about the impact of the Holocaust in the United States, and nonfiction books for high school and adult collections.

Sullivan, Edward T. *The Holocaust in Literature for Youth*. Lanham, MD: The Scarecrow Press, 1999. ISBN 0–8108–3607–6. 261 pages. Hardcover.

This reference work provides guidance to educators, classroom teachers, and public and school librarians in the selection of literature of the Holocaust. Following the introduction, where the author describes the work's purpose and emphasizes the importance of exploring Holocaust literature that goes beyond the most well-known works (such as *The Diary of Anne Frank*), the main section of the book is divided into nine subtopics: anthologies, autobiography and biography, drama, fiction, nonfiction, picture books, poetry and songs, reference works, and making connections (works about other genocides, prejudice, anti-Semitism, and related issues). Entries for each work listed are numbered consecutively, and provide full bibliographic information, as well as their purchase price. The scope of works included reflects a thorough knowledge of the available materials in the field, while the individual entries vary in length and complexity. A second section of the book entitled "Appendices" includes listings of professional resources for educators, electronic Holocaust resources, a select directory of Holocaust memorials, museums, organizations, and other institutions, some suggested activities for introducing Holocaust books and teaching about them to young people, and lists of core titles for inclusion in a school library. Although helpful, the "Appendices" are very selective and do not represent the same comprehensive command of the material as displayed in the main section of the work. Five indexes are provided: author, subject, geographic, subject, and title. This work is very helpful to its target audience in identifying core works concerning the Holocaust for young people, despite the inconsistencies evident in content about individual entries, which may force users to consult other bibliographies on the same topic.

NARRATIVE HISTORIES

Adler, David A. *We Remember the Holocaust.* New York: Henry Holt & Co., 1989. ISBN 0–8050–0434–3. 147 pages. Hardcover.

This narrative history of the Holocaust for young readers relies heavily on survivor memoirs, excerpts of which are integrated throughout the text. Photos of the survivors along with historical photos of the period 1933–1948 are frequently utilized to illustrate and personalize the narrative. The book includes a glossary, suggestions of books for young readers on the Holocaust, a select bibliography of books for in-depth study, and a chronology of events. Indexed. Young adult.

Altshuler, David A. *Hitler's War against the Jews—The Holocaust: A Young Reader's Version of* The War against the Jews 1933–1945 *by Lucy Dawidowicz.* West Orange, NJ: Behrman House, 1978. ISBN 0–87441–222–6. 190 pages. Paperback.

David Altshuler's version of Lucy Dawidowicz' *The War against the Jews 1933–1945* for young readers mirrors the design and contents of the longer work. Divided into two sections, "The Final Solution" and "The Holocaust," the book includes selected documents at the conclusion of each section to supplement the narrative. Among these are excerpts from *Mein Kampf* and Himmler's 1943 Poznan speech to the SS, along with letters and documents highlighting Jewish resistance in Germany and Occupied Eastern Europe. Many photos are integrated throughout the narrative, and a skeletal chronology of events is provided. The basic thesis of Dawidowicz' longer work—that Hitler had long desired the annihiliation of the Jews and put his aims into practice when running Nazi Germany—remains central to Altshuler's more elementary version. Most chapters conclude with a segment on "issues and values" where questions of enduring significance about the Holocaust are posed. Indexed. Young adult.

Bachrach, Susan D. *Tell Them We Remember: The Story of the Holocaust.* Boston: Little Brown & Co., 1994. ISBN 0–316–69264–6. 112 pages. Paperback.

Divided into three sections, "Nazi Germany," "The Final Solution," and "Rescue, Resistance and Liberation," this narrative history for young readers emphasizes the use of photos, notably of young people, to tell the story of the Holocaust. Utilizing the rich resources of the U.S. Holocaust Memorial Museum, Bachrach integrates the life histories of twenty young people who lived in the period 1933–1945 as sidebars to the historical narrative, thus personalizing the story from multiple perspectives. Both color and black-and-white photographs are used, with numerous photos of artifacts from the permanent exhibit at the U.S. Holocaust Memorial Museum. A chronology, suggestions for further reading, and a glossary are included. Indexed. Young adult.

Chaikin, Miriam. *A Nightmare in History: The Story of the Holocaust 1933–1945*. Boston: Houghton Mifflin, 1987. ISBN 0–89919–461–3. 150 pages. Hardcover.

Written for younger readers, this book traces the history of anti-Semitism from the ancient world to Nazi Germany. Chaikin emphasizes anti-Semitism as the fundamental rationale for the Holocaust, examining the Warsaw Ghetto and the death camp at Auschwitz-Birkenau as her primary illustrations of Nazi policy and their impact on Jewish life. She also discusses efforts to provide refuge and rescue for Jews, as well as the liberation of the camps and the formation of Israel. A brief bibliography of books for further study is included. Indexed. Young adult.

Grant, R.G. *New Perspectives: The Holocaust*. Austin, TX: Raintree Steck-Vaughn, 1998. ISBN 0–8172–5016–6. 64 pages. Hardcover.

This brief historical account of the Holocaust is written clearly and concisely, integrating many photos with captions into the historical narrative. Excerpts from memoirs and other primary sources are extensively employed to augment the narrative, which emphasizes the Holocaust as Nazi Germany's effort to destroy the Jews. The author begins the book with a chapter on the gas chambers, then links attempted annihilation of the Jews to the historical legacy of anti-Semitism, and the rise of Hitler and Nazism. The postwar period is addressed, with brief discussions of the Nuremberg Trials, the trial of Adolf Eichmann, and the significance of Holocaust remembrance. The work includes a source acknowledgment list, a glossary, very brief lists of recommended books and videos for further study, and a brief chronology. Indexed. Young adult.

The Holocaust. Woodbridge, CT: Blackbirch Press, 1998. Various ISBN. Various lengths. This nine part series includes six narrative histories, beginning with the history of Jews from ancient times to August 1935, moving forward in Books 2–6 to the end of World War II and the Holocaust's aftermath. Book 7 is a collection of primary sources (see entry in this chapter under "Primary Source Collections"), while Book 8 is a resource guide to media for further study on the Holocaust. Book 9 is a comprehensive index to the entire series, and a Teacher's Guide is available for purchase. The series has a solid scholarly foundation and is well-written for grades seven and higher, with extensive use of photographs and primary source excerpts throughout Books 1–6. Each volume contains a glossary, source notes, a select bibliography, and suggestions for further reading and study. Young adult.

The Holocaust Library. San Diego: Lucent Books, 1998. Various ISBN. Various lengths. Hardcover.

This series of seven books comprises a thematic history of the Holocaust. The book titles include: *The Death Camps, The Final Solution, The Nazis, Nazi War Criminals, The Resistance, The Righteous Gentiles,* and *The Survivors.* Each book includes a substantial number of photographs, and chapters contain many primary sources to highlight key themes in the narrative. Each book in the series contains chapter notes, a glossary, suggestions for further reading, a list of works consulted, and a brief author biography. All are indexed. Young adult.

The Holocaust Remembered Series. Springfield, NJ: Enslow Publishers, 1998. Various ISBN. All books in the series are 128 pages in length. Hardcover.

This series of five books presents the history of the Holocaust at a level appropriate for middle school. The book titles include: *The Holocaust Overview, The Holocaust Camps, The Holocaust Ghettos, The Holocaust Heroes,* and *The Holocaust Survivors.* Maps, graphics, and historical photographs are heavily employed in the series to illustrate key points in the narrative text, and each book includes a chronology, glossary of terms, chapter notes, and selected bibliography. Indexed. Young adult.

Meltzer, Milton. *Never to Forget: The Jews of the Holocaust.* New York: HarperCollins, 1991. ISBN 0–06–446118–1. 217 pages plus 4 pages of maps. Hardcover.

Written for middle school through high school grades and the general reader, Meltzer's general history of the Holocaust focuses almost exclusively on Nazi anti-Jewish policies. The author integrates excerpts from many first-person accounts in his chronological narrative, along with the texts of many songs that were sung by Jews in shtetls, ghettos, and death camps. Meltzer organizes the book in three sections. Book 1, the "History of Hatred," concerns Nazi policies against Jews in Germany up to 1938, as well as the minority status of Jews in Europe before 1933. Book 2, the "Destruction of the Jews," details the radicalization of Nazi policy against Jews following Kristallnacht, and continuing through to the "final solution's" implementation with mass industrial killing in death camps. Book 3, the "Spirit of Resistance," addresses Jewish resistance in ghettos, death camp revolts, and the eventual liberation of the death camps and concentration camps by Allied forces in 1944–1945. The author's first and final chapters in the book, entitled "Why Remember?" and "Never to Forget," respectively, clearly communicate the book's focus on helping the reader understand the enormity of the tragedy through use of survivor accounts and the preservation of memory. Selected maps, a chronology of the Holocaust, and a topical bibliography are provided, although the bibliography contains only works published prior to 1976. Young adult. Indexed.

Rogasky, Barbara. *Smoke and Ashes: The Story of the Holocaust.* New York: Dell Publishing Co., 1988. ISBN 0–8234–0697–0. 187 pages. Hardcover.

This history of the Holocaust is intended for a general audience, but can be employed at the secondary school level. The author examines the roots of Nazi racial anti-Semitism, and presents a chronological/thematic narrative, emphasizing the period 1939–1945, particularly the ghetto and camp experiences. Considerable attention is devoted to resistance movements, the roles of the U.S. and United Kingdom in responding to the Holocaust, rescuers and righteous Gentiles, and postwar trials of perpetrators. Unlike many other texts, this book includes a chapter on other genocides of the twentieth century, while concluding that the Holocaust is unique in terms of its scale, methods, and goals. Photographs are frequently used to supplement the narrative and a selected bibliography is included. Indexed. Young adult.

Rossell, Seymour. *The Holocaust: The Fire that Raged.* West Orange, NJ: Behrman House, 1992. ISBN 0–87441–526–8. 191 pages. Paperback.

Directed to a middle grades–high school audience, this history of the Holocaust relies heavily on the use of documentary excerpts, both print and photographic. Organized in three major sections with a postscript, "The Holocaust," "The World and the Jews and Resistance," "Rescue and Justice," the book begins with a brief introductory chapter on how to analyze documents. Each chapter contains a review and issues section, which summarizes key text themes and presents questions and activities for further study, respectively. Rescue, resistance, liberation, and war crimes trials are given considerable attention, as well as contemporary issues of Holocaust study and commemoration. Other victim groups such as Sinti and Roma (Gypsies) are briefly discussed. A chronology, list of source acknowledgments, and suggested bibliography of books and films for further study are provided. Indexed. A teacher's guide is available for use with the text. Young adult.

Stewart, Gail B. *Hitler's Reich.* San Diego: Lucent Books, 1994. ISBN 1–56006–235–5. 128 pages. Hardcover.

This historical account of the origins, development, and demise of the Third Reich emphasizes the central role of Adolf Hitler in the growth of Nazism, notably his lifelong anti-Semitism and the social problems in Germany after World War I that facilitated his rise to power. The implementation of mass murder during the Holocaust is addressed in Chapter 8 ("Descent into Hell"), while the origins and expansion of discrimination against Jews, the disabled, and other minorities are discussed in Chapter 5 ("Life in Nazi Germany"). Chapter notes are included, along with a works consulted section with brief annotations and a list of works for further reading. Many photographs and illustrations supplement the concise and well-organized text narrative. Indexed. Young adult.

Wigoder, Geoffrey, editor. *The Holocaust: A Grolier Student Library.* Danbury, CT: Grolier Educational, 1997. Series ISBN 0–7172–7637–6. 511 pages in 4 volumes. Hardcover.

This is a very well-written, scholarly reference work that is well suited to introducing the Holocaust to the young adult audience. The contributors are recognized experts in the field of Holocaust studies, and the subjects included in the text range across biography, history, literature, art, geography, and many other important aspects of the topic. Organized alphabetically, the work contains a brief historical overview of the Holocaust in Volume 1, as well as a glossary of key terms about the Holocaust and Nazism, also in Volume 1. Entries are cross-referenced, and each volume contains an index. Many photos, illustrations, maps, timelines, and sidebars with source excerpts from literature, first-person accounts, and documents are included. Volume 4 contains both cumulative and subject indexes for the complete series, as well as an annotated bibliography with recommended works categorized by recommendations for junior high or high school/adult users. While the bibliography emphasizes books, some mention is made of films for Holocaust study, although there is no discussion of sound recordings or computer software. This series is a very fine introduction to the Holocaust for its target audience, and encourages both teachers and students to pursue many avenues for further study. Young adult.

PRIMARY SOURCE COLLECTIONS

The Holocaust: A Historical Reader. Evanston, IL: McDougal Littell, 2000. ISBN 0–618–00363–0. 224 pages. Hardcover.

Designed for school use in middle through high school grades, this anthology of Holocaust sources contains six sections: The Situation of Jews Under Hitler, The Ghettos, The Concentration Camps, The Perpetrators of the Holocaust, Liberation, and Responding to the Holocaust. No section contains more than six selections, and the individual selections are given brief introductions that provide background information on the source and relate the source to the section theme, such as ghetto life. Sources employed range from interpretations by historians to eyewitness accounts and literary responses to the Holocaust, both during and after the era of the Third Reich. Brief photo collections are interspersed after three of the six sections, although the photo captions are limited and photo sources are not identified. Questions for consideration by the reader are provided for each source, and tend to focus more often than not on higher-level thinking skills. Specialized vocabulary words are highlighted within the text, while other words and phrases deemed essential for understanding of the sources are placed in bold and defined at the bottom of the page where they appear. A very limited index is provided, along with a list of source acknowledgments.

Shulman, Dr. William L. *Voices and Visions: A Collection of Primary Sources*. Woodbridge, CT: Blackbirch Press, 1998. ISBN 1–56711–207–2. 80 pages. Hardcover.

This anthology is Volume 7 in the Blackbirch Press series on the Holocaust. Intended for young readers, the anthology's chapters are correlated with the six volume chronological history of the Holocaust preceding this volume. Narrative introductions precede the document/source excerpts, many of which are drawn from survivor memoirs and eyewitness accounts from the period 1933–1945. Photos are employed to supplement the source excerpts, and in some cases they serve as the primary focus for analysis in the text. A brief chronology is included, along with a detailed glossary, brief biographies of the survivors whose excerpts are used, and a complete listing of source credits. Graphs of the estimated number of Jews killed in the Holocaust by country and the total number of Nazi and Axis camps are included. Indexed. Young adult.

WORKS ON SPECIALIZED TOPICS

Altman, Linda Jacobs. *Genocide: The Systematic Killing of a People*. Issues in Focus Series. Springfield, NJ: Enslow Publisher, 1995. ISBN 0–89490–664–X. 112 pages. Hardcover.

This book includes the Holocaust as one of the major genocides of the twentieth century; other genocides discussed concern Native Americans, Armenians within the Ottoman Empire, the forced famine in the Ukraine, and the genocide in Cambodia. The discussion of the Holocaust includes brief sections on Gypsies, Poles, and selected other victim groups. Periodically, black and white photographs are used to illustrate major points in the text. Chapter notes are included, and a selected bibliography is included along with an index. Young adult.

Ayer, Eleanor. *Parallel Journeys*. New York: Aladdin, 1995. ISBN 0–689–83236–2. 244 pages. Paperback.

Eleanor Ayer tells the story of two individuals who lived and suffered under Nazism: German Jew Helen Waterford, who was deported to Auschwitz, and

Alfons Heck, who grew up not far from Waterford but who joined the Hitler Youth and was an avid supporter of Nazism in his youth. In alternating chapters, the author tells each individual's story, showing how the policies and practices of Nazism affected each individual and his or her family in strikingly different ways. Historical photographs of each subject's family, as well as more recent photographs of their joint speaking engagements are included. The work closes with an epilogue that describes how Waterford and Heck agreed to make joint speaking presentations about the effects of Nazism and the Holocaust on their lives, and to serve as witnesses of the tragedies that totalitarianism and prejudice can produce if left unchecked. The book's unique structure and content makes it a very useful work for examination of how Nazism affected young people in markedly different ways. Chapter notes and a select bibliography are included. Indexed. Young adult.

Brager, Bruce L. *The Trial of Adolf Eichmann: The Holocaust on Trial.* San Diego: Lucent Books, 1999. ISBN 1–56006–469–2. 127 pages. Hardcover.

Included in Lucent Books' "Famous Trials" series, Bruce Brager's book presents the Adolf Eichmann trial in historical context as an effort not only to bring a major war criminal to justice, but to educate the nation of Israel and the world about the significance of the Holocaust. Extensive use of photos and historical sources on the trial illuminates the author's narrative text, which is clear and concise without unnecessarily simplifying the complex issues surrounding the trial itself. A list of sources consulted, chapter notes, suggestions for further reading, and a detailed index are included. Young adult.

Fox, Anne L., and Eva Abraham-Podietz. *Ten Thousand Children.* West Orange, NJ: Behrman House, 1999. ISBN 0–87441–648–5. 128 pages. Paperback.

Beginning with a chapter on life under Hitler, this book presents a chronological narrative about the Kindertransport program, which brought children from Germany and Austria to Great Britain in 1939. The two authors are Kindertransport survivors, and they have incorporated excerpts from first-person accounts, historical and contemporary photographs, and reproductions of historical documents and artifacts to enrich the survivor stories related in the text. Specialized vocabulary is defined on each page in the margins and the book concludes with a discussion of the reunion of Kindertransport survivors in London during 1989, and the subsequent founding of a Kindertransport association for survivors in the United States. Elementary grades. No index.

Gold, Alison Leslie. *Memories of Anne Frank: Reflections of a Childhood Friend.* New York: Scholastic, 1997. ISBN 0–590–90723–9. 135 pages. Paperback.

The author tells the story of the relationship between Hannah Pick-Goslar and Anne Frank, as told by Hannah Pick-Goslar to Alison Leslie Gold in interviews during the 1990s. Now living in Israel, Pick-Goslar was Anne Frank's closest friend and lived in the house next to the Franks' home. The work deepens our understanding of Anne Frank beyond the famous diary, as Pick-Goslar not only knew Anne Frank very well prior to the German occupation, but was interned in Bergen-Belsen and was able to meet Anne Frank again just before she died in April 1945. Eight pages of photographs about the two girls and Pick-Goslar's post–World War II life are included. No index. Young adult.

Holliday, Laurel. *Why Do They Hate Me? Young Lives Caught in War and Conflict.* New York: Pocket Books, 1999. ISBN 0–671–03454–5. 293 pages. Paperback.

This work by Laurel Holliday contains sections from three other books she has authored that detail the responses of young people to conflict during the Holocaust and World War II, the troubles in Northern Ireland, and the Israeli-Palestinian conflict. Brief introductions to the three sections of this anthology set the context for diary excerpts about how young people responded to the turmoil affecting their lives, while the author also provides introductions to the individual excerpts that contain biographical information about each contributor. Introductory maps to each section set a geographic context for the text that follows. No index. Young adult.

Mandell, Sherri Lederman. *Writers of the Holocaust.* New York: Facts on File, 1999. ISBN 0–8160–3729–9. 132 pages. Hardcover.

This book, part of the "Global Profiles" series by Facts on File, is intended as a reference book for libraries. The author has assembled ten major writers about the Holocaust, all of whom were victims of Nazi oppression. Three of the contributors—Hannah Senesh, Yitsak Katznelson, and Anne Frank—died in the Holocaust, but not before they authored works that shed light on their experiences. The remaining seven contributors—Abba Kovner, Primo Levi, Ida Fink, Arnost Lustig, Elie Wiesel, Aharon Appelfeld, and Jerzy Kosinski—are Holocaust survivors and have written works about the Shoah that range across genres (memoirs, fiction, essays). The book's introduction provides an historical overview of the Holocaust, and has a brief chronology of major events. Each of the ten contributor sections has an individual author's photo, a chronology of his or her life, text describing the contributor's accomplishments as an author, and items for further reading by the contributor and by experts about his or her work. Excerpts from each contributor's published works are included in sidebars to the narrative text. Young adult.

Newman, Amy. *The Nuremberg Laws: Institutionalized Anti-Semitism.* San Diego: Lucent Books, 1999. ISBN 1–56006–354–8. 96 pages. Hardcover.

Part of Lucent Books' "Words that Changed History" series, this book provides an historical overview of the Nuremberg Laws, establishing the critical connections between the Nuremberg Laws and related Nazi policies of racism and discrimination against Jews, the disabled, Gypsies, and other targeted minorities. The Holocaust is viewed as one outgrowth of the institutional racism and discrimination embedded in the Nuremberg Laws, and connections are discussed between the racist foundations of the Nuremberg Laws and contemporary racism, as exemplified by white supremacist hate groups, apartheid in South Africa, and "ethnic cleansing" in the former Yugoslavia. Many photos and source excerpts are included to augment the narrative text, as well as an appendix with the full text of the Nuremberg Laws and Decrees from 1935. Source notes, a recommended reading list for further study, an annotated list of works consulted by the author, and an index are included. Young adult.

Rice, Earle, Jr. *The Nuremberg Trials*. San Diego: Lucent Books, 1997. ISBN 1–56006–269–X. 112 pages. Hardcover.

Part of Lucent Books' "Famous Trials" series, this book presents the Nuremberg trials as an effort at international justice whose legacy has only partly been realized over the past fifty plus years. Beginning during World War II when the Allies declared that perpetrators of Axis war crimes would be held accountable, the author details the emergence of the International Military Tribunal, the creation of the Nuremberg Trial proceedings, and the dramatic presentations by both prosecution and defense during the trials of the twenty-one major criminals indicted and tried at Nuremberg in 1946. Brief chapters on the subsequent trials of Nazi war criminals and the mixed legacy of Nuremberg for international law are included. Throughout the text, historical photos and many excerpts from sources introduced at the trials are included to further illustrate the narrative text. A glossary, brief time line, list of works consulted, and suggestions of works for further study are included, along with an index. Young adult.

Rubin, Susan Goldman. *Fireflies in the Dark: The Story of Friedl Dicker-Brandeis and the Children of Terezin*. New York: Holiday House, 2000. ISBN 0–8234–1461–2. 48 pages. Hardcover.

This book presents the story of artist and teacher Friedl Dicker-Brandeis, who was deported to Terezin but who worked with other adult colleagues to give hope to children by having them create artworks that expressed their fears, hopes, and dreams while interned in the Terezin complex. The book includes many pieces of art by children who worked with Dicker-Brandeis, as well as art created by Dicker-Brandeis while in Terezin. The text is based upon documentary research and interviews with Terezin survivors, some of whom were taught by Dicker-Brandeis. An extensive list of references (books, videos, audio recordings, and Web sites) is provided for further study, and photos of some of the children who studied with Dicker-Brandeis are incorporated in the text. Indexed. Young adult.

Tito, E. Tina. *Liberation: Teens in the Concentration Camps and the Teen Soldiers who Liberated Them.* New York: Rosen Publishing Group, 1999. ISBN 0–8239–28462. 64 pages. Hardcover.

Telling the story of four teenagers, two who were survivors and two who were liberators, this book integrates many photographs with a concise text that draws heavily upon first-person accounts. The work contains a brief timeline of the Holocaust, a glossary of terms, a selected list of books for further reading, an annotated list of selected videos, and a list of recommended Web sites. Many of the photographs are very powerful, notably those from the Buchenwald and Dachau camps. The introduction by Holocaust scholar Yaffa Eliach discusses the teenagers' accounts as important due to their role as eyewitnesses and as purveyors of memory for the future. Young adult. No index.

Van der Rol, Ruud, and Rian Verhoeven. *Anne Frank: Beyond the Diary. A Photographic Remembrance.* Introduction by Anna Quindlen. Originally published by the Anne Frank House, Amsterdam. New York: Scholastic, 1995. ISBN 0–590–47447–2. 113 pages. Paperback.

This book presents a photographic history of the Frank family, including aspects of their life prior to and during World War II, the origin and eventual publication of *The Diary of Anne Frank,* and the emergence of the Anne Frank Foundation. Excerpts from *The Diary of Anne Frank* are interspersed within the narrative text, along with numerous historical photographs, maps, and photographs of Amsterdam. A chronology of the Frank family and the other families who hid in the secret annex is provided, along with notes on different versions of *The Diary of Anne Frank,* a list of sources for the photographs and quotes included in the work, and an index. The introduction by Anna Quindlen provides a personal perspective on the meaning of Anne Frank and her diary for young people today, particularly as illuminated by the photographs included in this book. Young adult.

FIRST-PERSON ACCOUNTS AND BIOGRAPHIES

Adler, David A. *Hilde and Eli: Children of the Holocaust.* Illustrated by Karen Ritz. New York: Holiday House, 1994. ISBN 0–8234–1091–9. 30 pages. Hardcover.

This illustrated children's book tells the story of two actual children, Hilde Rosenzweig (Germany) and Eli Lux (Czechoslovakia), who died in the Holocaust. It presents their stories with concise text and powerful illustrations, beginning in prewar Europe and continuing with the effects of Nazi rule on children. The afterword by author David A. Adler describes the sources for the work and their relationship to the contents of this illustrated book. Elementary grades. Indexed.

Axelrod, Toby. *Hans and Sophie Scholl: German Resisters of the White Rose*. New York: Rosen Publishing Group, 2001. ISBN 0–8239–3316–4. 112 pages. Hardcover.

This book relates the story of Hans and Sophie Scholl, who were among the few Germans to openly resist Nazi policies during the Third Reich. The introduction sets the context for their resistance to Nazism, and then the story of the White Rose group is told, with emphasis placed on the brother-and-sister team's role in developing distribution campaigns for anti-Nazi leaflets. The arrest of the White Rose group and the subsequent execution of Hans and Sophie Scholl are described, along with a discussion of the meaning of this small resistance movement for contemporary understanding of the Holocaust and Nazism. In addition to many photographs and excerpts from actual documents produced by the White Rose, a time line of key events, a glossary of terms, and selections for further reading are provided. Indexed. Young adult.

Bayer, Linda. *Elie Wiesel: Spokesman for Remembrance*. New York: Rosen Publishing Group, 2000. ISBN 0–8239–3306–7. 112 pages. Hardcover.

This is a biography of author and Holocaust survivor Elie Wiesel. His significance as a spokesperson about the Holocaust is emphasized, and excerpts from his most famous work, *Night*, as well as his memoir, *All Rivers Run to the Sea,* are integrated within the narrative. Photos are interspersed throughout the book, which also includes a time line of Wiesel's life, a glossary of key terms, and recommendations of books and videos for further study about Wiesel's life and works. Additionally, a selected listing of organizations and Web site addresses dealing with Holocaust study and research is included. Indexed. Young adult.

Boas, Jacob. *We Are Witnesses: Five Diaries of Teenagers Who Died in the Holocaust*. Foreword by Patricia C. McKissack. New York: Scholastic, Inc., 1995. ISBN 0–590–84475–X. 196 pages. Paperback.

Through the eyes of five teenagers whose diaries were found and published after 1945, Jacob Boas reveals the fears, hopes, and complex daily concerns of five Jewish children who perished in the Holocaust. Following a brief introduction where Boas relates stories about his own childhood during World War II in the Netherlands, the author presents a brief chronological overview of how the genocidal plans of the Third Reich affected each diarist. Rather than just presenting the diaries by themselves, Boas selects excerpts and interweaves them as he tells the story of each child and his or her family. Boas makes conscious comparisons among the experiences of the five teenagers to illustrate both common and unique aspects of their personal histories, as well as their treatment under Nazism. The effect of this approach is to place the emphasis squarely on how each individual's life experiences illustrated the dilemmas of Jewish families throughout Occupied Europe, and the very limited options available for survival. A complete list of source acknowledgments, extensive notes, and a detailed index complete the work. Young adult.

de Wijze, Louis. *Only My Life: A Survivor's Story*. Translated by Victor de Wijze. New York: St. Martin's Press, 1997. ISBN 0–312–14697–3. 183 pages. Hardcover.

This memoir by a Dutch Jew describes his experiences of deportation from the Westerbork transit camp to Auschwitz, his resourcefulness in surviving Auschwitz, his work details at the Buna-Monowitz slave labor complex, and his narrow escape from a grueling death march through Poland. Eventually able to evade the advancing Soviet army, he entered the U.S. military zone and was nursed back to health, returning to Holland in June 1945. The memoir's language and style are highly readable for a broad audience ranging from middle school through adults. No index. Young adult.

Drucker, Olga Levy. *Kindertransport*. New York: Scholastic, 1996. School edition of original published by Henry Holt & Company, 1992. ISBN 0–590–89745–4. 146 pages. Paperback.

This first-person account by a survivor of the Kindertransport refugee program tells the story of Olga Levy, who was sent by her parents to England under the auspices of the Kindertransport to escape Nazi oppression in the 1930s. Facing discrimination in her hometown of Stuttgart, Olga emigrated to England where she adjusted to life without her parents, who had remained in Germany in hopes of securing entrance as immigrants to the United States. Aided by a sympathetic British family, Olga adjusted to life in England and then emigrated to the United States in 1941, where she rejoined her parents. The story concludes with Olga's remembrance of the first Kindertransport survivors' reunion in 1989. The story is compelling and told in a style that appeals to young readers. No photographs or index. Elementary through young adult.

Eichengreen, Lucille. *Rumkowski and the Orphans of Lodz*. With Rebecca Camhi Fromer. San Francisco: Mercury House, 2000. ISBN 1–56279–115–X. 129 pages. Paperback.

This memoir of the Lodz ghetto focuses on the relationship between Chaim Rumkowski and the children of the ghetto, as viewed through Eichengreen's perspective, who was a teenager in Lodz and who later survived the Auschwitz, Bergen-Belsen, and Neuengamme camps. Eichengreen was deported from her homeland in Germany to Lodz with her mother in 1941. Eichengreen's father, a Polish national, had already been killed in Dachau when they were sent to the ghetto. The author views Rumkowski as an autocrat who abused his authority as head of the Jewish Council, and who functioned more as a tool of the Germans than as a protector of the Jews. Included in the text is an afterword by Rebecca Camhi Fromer, who assisted in publishing Eichengreen's memoir, along with selected photos of ghetto life in Lodz and a reproduction of the memorial plaque in Hamburg about Lucille Eichengreen's life. No index. Young adult.

Fluek, Toby Knobel. *Memories of My Life in a Polish Village*. New York: Alfred A. Knopf, Inc., 1990. ISBN 0–394–58617–4. 110 pages. Hardcover.

Written specifically for young readers, the author is herself a survivor of the Holocaust who emigrated to the United States in 1949. The text is clear and brief, organized as single-page entries under topics related to the chapter headings. Each page contains a drawing or painting about the text content. Both text and illustrations were created by the author. The book provides a very useful description of daily life for Jews in rural Poland before the Holocaust, as well as insights into life under Soviet rule prior to the German invasion of areas occupied by the Soviet Union on June 22, 1941. The illustrations effectively complement the poignant language of the text, making the book appealing for a broad range of young readers. No index. Elementary grades.

Frank, Anne. *The Diary of a Young Girl: The Definitive Edition*. Edited by Otto H. Frank and Mirjam Pressler. Translated by Susan Massotty. New York: Doubleday, 1995. ISBN 0–385–47378–8. 340 pages. Hardcover.

From June 12, 1942 to August 1, 1944, a young Jewish girl, Anne Frank, wrote diary entries that survived World War II through the efforts of a friend named Miep Gies, who placed the diary in safekeeping following the Frank family's deportation to Westerbork, and ultimately to Auschwitz in 1944. A shortened version of the full diary was edited and published by Otto Frank, Anne's father, in the 1950s, becoming one of the most widely read works on the Holocaust since its initial appearance. This edition draws upon the entire set of original diary entries, providing up to thirty percent more text and providing a more comprehensive, multidimensional view of Anne Frank than was evident in the first published version. An introduction explains the development of the various editions of the *Diary*, while the afterword explains the fate of the Frank family and the other Jews hiding in the famous attic in Amsterdam. No index. Young adult.

Friedman, Ina R. *Flying Against the Wind*. Brookline, MA: Lodgepole Press, 1995. ISBN 1–886721–00–9. 202 pages. Paperback.

This biography tells the story of courageous Cato Bjontes van Beek, who opposed Nazism in her native Germany and paid for her resistance activities with her life in 1943. Although she was one of a very few Germans who opposed Nazism and actively sought to defend individual civil liberties during the Third Reich, Cato's story illustrates that choices in favor of human rights and dignity were possible within Nazi Germany. Cato was arrested and sentenced to death for distributing anti-Nazi literature. Her martyrdom has served as a symbol of heroism and sacrifice for future generations. The book contains a chronology of events during the Third Reich, a glossary of terms, and an index.

————. *The Other Victims: First-Person Stories of Non-Jews Persecuted by the Nazis*. New York: Houghton Mifflin, 1990. ISBN 0–395–74515–2. 214 pages. Paperback.

The book is divided into five sections ("Unworthy of Life," "War against the Church," "Racial Purification: Breeding the Master Race," "Mind Control," and "Slaves for the Nazi Empire"). Friedman's accessible and flowing writing style incorporates brief contextual introductions to each story, followed by narratives of how individuals, families, or groups suffered from Nazi persecution—none of them being Jews. Included are Roma (Gypsies), Jehovah's Witnesses, the deaf, dissenters, slave laborers, and homosexuals, among others. Testimony by the subjects of the thirteen stories is regularly integrated into each narrative. A brief listing of related works for further study is provided. Indexed. Young adult.

Holliday, Laurel. *Children in the Holocaust and World War II: Their Secret Diaries*. New York: Pocket Books, 1995. ISBN 0–671–52054–7. 409 pages. Hardcover.

Containing entries from twenty-three children who lived during World War II, this book brings together in one collection some of the most poignant and tragic excerpts about the Holocaust and World War II. With the exception of the excerpts from Hannah Senesh's diary, the remainder of the entries are not well-known despite their power to illustrate aspects of the Holocaust that were much more indicative of children's experiences than those depicted in *The Diary of Anne Frank*. The author's introduction describes the varying circumstances under which the teenage diarists created their entries, along with introducing explanatory themes for understanding the diaries. In some cases the diaries were outlets for anger and rage; in other ways they served as palliatives for loneliness; while in all cases they illustrate how children endured and in some cases survived traumatic experiences. The variety of diary authors includes boys and girls, Jews and non-Jews, although the majority of entries are from Jewish children impacted by Nazi policies in Eastern Europe. A brief bibliography, two maps of Europe in 1942, and a complete listing of source credits are provided. No index. Young adult.

Hurwitz, Johanna. *Anne Frank: A Life in Hiding*. Decorations by Vera Rosenberry. New York: Avon Books, 1988. ISBN 0–380–73254–8. 56 pages. Paperback.

This is a brief version of Anne Frank's life story that provides a useful introduction to the famous diary. There is a useful discussion of the impact of *The Diary of Anne*

Frank as an entry point for study of the Holocaust. A list of important dates, one map, and illustrations are incorporated within the text. Indexed. Elementary grades.

Landau, Elaine. *We Survived the Holocaust*. New York: Franklin Watts, 1991. ISBN 0–531–11115–6. 144 pages. Hardcover.

This anthology of eyewitness accounts represents a range of geographical and historical experiences during the Holocaust. Some document facsimiles are included that help to illustrate specific issues within individual survivor accounts. Accompanying the individual survivor accounts are a selected bibliography, glossary, and appendix of selected Holocaust organizations. Indexed. Young adult.

Leapman, Michael. *Witnesses Go to War: Eight True-Life Stories of Nazi Persecution*. New York: Viking, 1998. ISBN 0–670–87386–1. 127 pages. Hardcover.

This anthology begins with a brief introduction that describes Europe in the 1930s, when the growth of Nazism threatens continental peace, and later during World War II, as the aggressive war waged by Nazi Germany devastates Europe. Eight true stories of children affected by World War II in Europe follow, including Jews such as Anne Frank, a Gypsy, children hidden and transported to safety, and the children of the Czech town of Lidice, destroyed by the Nazis in retaliation for the assassination of SS leader Reinhard Heydrich in 1942. The stories are told in the third person, but testimony from the subjects of each story is regularly incorporated in each chapter. Photographs are heavily employed to augment the narrative, and maps are included to help the reader locate places referenced in each story. Source acknowledgments and an index complete the book. Young adult.

Lobel, Anita. *No Pretty Pictures: A Child of War*. New York: Greenwillow Books, 1998. ISBN 0–688–15935–4. 193 pages. Hardcover.

Born in Krakow to a middle-class family, the author describes her wartime experiences from the beginning of the Nazi occupation of Poland through her experiences as a hidden child to her deportation to a series of camps in the Nazi system. The most unique aspect of the narrative concerns her transfer, under the auspices of the International Red Cross, to Sweden in 1945 just before the war ended. The final third of the memoir describes her reunification with her parents, their adjustment to refugee life in Sweden, and her eventual emigration to the United States. A collection of family photographs from the prewar and postwar periods complements the text narrative. No index. Young adult.

McDonough, Yona Zeldis. *Anne Frank*. Illustrated by Malcah Zeldis. New York: Henry Holt & Co., 1997. ISBN 0–8050–4924–X. 32 pages. Hardcover.

This illustrated children's book presents the life story of Anne Frank, and includes a listing of important dates in Anne Frank's life and in the development of *The Diary of Anne Frank*. A concluding author's note provides an explanation why the author and illustrator felt it was important to present Anne Frank's life story to young children. No index. Elementary grades.

Mochizuki, Ken. *Passage to Freedom: The Sugihara Story*. Illustrated by Dom Lee. Afterword by Hiroki Sugihara. New York: Lee & Low Books, 1997. ISBN 1–880000–49–0. 33 pages. Hardcover.

This illustrated children's book relates the efforts of Japanese diplomat Chiune Sugihara to provide thousands of visas to Jewish refugees in Lithuania against the recommendations of his government. The afterword by Sugihara's son takes the story of his father's life beyond World War II, noting that a monument was built to him in his Japanese birthplace and that by the 1980s, honors were finally being given to him for his selfless efforts to save Jews. No index. Elementary grades.

Nieuwsma, Milton J. *Kinderlager: An Oral History of Young Holocaust Survivors*. New York: Holiday House, 1998. ISBN 0–8234–1358–6. 161 pages. Hardcover.

This book is based upon interviews with three female child survivors of Auschwitz, and discusses not only their lives before deportation and as prisoners in Auschwitz, but during the postwar period as they rebuilt their lives following liberation. Included in the book is a glossary, maps of the Auschwitz kinderlager and surrounding area in Poland, and a selected bibliography of narratives by Auschwitz survivors. Many photos are incorporated within the text to highlight specific aspects of the first-person accounts used by the author. No index. Young adult.

Rabinovici, Schoschana. *Thanks to My Mother*. New York: The Dial Press, 1998. ISBN 0–8037–2233–4. 246 pages. Hardcover.

As a survivor from Vilnius, Lithuania, the author discusses how her mother acted to save her from various dangers in the deportation process, and later protected her in three separate camps, as well as during a death march. The story commences prior to the Holocaust in Vilnius during the late 1930s, where her parents divorce and her mother remarries, continuing through the Soviet occupation of Lithuania (1939 to mid-1941) and into the German occupation of Lithuania. Some photographs and document facsimiles are provided to augment the narrative, as well as maps of the Stutthof camp and the death march. No index. Young adult.

Rosengarten, Israel J. *Survival: The Story of a Sixteen-Year-Old Jewish Boy*. Translated from the Dutch. Syracuse: Syracuse University Press, 1999. ISBN 0–8156–0580–3. 218 pages. Hardcover.

Telling his life story in precise detail, Israel Rosengarten's memoir describes his early life in Belgium, the German occupation, the deportations of Jews to camps in Belgium, and the eventual transfer he endured to camps in Poland and Germany. Enduring life in Blechhammer, a subcamp of Auschwitz, and the two large camps of Gross-Rosen and Buchenwald, Rosengarten describes the difficulties of survival in a system designed for dehumanization. Liberated by U.S. troops in April 1945, he seeks repatriation to Belgium, but his return is delayed because his father (now dead) was born in Poland. Eventually returned to Belgium by train, the author finds that he was the sole survivor of his family of seven. A compelling and often disturbing story, the memoir is unsparing in its portrayal of the tragedy and loss the author encountered as a teenager. No index. Young adult.

Siegal, Aranka. *Upon the Head of the Goat: A Childhood in Hungary, 1939–1944*. New York: Penguin, 1994. ISBN 0–14–036996–X. 215 pages. Paperback.

This memoir describes life in Hungary from a nine-year-old child's perspective during World War II, with the emphasis placed upon the predeportation experiences of the author, including life in the ghetto. The work is based upon the author's own life experiences as a survivor of Auschwitz, Christianstadt, and Bergen-Belsen, and considerable attention is devoted to the influence of anti-Semitism and war on Jewish families in Hungary. Elementary grades. No index.

Streissguth, Thomas. *Raoul Wallenberg: Swedish Diplomat and Humanitarian*. New York: Rosen Publishing Group, 2001. ISBN 0–8239–3318–0. 112 pages. Hardcover.

This life of Raoul Wallenberg places emphasis on his rescue work in Hungary and the mystery surrounding his disappearance following his arrest by the Soviets after World War II. Maps, photos of events in Hungary during the German occupation, and photos of key documents augment the text. The biography does not, however, include evidence from the most recent Swedish-Soviet inquiry into Wallenberg's disappearance. Recommendations for further reading, a list of recommended Web sites, a glossary, and a time line about Wallenberg's life are included. Indexed. Young adult.

FICTION AND POETRY

Bishop, Claire Huchet. *Twenty and Ten*. Illustrated by William Pene DuBois. New York: Penguin, 1978. Originally published by Viking Press, 1952. ISBN 0–14–031076–2. 76 pages. Paperback.

Claire Huchet Bishop's story relates how ten Jewish refugee children were protected by a Catholic nun and her students in a French school during 1944. The book is based upon a true story from World War II. The author and illustrator effectively describe the difficulties and fears encountered by the host school community in providing refuge to the Jewish children, along with the strange twist of fate that helped the Jews and their protectors survive Nazi oppression. No index. Elementary.

Koehn, Ilse. *Mischling, Second Degree: My Childhood in Nazi Germany.* With a foreword by Harrison E. Salisbury. New York: Penguin, 1990. ISBN 0–14–034290–7. 240 pages. Paperback.

This is a true story about a young woman whose father's mother was Jewish in Nazi Germany. Blending historical fiction with elements of a memoir, the story is told in the first person and relates how the narrator's Jewish heritage was kept a secret during her wartime life in Germany, where she survives with support from her mother's parents. Young adult.

Lowry, Lois. *Number the Stars.* New York: Bantam Doubleday Dell, 1989. ISBN 0–440–22753–4. 137 pages. Softcover.

This Newbery Award–winning work of historical fiction tells the story of Jewish persecution during the German occupation in Denmark, and how over ninety percent of all Danish Jews were rescued by Danes and transported to Sweden on the eve of their planned deportation to death camps in the East. Lois Lowry mixes fictional characters with an accurate description of the historical setting and events to create a work that is suspenseful and inspirational. Her rendering of the motivations and actions of the Danish resistance is particularly effective. The author includes an afterword where she explains the relationship between the work and the history of the Holocaust in Denmark. No index. Elementary.

Mazer, Norma Fox. *Good Night, Maman.* New York: HarperCollins, 1999. ISBN 0–06–440923–6. 185 pages. Paperback.

This work of historical fiction concerns the plight of Jewish refugees in Paris who survive the Nazi occupation, travel to the Allied occupation zone in Italy, and eventually emigrate to the United States. The main characters of the work, Karin and Marc Levi, are two members of the 982 refugees who were admitted into the United States in 1944 as the only government-sponsored refugees brought to the United States in World War II. The final section of the novel describes their adjustment to the United States at the resettlement camp in Oswego, New York, and their permanent settlement in the United States after World War II. Elementary grades.

Nolan, Han. *If I Should Die before I Wake.* New York: Harcourt Brace & Co., 1994. ISBN 0–15–238040–X. 225 pages. Hardcover.

This novel presents the transformation of a young neo-Nazi into a person who gains an understanding of the suffering and pain endured by Holocaust survivors. Close to death in a Jewish hospital, neo-Nazi Hilary falls into a coma and her memory is dominated by the experiences of Chana, a young woman in Poland during World War II. The transformation of Hilary occurs after the memories of Chana's experiences in the ghetto and camps bring her to the realization that all humans have a common bond, and that hate and prejudice are ultimately self-destructive behaviors. Young adult.

Orgel, Doris. *The Devil in Vienna.* New York: Puffin, 1988. ISBN 0–14–032500–X. 246 pages. Paperback.

Drawing upon experiences of her youth, the author has fashioned a novel that illustrates the importance of friendship between a Jew and Gentile, despite the presence of the "devil" (Nazism) in their home city of Vienna. Young adult.

Orlev, Yuri. *The Island on Bird Street.* Translated from Hebrew by Hillel Halkin. Boston: Houghton Mifflin, 1984. ISBN 0–395–33887–5. 162 pages. Paperback.

This novel by one of Israel's most distinguished authors is based upon the author's own experiences in the Warsaw Ghetto. The story revolves around the hopes of a young boy who awaits his father's return to the ghetto. Gradually, the young boy becomes resilient and resourceful in his struggle for survival, and when his father does return, the young boy has become an adult in everything but name. Young adult.

Pausewang, Gudrun. *The Final Journey.* Translated by Patricia Crampton. New York: Penguin, 1998. ISBN 0–14–130104–X. 155 pages. Paperback.

This novel is a compelling account of the deportation of a young girl and her grandparents, with emphasis placed on the experiences they endure in the deportation train car. As they arrive in a death camp, they are processed and the story ends as Alice, the young girl, is about to experience what she believes is a shower. The novel is characterized by feelings of trepidation, uncertainty, and false hopes, which are ultimately crushed as the deportees await their fate in the death camp. Young adult.

Richter, Hans Peter. *Friedrich.* Translated by Edite Kroll. New York: Puffin Books, 1987. ISBN 0–14–032206–X. 149 pages. Paperback.

————. *I Was There.* Translated by Edite Kroll. New York: Puffin Books, 1987. ISBN 0–14–032205–1. 204 pages. Paperback.

These two works by Hans Peter Richter relate stories of how Nazism influenced the lives of young people during the Third Reich. *Friedrich* tells the story of the gradual destruction of the Schneider family, a German Jewish family. As Nazi policies and practices designed to isolate and destroy Jews evolve, Friedrich's world collapses and his family's life disintegrates in a Germany engaged in total war. *I Was There* presents the story of three young boys in Nazi Germany, illustrating how Germans became enamored with Nazism and detailing the destructive impact of the Third Reich on the hopes and dreams of the younger generation. *Friedrich* contains a chronology of key dates relevant to the story, while *I Was There* also contains a chronology, but supplements this with notes concerning Nazi terminology and key people, organizations, and events during the Third Reich. Young adult.

Vos, Ida. *The Key Is Lost*. Translated by Terese Edelstein. New York: HarperCollins, 2000. ISBN 0–688–16283–5. 271 pages. Hardcover.

This account of historical fiction relates how two Jewish girls in the Netherlands changed their identities and hid from the Nazis, while their families lost their homes, businesses, and possessions under the German occupation. The novel draws upon the author's personal experiences as a Jew who went into hiding with her younger sister during World War II. Elementary grades.

Yolen, Jane. *The Devil's Arithmetic*. New York: Puffin, 1990. ISBN 0–14–034535–3. 170 pages. Paperback.

Transporting a contemporary Jewish girl back in time to 1940, the author develops a compelling story about how a young Jewish girl who had tired of her relatives' Holocaust stories now finds herself in a life-threatening situation during the Shoah. The personal awakening of the young Hannah about the continuity and power of Jewish history through the medium of the Holocaust is a major theme of this novel. Young adult.

6

PERIODICALS

OVERVIEW

The journals included here are the key periodicals in the field of Holocaust studies. These periodicals are highly respected by scholars and practitioners because they offer insightful commentary, book reviews, and articles that advance scholarly understanding of the Holocaust and genocides. Selected special issues of other professional journals are included because of the important contributions these thematic issues have made to study and teaching of the Holocaust, whether that be in Europe, North America, or Israel. Recognizing the changing landscape of academic scholarship, this chapter includes a special issue on genocide of *Other Voices*, a refereed electronic scholarly journal published at the University of Pennsylvania.

KEY PERIODICALS IN HOLOCAUST STUDIES

Dimensions: A Journal of Holocaust Studies. Published by the Anti-Defamation League's Braun Holocaust Institute. ISSN 0882–1240. Available via subscription from Braun Holocaust Institute, 823 United Nations Plaza, New York, NY 10017–3560. Phone: 212-885-7792.

Dimensions: A Journal of Holocaust Studies publishes articles and reviews of books, audiovisual materials, and articles appearing in other periodicals regarding Holocaust studies. Contributors are drawn from a range of disciplines, encompassing precollegiate through postgraduate educational levels. Issues are organized thematically, with additional articles and reviews often included on related topics. Beginning in 2002, *Dimensions* will be available as an online journal only.

Holocaust and Genocide Studies. Published by Oxford University Press in association with the United States Holocaust Memorial Museum. ISSN 8756–6583. Available via subscription from Oxford University Press, Journals Customer Service, 2001 Evans Road, Cary, NC 27513. Phone: 1-800-852-7323.

Holocaust and Genocide Studies is the leading scholarly journal for the study of the Holocaust. Produced in collaboration with the U.S. Holocaust Memorial Museum, this quarterly journal is an international interdisciplinary journal that addresses the implications of the Holocaust and of genocide in the areas of human behavior, the moral aspects of science and technology, and various dimensions of social and political organization. Issues of the journal contain essays, book reviews, listings of recently published books on the Holocaust and genocides, obituaries, a catalogue of major research centers with an emphasis on the Holocaust, and contributor biographies. Materials submitted for publication are evaluated using a peer review process.

Holocaust Studies Series. Published by Kluwer Academic Publishers, Postbus 17, 3300 AA Dordrecht, Netherlands. ISSN 0924–5022. Phone: 31-78-6392392.

Commencing in 1983, this series of monographs presents diverse perspectives on the Holocaust. Manuscripts undergo peer review and the series is not indexed.

Journal of Genocide Research. Published by Carfax Publishing Limited, PO Box 25, Abington Oxon OX14 3UE, England. Phone: 44-123-540-1000.

This refereed interdisciplinary journal seeks to promote multidimensional and comparative inquiry into the topic of genocide. Articles addressing the investigation of genocidal thinking and behavior are welcomed.

The Journal of Holocaust Education (formerly *British Journal of Holocaust Education*). Published by Frank Cass, Newbury House, 900 Eastern Avenue, Newbury Park, Ilford, Essex 1G2 7HH, England. ISSN 1359–1371. Phone: 44-181-599-8866.

This refereed journal provides a forum for debate on a range of topics about Holocaust education and research, including historical, educational, philosophical, religious, and sociological perspectives. The journal is indexed and includes book reviews.

Simon Wiesenthal Center Annual.

Published by the Simon Wiesenthal Center, Los Angeles, California, this journal includes a broad range of articles and reviews on the Holocaust, defined as Nazi Germany and the "final solution," 1933–1934; European Jewry during World War II; refugees, rescue, and immigration; displaced persons and post-war trials; and modern anti-Semitism. The editors have invited papers from every academic discipline. The full contents of Volumes 1–7 are accessible on the Simon Wiesenthal Center Web site at http://www.wiesenthal.com. For further information, contact the Simon Wiesenthal Center at 310–553–9036 or via e-mail at library@wiesenthal.net.

Yad Vashem Studies. Published by the Yad Vashem Martyrs' and Heroes' Remembrance Authority, PO Box 3477, Jerusalem 91034, Israel. ISSN 0084–3296. Phone: (972) 2-644-3505. FAX: (972) 2-644-3506.

This refereed journal begun in 1957 presents multifaceted perspectives on Holocaust studies. Book reviews are included and the journal is fully indexed, with back issues available for purchase.

SPECIAL ISSUES OF PROFESSIONAL JOURNALS

"On Genocide." Thematic issue of *Other Voices: The (e)Journal of Cultural Criticism.* http://dept.english.upenn.edu/~ov. Volume 2, Number 1, February 2000.

This issue of the peer-reviewed electronic journal *Other Voices* contains a series of commentaries, articles, interviews/lectures, and book reviews on the Holocaust and genocide. Contributions encompass topics as diverse as Holocaust art, the Museum of Tolerance, the experiences of Holocaust survivors, literary criticism and the Holocaust, Bosnian survivor experiences, genocide prevention, and others. The editorial address is: ov@dept.english.upenn.edu. (online) and Other Voices Attn: Vance Bell, PO Box 31907, Philadelphia, PA 19104–1907.

Parsons, William S., and Samuel Totten, editors. "Teaching about Genocide." Thematic issue of *Social Education,* Volume 55, Number 2, February 1991. Published by the National Council for the Social Studies, 8555 Sixteenth Street, Suite 500, Silver Spring, MD 20910. Phone: 301-588-1800.

This thematic issue of the leading social studies professional journal in the United States provides a comprehensive examination of the topic of genocide studies, including articles on instructional and curricular rationales, historical overviews of twentieth century genocides ranging from the Ottoman genocide of the Armenians and the Holocaust to the genocide in East Timor during the 1980s, brief first-person accounts of selected genocides, and teaching units on defining genocide and other aspects of genocide study.

"Teaching the Holocaust." Thematic issue of *International Textbook Research Journal*. Volume 22, Number 1, January 2000. ISSN 0172–8237. 168 pages.

This thematic issue of *International Textbook Research Journal* includes essays by authors from Germany, Israel, Austria, Russia, and the United States regarding how the Holocaust is taught in these countries. Topics include textbook analyses, patterns of curriculum and instruction, museum education, and the relationship of Holocaust studies to reflective citizenship education. Articles are presented in either German or English with abstracts in English, French, and German. Brief book reviews and reports on educational projects complete this special thematic issue. Available from the Georg Eckert Institute, Celler Strasse 3 D-38114, Braunschweig, Germany.

Totten, Samuel, Stephen Feinberg, and Milton Kleg, editors. "Teaching about the Holocaust." Thematic Issue of *Social Education*, Volume 59, Number 6, October 1995. Published by the National Council for the Social Studies, 8555 Sixteenth Street, Suite 500, Silver Spring, MD 20910. Phone: 301-588-1800.

Including a broad range of articles on theory and practice, this special issue of *Social Education* addresses issues of rationale and guidelines for classroom practice, as well as a comprehensive chronology on the history of the Holocaust and detailed listings of instructional resources. The editors have made a special effort to incorporate articles addressing the study of the Holocaust in other subject fields, such as language arts and interdisciplinary curricula.

PART II

PRIMARY SOURCES: PRINT AND RELATED RESOURCES

7

COLLECTIONS AND ANTHOLOGIES OF DOCUMENTS AND FIRST-PERSON ACCOUNTS

This chapter contains three interrelated sections: anthologies of documents, anthologies of first-person accounts, and collections of oral testimonies. All three sections provide important firsthand evidence concerning the Holocaust to complement the more broad-based narrative histories discussed in Chapter 2. Section overviews discuss the unique contributions made by the anthologies and oral testimony collections to our deepening understanding of the Shoah.

ANTHOLOGIES OF DOCUMENTS

Overview

The Holocaust ended in 1945 with the defeat of Nazi Germany. But the legacy of the Holocaust has in many ways been shaped by study of the huge quantity of documents and sources on this topic, which continues to grow as archives and other repositories yield their contents to scholars. The works included in this chapter encompass not only documents and related sources on the Holocaust, but by necessity one must engage the history of the Third Reich to gain a comprehensive understanding of how genocide became a central focus of the Nazi regime. Most often, the anthologies discussed here present documents and sources within an interpretive framework that is put forth by the editor in one or more essays in each anthology. Additionally, these anthologies typically organize their contents thematically or topically to help the user establish connections between specific documents, and to broader historical patterns of change. The anthologies of first-person accounts typically contain interpretive introductions that help readers understand the historical context in which the works were created, and many anthologies provide bibliographies that encourage further study of related works.

Teachers and scholars will find this section particularly helpful as they plan for instruction about the Holocaust, given the importance of primary document and source analysis in developing a critical approach to historical understanding.

Abzug, Robert. *America Views the Holocaust: A Brief Documentary History*. Boston: Bedford/St. Martin's, 1999. ISBN 0–312–13393–6. 236 pages. Paperback.

Part of the multivolume Bedford Series in History and Culture, Robert Abzug's work is an effort, through use of historical documents, to address serious questions about the relationship of the United States to the Holocaust. The overriding emphasis is placed on questions about the moral responsibilities of nations and individuals when genocide is recognized but less often confronted. The book's purposes are to reveal how Americans viewed the Holocaust as it emerged from the rise of Nazism to the end of World War II and to provide a survey of contrasting approaches by historians to the issues of historical reconstruction and moral responsibility since 1945. Each of the three major sections in the anthology—"The First Years of the Nazi Regime (1933–1935)"; "Exclusion, Emigration and War (1935–1941)"; and "Imagining the Unimaginable (1942–1945)"—has an introduction that defines the context of that chronological segment and its thematic emphasis. Each document receives a brief introduction as well. The volume includes a brief chronology, questions for consideration by the reader, and a select bibliography on the topic, as well as complete references for all sources (acknowledgments). Indexed.

Adelson, Alan, and Robert Lapides, editors. *Lodz Ghetto: Inside a Community under Siege*. New York: Penguin, 1989. ISBN 0–14–013228–7. 525 pages. Paperback.

Drawing upon over 10,000 pages of material and over 2,000 photographs compiled after a worldwide search, the contents of this anthology offer a wide-ranging selection of eyewitness accounts on life in the Lodz ghetto. More broadly defined than *The Chronicle of the Lodz Ghetto*, which was written under the official sponsorship of the ghetto administration, this anthology presents diary entries, personal notebooks, color and black-and-white photographs, and other sources depicting the gradual destruction of the Lodz Jewish community and the daily efforts at survival by the inhabitants. This work is an important supplement to the film on the same subject (see Chapter 10 on films and videotapes), but it also stands alone as one of the best sources on ghetto life during the Holocaust. Notes on Jewish Council leader Chaim Rumkowski, brief biographical sketches of authors included in the anthology, an afterword by Holocaust scholar Geoffrey

Hartman, and a glossary are included, along with a list of source acknowledgments and a street map of the Lodz ghetto. The index is limited to noting entries by specific anthology authors.

Arad, Yitzhak, Yisrael Gutman, and Abraham Margaliot, editors. *Documents on the Holocaust: Selected Sources on the Destruction of the Jews of Germany and Austria, Poland and the Soviet Union.* Translations by Lea Ben Dor. Introduction by Steven T. Katz. Eighth edition. Lincoln: University of Nebraska Press, 1999. ISBN 0–8032–5937–9. 508 pages. Paperback.

This comprehensive anthology of 213 sources is organized geographically. Sections on Germany and Austria, Poland, and the Soviet Union present documents about the Holocaust primarily from perpetrator and victim perspectives, although a limited number of bystander accounts are included. Sources are numbered consecutively from beginning to end, and each geographic section of the anthology begins with an introduction to the documents and how they illustrate the development of the Holocaust in that country (or in the case of Germany and Austria, as separate countries prior to the Anschluss of 1938). The wealth of materials from the Yad Vashem archives constitutes the strength of this anthology, particularly in the selection of sources on resistance efforts in Eastern Europe. A selected bibliography, three indices (names, organizations/institutions, places), and a comprehensive bibliography are also included. The sources of the documents follow each document entry.

Arad, Yitshak, Shmuel Krakowski, and Shmuel Spector, editors. *The Einsatzgruppen Reports.* New York: The Holocaust Library, in cooperation with Yad Vashem Martyrs Remembrance Authority, 1988. ISBN 0–89604–058–5. 378 pages. Paperback.

One of the most important compilations of Holocaust sources documenting the genocidal policies of Nazi Germany, *The Einsatzgruppen Reports* consist of excerpts from dispatches sent by German death squads operating in Eastern Europe from June 1941 through January 1943. The book begins with a thorough introduction that defines the purposes, organization, and composition of the Einsatzgruppen, their relationship to the German army, their geographic areas of operation, how their reports were compiled and transmitted, and how the reports were employed as evidence in post-1945 war crimes prosecutions. A table of comparable ranks among the Einsatzgruppen, the Wehrmacht, and the U.S. military is provided, along with a map displaying the routes taken and the major areas affected by Einsatzgruppen operations, primarily in the USSR. The report excerpts range across all four Einsatzgruppen (A, B, C, and D) areas of operations, and they describe in murderous detail the effectiveness of Nazi genocidal policies. Few other sources created by perpetrators so effectively depict the systematic efforts of Nazi Germany to eradicate the Jews of Europe, making these sources invaluable for understanding both the scope and nature of Nazi genocidal policies. The book is fully indexed.

Berenbaum, Michael. *Witness to the Holocaust: An Illustrated Documentary History of the Holocaust in the Words of Its Victims, Perpetrators and Bystanders.* New York: HarperCollins, 1997. ISBN 0–06–270108–8. 364 pages. Hardcover.

Containing sources that effectively complement the author's well-known narrative history of the Holocaust *The World Must Know*, this anthology incorporates ninety-four sources that address not only the preconditions of the Holocaust in Germany and the implementation of the genocide by Nazi Germany and collaborators, but the responses of Jews and world societies to the "final solution." Special attention is given to efforts at resistance, such as the Warsaw Ghetto uprising and the problem of what was or was not known about the Holocaust in the West. Sections on the controversy regarding the decision not to bomb Auschwitz, liberation of the camps, and the Nuremberg Trials, all significant topics that are often excluded from source anthologies, are well-represented in this book. A contextual overview is provided at the beginning of the anthology, and all twenty-one chapters begin with introductions that place their contents in a chronological sequence, while also discussing the historical themes they illustrate. A detailed chronology of the period encompassed in the sources is provided, along with a detailed index. Documentation of each source is provided at the end of individual source entries.

Chartock, Roselle, and Jack Spencer. *Can It Happen Again? Chronicles of the Holocaust.* New York: Black Dog and Leventhal Publishers, Inc., 1995. ISBN 1–884882–26–6. 376 pages. Hardcover.

Divided into six sections, this anthology encompasses a broad range of excerpts from survivor accounts, music, fiction, poetry, encyclopedia entries, works of philosophers and psychologists, selections by historians, and newspaper accounts. Works created during the period of the Third Reich are mixed with analytical entries of more recent creation. The six sections—"What Happened?," "Victims and Victimizers," "How and Why?," "What Does the Holocaust Reveal about the Individual and Society?," "Aftermath," and "Could It Happen Again?"—are subdivided into discrete chapters, each of which has very brief introductions to the excerpts that follow. Each major section begins with an extended quoted excerpt from a document, although these quotes are not accompanied by contextual explanations. The book contains a very brief introduction of three pages that raises questions about the causes, processes, and consequences of the Holocaust, and it concludes with a limited glossary of terms and an index. All sources used in the book are fully referenced in the acknowledgments section.

Czech, Danuta. *Auschwitz Chronicle, 1939–1945*. Foreword by Walter Laqueur. New York: Henry Holt & Co., 1990. ISBN 0–8050–5238–0. 855 pages. Paperback.

This collection includes entries on the Auschwitz camp complex drawing from the records of the Auschwitz State Museum. Organized as a chronicle beginning in 1939 and ending on January 27, 1945, when Soviet troops liberated Auschwitz, the book reconstructs the events and growth of the camp complex in that period. Each descriptive entry is accompanied by its source citation in the margin and all photos include descriptive captions. The introductory essay comprehensively describes how the Auschwitz Museum's resources were gathered, organized, and utilized to form the basis of the *Chronicle*, while the foreword by Walter Laqueur discusses the significance of Auschwitz in the conduct of the "final solution" and the great range of material on Auschwitz that has emerged since liberation in 1945. Biographical sketches of some of the perpetrators, a glossary of general and camp terms, a detailed bibliography, and a name index conclude the work, which is an essential reference source on the largest, most complex of Nazi death camps.

Dawidowicz, Lucy S., editor. *A Holocaust Reader*. West Orange, NJ: Behrman House, 1976. ISBN 0–87444–236–6. 397 pages. Paperback.

Dawidowicz' anthology begins with an outstanding introduction that discusses the origins of Holocaust documents, presents methodological concerns in the use of eyewitness accounts and partisanship of some documents, and addresses concerns about Nazi language, as well as the muted, somewhat censored language of Jews in Occupied Europe. The anthology's sources are divided into two sections: "The Final Solution," as displayed in documents of perpetrators (including preconditions for the rise of Nazi genocide and the first stage of anti-Jewish legislation in Germany), and "The Holocaust," or evidence of Jewish responses to Nazi policies of genocide (beginning in pre–World War II Germany and continuing through most of World War II). Introductions are provided for each chapter that discuss the significance of each document and its place in the processes of destruction initiated by Nazi Germany and resisted by Jews. Suggestions for further reading, an appendix of the estimated number of Jews killed in the "final solution," selected maps, and a list of sources conclude the book, which is also fully indexed.

Ehrenburg, Ilya, and Vasily Grossman, editors. *The Black Book*. Translated from the Russian by John Glad and James S. Levine. New York: Holocaust Library, 1981. ISBN 0–89604–031–3. 595 pages. Hardcover.

This anthology of sources on the experiences of Jews in the USSR during the Holocaust was never published as a complete text in the former Soviet Union. Some segments were published in the Soviet press, but this edition was compiled from various editions in the former USSR and Romania by experts at Yad Vashem. The brief introduction by historian Yitshak Arad places *The Black Book* in its historical context as an invaluable source of the experiences of Soviet Jews between 1939 and 1945. *The Black Book* challenges the Soviet silence on the Holocaust and the suffering of Jews in particular by including detailed accounts from the Ukraine, Byelorussia, the Russian Republic, Lithuania, and Latvia, most written by eyewitnesses and/or survivors of Nazi oppression. Testimonies of individuals who helped Jews, of death and concentration camp survivors, evidence drawn from interrogations of perpetrators, perpetrator documents, and fourteen pages of photographs are also included. Notes on the text, brief biographical sketches of the contributors, and two indices (names and geographic locations) are provided.

Housden, Martyn. *Resistance and Conformity in the Third Reich*. New York: Routledge, 1997. ISBN 0–415–12133–7. 199 pages. Hardcover.

This source anthology is organized thematically, and places emphasis on how daily life was experienced in Nazi Germany. The eight sections address the character and appeal of National Socialism; the responses of workers, churches, youth, and conservative elites to Nazism; the response of Germany's Jews to policies and practices of the Third Reich; how ordinary Germans reacted to Nazi racial policies; and the nature of resistance to Nazism in various segments of German society. Extensive introductions to each document are provided and references to major works in the book's bibliography are included in each chapter. Helpful interpretive and analytical questions for discussion are included in the editor's preface. Suggestions for further reading on each thematic topic are provided as well. Indexed.

Kaes, Anton, Martin Jay, and Edward Dimendberg, editors. *The Weimar Republic Sourcebook*. Berkeley: University of California Press, 1994. ISBN 0–520–06775–4. 806 pages. Paperback.

This massive volume contains 327 sources on the Weimar period in Germany history, representing a very broad spectrum of political, social, economic, and cultural perspectives on the era from 1919 to 1933. Concise but authoritative introductions precede each of the nine sections in the anthology, where the contents of each section are discussed within the context of changing interpretations of the historiography of the Weimar Republic. A comprehensive set of biographical sketches follows the final section of sources, which helps the reader acquire background information on the many individuals discussed in the volume. An extensive chronology of political events during the Weimar Republic, a selected bibliography for further study, source acknowledgments, and a detailed index conclude the volume. For students and individuals seeking understanding of the prelude to Nazism in the words of eyewitnesses, this is an essential book.

Klee, Ernst, Willi Dressen, and Volker Riess, editors. *The Good Old Days: The Holocaust as Seen by Its Perpetrators and Bystanders*. New York: Free Press, 1991. ISBN 0–02–917425–2. 314 pages. Hardcover.

This compilation of letters, memoranda, diary excerpts, photographs, and confidential reports by perpetrators of Nazi genocidal policies and bystanders juxtaposes the mundane with the murderous. Mixed together are perpetrator concerns for their daily needs (examples include the quality of their food, the type of accommodations they encountered when touring extermination camps and euthanasia facilities, and concerns for their families) and their businesslike, everyday completion of tasks central to the conduct of the "final solution" (observing massacres of Jews, selecting victims for gassing, and finding better ways of killing large numbers of people, among others). Little remorse or horror is expressed by the authors of the sources; the evidence of willing participation in mass murder far outweighs the limited number of sources attesting to reservations raised by the very few perpetrators who questioned their orders and sought reassignment elsewhere. Clearly, those who questioned and sought such reassignments away from the killing process suffered no serious repercussions, as is clearly shown in this book. The two sections of the book are primarily composed of text sources, although photographs are regularly included to demonstrate the open, public nature of the killing process, as well as the desire of many perpetrators to memorialize their involvement with visual reminders. Part I focuses on the actions of the Einsatzgruppen while Part II concentrates on activities of the extermination centers. The contents also include a thorough glossary and list of abbreviations, a listing of document sources, a detailed chronology, a set of brief biographical sketches of source authors, and an index of persons and places.

Kowalski, Isaac, compiler and editor. *Anthology of Armed Jewish Resistance, 1939–1945*. Brooklyn: Jewish Combatants Publishers House, 1984. ISBN 0-961-32190-3. 647 pages. Hardcover.

This is an anthology of works about Jewish resistance in World War II compiled by a partisan and survivor. The work contains excerpts from previously published works as well as documents and testimonies collected by the editor. Historian Yitshak Arad provides an introduction that discusses key patterns in Jewish resistance during the period 1939–1945. There is extensive use of photographs of author contributors to the anthology and of events, groups, and individuals associated with the specific articles in the text. No source citations for photographs are provided. A glossary, abbreviations list, and acknowledgments are included, along with selected maps. Indexed.

Levy, Richard S., editor. *Antisemitism in the Modern World: An Anthology of Texts*. Lexington: D. C. Heath & Co., 1991. ISBN 0–669–24340–X. 270 pages. Paperback.

This anthology provides a comprehensive introduction to the development of historic anti-Semitism. Following a detailed explanation of anti-Semitism's origins and a brief discussion of historic relationships between Jews and Christians from the ancient world to the twentieth century, the book is organized into five

major sections, beginning with the anti-Jewish tradition (eighteenth-century documents) and continuing forward chronologically to the period following the Holocaust. Each document is preceded by a detailed introduction explaining its origins
and historical significance in the development of anti-Semitism. A major contribution of the book is its assembling of important pre-Holocaust statements by anti-
Semitic politicians, philosophers, and ideologues, which established the foundation for development of the Nazi racial anti-Semitic program. Key documents
from the Holocaust itself include speeches by Hitler and the Protocol of the
Wannsee Conference, an anti-Semitic statement from Vichy France, and an eyewitness account of the persecution of Jews in Romania. An important component
of the book that reinforces the text materials is a selection of anti-Semitic nine-
teenth- and twentieth-century cartoons and other visual depictions of Jews, all of
which are thoroughly introduced and related to key ideas in the text documents. A
series of suggestions for further reading is provided along with a chronology of
major anti-Semitic publications and activities, beginning in 1710 and extending to
1987. No index.

Marrus, Michael R. *The Nuremberg War Crimes Trial, 1945–46: A Documentary History.* Boston: Bedford/St. Martin's, 1997. ISBN 0–312–13691–
9. 240 pages. Paperback.

This entry in the Bedford Series in History and Culture provides a well-organized
selection of key documents concerning the Nuremberg War Crimes Trial of 1945–
1946, accompanied by concise introduction and commentary. Michael Marrus
divides the book into nine sections, beginning with historical precedents and
concluding with assessment of the trial. Over seventy documents, either complete
or excerpted, are included in the volume, with major sections devoted to the three
core indictments issued by the International Military Tribunal: crimes against
peace, war crimes, and crimes against humanity. Full bibliographic citations for all
documents are provided, encouraging the reader to pursue in-depth study of the
vast amounts of published materials created or used at the trial. A detailed
chronology, summary of the defendants, their fate, and a chart of the charges,
verdicts, and sentences are provided, along with a select bibliography. Indexed.

Noakes, Jeremy, editor. *Nazism 1919–1945: A Documentary Reader.
Volume 1: The Rise to Power, 1919–1934.* Revised edition. Evanston:
Northwestern University Press, 1998. ISBN 0–85989–598–X. 220 pages.
Paperback.

This is the first of four very detailed and comprehensive documentary histories of
Nazism, representing a revised version of the original two-volume set *Documents
on Nazism 1919–1945*, published in 1983. Following a thorough introduction
setting the context for the volume's contents, with particular emphasis placed on
the virulent anti-Semitism sweeping Germany after 1876 and the emergence of
right-wing Pan-German nationalist movements, the book is organized chronologically beginning with the founding of the Nazi Party and the seizure of power in

1933–1934. Each chapter consists of a narrative interspersed with excerpted documents, presented in chronological sequence. The documents are numbered consecutively, a pattern that continues through the remaining three volumes of the series. A list of sources and selected bibliography conclude the volume, which is fully indexed.

Noakes, Jeremy, and Geoffrey Pridham, editors. *Nazism, State, Economy and Society, 1933–1939: A Documentary Reader.* Evanston: Northwestern University Press, 1995. ISBN 0–85989–461–4. 430 pages. Paperback.

This book is organized in the same fashion as Volume 1 of this documentary reader series. The development of Nazi policies designed to segregate and discriminate against Jews is thoroughly documented in the chapter on "Antisemitism 1933–1939" and reinforced by documents included in the sections "Propaganda and Indoctrination" and "Youth and Education." The documents include explanatory introductions and often represent eyewitness accounts as well as letters, official reports, and tables of statistics. The documents are numbered consecutively, a pattern that commenced in Volume 1 and continues through the remaining two volumes of the series. A list of sources and selected bibliography conclude the volume, which is fully indexed.

————. *Nazism: Foreign Policy, War and Racial Extermination.* Evanston: Northwestern University Press, 1995. ISBN 0–85989–474–6. 640 pages. Paperback.

Within the four-volume set of documentary readers prepared by Noakes and Pridham, this volume contains the most significant material on the planning and implementation of Nazi genocidal policies. Including over 200 separate documents and document excerpts, many of them eyewitness accounts, the editors provide a detailed view of how mass murder commenced in the "euthanasia program" and continued through intensified persecution of Jews, the transition to mass extermination during 1941–1942, and the extensive network of slave labor and death camps. A series of maps illustrating German military campaigns in Europe as well as Soviet counteroffensives is provided, along with a comprehensive listing of source acknowledgments and a selected bibliography for further study. Documents are numbered consecutively, following the pattern introduced in Volume 1 and continuing throughout the entire four-volume series.

Noakes, Jeremy, editor. *Volume 4: The German Home Front in World War II.* Exeter: University of Exeter Press, 1998. ISBN 0–85989–311–1. 698 pages. Paperback.

This is the concluding volume of the most comprehensive set of readily available sources on Nazism for general use. Similar to the other volumes in the series, all documents are numbered consecutively, beginning with source 919 and concluding with source 1399. Chapters on "Law and Terror" and "Propaganda" have very direct relationships to the Holocaust, notably the policies enacted by the Nazi state to suppress dissent and reinforce stereotyping, discrimination, and dehumanization of targeted victim groups. The chapter on "Defeat" includes Hitler's last will and testament, where his implacable hatred of Jews remained constant to the end. A selective bibliography concludes the book, which also is fully indexed.

Parsons, William S., Samuel Totten, and Israel W. Charny, editors. *Century of Genocide: Eyewitness Accounts and Critical Views*. New York: Garland Publishing, 1997. ISBN 0–8153–2353–0. 488 pages. Paperback.

This anthology juxtaposes fourteen extended critical essays with selected eyewitness accounts on genocides of the twentieth century. Beginning with the genocide of the Hereros in German Southwest Africa during the first decade of the twentieth century and extending through the Rwandan genocide of the 1990s, the editors have developed a comprehensive approach to understanding both the history and the impact of these genocides, with the emphasis placed on interpretation of the atrocities through eyewitness accounts of survivors. The Holocaust is represented by three chapters (on Jews, Gypsies, and the disabled), the only genocide to receive multiple perspectives. Introductory essays by the editors raise questions about how the focus of human caring can become more extensive and thus serve as an impediment to genocidal acts, and provide insights about efforts to limit the spread of genocide through development of a genocide early-warning system. The key questions addressed by each contributor are identified, and issues of definition regarding the term "genocide" are thoroughly discussed. The book concludes with a comprehensive index, extensive notes, and detailed bibliographies for each chapter that facilitate further in-depth study.

Steinhoff, Johannes, Peter Pechel, and Dennis Showalter. *Voices from the Third Reich: An Oral History*. Preface by Helmut Schmidt. New York: Da Capo Press, 1994. ISBN 0–306–80594–4. 550 pages. Paperback.

This anthology of interview excerpts focuses on individuals who were teenagers or in their early twenties during the years of the Third Reich. Each section has a brief introduction placing that section's interviews in an historical context during the period 1933–1945. Brief headnotes provide biographical information on the informants. Part III, "Defeat and Crimes," contains many interview excerpts dealing with the Nazi policies of genocide, notably in Chapter 10, "Genocide." Earlier sections, notably Chapter 2 in Part I, "Jews Get Out," details how average Germans collaborated with Nazi anti-Jewish policies prior to World War II. A glossary and chronology are provided to assist the reader in understanding the many references to terms, organizations, places, and individuals within the interview excerpts. Indexed.

ANTHOLOGIES OF FIRST-PERSON ACCOUNTS

Audio Documentaries

Notowitz, David. *Voices of the Shoah: Remembrances of the Holocaust*. Rhino CD Set R2/R4 75600. Los Angeles: Rhino Records, 2000. ISBN 0–

7379–0031–8. 4-CD set. TT: CD 1 = 58:46; CD 2 = 47:56; CD 3 = 68:57; CD 4 = 60.29.

This audio documentary consists of four audio compact discs and an accompanying book. Narrated by actor Elliott Gould, the documentary thematically interweaves survivor testimony, musical excerpts, and narration to tell the story of the Shoah, relying primarily on oral historical memoirs. Volumes 1 and 2 (Remembrances of the Holocaust) survey major topics such as "Life before the Shoah," "Life in the Ghettos," "Deportations to Labor and Death Camps," "Resistance," "Death Marches and Liberation," "Postwar Sickness and Recovery," and others. Volume 3 includes related topics such as the Kindertransport program and three accounts of camp liberation by American soldiers, while Volume 4 addresses the impact of the Shoah on children of survivors and Jews hidden as children, concluding with an epilogue. The booklet contains a time line, supplementary essays, transcript excerpts from the audio tracks, photos, discussion questions and activities, a bibliography, a glossary, and a selected list of learning resources for high school and adult audiences.

Books

Anderson, Mark M., editor. *Hitler's Exiles: Personal Stories of the Flight from Nazi Germany to America.* New York: New Press, 2000. ISBN 1–56584–591–9. 354 pages. Paperback.

The editor has created a kaleidoscope of first-person accounts, many reprinted over fifty years after their original publication, dealing with the refugee experience of individuals and families fleeing Nazism. The contents include the very famous (Albert Einstein, Stefan Zweig, Hannah Arendt) and the not-so-famous, who relate the obstacles they encountered in seeking refuge, as well as how they readjusted to life in the United States. A broad cross-section of vocations is represented, and the entries achieve a good balance of male and female perspectives. The editor's introduction places the contents within a context not only of the rise of Nazism and its effects on German society, but also within the long history of immigration to the United States, where these German refugees shared characteristics with some other immigrants while retaining unique cultural attributes of their own. Each of the book's three sections contains a brief introduction, and there is a detailed chronology of events provided for reference. A select bibliography and list of source acknowledgments conclude the book. No index.

Geier, Arnold. *Heroes of the Holocaust: Extraordinary True Accounts of Triumph.* New York: Berkley Books, 1993. ISBN 0–425–16029–7. 280 pages. Paperback.

This anthology presents twenty-eight stories of how Jews were hid, assisted, and/or rescued by individuals in Germany and Occupied Europe during the Holocaust. In some cases, the stories were compiled by others and shared with the author, but most were drawn from interviews done by the author, or from manuscripts solicited by him from informants. The majority of stories address righteous activities in Germany and Poland, although some submissions concern cases from Hungary, Romania, France, and Holland. Pen-and-ink drawings are incorporated into the text as illustrations for the stories, and when available, photos of the survivors and those who assisted them are included. A map of main camps in the Third Reich and Occupied Europe, a chronology of the Holocaust, and a select bibliography (divided into general sources and sources on courage, rescue, and heroism) are included. No index.

Greene, Joshua M., and Shiva Kumar, editors. *Witness: Voices from the Holocaust.* Foreword by Lawrence L. Langer. New York: Free Press, 2000. ISBN 0–684–86525–4. 270 pages. Hardcover.

This series of interview excerpts from the Yale Fortunoff Archives uses twenty-seven of the 100 interviews screened by the editors. They are not organized as independent narratives, but instead in thematic chapters drawing from a variety of the informants depending upon the chapter theme (ghettos, liberation, and others). The excellent introduction by Lawrence Langer addresses the significance of testimonies as a source for Holocaust study, noting the complexity and multiple layers of meaning evident in personal remembrances. Langer also notes the significance of providing access to personal histories to insure that the history of the Holocaust won't be forgotten. A select bibliography and a brief description of the Yale Fortunoff Archives are included, along with a detailed index.

Halter, Marek. *Stories of Deliverance: Speaking with Men and Women who Rescued Jews from the Holocaust.* Translated by Michael Bernard. Chicago: Open Court Publishing Co., 1998. ISBN 0–8126–9364–7. 304 pages. Paperback.

Combining personal reflections on his own life experiences and the moral choices of individuals in difficult circumstances with excerpts from his discussions with people who aided Jews during the Holocaust, Marek Halter presents a multifaceted picture of how some people risked their lives to defy Nazism. The over forty separate stories in the book encompass a diverse geographic context: North Africa, the Jewish community in Shanghai, Rhodes, Yugoslavia, Denmark, France, and many others. Unifying the stories is Halter's search for explanations about the motivations and actions of the "just" (his term for righteous people) and letting the informants speak for themselves in extended quotes about their activities. The book contains a thorough index, but no photographs.

Laska, Vera, editor. *Women in the Resistance and in the Holocaust: The Voices of Eyewitnesses.* Foreword by Simon Wiesenthal. Westport, CT: Greenwood Press, 1983. ISBN 0–313–23457–4. 330 pages. Hardcover.

This work by the Czech Holocaust survivor provides an introductory essay and selections from firsthand accounts divided into three sections: "Women in the Resistance," "Women in Concentration Camps," and "Women in Hiding." The editor has made a concerted effort to include a broad cross-section of female eyewitnesses, and a selection of illustrations are included to highlight specific stories in the work. A comprehensive bibliography is provided, along with a detailed index.

Lewin, Rhoda G., editor. *Witnesses to the Holocaust: An Oral History.* Afterword by Deborah E. Lipstadt. Boston: Twayne Publishers, 1990. ISBN 0–8057–9100–0. 241 pages. Hardcover.

Divided into three sections, this volume in Twayne Publishers Oral History Series includes fifty-eight edited interview excerpts from Holocaust survivors and U.S. liberators of Nazi camps, which were based upon interview materials held at the Jewish Community Relations Council in Minneapolis, Minnesota, or which the author conducted on her own. The work begins with a preface where she describes her research methods and discusses the value of oral history. Photos of selected survivors and scenes of liberation are included with the interviews. Each section begins with a very brief introduction, and the individual interview excerpts are introduced with headnotes about the informants. Each of the chapters in Part I includes subheadings to organize the excerpts and facilitate comparative analysis ("Auschwitz," "The Transport," "Deportations," and other subheadings). The afterword by Deborah Lipstadt addresses the significance of witness testimonies in combating Holocaust denial. A glossary, interviewing guide, and discussion questions for classroom use, along with a detailed index, conclude the book.

Niewyk, Donald, editor. *Fresh Wounds: Early Narratives of Holocaust Survival.* Chapel Hill: University of North Carolina Press, 1998. ISBN 0–8078–2393–7. 414 pages. Hardcover.

Bringing to readers thirty-six interviews done by pioneering American psychologist David P. Boder with Holocaust survivors in 1946, historian Donald Niewyk has made an important contribution to the understanding of the Holocaust through the medium of first-person accounts. The significance of Boder's interviews, as reconstituted in this edition, rests with their collection very soon after the end of World War II, thus limiting the decay and distortion of memory that is likely to occur in survivor testimonies gathered many years after the end of the Holocaust. Niewyk's introduction places the Boder interviews in their historical and methodological context, noting how their editing for this volume was accomplished. Most importantly, Niewyk discusses the thirty-six interviews and their relationships to core themes in Holocaust history, such as the processes of identification, expropriation, concentration, and annihilation articulated by Raul Hilberg, as well as the massive involvement of German social institutions in genocide, which ranged from collaboration by German businesses to the daily brutalities of life in the camps. Each interview contains an introduction that describes the personal and family background of the interviewee and relates how that person was affected by Nazi policies of persecution. All of the interviewees are Jews, and all are from Central or Eastern Europe, with Poland represented most often. Two glossaries are provided, one of specialized terms and the other of ghettos and camps. A selected bibliography is included, along with an index.

Owings, Alison. *Frauen: German Women Recall the Third Reich.* New Brunswick: Rutgers University Press, 1993. ISBN 0–8135–1992–6. 494 pages. Hardcover.

Consisting of portraits based upon interviews with twenty-nine German women who lived during the Third Reich, this book reveals various dimensions of how women experienced life under Nazi rule. Considerable attention is given to the treatment of Jews in Nazi Germany, with diverse responses from the informants: ranging from efforts to downplay the atrocities perpetrated on Jews, to feelings of helplessness in the face of brutality, to many others. The author succeeds in soliciting detailed responses from the informants and is quite effective at challenging the informants to rethink their assumptions and assertions with probing questions highlighting difficult, perplexing topics. The final chapter presents an analysis of the twenty-nine portraits, focusing on patterns of exoneration and repression in the informant comments. A brief glossary is included, along with an acknowledgments section. Indexed.

COLLECTIONS OF ORAL TESTIMONIES

Overview

Even prior to the end of World War II, the collection of oral testimonies about the Holocaust had commenced. When the Soviet military liberated death camps in Poland, survivors of those camps were offered the opportunity to relate their experiences to Soviet personnel, in the event such information could be employed in trials of perpetrators. Since the end of World War II, and at an accelerating pace since the 1960s, survivors of the Holocaust and some perpetrators have been interviewed and their memoirs preserved for posterity. Most recently, the large-scale efforts of Steven Spielberg's Survivors of the Shoah Visual History Foundation have generated increased public awareness about the significance of preserving Holocaust survivor testimonies, now that many survivors are at a very advanced age. However, the collection of testimonies, whether they be on audiotape or videotape, has been an important function of Holocaust centers, museums, libraries, and archives for decades. The listings of repositories of Holocaust testimonies in this chapter are based upon a comprehensive review of directories of Holocaust institutions, as well as examination of printed works whose contents have been drawn heavily from testimonies available in selected repositories worldwide. For each listing, the title, location, phone, fax number, address, and Web site/e-mail addresses (where applicable) are provided, along with a parenthetical notation if the repository contains videotaped testimonies as well as those preserved on audiotape. Readers desiring a more detailed, but somewhat dated catalog of oral testimonies primarily held in the United States should consult Joan Ringelheim, compiler, *A Catalogue of Audio and Video Collections of Holocaust Testimony* (second edition). Westport, CT: Greenwood Press, 1992. ISBN 0–313–28221–8.

Australia

Jewish Holocaust Museum and Research Center of Melbourne, Australia. 13 Selwyn Street, Elsternwick Melbourne VIC 3185, Australia. Phone (61) 3-952-81985. FAX (61) 3-952-83758. http://www.arts.monash.edu.au/affiliates.hlc.

Belgium

Memorial National du Fort de Breendonk (Fort Breendonk). Willebroek B-2830, Belgium. Phone (32) 3-886-62-09. FAX (32) 3-866-53-91. http://www.breendonk.be. e-mail: info@breendonk.be.

Brazil

Nucleo de Historia Oral—Arquivo Historeico Judaico Brasileiro (Oral History Department of the Brazilian Jewish Historical Archives). Rua Prates, 790 Sao Paulo 01121-000, Brasil. Phone (55) 11-228-8769. FAX (55) 11-228-9769. e-mail: ahjb@uol.com.br.

Canada

Living Testimonies Holocaust Video Archive at McGill University. New Chancellor Day Hall, Suite 514, McGill University, 3644 Peel Street, Montreal, Quebec H3A 1W9, Canada. Phone 514-398-3294. FAX 514-488-8932. http://www.arts.mcgill.ca/programs/livingt/. e-mail: livingt@leacock.lan.mcgill.ca. (Videotaped testimonies)

The Montreal Holocaust Memorial Center. 1 Carre Cummings Square, Montreal, Quebec H3W 1M6, Canada. Phone 514-345-2605, ext. 3026. FAX 514-344-2651. e-mail: natashal@fedcjamtl.org. (Videotaped testimonies)

Vancouver Holocaust Education Center. #50-950 West 41st Avenue, Vancouver, British Columbia V5Z 2N7, Canada. Phone 604-264-0499. FAX 604-264-0497. http://www.vhec.org. e-mail: info@vhec.org. (Videotaped testimonies)

France

Musee de la Resistance et de la Deportation (Museum of the Resistance and Deportation). La Citadelle, 15000 Besancon, France. Phone (33) 03-816-50755. FAX (33) 03-816-50756. http://www.besancon.com. e-mail: elizabeth. pastwa@besancon.com.

Germany

Dokumentations-und Informationszentrum Emslandlager (DIZ) (The Emsland Camps Documentation and Information Center). Postfach 1132, Papenburg D-26821, Germany. Phone (49) 04961-916306. FAX (40) 04961-916308. http://www.diz-emslandlager.de. e-mail: mail@diz-emslandlager.de.

Israel

Beit Theresenstadt. Kibbutz Givat Hayim-Ichud Mobile Post Emek Heffer 39395 Israel. Phone (972) 04-636-9515. FAX (972) 04-636-9611. http:// www.bterezin.org.il. e-mail: bterezin@inter.net.il.

Ot Va'ed—An Educational Enterprise Dedicated to the Significance of the Holocaust on the Jewish Spirit. 58 King George Street, PO Box 71197, Jerusalem 91711, Israel. Phone (972) 2-625-2689. FAX (972) 2-625-2703.

Yad Vashem—The Holocaust Martyrs' and Heroes' Remembrance Authority. PO Box 3477, Jerusalem 91034, Israel. Phone (972) 2-644-3400. FAX (972) 2-643-3443. http://www.yadvashem.org.il.

Lithuania

Atminties Namai (The House of Memory). Klaipidos g. 6-406 Vilnius 2600, Lithuania. Phone (370) 8-2-227-183. FAX (370) 8-2-227-173. e-mail: mtc@osf.lt.

Vilna Gaon Jewish State Museum of Lithuania. Pamenkalnio 12, Vilnius LT-2001, Lithuania. Phone (370) 2-620-730. FAX (370) 2-227-083. http:// muziejai.mch.miilt/Vilnius/zydu_muziejus.en.htm. e-mail: jmuseum@delfi.lt.

The Netherlands

Nederlands Instituut voor Oorlogsdocumentatie (NIOD) (Netherlands State Institute for War Documentation). Herengracht 380, Amsterdam 1016, CJ, The Netherlands. Phone (31) 20-523-3800. FAX (31) 20-523-3888. http:// www.oorlogsdoc.knaw.nl. e-mail: info@oorlogsdoc.knaw.nl.

New Zealand

Holocaust Oral History Group. PO Box 63, Auckland, New Zealand. Phone (64) 9-521-3526. FAX (64) 9-521-3526. e-mail: narev@clear.net.nz.

Poland

Muzeum Gross-Rosen (The State Museum of KL Gross-Rosen). Skrytka Pocztowa 217, Walbrzych 58-300, Poland. Phone (48) 74-855-9007 and (48) 74-846-4566. FAX (48) 74-842-1580. http://www.region-walbrzych.org.pl/grosrosen. e-mail: pmgr@wb.onet.pl.

Panstwowe Muzeum Auschwitz-Birkenau (State Museum of the KL Auschwitz–Birkenau). ul. Wiezniow Oswiecimia 20, Oswiecim 32-603, Poland. Phone (48) 33-843-2022. FAX (48) 33-843-1934. http://www.auschwitz.org.pl. e-mail: muzeum@auschwitz-muzeum.oswiecim.pl.

Panstwowe Muzeum na Majdanku (The State Museum of Majdanek). ul. Dr. Meczennikow Majdanka 67, Lublin 20-325, Poland. Phone (48) 81-744-2640. FAX (48) 81-744-0526. http://www.majdanek.pl. e-mail: dyr@majidanek.pl.

Panstwowe Muzeum Stutthof w Sztutowie (State Museum Stutthof in Sztutowo). ul. Muzealna 6, Sztutowo 82-100, Poland. Phone (48) 55-247-8353. FAX (48) 55-247-8358. http://www.kki.net.pl.museum/. e-mail: museum@kki.net.pl.

Zydowski Instytut Historyczny. Instytut Naukowo-Badawczy (Jewish Historical Institute). ul. Tolmackie 3/5, Warszawa 00-090 Poland. Phone (48) 22-827-8372 and (48) 22-827-9221. FAX (48) 22-827-8372. http://www.jewishinstitute.org.pl/ OZIH1E.html. e-mail: zihinb@ikp.atom.com.pl.

United Kingdom

Holocaust Survivor Centre. Parson Street, London NW4 1QA, United Kingdom. Phone (44) 181-202-9844. FAX (44) 181-201-5534.

Imperial War Museum. Lambeth Road, London SE1 6HZ, United Kingdom. Phone (44) 020-741-65204 and (44) 020-741-65285. FAX (44) 020-741-65278. http://www.iwm.org.uk. e-mail: sbardgett@iwm.org.uk.

Institute of Contemporary History and Wiener Library. 4 Devonshire Street, London W1W 5BH, United Kingdom. Phone (44) 020-7636-7247. FAX (44) 020-7436-6428. http://www.wienerlibrary.co.uk. e-mail: info@wienerlibrary.co.uk.

United States

ADL Braun Holocaust Institute. 823 United Nations Plaza, New York, New York 10017, United States of America. Phone 212-885-7792. FAX 212-867-0779. http://www.adl.org. e-mail: webmaster@adl.org.

Bagby Videotape Archives of Early Christian Resisters to the Hitler Regime. 1501 Lakeside Drive, Lynchburg, Virginia 24501-3199, United States of America. Phone 804-544-8441. FAX 804-844-8499. http://www.loc.gov/rr/main/religious/ lyn.html. e-mail: JKelly934@aol.com.

Bay Area Holocaust Oral History Project. 1700 Alameda de las Pulgas, San Mateo, California 94403, United States of America. Phone 650-570-6382. FAX 650-570-7183. http://dai.sfsu.edu/012/holocaust/prototype. e-mail: bahohp@aol.com (Videotaped testimonies)

Center for Holocaust and Genocide Studies—Ramapo College of New Jersey. Ramapo College Library, 404 Ramapo Valley Road, Mahwah, New Jersey 07446, United States of America. Phone 201-684-7409. FAX 201-684-7953. http:// www.ramapo.edu/content/campus.resources/Holocenter/holocaust.html. e-mail: mriff@ramapo.edu.

Center for Holocaust and Genocide Studies—University of Minnesota. 100 Nolte Hall West, 315 Pillsbury Drive, University of Minnesota, Minneapolis, Minnesota 55435, United States of America. Phone 612-626-2235. FAX 612-626-9169. http:// chgs.hispeed.com. e-mail: chgs@tc.umn.edu.

Center for Holocaust Studies at Brookdale Community College. 765 Newman Springs Road, Lincroft, New Jersey 07738, United States of America. Phone 732-224-2769. FAX 732-224-2045. http://www.holocaustbcc.org. e-mail: HoloCenter@Brookdale.CC.NJ.US.

Dallas Holocaust Memorial Center. 7900 Northaven Road, Dallas, Texas 75230, United States of America. Phone 214-750-4654. FAX 214-750-4672. http://www.dallasholocaustcenter.org. e-mail: dmchs@mail.swbellnet. (Videotaped testimonies)

Edna Silberman Holocaust Oral History Project of the Greater Harrisburg Jewish Community. 3301 West Front Street, Harrisburg, Pennsylvania 17110, United States of America. Phone 717-236-9555. FAX 717-236-2552.

Eyes from the Ashes. Box 1133, Bryn Mawr, Pennsylvania 19010-7133, United States of America. Phone 610-527-3131. FAX 610-527-9334. http://www.eyesfromtheashes.com. e-mail: ann@eyesfromtheashes.com.

Fortunoff Video Archives for Holocaust Testimonies. PO Box 208240, Sterling Memorial Library, Yale University, New Haven, Connecticut 06520-8240, United States of America. Phone 203-432-1879. FAX 203-432-7441. http://www.library.yale.edu/testimonies. e-mail: fortunoff.archive@yale.edu. (Videotaped testimonies)

The Foundation for the Advancement of Sephardic Studies and Culture. PO Box 092-272, Brooklyn, New York 11209, United States of America. http://www.sephardicstudies.org.

Fred R. Crawford Witness to the Holocaust Project—Emory University. Special Collections Department, Robert W. Woodruff Library, Emory University, Atlanta, Georgia 30322-2870, United States of America. Phone 404-329-6428. http://gtel.gatech.edu/projects/holocaust. (Videotaped testimonies)

Halina Wind Preston Holocaust Education Center. 100 West 10th Street, Suite 301, Wilmington, Delaware 19801-1628, United States of America. Phone 302-427-2100. FAX 302-427-2438. e-mail: Delawarejfd@jon.cjfny.org.

Holocaust Center of the United Jewish Federation of Greater Pittsburgh. 5738 Darlington Road, Pittsburgh, Pennsylvania 15217-1512, United States of America. Phone 412-421-1500. FAX 412-422-1996. http://www.ujf.net. e-mail: information@ujf.net. (Videotaped testimonies)

The Holocaust Commission of the United Federation of Tidewater. 5029 Corporate Woods Drive, Suite 225, Virginia Beach, Virginia 23462, United States of America. Phone 757-671-1600. FAX 757-671-7613. http://www.holocaustcommission.org. e-mail: betsyk@ujft.org. (Videotaped testimonies)

Holocaust Documentation and Education Center, Inc. Florida International University, North Miami Campus, 3000 N. E. 151 Street, North Miami, Florida 33181, United States of America. Phone 305-919-5690. FAX 305-919-5691. http://

holocaust.FIU.edu/history1.html. e-mail: xholocau@fiu.edu. (Videotaped testimonies)

Holocaust Library and Resource Center—Albright College. F. Wilbur Gingrich Library, 13th and Bern Streets, PO Box 15234, Reading, Pennsylvania 19612-5234, United States of America. Phone 610-921-7214. FAX 610-921-7509. http://www.albright.edu/library/holocaust.html. e-mail: dant@alb.edu.

Holocaust Memorial Center. 6602 West Maple Road, West Bloomfield, Michigan 48322-3005, United States of America. Phone 248-661-0840. FAX 248-661-4204. http://www.holocaustcenter.org. e-mail: info@holocaustcenter.org. (Videotaped testimonies)

Holocaust Museum Houston. 5401 Caroline Street, Houston, Texas 77004-6804, United States of America. Phone 713-942-8000. FAX 713-942-7953. http://www.hmh.org. e-mail: sllanes@hmh.org.

Holocaust Oral History Archive of Gratz College. Old York Road and Melrose Avenue, Melrose Park, Pennsylvania 19027, United States of America. Phone 215-635-7300, ext. 130. FAX 215-635-7320. e-mail: archives@gratz.edu.

Holocaust Resource Center and Archives of Queensborough Community College. 222-05 56th Avenue, Bayside, New York 11364, United States of America. Phone 718-225-1617. FAX 718-631-6306. e-mail: hrcaho@worldnet.att.net.

Holocaust Resource Center of Buffalo. 1050 Maryvale Drive, Room 464, Cheektowaga, New York 14225, United States of America. Phone 716-634-9535. FAX 716-634-9625. http://www.holocaustcenterbuff.com. e-mail: hrc1050@aol.com.

Holocaust Resource Center of Kean University. Thompson Library, Second Floor, Kean University, Union, New Jersey 07083, United States of America. Phone 908-527-3049. FAX 908-629-7130. http://www.kean.edu/hrc/. e-mail: keanhrc@turbo.kean.edu. (Videotaped testimonies)

Holocaust Resource Center of the Richard Stockton College of New Jersey. The Richard Stockton College, PO Box 195, Pomona, New Jersey 08240, United States of America. Phone 609-652-4699. FAX 609-748-5543. http://loki.stockton.edu/~holocaus/hrc.htm. e-mail: iaoprod446@stockton.edu.

Jewish Teacher Resource Center. 3301 West Front Street, Harrisburg, Pennsylvania 17110, United States of America. Phone 717-236-9555. FAX 717-236-2552. e-mail: leebaleh@aol.com.

Lillian and A.J. Weinberg Center for Holocaust Education of the William Breman Jewish Heritage Museum. The Selig Center, 1440 Spring Street, Atlanta, Georgia 30309, United States of America. Phone 404-870-1872. FAX 404-881-4009. http://www.atlantajewishmuseum.org/holocaust.html. e-mail: csinger@atljf.com. (Videotaped testimonies)

Los Angeles Holocaust Museum. 6006 Wilshire Boulevard, Los Angeles, California 90036, United States of America. Phone 323-761-8170. FAX 323-761-8174. http://www.remembertoteach.com/museum.htm#. e-mail: kjosephy@earthlink.net.

Midwest Center for Holocaust Education. 5801 West 115th Street, Suite 106, Overland Park, Kansas 66211-1800, United States of America. Phone 913-327-8190. FAX 913-327-8193. http://www.mchekc.org. e-mail: info@mchekc.org.

New York Public Library. Dorot Jewish Division, Fifth Avenue and 42nd Street, Room 84, New York, New York 10018-2788, United States of America. Phone 212-930-0601. FAX 212-642-0141. http://www.nypl.org. e-mail: freidus@nypl.org.

Oral History Institute (OHI). 56 East 300, South Salt Lake City, Utah 84111, United States of America. Phone 801-355-3903. FAX 801-355-3903. e-mail: lejodajo@utah.USWest.net.

Oregon Holocaust Resource Center. Pacific University, 2043 College Way, Forest Grove, Oregon 97116, United States of America. Phone 503-359-2930. FAX 503-359-2246. http://nellie.pacificu.edu/ohrc. e-mail: ohrc@pacificu.edu.

Rabbi Leib Geliebter Memorial Foundation, Inc. 1663 East 17th Street, Brooklyn, New York 11229, United States of America. Phone 718-998-4437. FAX 718-998-2137. e-mail: carenet@aol.com. (Videotaped testimonies)

Ruth Sajerman Markowicz Holocaust Resource Center of Greater Toledo. 6465 Sylvania Avenue, Sylvania, Ohio 43560, United States of America. Phone 419-885-4485. FAX 419-885-3207. e-mail: markow@msn.com.

San Francisco Holocaust Oral History Project. PO Box 77603, San Francisco, CA 94107, United States of America. Phone 415-882-7092. e-mail: hohp@mailexcite.com.

Simon Wiesenthal Center—Museum of Tolerance. 9786 Simon Wiesenthal Plaza, West Pico Boulevard, Los Angeles, CA 90035-4792, United States of America. Phone 310-553-8403. FAX 310-772-7655. http://www.museumoftolerance.com. e-mail: library@wiesenthal.net.

South Carolina Council on the Holocaust. 1429 Senate Street, 801 Rutledge Building, Columbia, South Carolina 29201, United States of America. Phone 803-734-0322. FAX 803-734-6142. e-mail: mwalden@richland2.org.

Southern Institute for Education and Research at Tulane University. Tulane University, MR Box 1692, 31 McAlister Drive, New Orleans, Louisiana 70118, United States of America. Phone 504-865-6100. FAX 504-862-8957. http://www.tulane.edu/~so-inst. e-mail: lhill@tulane.edu.

Survivors of the Shoah Visual History Foundation. PO Box 3168, Los Angeles, California 90078-3168, United States of America. Phone 888-241-0772 (USA and Canada) and 818-777-7802 (other countries). FAX 818-866-3766. http://www.vhf.org. e-mail: educationalresources@vhf.org. (Videotaped testimonies)

United States Holocaust Memorial Museum. 100 Raoul Wallenberg Place, SW, Washington, DC 20024-2156, United States of America. Phone 202-488-6103. FAX 202-288-2690. http://ushmm.org. e-mail: oralhistory@ushmm.org. (Videotaped testimonies)

Virginia Holocaust Memorial Museum. 213 Roseneath Road, Richmond, Virginia 23221, United States of America. Phone 804-257-5400. FAX 804-257-4314. http://www.va-holocaust.com. e-mail: info@va-holocaust.com. (Videotaped testimonies)

Washington State Holocaust Education Resource Center. 2031 Third Avenue, Seattle, Washington 98121, United States of America. Phone 206-441-5747. FAX 206-956-0881. http://www.wsherc.org. e-mail: info@wsherc.org. (Videotaped testimonies)

Uruguay

Centro Recordatorio del Holocausto Soc. Amigos de Yad Vashem (Holocaust Memorial Center, Friends of Yad Vashem). Canelones 1084, Piso 3, Montevideo 11100, Uruguay. Phone (598) 2–902–5750, ext. 124. FAX (598) 2–203–1746. e-mail: benvin@redfacil.com.uy. (Videotaped testimonies)

8
INDIVIDUAL WORKS:
FIRST-PERSON ACCOUNTS
AND BIOGRAPHIES

OVERVIEW

For students of the Holocaust, first-person accounts provide a very rich source of information and insights about this historical period. The works included in this chapter are only a small sample of the many first-person accounts available in print, but at the same time they help the reader address the diversity of the authors (age, geographic area, gender, cultural status, class, and religion) as well as the mixture of genres evident (diaries, memoirs, autobiographies, collections of letters, and interrogation records). Both perpetrators and victims are represented to help the reader encounter their perspectives on the Holocaust in their own words. The voices of adults and children are present, as are the words of the famous (Anne Frank, Elie Wiesel) and the less well-known. Used in conjunction with the narrative histories and source anthologies discussed in Chapters 2 and 7 respectively, these first-person accounts are valuable contributions to an in-depth understanding of this complex historical period.

BIBLIOGRAPHIC WORKS

Totten, Samuel. *First-Person Accounts of Genocidal Acts Committed in the Twentieth Century: An Annotated Bibliography*. Westport, CT: Greenwood Press, 1991. ISBN 0–313–26713–8. 351 pages. Hardcover.

This authoritative work annotates entries for many Holocaust first-person accounts, including bibliographies, individual accounts, anthologies, essays about first-person accounts, entries of books, and other print materials where first-person accounts are referenced and films. The extensive introductory essay addresses important concerns about the use and value of first-person accounts for research, study, and teaching, and includes a list of references on oral history depositories. Among the lesser-known genocides included from the early to the late twentieth century are the German genocide of the Hereros in Africa, the genocides in Cambodia and East Timor, and the genocide of Bahais and of indigenous peoples, such as the Ache culture in Paraguay. Two sections on Holocaust first-person accounts are included: one on the Holocaust overall (primarily focused on Jews), and a separate chapter on Gypsies. Given the vast literature on Holocaust first-person accounts, these two chapters account for more than half of the book's total pages. Both subject and author indexes are provided.

DIARIES AND JOURNALS

Adelson, Alan. *The Diary of David Sierakowiak: Five Notebooks from the Lodz Ghetto.* New York: Oxford University Press, 1996. ISBN 0–19–510450–1. 271 pages. Hardcover.

This diary depicts life in the Lodz ghetto between June 28, 1939 and April 15, 1943 through the eyes of young David Sierakowiak, who died of tuberculosis, starvation, and exhaustion in the Lodz ghetto on August 8, 1943. The entries are not continuous over the entire span of the diary, but the compelling nature of the author's prose holds the reader's attention. This is not an uplifting or hopeful story, but rather one that reveals the relentless, unfolding tragedy and misery of the population destined for death in the Lodz ghetto. This edition includes a concise and insightful foreword by Lawrence Langer, as well as photos of life in the Lodz ghetto that are linked to captions excerpted from the diary entries. The photos were taken by ghetto photographers Mendel Grossman and Henryk Ross prior to the final deportations from Lodz in 1944. No index.

Berg, Mary. *Warsaw Ghetto: A Diary by Mary Berg.* Edited by S.L. Shneiderman. New York: L.B. Fischer, 1945. No ISBN. 253 pages. Hardcover.

Mary Berg, the daughter of an American citizen, resided in Lodz and was sixteen years old when she and her mother arrived in the Warsaw ghetto. Berg's diary was the first eyewitness account to be published of the Warsaw Ghetto uprising, and is a very detailed diary originally written in Polish, and translated to English after Berg and her mother arrived in the United States in 1944. Exchanged with U.S. prisoners of war for German prisoners of war, Mary Berg and her mother returned to the United States through Portugal in 1944, when Mary was twenty years old. No index.

Dorian, Emil. *The Quality of Witness: A Romanian Diary, 1937–1944.* Selected and edited by Marguerite Dorian. Translated by Mara Soceanu

Vamos. Introduction by Michael Stanislawski. Philadelphia: The Jewish Publication Society of America, 1982. ISBN 0–8276–0211–1. 350 pages. Hardcover.

This diary chronicles the experiences of the Romanian Jewish community for seven years through the eyes of Emil Dorian, a noted writer and medical doctor. The preface by the author's daughter establishes a context for the diary, noting that Romanian Jews suffered from living in the last country in Europe to emancipate Jews, as well as from the brutality of the fascist Antonescu regime, which allied with the Third Reich during World War II. The tragedy of Romanian Jews, particularly those living in Transnistria, is discussed in the diary, along with the efforts of the Romanian government to protect Jews in the "old kingdom" of Romania from deportation to death camps. At the same time, the author recognized that the life of Jews in Romania could never truly be restored, given the persecution and oppression visited upon them by the Nazis and their Romanian collaborators. Although Emil Dorian remained in Romania and practiced medicine until his death in 1956, the diary was only published following its transmission to his daughter, who was living outside of communist-dominated Eastern Europe following her father's death. No index.

Flinker, Moshe. *Young Moshe's Diary.* Introductions by Shaul Esh and Geoffrey Wigoder. Jerusalem: Yad Vashem, 1971. No ISBN. 126 pages. Hardcover.

Moshe Flinker's diary tells the story of how he and his family attempted to survive by living under false Aryan identities in Belgium. Originally from Poland, Flinker and his family had relocated to the Netherlands before the beginning of World War II. The story depicts how a teenager living under the Nazi occupation experienced oppression, but also strongly expressed his faith in the survival of the Jewish people and articulated his belief in their redemption through a return of the Jewish people to their ancestral home in Palestine. Deported to Auschwitz with his parents in 1944, he was murdered in the Auschwitz camp. His five sisters and youngest brother survived, eventually emigrating to Israel after the war. The introductions by Shaul Esh and Geoffrey Wigoder discuss the significance of Flinker's diary as a testimony of Jewish youth during the Holocaust, and as an example of the continuity of Jewish faith in the most difficult of circumstances. No index.

Frank, Anne. *The Diary of a Young Girl: The Definitive Edition.* Edited by Otto H. Frank and Mirjam Pressler. Translated by Susan Massotty. New York: Doubleday, 1995. ISBN 0–385–47378–8. 340 pages. Hardcover.

From June 12, 1942 to August 1, 1944, a young Jewish girl, Anne Frank, wrote diary entries that survived World War II through the efforts of a friend named Miep Gies, who placed the diary in safekeeping following the Frank family's deportation to Westerbork, and ultimately to Auschwitz in 1944. A shortened version of the full diary was edited and published by Otto Frank, Anne's father, in the 1950s, becoming one of the most widely read works on the Holocaust since its initial appearance. This edition draws upon the entire set of original diary entries, providing up to thirty percent more text and providing a more comprehensive, multi-dimensional view of Anne Frank than was evident in the first published version. An introduction explains the development of the various editions of *The Diary*, while the afterword explains the fate of the Frank family and the other Jews hiding in the famous attic in Amsterdam. No index.

Friedman, Saul, editor. *The Terezin Diary of Gonda Redlich*. Foreword by Nora Levin. Lexington: University Press of Kentucky, 1992. ISBN 0–8131–0960–4. 173 pages. Paperback.

Providing a first-hand record of what transpired in the "model camp" of Terezin from January 1, 1942 through August 2, 1944, this book also includes a concurrent diary kept by the author for his son Dan, from March 16, 1944 through October 6, 1944, the day before their final deportation from Terezin to Auschwitz. The diary is a record of the author's experiences on camp committees and as director of the camp's Youth Welfare Department, as well as his role as a husband and father in a camp that served as a cruel hoax for Jews who expected it to be a temporary haven prior to permanent resettlement. The great value of this diary rests not only in its first-hand depictions of the desperate struggle for survival in Terezin, but in the excellent, comprehensive notes accompanying each entry by noted Holocaust scholar Saul Friedman. Friedman also provides a detailed bibliographic note following the diary to encourage further study in related sources. A detailed index and map of Terezin are also included.

Herzberg, Abel J. *Between Two Streams: A Diary from Bergen-Belsen*. Translated from the Dutch by Jack Santcross. New York: St. Martin's Press, 1997. ISBN 1–86064–121–0. 221 pages. Hardcover.

The author was deported from Westerbork camp in the Netherlands to Bergen-Belsen in 1944, and this diary is the record of his fifteen months in Bergen-Belsen. Following a brief biographical sketch of the author, who died in 1989, the diary commences and presents a very detailed portrait of the author's experiences from arrival in Bergen-Belsen to his liberation from a death train that had departed from Bergen-Belsen prior to the arrival of Allied troops in 1945. The book was originally published in 1950 in the independent weekly newspaper *De Groene Amsterdammer*. The author states that the critical theme in the diary is the contest between two streams—Nazism and Judaism—and how those two streams pervaded daily life in the Bergen-Belsen camp complex. No index.

Hilberg, Raul, Stanislaw Staron, and Josef Kermisz, editors. *The Warsaw Diary of Adam Czerniakow*. New York: Stein & Day, 1982. ISBN 0–8128–6110–8. 420 pages. Hardcover.

The diary of the leader of the Warsaw Jewish Council, Adam Czerniakow, consists of a collection of nine notebooks kept by Czerniakow from September 6, 1939 to July 23, 1942. One notebook, number five in the series dealing with the period December 14, 1940 to April 22, 1941, was never recovered. The notebooks record major events outside the ghetto, the author's impressions, experiences, and key directives. Clearly, the notebooks were intended to serve as a record for Czerniakow's future reference, and addenda were added to the notebooks to substantiate key points or amplify ideas he recorded. The documentary value of the diary rests in its daily chronicle of the impact of Nazi policies on the over 300,000 ghetto residents, and the responses of the ghetto administration and residents to those policies. Czerniakow carefully and concisely reports resistance efforts, as well as the vitality and commitment of ghetto residents in the face of tragedy. The extensive introductions by the editors place both the diary and its author in an historical context and provide a detailed understanding of the diary as a source on ghetto life. A documentary appendix of related sources is included, along with a listing of annotated sources. A very detailed index concludes this critical work on the Holocaust.

Hillesum, Etty. *An Interrupted Life and Letters from Westerbork*. With a foreword by Eva Hoffman. New York: Henry Holt & Company, 1996. ISBN 0–8050–5087–6. 376 pages. Paperback.

This edition of Etty Hillesum's work contains both her diary and letters written while she was in the Westerbork transit camp, from where she was deported to Auschwitz in 1943. This edition includes a foreword by writer Eva Hoffman, which discusses critical themes in Hillesum's diary and letters, notably the attainment of a deep personal knowledge in response to what she observed in occupied Holland. The introduction and notes on the contents by Jan G. Gaarlandt are very helpful in placing Hillesum's work within an historical context of the Holocaust's development, and in helping the reader identify the many individuals she references in her diary and letters. In contrast to *The Diary of Anne Frank*, Hillesum's diary and letters are the work of an older, more mature woman, thus providing an important additional dimension on the Holocaust in the Netherlands. No index.

Klemperer, Victor. *I Will Bear Witness: A Diary of the Nazi Years, 1933–1941*. New York: Random House, 1998. ISBN 0–679–45696–1. 519 pages. Hardcover.

———. *I Will Bear Witness: A Diary of the Nazi Years, 1942–45*. New York: Random House, 1999. ISBN 0–375–50240–8. 556 pages. Hardcover.

These two volumes provide one of the most comprehensive and detailed records of daily life in Nazi Germany available. The author, a Jew who was married to a Gentile and who had converted to Protestantism, remained in Germany for the entire length of the Third Reich, avoiding deportations as a Jew married to an

Aryan. The level of precision and thick description provided in the diaries is impressive, revealing Klemperer's considerable gifts as a writer and his ability to "bear witness" to the dehumanizing effects of Nazi policies and practices on fellow Jews as well as his own family. Few other accounts offer as compelling a portrait of the daily degradation that Jews encountered under Nazism. Detailed notes are provided in each volume, along with a chronology of Klemperer's life. Both volumes are fully indexed.

Korczak, Janusz. *Ghetto Diary*. Preface by Igor Newerly. Includes Aaron Zeitlin, *The Last Walk of Janusz Korczak*. New York: Holocaust Library, 1978. ISBN 0–89604–004–6. 192 pages. Hardcover.

This is the final literary work of educator and children's rights theorist Janusz Korczak, born Henrik Goldzmit. The diary relates how the Nazi occupation of Warsaw gradually destroyed the safe environment Korczak had created in his "children's republic," otherwise known as the Children's House, a ghetto orphanage run by Korczak and his staff. This version includes a prose poem by Israeli poet Aaron Zeitlin, which discusses *Ghetto Diary* within the overall context of Korczak's life and publications. Igor Newerly's preface discusses the conditions under which Korczak wrote the diary, knowing full well that he and his children at the orphanage were targeted for murder by the Nazis. Selected photographs of Korczak and his staff are included in this edition. No index.

Novac, Ana. *The Beautiful Days of My Youth: My Six Months in Auschwitz and Plaszow*. Translated from the French by George L. Newman. New York: Henry Holt & Co., 1997. ISBN 0–8050–5018–3. 314 pages. Hardcover.

Deported from Transylvania in 1944, Zimra Harsanyi (Ana Novac) kept a diary of her experiences as a young woman who endured both Auschwitz and Plaszow camps. One of the very few journals that survived the camp experience, the contents include numerous descriptions of other prisoners, of the SS guards and officers, and of the daily struggle for survival. Combining humor, philosophical reflection, and a determination to record the events and behaviors evident in the camp system, the author's journal stands as a document of resistance to the dehumanizing forces all around her. The preface by Holocaust scholar Myra Goldenberg and the introduction by the author set forth themes about the journal's contents and explain the author's origins, respectively. A brief glossary and set of explanatory notes concludes the book. Indexed.

Senesh, Hannah. *Her Life and Diary*. Introduction by Abba Eban. New York: Schocken, 1972. ISBN 0–8052–0410–5. 257 pages. Paperback.

This edition of the famous diary by Jewish patriot Hannah Senesh includes her diary, letters written by Hannah from October 1939 to March 1944, plus chapters about her life by Reuven Dafne and Yoel Palgi, both of whom parachuted with Hannah into Occupied Europe in 1944 to assist Jews in seeking refuge from the

Nazis following the occupation of Hungary by German forces. A reflection on Hannah's life by her mother Catherine is also included, along with a selection of Hannah Senesh's poems. No index.

Sloan, Jacob, editor and translator. *Notes from the Warsaw Ghetto: The Journal of Emmanuel Ringelblum.* New York: Schocken Books, 1989. Reprint of 1958 edition published by the McGraw-Hill Book Co., Inc. ISBN 0–805–20460–1. 369 pages. Paperback.

Buried in the Warsaw ghetto and discovered between 1946 and 1950, *The Journal of Emmanuel Ringelblum* presents a young historian's perspective on the destruction of Jewish life in the Warsaw ghetto as he witnessed it. Writing for posterity, Ringelblum's report, "The Oneg Shabbat" (Sabbath Celebrants) records the daily life of the Warsaw Ghetto with the trained eye of a practicing social historian, which was Ringelblum's profession by training. Working with a staff, Ringelblum and his associates created a ghetto archive to provide testimony and evidence of what actually transpired in the ghetto. This book contains Ringelblum's detailed notes, actually a working draft of what eventually could have been a history of the ghetto itself. In the truest sense, the *Notes* are a reflection of daily life in the ghetto, often fragmented and lacking continuity, but always revealing and illuminating about the daily struggles to forestall catastrophe. The editor includes a detailed introduction describing Ringelblum and the origins of the *Notes*, a street map of the Warsaw Ghetto, a map of Poland, a pronunciation guide, four sets of brief prefatory editorial comments before each section of the *Notes*, and a detailed chronology that juxtaposes events in Warsaw and those occurring outside of the city from August 1938 through December 1950, when the second cache of hidden Oneg Shabbat archives was discovered in Warsaw. Indexed.

Tory, Avraham. *The Kovno Ghetto Diary.* Edited with an introduction by Martin Gilbert. Textual and historical notes by Dina Porat. Translated by Jerzy Michalowicz. Cambridge: Harvard University Press, 1990. ISBN 0–674–85811–5. 554 pages. Paperback.

From June 22, 1941 through January 9, 1944, Avraham Tory recorded in considerable detail the life of Jews in Kovno, Lithuania. In August 1941, Jews in Kovno were forced to relocate to a ghetto in the suburb of Valijampole. Tory's diary relates the story of the ghetto in entries of varied length, sometimes substituting documents about particular events or topics where sections of the original diary were lost. The original diary, written in Yiddish, was recovered from its hiding place in the ghetto after Soviet troops had entered Kovno in August 1944. Tory, who had escaped just before the final liquidation and destruction of the Kovno ghetto in 1944, found three of the five crates of material he had originally hidden in the rubble of the burned-out ghetto. The comprehensiveness of this diary and its chronological scope provide readers with one of the most complete records of ghetto life during the Holocaust. Historian Martin Gilbert's excellent introduction places the diary within the overall efforts of Nazi Germany to exterminate European Jews, as well as emerging Jewish resistance activities. This edition contains maps of the region where Kovno was located, as well as detailed maps of the ghetto. The historical photos and drawings included were created by ghetto inhabitants before the final destruction of the ghetto. Thorough notes and a comprehensive index are included.

AUTOBIOGRAPHIES AND MEMOIRS

Appleman-Jurman, Alicia. *Alicia: My Story*. New York: Bantam Books, 1988. ISBN 0–553–28218–2. 433 pages. Paperback.

The author's autobiographical account describes her youth in Poland and her experiences in avoiding capture and deportation to the death camps. The work is particularly effective in illuminating the difficulties of survival for Jews in Occupied Eastern Europe when collaborators, in this case most often Ukrainians, were everywhere. The narrative continues through the end of World War II into the establishment of Israel, where the author served in the Israeli navy during the war of independence. The sections of the work on survival during the post–World War II period are particularly valuable, given the level of detail provided in the text and the author's insightful accounts of overcoming anti-Semitism, as well as vignettes about the kindness she encountered from many individuals who helped her survive. No index.

Cohen, Elie A. *The Abyss*. Translated by James Brockway. New York: W.W. Norton & Company, 1973. ISBN 0–393–07477–3. 111 pages. Hardcover.

This memoir by a Dutch medical doctor was written as an "admonitory monument," or a warning to others that what the author experienced (depravity, criminality, immorality) can occur again if human beings are willing to descend to the depths of human behavior. Deported from Westerbork to Auschwitz in 1943, the author's wife and four-year-old son were immediately sent to the gas chambers, while the author survived by working as a prisoner doctor in Auschwitz. Later deported to Mathausen, Melk, and Ebensee (from where he was liberated), Cohen returned to the Netherlands and eventually earned an advanced degree, publishing a detailed study of the medical and psychological dimensions of life in the Nazi camp system. Rather than providing a day-by-day account of his life in the camps, Cohen presents selected images of his life ("Life at Westerbork," "Transport to Auschwitz," "The Last Selection"), at times reflecting on broader issues about the Holocaust by making reference to controversies and events that occurred in the post-World War II period, such as the role of the Jewish Councils. No index.

Demetz, Hanna. *The House on Prague Street*. Translated from the German by the author. New York: St. Martin's Press, 1980. ISBN 0–312–39322–9. 186 pages. Hardcover.

This memoir was written by the daughter of a Jewish mother and a non-Jewish German father, and relates how the child of a mixed marriage survived the German occupation of Czechoslovakia. The memoir includes a vivid description of the family's life before the German occupation, followed by the story of how Jews were persecuted under Nazi rule. Following liberation, a new wave of oppression begins at the hands of the communists, while revelations of Auschwitz and other extermination camps emerge when survivors return to Prague and other Czech towns and cities. No index.

Finkelstein, Genya. *Genya*. Translated from the Hebrew by Shuli Sharvit. New York: GT Publishing, 1998. ISBN 1–57719–616–3. 142 pages. Hardcover.

This memoir relates the experiences of Genya Finkelstein, a Ukrainian Jew whose parents and three brothers were killed by the Nazis, leaving the author orphaned at age eleven. Relying upon her own resourcefulness, the author posed as a Gentile, suffering humiliation while working surreptitiously as a servant in the home of people connected to the men who killed her family. Her story continues following the war with her eventual emigration to Israel, her marriage, and eventual development of her own family. The book contains a collection of family photos depicting the author's family before World War II, as well as images of the author's friends and family during the pre-emigration period to Israel, and during her life in Israel. Maps of the author's travels during World War II and genealogical charts of her family are included. No index.

Frankl, Viktor. *Man's Search for Meaning*. Updated edition. New York: Washington Square Press, 1985. ISBN 0–671–66736–X. 221 pages. Paperback.

Written in nine days during 1945, Victor Frankl's account of how he found the "will to meaning" as a concentration camp inmate served as the basis for his development of the psychiatric approach labeled "logotherapy." Frankl's experiences in the camp constitute two-thirds of the book, with the remainder consisting of an introduction to logotherapy and a postscript written by the author for the 1985 edition. Frankl's account of his camp experiences stresses the individual's freedom to "choose one's attitude in a given set of circumstances." Consistent with core elements of existentialist philosophy, Frankl's interpretation of his survival rests on the individual's acceptance of the need to define a personal reason for living; having accepted this responsibility, individuals could then rise above their fate and find meaning in their suffering. The tone of the narrative is uplifting, based upon Frankl's core conviction that there is meaning in life itself no matter how grim and cruel the circumstances one may encounter. An extensive bibliography of English language sources on logotherapy is included. No index.

Frister, Roman. *The Cap: The Price of a Life*. Translated by Hillel Halkin. Originally published in Hebrew in 1993. New York: Grove Press, 1999. ISBN 0–8021–3762–8. 380 pages. Paperback.

This survivor memoir is brutally honest regarding the details of ghetto life in Plaszow-Cracow, how the author survived in the forest as an escapee from the ghetto, his camp experiences, and the patterns of anti-Semitism evident among many factions of Poles who resisted Nazism. At the same time, the author takes pains to discuss Poles who helped Jews during the Nazi occupation. The author's style is at times difficult to follow, since he intersperses discussion of World War II experiences with postwar activities and events. No index.

Fromer, Rebecca Camhi. *The House by the Sea: A Portrait of the Holocaust in Greece.* San Francisco: Mercury House, 1998. ISBN 1–56279–105–2. 162 pages. Paperback.

Based upon extensive interviews with Elia Aelion and including many photographs of the Aelion family, this book provides a vivid picture of the Holocaust in Greece, primarily rendered through Aelion's experiences. The book is introduced with a brief chapter explaining the historical role of Jews in Salonika, first under Ottoman control (until 1913) and then as part of the Greek state. Beginning with a chapter on Aelion's early life and family background, the narrative then describes the family's life and difficulties during Italian and German occupation, focusing on Salonika and Athens. The loss of ninety-six percent of Salonika's Jewish population is tragically conveyed through the lens of the family's experiences. The book contains tables of statistical data, some document reproductions, a glossary and selected bibliography, and brief chronologies about the history of Jews in Salonika and the Holocaust in Greece No index.

Gershon, Karen. *A Lesser Child.* London: Peter Owen, 1994. ISBN 0–7206–0899–6. 198 pages. Hardcover.

This autobiography presents the author's young life in Bielefeld, Germany from early childhood to emigration via the Kindertransport program to Great Britain in 1939. The author describes how life for Jews changed markedly when Nazism took control of the small German city of Bielefeld, notably owing to the imposition of racial laws and state-sponsored discrimination. The informal isolation of Jews by other residents of Bielefeld is clearly recounted, along with the development of strong Zionist sentiments among German Jews during the Third Reich. Particularly compelling is the author's description of the implications of Kristallnacht for the status of German Jews. Two family photos are included with the text. No index.

Geve, Thomas. *Guns and Barbed Wire: A Child Survives the Holocaust.* Chicago: Academy Chicago Publishers, 1987. ISBN 0–89753–261–X. 220 pages. Hardcover.

Born in 1929 in northern Germany, the author was imprisoned in 1943 and deported to Auschwitz. The memoir describes how the Holocaust influenced his early life, which included not only internment in Auschwitz, but periods spent in Gross-Rosen and Buchenwald as well. During his experiences, the author created seventy-nine miniature pictures of life in the camps and later wrote this memoir in

1958. Four appendices are included with the memoir text: the words to the resistance song "Peat-Bog Soldiers," two drawings of the Auschwitz camp complex, and one of the area where camps were located that the author endured. Eight pages of the author's camp pictures are included to augment the memoir text. No index.

Heimler, Eugene. *Night of the Mist*. London: Bodley Head Ltd., 1959. No ISBN. 192 pages. Hardcover.

This memoir by a Hungarian survivor of the Holocaust depicts the author's deportation to a ghetto, and eventually to Auschwitz along with hundreds of thousands of other Hungarian Jews in 1944. Transferred to a slave labor facility in Troeglitz where he worked for the I.G. Farben conglomerate, the author was later deported again to Buchenwald and finally placed on a death march toward Mauthausen. This memoir ends with the author's escape from the SS and his flight to Czechoslovakia as the war comes to an end. The author provides many details about the daily struggles of slave laborers in the camps, while confirming that survival in the camp system was unpredictable and difficult at best. No index.

Hoss, Rudolph. *Death Dealer: The Memoirs of the SS Kommandant at Auschwitz*. Edited by Steven Paskuly. New York: Da Capo Press, 1992. ISBN 0–306–80698–3. 390 pages. Paperback.

The memoir of the former commandant of Auschwitz is one of the key testimonies by perpetrators, revealing the essence of the middle-management-murderer mentality: blind obedience to duty, combined with commitment to an evil ideology. This edition contains a helpful introduction that places the memoir in context and notes Hoss's attempts at distortions and omissions of key facts that are substantiated by other sources. Additionally, the introduction debunks Holocaust denier claims that the Hoss memoirs are fraudulent. The thorough annotations help the reader make sense of the many terms, events, names, and other references made by Hoss in the text, and this edition includes three appendices: incident at Budy, a chronology of important events at Auschwitz-Birkenau, and the Wannsee Conference protocol. Indexed.

Kielar, Wieslaw. *Anus Mundi: 1,500 Days in Auschwitz/Birkenau*. Translated from the German by Susanne Flatauer. New York: Times Books, 1980. ISBN 0–8129–0921–6. 312 pages. Hardcover.

This detailed memoir describes in horrifying detail the treatment of Jews, Soviet prisoners of war, and political prisoners by the Nazis, and includes two line drawings of the Auschwitz-Birkenau camp for reference by the reader. A non-Jewish Pole, the author was first interned in Auschwitz-Birkenau and later was sent as a slave laborer to the Oranienburg camp in Germany and later to the Philps works in Germany's Weser Valley. He was liberated by U.S. troops. The memoir ends as the author and his fellow Polish prisoners are seeking to return to Poland, and news of Germany's surrender is announced. No index.

Klein, Gerda Weissman. *All But My Life*. Revised edition. New York: Hill & Wang, 1995. ISBN 0–8090–1580–3. 263 pages. Paperback.

This classic memoir was first published in 1957. The expanded edition of *All But My Life* includes an epilogue with reflections on Gerda Weissman Klein's life since the end of World War II and her liberation by U.S. military forces. The narrative of Gerda Weissman's three years as a prisoner following deportation from her home in Bielitz, Poland is a testament to her spiritual strength and the intervention of various individuals who unexpectedly acted to help her survive. The level of detail and her fluid, well-constructed prose style makes the narrative accessible to a wide range of readers, from middle school through adults. Two pages of family photos representing her pre-war and post-war families are included. No index.

Kofman, Sarah. *Rue Ordener, Rue Labat*. Lincoln: University of Nebraska Press, 1996. ISBN 0–8032–7780–6. 85 pages. Paperback.

This memoir reveals the life of Sarah Kofman, beginning in 1942 at the age of eight, when the arrest and deportation of her father occurred. Hiding with her mother in the home of a Christian woman on Rue Labat in Paris, the author describes how she and her mother survived until liberation, later learning that her father died in Auschwitz. The narrative continues by discussing the author's attachment to the woman who hid her and her mother, and her eventual estrangement from her birth mother. The author's entrance into her own scholarly career through matriculation at the Sorbonne in the mid-1950s brings the work to a close. No index.

Korn, Abram. *Abe's Story: A Holocaust Memoir*. Edited by Joseph Korn. Annotated by Richard Voyles. Atlanta: Longstreet Press, 1995. ISBN 1–56352–206–3. 197 pages. Hardcover.

Left as an unpublished manuscript in 1982, *Abe's Story* is the testimony of Abram Korn, as compiled by his son Joseph Korn. The narrative describes the young Abram's encounter with invading Nazis in his hometown of Lipno, Poland in 1939, and his subsequent deportation to a series of camps in Germany and Poland, including almost two years in Auschwitz. Transported to Buchenwald in March 1945, he was liberated by U.S. military forces in April 1945. Korn's story includes chapters on his readjustment following liberation, his marriage and emigration to the United States, and his development of a successful business career in the United States. The book's Epilogue and Afterword carry the story forward in Joseph's words to the date of publication, including reflections on his father's life and legacy as a survivor. A brief listing of books and videotapes is provided for further study. No index.

Kralovitz, Rolf. *TenZeroNinety in Buchenwald: A Jewish Prisoner Tells His Story*. Translated by Eva R. Cohn. Cologne: Walter Meckauer Kreis e. V., 1998. ISBN 3-923622-13-9. 78 pages. Paperback.

This brief memoir details the experiences of a Jewish teenager deported to Buchenwald in 1943. By virtue of his father's Hungarian origin, the Kralovitz children and his mother were granted citizenship papers by the Hungarian consulate. These papers led to their being deported to camps in Germany, although his father was eventually sent back to Hungary. The author's sister, mother, and father all perished. The memoir describes Kralovitz' experiences in Leipzig following the segregation of his family into "Jewish housing," their subsequent deportations, and his life in Buchenwald. The book contains selected photographs of documents regarding Kralovitz' life under Nazism, such as his ID card, letters sent to him by his mother and father, and photos of his family, some taken prior to World War II and others by German authorities. A brief name index is included.

Leitner, Isabella. *From Auschwitz to Freedom*. New York: Anchor Books, 1994. ISBN 0-385-47318-4. 233 pages. Paperback.

Combining two books, *Fragments of Isabella* and *Saving the Fragments*, into one volume, this edition of Isabella Leitner's memoir on the Holocaust integrates her family's deportation and death camp experiences with the story of how Isabella and her two sisters were liberated by Soviet troops and eventually emigrated to the United States as the first Auschwitz survivors to arrive in this country. Included in this edition is a brief introduction by the author (1993) and a series of photographs illustrating the author and her family prior to their 1944 deportation from Hungary, and their post–World War II readjustment to life in the United States. Leitner's descriptions of her experiences are compelling and written as a series of brief snapshots, or "fragments," in contrast to a flowing chronological narrative. Included in this edition is an epilogue written by Leitner's husband, Irving, relating the difficulties faced by the family in encountering Holocaust memories during a European trip in the 1970s. An afterword by the author Howard Fast and a brief discussion of camp (*lager*) language, as well as a brief lexicon of *lager* terms employed in the text are also included. No index.

Lengyel, Olga. *Five Chimneys*. New York: Howard Fertig, 1983. Originally published in 1947 by Ziff-Davis Publishing Company. ISBN 08652-7343-X. 213 pages. Hardcover.

This memoir was written by a Hungarian Jewish surgical assistant who was deported with her family and parents to Auschwitz in 1944. She was the sole survivor of Auschwitz among her family, and in the memoir discusses a wide range of topics, including love and sexual relations in the camp. She also provides detailed descriptions of perpetrators such as Josef Mengele, Irma Griese, Dr. S. Klein, and Josef Kramer. A glossary of terminology unique to discussions of the camp system is provided. No index.

Levi, Primo. *Survival in Auschwitz*. With a New Afterword—"Primo Levi and Philip Roth: A Conversation." New York: Simon & Schuster, 1996. ISBN 0–684–82680–1. 187 pages. Paperback.

A personal memoir of Levi's experiences as an Italian Jew deported to Auschwitz in 1944, this book stands out as one of the most profound and significant of all Holocaust memoirs. Originally written soon after the end of World War II, Levi's tone is philosophical and his writing avoids detailed descriptions of the cruelties and bestialities he witnessed first-hand in Auschwitz. Instead, Levi examines human interaction in the camp and during the liberation of Auschwitz by the Soviet military, providing insights into how humanity was challenged on a daily basis by the actions of Nazis and prisoners. Levi's character portraits of other prisoners illuminate universal themes of human dignity and compassion, the attempts by prisoners to maintain individual identity, and the ways in which the camp system functioned to degrade all of its participants. Without exception, each chapter in *Survival in Auschwitz* contains deeply moving passages of timeless significance, many of which are excerpted in other studies of the Holocaust because they illustrate the ongoing struggle of average people to retain their humanity in an inhuman setting. No index.

Leyens, Erich, and Lotte Andor. *Years of Estrangement*. Translated by Brigitte Goldstein. Evanston: Northwestern University Press, 1996. ISBN 0–8101–1166–7. 115 pages. Paperback.

This book contains two memoirs, one each by Erich Leyens and Lotte Andor. Both discuss the impact of the Holocaust on their lives in Germany, with greater attention to Nazi policies in the Leyens work. These memoirs are valuable for their revelations about the impact of Nazism on daily life in Germany during the period 1933–1938, the critical period when opposition to Nazism was crushed and the institutionalization of anti-Jewish persecution became a fact. Both authors emigrated to the United States before World War II began. The book contains an authoritative introduction by the German historian Wolfgang Benz, which places the memoirs in historical context. No photos or index.

Liebster, Simone Arnold. *Facing the Lion: Memoirs of a Young Girl in Nazi Europe*. Foreword by Sybil Milton. New Orleans: Grammaton Press, 2000. ISBN 0–9679366–5–9. 408 pages. Hardcover.

One of the very few published life stories of Jehovah's Witnesses who endured Nazi persecution, Simone Arnold Liebster's memoir illustrates how Jehovah's Witnesses were victimized by the Nazi state in occupied France. The account illuminates the extensive measures employed by Nazi Germany to isolate and, in Liebster's case, to reeducate Jehovah's Witnesses. Removed from her home because of her unwillingness to conform to Nazi educational practices and ideological indoctrination, such as joining the League of German Maidens, Liebster remained steadfast in her convictions, despite her tenure in a German reform school. The book contains appendices with relevant documents regarding Nazi persecution of the author's family and other Jehovah's Witnesses in Alsace, along with sample excerpts from Nazi school textbooks and related indoctrination materials to which youth were exposed during the occupation. No index.

Meed, Vladka. *On Both Sides of the Wall: Memoirs from the Warsaw Ghetto.* Introduction by Elie Wiesel. New York: Holocaust Library, 1993. ISBN 0–89604–013–5. 276 pages. Paperback.

This classic memoir relates the experiences of Feigele Peltel-Miedzyrzecki (Vladka Meed) during the days of the Warsaw Ghetto, the Ghetto Uprising, and her subsequent work as a courier of the Coordinating Committee of Jewish Organizations. Passing for an "Aryan" using forged documents, she survived many narrow escapes and aided many survivors in their efforts to find refuge beyond the Nazis' grasp. The level of detail and the flow of the narrative make the book accessible to both high school and adult readers. Complementing the text are over forty historical photographs concerning the Warsaw Ghetto, Meed's family, and Jewish partisan efforts. Indexed.

Michelsen, Frida. *I Survived Rumbuli.* Translated and revised by Wolf Goodman. New York: Holocaust Library, 1979. ISBN 0–89604–030–5. 232 pages. Paperback.

Originally written during the author's postwar years in the Soviet Union and later revised and expanded following Michelsen's emigration to Israel, *I Survived Rumbuli* is a detailed memoir of the Holocaust in Latvia through the eyes of one of the very few survivors of mass extermination in the Rumbuli Forest. The author begins her story on the day of the German invasion, June 22, 1941, and concludes it with her emigration to Israel in 1971. The efforts of selected Latvian families who provided refuge to Michelsen are a major element in the narrative, contrasting with the brutal efforts of the Nazis to annihilate the Latvian Jewish population. Selected photographs of the author and her family are included. No index.

Muller, Filip, with Helmut Freitag. *Eyewitness Auschwitz: Three Years in the Gas Chambers.* Edited and translated by Suzanne Flatauer. Chicago: Ivan R. Dee, 1999. ISBN 1–56663–271–4. 180 pages. Paperback.

This memoir by the only Auschwitz inmate to survive the entire period of the gassings in Auschwitz describes in precise detail the daily activities of mass extermination. Muller survived to relate his study through sheer luck, and he drew upon his experience as a *sonderkommando* to testify at the Frankfurt "Auschwitz" trial in 1964. Muller's detailed descriptions include the assistance he gave to Wetzler and Rosenberg-Vrba, two prisoners who escaped in 1944 and provided one of the first eyewitness accounts of Auschwitz to Western sources, as well as his account of the 1944 *sonderkommando* revolt. The appendix includes diagrams of Auschwitz and the book concludes with a glossary of terms about life in Auschwitz. No index.

Nir, Yehuda. *The Lost Childhood: A Memoir.* New York: Harcourt Brace Jovanovich, 1989. ISBN 0–15–158862–7. 256 pages. Hardcover.

Yehuda Nir's memoir tells the story of a young man who is one of only two survivors from the ZTSL grammar school in Lwow, Poland as a result of the Holocaust. The story begins in the summer of 1939, continuing through the family's deportation to the Lwow ghetto in 1942. Aided by his sister Lola's boyfriend, Ludwig Selig, the family escapes from the Lwow ghetto to Krakow. Hiding their identity and adopting Christian ways, they move to Warsaw and soon thereafter become laborers for a German businessman in Poland. Following their liberation by Soviet soldiers, and efforts by Soviet soldiers to rape Lola, the family returns to Poland to rebuild their lives. No index.

Nomberg-Przytyk, Sara. *Auschwitz: True Tales from a Grotesque Land.* Edited by Eli Pfefferkorn and David H. Hursch. Translated by Roslyn Hirsch. Chapel Hill: University of North Carolina Press, 1985. ISBN 0– 8078–4160–9. 185 pages. Paperback.

This collection of forty tales based upon true experiences illuminates life in Auschwitz between 1943 and early 1945, when the author was moved to Ravensbruck, soon to be liberated by advancing Soviet troops. Each brief tale presents a vignette of camp life, with considerable attention devoted to examining the moral and ethical dimensions of the characters' behavior. The book begins with a brief description of how the manuscript was found and translated and it concludes with an extended afterword that discusses the place of Nomberg-Przytyk's work in the larger body of Auschwitz and camp memoirs and literature. Notes and a glossary are included. No index.

Nyiszli, Dr. Miklos. *Auschwitz: A Doctor's Eyewitness Account.* Translated by Tibere Kremer and Richard Seaver. Foreword by Bruno Bettelheim. New York: Arcade Publishing Inc., 1993. ISBN 1–55970–202–8. 222 pages. Paperback.

This eyewitness account of Auschwitz, originally written in 1946, was authored by the Jewish medical doctor Miklos Nyiszli, who upon arrival at Auschwitz from Hungary was named Dr. Josef Mengele's personal research pathologist. His descriptions of daily activities in Auschwitz, most notably the work of the *sonderkommando*, are harrowing. The account is preceded by an extensive introductory essay by Bruno Bettelheim, who recognizes the importance of Nyiszli's account while lamenting the doctor's moral ambiguity in the face of Nazi policies of mass murder. Bettelheim also raises questions about the attitudes of European Jews during the Holocaust, criticizing their willingness to endure persecution and praising the minority who actively resisted Nazism, such as the *sonderkommando* who revolted and destroyed crematoria at Auschwitz in 1944. No index.

Opdyke, Irene Gut, with Jennifer Armstrong. *In My Hands: Memories of a Holocaust Rescuer.* New York: Anchor Books, 2001. ISBN 0–385–72032–7. 248 pages. Paperback.

Based upon interviews conducted by Jennifer Armstrong with Irene Gut Opdyke, this memoir tells the story of a young woman during the Nazi occupation of Poland, who worked as both a housekeeper and a waitress for German officers. Although she had already suffered physical and emotional abuse at the hands of Soviet soldiers during the Soviet occupation of Poland from September 1939 to June 1941, Irene Gut refused to turn her back on those in need. Smuggling food and providing encouragement to Jews in the ghetto, and later hiding a dozen Jews in the home where she worked as housekeeper for a German officer, Irene Gut risked her life on a daily basis to help those threatened with extermination. Following the end of World War II, she is aided by friends in relocating to a displaced-persons camp in Germany, and ultimately to the United States. Included in this story of bravery and compassion are pronunciation guides to German and Polish terms within the narrative, a brief section providing historical background to Gut Opdyke's story, and two maps that detail the boundaries of Poland during the occupation period (1939–1945) and in the pre- and post-war periods.

Perl, Gisella. *I Was a Doctor in Auschwitz.* Salem: Ayer Company Publishers Inc., 1992. Reprint of 1948 edition. ISBN 0–405–12300–0. 189 pages. Hardcover.

This is a detailed account of a Hungarian female doctor assigned after deportation to Auschwitz as Josef Mengele's staff gynecologist. She describes her life in Auschwitz from the entry to exit stages, noting the indignities and horrors of medical experimentation done by Mengele, as well as the processes used to dehumanize and eventually murder camp inmates. Great emphasis is placed on how the inmates were used to service the Nazi state before their destruction, whether in the role of providing blood plasma for wounded German soldiers, via confiscation of their belongings for transport back to Germany, or in innumerable other ways. The memoir closes with her departure from Auschwitz, her transfer to Bergen-Belsen, and her eventual liberation. No photos or index.

Rosenberg, Carl. *As God Is My Witness.* Washington: U.S. Holocaust Memorial Museum, 2000. Reprint of 1990 edition published by The Holocaust Library. ISBN 0–89604–143–3. 133 pages. Paperback.

This memoir of a Polish Jew who served in the Polish army details how Carl Rosenberg was captured by the Nazis, survived Auschwitz and two other camps, and later told his story to help others understand what he endured. Keeping his promise to his mother that he would serve as a witness to the tragedy of the Holocaust, Rosenberg's memoir includes content on Polish anti-Semitism that he endured before World War II, as well as ten pages of photos, primarily focused on what Allied troops encountered during liberation of the camps. A brief glossary is provided, but there is no index.

Rotem (Kazik), Simha. *Memoirs of a Warsaw Ghetto Fighter: The Past Within Me*. Translated from the Hebrew and edited by Barbara Harshav. New Haven: Yale University Press, 1994. ISBN 0–300–05797–0. 180 pages. Hardcover.

This memoir tells the story of the author's upbringing in Warsaw, followed by his segregation in the Warsaw Ghetto, his participation in the Zionist Youth Organization resistance group, and his role as a key courier during the Ghetto uprising of 1943. The memoir also discusses how the author hid on the Aryan side of Warsaw, his involvement in underground resistance activities, the results of the Polish Home Army uprising in 1944, and his eventual emigration to Israel in 1946. Readers will find much in this memoir that augments the contents of other Warsaw Ghetto participant memoirs, such as *On Both Sides of the Wall* by Vladka Meed. Maps, photos, and an appendix (a journal of the Ghetto uprising from 1943) are included. Indexed.

Schloss, Eva, with Evelyn Julia Kent. *Eva's Story*. New York: Berkley Books, 1990. ISBN 0–425–12272–7. 224 pages. Paperback.

This memoir relates the story of Eva Schloss, born Eva Geiringer in Vienna, Austria in 1929. Detailing the family's middle class life in Austria, the narrative tells how the family emigrated first to Brussels, then to Amsterdam in search of improved economic opportunities and to escape Nazi persecution of Jews. Following the German invasion of Holland, the family went into hiding until discovered and deported to death camps in Eastern Europe. Eva Schloss's story of survival has a direct connection to the family of Anne Frank, since her mother Fritzi married Otto Frank in 1953. The epilogue discusses the impact of the Holocaust on the author's family members and how the survivors readjusted following World War II. A postscript by the author's mother, Fritzi Frank, briefly discusses how she met and married Otto Frank and helped him prepare the first publication of Anne Frank's diary. No index.

Schumann, Willy. *Being Present: Growing Up in Hitler's Germany*. Kent: Kent State University Press, 1991. ISBN 0–87338–493–8. 212 pages. Paperback.

In vivid detail, the author describes his young years growing up in Hitler's Germany: participation in Hitler Youth activities, education and the influence of Nazi ideology, the efforts by the Nazi regime to maintain popular support for the war despite setbacks beginning in 1942, and the author's firm belief in Nazism. The author's rejection of Nazism following the German defeat in World War II emerges as the result of his ability to reflect on his actions, engage in scholarship, and examine the years of his youth from a broader perspective, particularly through his teaching of German language and literature at Smith College. Detailed notes accompany the text. Indexed.

Semprun, Jorge. *Literature or Life.* Translated by Linda Coverdale. New York: Penguin, 1997. ISBN 0–14–02.6624–0. 310 pages. Paperback.

This memoir by the Spanish resistance fighter Jorge Semprun integrates discussions of his experiences as a prisoner at Buchenwald from 1943 to liberation by U.S. troops in 1945 with his struggles to write about camp life during the fifty years following World War II. Semprun demonstrates convincingly that his daily life is in many ways continually influenced by his wartime experiences, and that his life in Buchenwald has remained a haunting obsession for him. This book is an effective complement to Semprun's memoir *The Long Voyage,* which relates the influence of his Holocaust experiences on Semprun's distinguished literary career. No index.

———. *The Long Voyage.* New York: Penguin, 1997. ISBN 0–14–118029–3. 236 pages. Paperback.

Jorge Semprun's memoir alternates between renderings of his inner thoughts and descriptions of behavior he witnessed and enacted in the camp, as well as how the camp experience influenced his later life. The author was a Spaniard captured by the Nazis when he was fighting for the French resistance in 1943, and was later deported to Buchenwald, which he endured and survived. Much in the spirit of Wiesel's *Night, The Long Voyage* alternates between genres (memoir and novel), while providing a vivid depiction of the terror and uncertainty encountered by prisoners during the deportation process and within the camp system. Not indexed.

Szpilman, Wladyslaw. *The Pianist.* Translated by Anthea Bell. New York: Picador, 2000. Polish edition published in 1999. ISBN 0–312–26376–7. 222 pages. Paperback.

Written in 1945, this memoir by a Polish Jew was not published until 1999. It tells the story of a Polish Jewish musician who survived in hiding after the destruction of the Warsaw ghetto, despite the loss of his entire family. The person who saved him and others in Poland, Wilm Hosenfeld, was a German Wehrmacht officer. This edition includes extracts from Hosenfeld's diary, a foreword by the author, and an epilogue by German writer Wolf Biermann. No index.

Ten Boom, Corrie, with John and Elizabeth Sherrill. *The Hiding Place.* New York: Bantam, 1974. ISBN 0–553–25669–6. 242 pages. Paperback.

Corrie Ten Boom's memoir relates how the author and her family worked to hide Jews in Haarlem, the Netherlands during the German occupation in World War II. Eventually discovered and interned by the occupation forces, Corrie and her sister Betsie were deported to Ravensbruck concentration camp, a camp for female prisoners. Despite the loss of her sister and other members of her family during the Holocaust, Corrie Ten Boom did not lose faith and she survived. Following the war, she participated in Christian missionary work and authored this memoir in collaboration with John and Elizabeth Sherrill. Included in this edition are sixteen pages of photographs accompanied by excerpts from the memoir that illustrate segments from the story, including life in the Netherlands during the occupation and the two sisters' experiences in Ravensbruck concentration camp. No index.

Velmans, Edith. *Edith's Story*. New York: Bantam, 2001. ISBN 0–553–38110–5. 239 pages. Paperback.

Edith Van Hessen was a young girl in the Netherlands when World War II began, and as a fourteen-year-old she kept a diary with details of a teenager's life. Hidden by a Christian family and forced to deny her Jewish identity, Edith endured the deportation of her family to the Westerbork transit camp, from which her mother and grandmother were deported to Sobibor and murdered in 1943. The text integrates Edith Velmans' memoirs with excerpts from her wartime diaries and selected letters received from her family when she was being hidden. Surviving the war, Edith Velmans eventually emigrated to the United States and became a psychologist. Tine Zur Kleinsmede, the wife in the Christian family who hid Edith from the Nazis, was recognized as a Righteous Gentile by Yad Vashem in 1983 on her ninetieth birthday, and Edith Velmans accompanied her to the ceremony in Jerusalem. No index.

Werner, Harold. *Fighting Back: A Memoir of Jewish Resistance in World War II*. Edited by Mark Werner. Foreword by Martin Gilbert. New York: Columbia University Press, 1992. ISBN 0–231–07883–8. 253 pages. Paperback.

Following the introduction by Martin Gilbert, which explains how the memoir originated, this extensive and detailed account of Jewish partisan activities also includes chapters on life in Poland for Jews prior to World War II and during the Soviet occupation prior to the invasion of the Soviet Union by Nazi Germany on June 22, 1941. Photos are included of the author and other partisans, along with photos of the author's family before and after World War II. A name glossary is included along with a detailed index.

Wiesel, Elie. *Night*. Preface for the twenty-fifth edition by Robert McAfee Brown. New York: Bantam Books, 1986. ISBN 0–553–27253–5. 109 pages. Paperback.

Wiesel's autobiographical account of his experiences in the Holocaust relates his deportation from Hungary in 1944 to Auschwitz, his subsequent transfer to Buchenwald, and his eventual liberation in April 1945. Written only after a long period of reflection about his experiences, the novel provides powerful glimpses of the protagonist's inner feelings, as well as detailed portraits of camp life. Throughout the text, there is a questioning of certainty and of religious faith, which has been a continuing motif in much of Wiesel's literary output. As an account of one teenage boy's encounter with evil, *Night* is a compelling and often terrifying journey that challenges readers to reexamine their beliefs about the essential nature of human beings and the power of the institutions they create for both good and evil. No index.

Zable, Arnold. *Jewels and Ashes.* New York: Harcourt Brace, 1994. ISBN 0–15–600147–0. 210 pages. Paperback.

This autobiographical work was written by the son of Jewish refugees from Poland who left Europe before World War II, settling in Melbourne, Australia. Returning to Europe to visit remnants of what was left behind, the author journeys to Krakow, Bialystok, Auschwitz, and Orla, blending a modern sense of loss with an effort to reconstruct the world of Eastern European Jewish life. The work is based upon memoirs of the author's parents, as well as historical research and personal observations as he retraces his parents' steps and, in the process, gains a deeper understanding of how Holocaust survivors and refugees from Nazism reconstructed their lives despite losing so much of a once thriving culture. No index.

RELATED WORKS

Schapiro, Raya Czerner, and Helga Czerner Weinberg. *One Family's Letters from Prague, 1939–1941.* Chicago: Academy Chicago Publishers, 1991. ISBN 0–89733–427–2. 218 pages. Paperback.

This series of seventy-seven letters represents the correspondence between Paula and Erwin Froelich, Jews from Prague, Czechoslovakia. The scope of the correspondence is from June 1939 to the deportation of Erwin and Paul in July 1942. The final letter in the collection is a 1946 letter from a family relative, Pranta Porger (cousin to the book's compilers), who relates the fate of Paula, Erwin and other family members who were unable to emigrate prior to the implementation of Nazi anti-Jewish policies in Czechoslovakia. The letters describe the degradation of Jewish life under Nazism and the frustration experienced by the U.S. resident family members in seeking assistance to bring Paul and Erwin to safety, particularly in their dealings with U.S. government agencies. The appendix provides facsimile reproductions of letters and Nazi deportation records about the fate of Paula and Erwin, with brief explanatory notes. A list of transports from Terezin to the East is also provided for reference purposes concerning the fate of Paula and Erwin. A thorough name index is provided.

Von Lang, Jochen, and Claus Sibyll, editors. *Eichmann Interrogated: Transcripts from the Archives of the Israeli Police.* New foreword by Michael Berenbaum. Translated by Ralph Manheim. New York: Da Capo Press, 1999. Reprint of original edition published in 1983 by Farrar, Straus & Giroux. 320 pages. ISBN 0–306–80916–8. Paperback.

During the year prior to his trial in Israel, Adolf Eichmann was interrogated by Captain Avner W. Less of the Israeli police. This book contains an edited condensation of the 275 hours of questions and answers, approximately ten percent of the over 3,500 transcript pages. The contents reveal Eichmann as the bureaucrat who claimed he was not an anti-Semite, that he was just "following orders." It also reveals a series of lies, distortions, evasions, and admissions of the truth, all directed to limiting his role at the center of Nazi policies of mass murder. The new foreword by Michael Berenbaum places the Eichmann trial as well as his SS career within an historical context and correctly notes that studies of perpetrator behavior are essential aspects of efforts to fully understand the Holocaust. No index.

Weiss, David W. *Reluctant Return: A Survivor's Journey to an Austrian Town.* Bloomington: Indiana University Press, 1999. ISBN 0–253–33584–1. 189 pages. Hardcover.

The author, an Austrian survivor living in Israel, tells the story of how he returned to his hometown of Weiner Neustadt to reexamine memories and forge a collaboration with Christians who desire a restoration of God's work in the town. To achieve this restoration, the Christians require the return of a Jewish presence, which was virtually obliterated in Weiner Neustadt during the period after the Anschluss in 1938, when Austria became part of the Third Reich. The author details his initial skepticism about the project, but then explains how he was convinced to participate in the effort to bring Jewish life back into this small Austrian town, albeit through the efforts of Christians who lament the tragic consequences of Nazism. No index.

BIOGRAPHIES

Overview

The biographies in this section offer readers the opportunity to explore how the Holocaust intersected and forever changed the lives of selected individuals. Major figures such as Adolf Hitler are included, given his central role in the rise of Nazism and the creation of the Holocaust, as well as Heinrich Himmler, who oversaw the planning and implementation of the genocide. Other figures, such as the Italian survivor and author Primo Levi and the teenager Anne Frank, represent victims whose literary contributions are essential to understanding the tragedy of this period for European Jews, while the German cleric Dietrich Bonhoeffer was a resolute opponent of Nazism and suffered the ultimate penalty for his resistance. Rescuers also are represented, such as the American Varian Fry and the Japanese diplomat Sempo Sugihara, two men whose valiant efforts went virtually unrecognized for decades. And then there is the Swedish diplomat Raoul Wallenberg, known worldwide for his desperate efforts to save Hungarian Jews from deportation in 1944 while the facts surrounding his death have, until very recently, been shrouded in mystery. The continuing struggle to bring perpetrators to justice has been the life's work of Simon Wiesenthal, while SS doctor Josef Mengele evaded capture and was never brought to justice. These books demonstrate how individuals transform history, and are transformed by it.

Anissimov, Myrian. *Primo Levi: Tragedy of an Optimist.* Translated by Steve Cox. Woodstock, NY: Overlook Press, 1999. ISBN 9–87951–806–5. 452 pages. Paperback.

This biography of Primo Levi is a comprehensive study of the famed author's life, integrating study of his many autobiographical and literary works throughout the text. Levi's early life as an Italian Jew, his education, and the discrimination he faced under the Mussolini regime's anti-Semitic laws set the context for his later partisan activites, arrest, deportation, and arrival in Auschwitz-Birkenau, where he worked in the Buna-Monowitz complex run by I.G. Farben. Levi's fame as an author, beginning with the publication of *If This Is a Man* (1947), later retitled *Survival in Auschwitz,* gradually developed while he continued his career as an industrial chemist upon return from the camps to Italy. Marrying in 1947, Levi worked as a chemist for thirty years, all the while continuing to write and remaining active in the ongoing struggle to attain a deeper understanding of the Holocaust's impact on modern life. This biography draws substantially upon Levi's correspondence, the recollections of friends and other survivors, and other unpublished sources, illustrating how Levi's poetry, memoirs, essays, and other writings reflected his constant concern that humans could create another Auschwitz and not learn from the tragedies he and millions of others had endured. A selection of photographs about Levi's life are included, along with two appendixes: Levi's preface to the book *The Jews of Turin,* and an unpublished contribution by Levi to the Italian newspaper *La Stampa* entitled "The Marital Web." The book contains a select bibliography of works about Primo Levi, a glossary of concentration camp terms, and chapter notes. Indexed.

Bierman, John. *Righteous Gentile: The Story of Raoul Wallenberg, Missing Hero of the Holocaust.* Revised edition. New York: Penguin, 1995. ISBN 0–14–024664–9. 221 pages. Paperback.

This study of Raoul Wallenberg's life was initially published in 1981, and the revised edition contains updated material on the continuing search for evidence about Wallenberg's fate while in Soviet captivity. The author concludes that Raoul Wallenberg's Soviet file was likely destroyed, thus obscuring the efforts of scholars and investigators to find the entire truth. Bierman's biography sets Wallenberg's life story within the context of the Holocaust, beginning with the planning for the Nazi invasion of Hungary in 1944 and Adolf Eichmann's goal of deporting all Hungarian Jews to death camps. Bierman argues that Wallenberg's efforts, and those of other Swedish diplomats, helped to frustrate Eichmann's zealous efforts to achieve the total annihilation of Hungarian Jews. The second half of the book is an attempt to reconstruct Wallenberg's life in captivity, following his capture by Soviet forces in 1945 and his relocation to Moscow's notorious Lubyanka prison that same year. Bierman examines the competing views about Wallenberg's fate, and concludes that despite the revelations brought forth from Soviet archives resulting from glasnost, a full understanding of Wallenberg's life story in Soviet captivity may never be known. A selected bibliography is provided, along with eight pages of family and Holocaust-era photographs about Wallenberg's life. Not indexed.

Breitman, Richard. *The Architect of Genocide: Himmler and the Final Solution.* Hanover: University Press of New England, 1991. ISBN 0–87451–596–3. 335 pages. Paperback.

This very significant biography of Heinrich Himmler, leader of the SS and the man responsible for overseeing the mass murder of European Jews, illuminates how Himmler rose to power within the Nazi regime, articulated and developed a world view dominated by a racist, anti-Semitic ideology, and eventually became the second most powerful man in the Third Reich, answering only to Adolf Hitler. Breitman describes Himmler's early life, his rise within the ranks of the Nazi party, his effectiveness in competing for power, his ideological fanaticism, and his role as the "ultimate bureaucrat" in devising and implementing mass murder on an unprecedented scale. Relying upon a wide range of sources, and drawing heavily upon major archival collections held in the United States and Europe, Breitman's biography demonstrates how an ordinary German rose to power, learned to be a brutal and uncompromising ideologue, and in the process organized the killing of millions of people. Additionally, it is clear from Breitman's work that Adolf Hitler's role as the mastermind behind the Holocaust is no longer in dispute. Extensive chapter notes are provided, along with a glossary of terms and a listing of archival collections utilized in the study. Indexed.

Bullock, Alan. *Hitler: A Study in Tyranny.* New York: HarperCollins, 1991. Abridged edition of 1971. ISBN 0–06–092020–3. 489 pages. Paperback.

As one of the first major scholarly biographies of Hitler, Alan Bullock's work has influenced many subsequent works on Hitler's life. Bullock presents Hitler's life as a chronological narrative, emphasizing Hitler's talents as a charismatic leader: his willingness to grasp opportunities, take political risks, present a simple but powerful message to the public; his determination to achieve his goals; and his ability to exploit the weaknesses of his opponents. At the same time, Bullock illuminates Hitler's flaws: his narcissism and belief that Germany's destiny and his own were inextricably related; his cruelty and indifference to suffering; his egotism and lack of intellectual interests; and his commitment to an ideology of racist domination that had no uplifting or socially redeeming qualities. Throughout the work, Bullock argues that Nazism could not have prevailed in the manner it did without Hitler's leadership, but that Hitler's career also reflected powerful German political and cultural traditions that favored authoritarianism, militarism, and state power that crushed individual liberties. The Holocaust does not receive substantial attention in Bullock's biography, although he makes it clear that the mass murder of European Jews was the outgrowth of Hitler's racial vision, and he cannot escape responsibility for the results of that policy. This abridged version does not contain notes or an index. Readers desiring those components are advised to consult the unabridged edition.

Kaniuk, Yoram. *Commander of the Exodus*. Translated by Seymour Simckes. New York: Grove Press, 1999. ISBN 0–8021–1664–7. 214 pages. Hardcover.

This biography relates the story of Yossi Harel, commander of the ship *President Warfield* (also known as *Exodus*), which brought Jews to Palestine following the end of World War II. Despite British opposition to the entrance of Jewish refugees into Palestine, Harel commanded the *Exodus* and other ships and confronted the might of the British navy in an effort to help Jews leave Europe and start a new life in Eretz Israel. The biography relates how Harel and his companions overcame both diplomatic and logistical difficulties, and eventually helped bring thousands of Jewish refugees, many of them concentration and death camp survivors, to Palestine in search of a new life. The author has drawn heavily from interviews with Yossi Harel, along with published sources in Hebrew and English. A brief glossary of terms and a select bibliography are provided. Not indexed.

Kershaw, Ian. *Hitler 1889–1936: Hubris*. New York: W.W. Norton, 1999. ISBN 0–393–04671–0. 700 pages. Hardcover.

———. *Hitler 1936–1945: Nemesis*. New York: W.W. Norton, 2000. ISBN 0–393–04994–9. 1115 pages. Hardcover.

These two volumes by Ian Kershaw offer a detailed view of Hitler's life, drawing heavily upon previously unpublished sources, such as the diary of Joseph Goebbels, recently located in former Soviet archives in Moscow. Kershaw, a distinguished scholar of modern German history, emphasizes the personal leadership style of Hitler and how the functioning of the Nazi state in many ways depended upon his personal idiosyncracies. Hitler's pattern of leadership reflected his lack of interest in details, a distaste for organization, and a firm belief that Germany's destiny was directly linked to Hitler's own life journey. Kershaw shows convincingly that Hitler's obsessive racial anti-Semitism was the foundation for genocide, and that the violence and cruelty unleashed on European populations in Eastern Europe was integral not only to Hitler's vision of a revamped European population but to the German war strategy itself. Simultaneously, Kershaw demonstrates that the German population, not just Nazi party members, provided widespread and continuing support for Hitler and the Nazi state from 1933 to the defeat of Germany in 1945. Ultimately, Kershaw views Hitler as the architect of a tragic "collapse of civilization," a man whose actions and beliefs received the widespread support of one of Europe's most advanced societies and who engendered a führer cult that removed limits on power that made the excesses of Nazism possible. In both volumes sections of photographs are provided that illuminate themes in the text, along with very extensive chapter notes and selected bibliographies. These two volumes are essential reading for students of both modern German and European history and the Holocaust. Indexed.

Levine, Hillel. *In Search of Sugihara*. New York: Free Press, 1996. ISBN 0–684–83251–8. 232 pages. Hardcover.

This biography presents the life of Chiune Sugihara, the Japanese diplomat whose visas helped to save the lives of over 2,000 Jews while he was based in Kovno, Lithuania, and smaller numbers of Jews when he was based in Prague and Konigsberg. Hillel Levine explores the education and rise in the Japanese diplomatic service of Sugihara, whose formative experiences were in the Far East, primarily Manchuria. Sent to Lithuania to spy on the Germans and Soviets during the period of planning for the Japanese attack on Pearl Harbor, Sugihara made the decision to grant visas to Jews seeking refuge from the German occupation of Poland and the Soviet occupation of Lithuania. The author not only reconstructs the events of the critical period when Sugihara issued the "visas that saved lives," but relates how Sugihara was asked to resign from the Japanese foreign service following World War II and how he rebuilt his life during the post-war period. Recognized in the 1980s as a Righteous Gentile by Yad Vashem, Sugihara accepted the thanks of those he had helped survive, but never sought the limelight before his death in 1986. The author includes brief vignettes about individuals who received visas from Sugihara, and how they survived the Holocaust following their departure from Lithuania, ending up in Japan, Shanghai, or other destinations. Extensive chapter notes and a detailed bibliography are provided. Indexed.

Lifton, Betty Jean. *The King of Children: A Biography of Janusz Korczak*. New York: Random House, 1989. ISBN 0–8052–0930–1. 404 pages. Paperback.

This comprehensive biography of Janusz Korczak examines the life of one of the twentieth century's major theorists and authors on the rights of children. Korczak, born Henryk Goldsmit, developed his ideas about the rights of children through his work as a medical doctor and later as an orphanage director in Warsaw. Korczak emphasized the dignity and respect that children warranted from adults, and he instituted practices in his Warsaw orphanages reflecting this perspective. In Korczak's two Warsaw orphanages, he instituted reforms that provided children with institutions of self-government (i.e., a court system) and a weekly forum for their writing in a supplement to the Jewish daily *Nasz Przeglad*. Despite the entreaties of friends in the Warsaw community, Korczak refused to leave the orphanages during the Nazi occupation, and he labored unceasingly to provide them with support during the privations of the Warsaw Ghetto. When the deportation order was issued in 1942 for the children in the orphanage, Korczak and his devoted colleague Stefania Wilczynska refused to abandon them and marched with the children to the train, which took them to Treblinka and their death. This biography draws upon a broad range of written sources, as well as interviews with surviving alumni of Korczak's Children's Home in Warsaw. Extensive chapter notes and a selected bibliography are provided, in addition to photographs of Korczak and his key associates. Indexed.

Marino, Andy. *A Quiet American: The Secret War of Varian Fry.* New York: St. Martin's Griffin, 2000. ISBN 0–312–26767–3. 403 pages. Paperback.

This biography of Varian Fry, the only U.S. citizen recognized as a Righteous Gentile at Yad Vashem, offers a comprehensive portrait of the complex man whose actions helped save the lives of over 1,500 European intellectuals trapped in Vichy France. Author Andy Marino describes Fry's upbringing in New Jersey, his elite education at Harvard, and his subsequent activities as a journalist in New York, where he received the opportunity to cover political events in Nazi Germany. One of the first U.S. journalists to thoroughly report the serious threats to Jewish life in Nazi Germany, Fry later returned to Europe as the representative of the Emergency Rescue Committee, and in this role he provided financial and other forms of support for European intellectuals targeted by the Nazis. Marino's book details how Fry and his small circle of assistants helped political prisoners, Jews, and others targeted for arrest by the Nazis and their Vichy allies escape to neutral countries, and eventually make their way to safety in the United States. The experiences of the refugees helped by Fry, among whom were Marc Chagall, Leon Feuchtwanger, Max Ernst, Hannah Arendt, and others, are integrated within the narrative, as are insights from people who worked with Fry while he was in Marseilles. Chapter notes and a selected bibliography are provided, along with sixteen pages of photographs about Fry's family and activities. Indexed.

Muller, Melissa. *Anne Frank [The Biography].* Translated by Rita and Robert Kimber. New York: Henry Holt & Co., 1998. ISBN 0–8050–5996–2. 330 pages. Hardcover.

Melissa Muller's biography of Anne Frank begins with the arrest of the Frank family and others hiding in the secret annex at 263 Prinsengracht, Amsterdam and the salvaging of the diary pages by Miep Gies. From that point, the life story of Anne Frank is related, informed by extensive interviews with survivors, use of correspondence, and other documentary records of the Frank family. Melissa Muller does not seek to replicate the world-famous diary of Anne Frank, but rather attempts to paint a richer, more nuanced picture of the life of this teenager who died in the Bergen-Belsen camp in 1945. The epilogue discusses other key individuals mentioned in the biography, offering brief descriptions of each person's fate during the Holocaust and how they are connected to Anne Frank's life story. Additionally, an extensive account of how the famed diary was created and later published by Anne's father Otto Frank is provided. A poignant note by Miep Gies, the key supporter for the Frank family while they were in hiding, is included along with chapter notes and eight pages of photographs about Anne Frank's brief life. Indexed.

Pick, Hella. *Simon Wiesenthal: A Life in Search of Justice.* Boston: Northeastern University Press, 1996. ISBN 1–55553–273–X. 349 pages. Hardcover.

Hella Pick's biography of Simon Wiesenthal presents a balanced portrayal of one of the world's most well-known advocates of bringing Nazi participants in the Holocaust to justice. The author describes Wiesenthal's early life, his successful career as an architect before World War II, his experiences in thirteen concentration and labor camps, and his efforts since the end of World War II to locate and bring war criminals to justice. The actions taken by Wiesenthal to track down individuals such as Adolf Eichmann and Franz Stangl are included, along with Wiesenthal's controversial investigative methods and his conflicts with Austrian politicians such as Bruno Kreisky and Kurt Waldheim. Providing ample space for the critics of Wiesenthal, the author emerges as an advocate of Wiesenthal, believing that his integrity and strong sense of justice outweigh criticisms of his methods and penchant for notoriety. Wiesenthal's sense of mission, his dedication to justice, and his charismatic personality are three key characteristics that pervade the narrative, and on balance suggest that his categorization as a heroic figure has a firm basis in truth. Sixteen pages of photographs, chapter notes, and a selected bibliography and source note are included. Indexed.

Posner, Gerald L., and John Ware. *Mengele: The Complete Story.* New York: McGraw-Hill, 1986. ISBN 0–07–050598–5. 364 pages. Hardcover.

This life of Josef Mengele is primarily focused on the efforts to locate and bring Mengele to justice following the defeat of Nazi Germany. Mengele emerges as an avid Nazi with career ambitions that are served by his involvement in the SS and his family's support of Nazism. His direct involvement in selections at Auschwitz and in the use of cruel, sadistic experiments on humans at Auschwitz is described, along with his family's efforts to hide his whereabouts in the immediate post-war period when they feared he would be prosecuted for war crimes by the U.S. occupation authorities in Germany. The remainder of the book describes how Mengele escaped to Latin America, residing first in Argentina, then in Paraguay and later in Brazil, and at times returning to Europe surreptitiously for meetings with family. The efforts to locate Mengele, the activities of his friends to hide him, and his eventual death by drowning in Brazil are related in vivid detail. Chapter notes, a selected bibliography, and fourteen pages of photographs about Mengele's life, including photos from his service in the SS, are included. Indexed.

Robertson, Edwin. *The Shame and the Sacrifice: The Life and Martyrdom of Dietrich Bonhoeffer.* New York: Macmillan, 1988. ISBN 0–02–603650–9. 288 pages. Hardcover.

Edwin Robertson's biography of Dietrich Bonhoeffer presents the life of this courageous Protestant theologian, who refused to be seduced by Nazism and opposed its racist, anti-Semitic messages as a leading cleric in the Confessing

Church of Germany. Beginning with a brief contribution by Renate Bethge, the younger sister of Bonhoeffer's lifelong friend Eberhard Bethge, the biography explores Bonhoeffer's early life, his education in Germany and the United States, the development of his theological perspective and its connections to the ecumenical movement within Protestant thought, the emergence of his opposition to Nazism, his involvement in the high-level conspiracy with selected military officers to overthrow the Hitler regime, and his eventual arrest, imprisonment, and execution in April 1945, less than two months before the end of World War II in Europe. Bonhoeffer's letters are used extensively in the text to highlight the development of his theology, along with his involvement in the resistance movement against Nazism. While chapter notes are provided, there is no select bibliography. Indexed.

Toland, John. *Hitler.* Ware, UK: Wordsworth Editions, 1997. Reprint of 1976 edition. ISBN 1–85326–676–0. 1,035 pages. Paperback.

John Toland's biography of Adolf Hitler builds upon earlier studies, such as the biography by Alan Bullock, but draws heavily upon over 200 interviews conducted by the author with Hitler's close associates, as well as previously unpublished sources. Toland views Hitler as a man of profound contradictions, but with at least one consistent obsession, his hatred of the Jews, which became a defining characteristic of Hitler's worldview following the defeat of Germany in World War I. In contrast to Bullock's study, Toland provides much more detail on the central role of Hitler in the development of the "final solution of the Jewish question," documenting his claims with reference to Goebbels' diaries and other sources from individuals close to Hitler. Additionally, Toland returns to the annihilation of the Jews and the genocidal plans for other targeted victim groups (Soviet POWS, for example) throughout his biography, demonstrating its central role in Hitler's utopian racist vision for Europe. The work contains a glossary, maps, extensive chapter notes, sixty-four pages of photographs about Hitler's life, and a very detailed index.

Waite, Robert L.G. *The Psychopathic God: Adolf Hitler.* New York: Da Capo Press, 1992. Reprint of original edition published by Basic Books in 1977. ISBN 0–306–80514–6. 482 pages. Paperback.

Robert L.G. Waite's biographical study of Adolf Hitler integrates psychological methods with historical inquiry to develop a psychopathological portrait of Hitler. Waite emphasizes study of Hitler's personality while not ignoring the broader historical context within which he lived. At the same time, Waite argues that Hitler cannot be understood without a comprehensive analysis of his personal life, in this case viewed through the lens of formal psychology. Viewing Hitler as a mentally deranged human being but also a very talented and skillful politician, Waite believes that the complexity of Hitler's actions and beliefs cannot be understood without recognizing the coexistence of both rational and irrational elements. Throughout the book, the author draws heavily upon Freudian psychology in an effort to demonstrate how Hitler's political career was rooted in the pathologies that were formed during his early life, particularly his years in Vienna. As an example, Waite sees Hitler's ideology as having deep roots in traumas and fantasies from Hitler's early life, and which heavily influenced his sense of personal destiny, as well as his conviction that Germany's destiny was directly linked to his life's work. As a complementary work to other biographies of Hitler, such as those by Bullock, Kershaw, and Toland, Waite's book illuminates the complexity of Hitler's beliefs and behavior in ways that traditional historical studies do not. A note on sources, as well as extensive chapter notes, is provided. Indexed.

Wood, E. Thomas, and Stanislaw M. Jankowski. *Karski: How One Man Tried to Stop the Holocaust*. Foreword by Elie Wiesel. New York: John Wiley & Sons, 1994. ISBN 0–471–01856–2. 316 pages. Paperback.

This biography of Jan Karski places the greatest emphasis on his wartime activities, when he served as a courier for the Polish underground and was an eyewitness to the atrocities of the Holocaust. During World War II, Karski reported the horrors of the mass murder of the Jews in considerable detail to high officials in Great Britain and the United States, but little action was taken in light of his reports. The authors also explain how Karski gained fame through writing and speaking activities, but after World War II earned his doctorate and taught for decades at Georgetown University, while not speaking about his wartime experiences. In the 1970s, he was interviewed for Claude Lanzmann's epic film *Shoah*, and he finally broke his silence about his Holocaust experiences. The epilogue details how he never swayed from opposing anti-Semitism, and how he finally was able to discuss his wartime experiences and overcome the repressed anger he had contained for decades about the inaction of the Allies to save the Jews. The work includes a glossary of names mentioned in the text, along with extensive chapter notes and sources for each chapter. Indexed.

PART III

GENERAL ELECTRONIC
RESOURCES

9

INTERNET-BASED RESOURCES

OVERVIEW

The rapid expansion of Internet access throughout much of the world has opened up new vistas for the presentation and delivery of content and resources about the Holocaust and its legacy. Listserves and newsgroups provide opportunities for users to communicate with colleagues and other interested individuals about issues of common concern in the study of the Holocaust, irrespective of geographic location. Only a computer with Internet access and a successful subscription to the listserve or newsgroup are required. The databases and World Wide Web sites make information readily available in electronic form that in earlier decades was available only in print, graphic, photographic, audio, or motion video formats. Now, World Wide Web sites can deliver multimedia capability to users on a global scale, facilitating the creation and exchange of information in a manner that is both dynamic and limitless in its scope. The Internet-based resources included in this chapter have been selected based upon the following criteria: (1) their primary mode of information delivery is through the Internet, (2) their contents meet accepted scholarly standards for documentation, or in the case of online messaging and discussion forums (listserves), they are moderated by individuals with expertise in the field, (3) their contents inform users regarding one or more aspects of Holocaust study, and (4) they provide contact information concerning the development, maintenance, and/or revision of their content. A systematic effort has been made to limit repetition with sites listed in other chapters of this book. The Internet resources listed in this chapter, if also listed elsewhere in this work, are described because they possess unique aspects that were not highlighted in other chapter listings. Unless otherwise noted, all Internet resources are presented in English.

DATABASES

Holocaust Education, Remembrance, and Research. http://ntdata.ushmm. org/ad/.

Located within the very extensive Web site of the U.S. Holocaust Memorial Museum, this online database provides information on over 1,000 organizations around the world concerned with Holocaust education, remembrance, and research. The listing was compiled by the Task Force for International Cooperation on Holocaust Education, Remembrance, and Research. The database can be searched by organization name, country, and/or city.

MODERATED LISTSERVES AND NEWSGROUPS

H-NET List for History of the Holocaust. http://www.h-net.msu.edu/ ~holoweb/.

This moderated electronic discussion list provides an opportunity for scholars, educators, and interested participants to communicate regarding the study of the Holocaust and related topics, such as anti-Semitism and Jewish history of the 1930s and 1940s, as well as the history of World War II, the history of Germany, and international affairs. The focus of the discussions is on academic topics. Book reviews, course syllabi, professional papers, and links are available on the H-Holocaust homepage. The H-Holocaust discussion list also is searchable, and a list of discussion logs is provided for easy reference. Subscription information is located on the Web site.

H-NET List for Study of Antisemitism. http://www.h-net.msu.edu/~antis/.

This electronic discussion list encourages communication among scholars regarding the broadly defined history of anti-Semitism. H-Antisemitism provides bibliographic, research, and teaching aids to its subscribers, along with a set of links to related Web sites, access to documents, occasional papers, and reviews of books. The H-Antisemitism discussion list is searchable, and a list of discussion logs is provided for easy reference. Subscription information is located on the Web site.

Holocaust ListServer. http://fido.seva.net:8090/mailman/listinfo/holocaust.

This moderated listserve is open to all Holocaust educators and students, with its purpose being to give Holocaust educators opportunities to share ideas, queries, and issues about their programs and activities. The list is an adjunct to the Holocaust Teacher Resource center Web site located at http://www.Holocaust-trc.org.

Soc.culture.jewish.holocaust.

This moderated newsgroup offers subscribers the opportunity to discuss issues of Holocaust history, anti-Semitism, religious and philosophical responses to the Holocaust, and other topics. Survivors and liberators of concentration and death camps also participate, and book reviews are discussed as well. To subscribe, contact the list moderator at shoahmod@verdad.org. This moderated Usenet newsgroup can also be reached via www.Holocaust-history.org.

WORLD WIDE WEB SITES

American Memory: The Hannah Arendt Papers at the Library of Congress. http://memory.loc.gov/ammem/arendthtml.

This Web site contains a selection of the over 75,000 digital images in the Hannah Arendt papers, which are located in the Manuscript Division of the Library of Congress. Among the sections of the Hannah Arendt papers currently available on this Web site is a special presentation on "The World of Hannah Arendt," a chronology of her life and works, and an index of all folders in the Arendt Papers, which includes extensive listings of materials on her controversial book *Eichmann in Jerusalem*. User information for the final version of the complete digitized collection of the Hannah Arendt papers is included on this Web site.

Austria: National Fund for Holocaust Victims. http://www. nationalfonds. org.

This Austrian government Web site contains information about reparations and efforts at restitution for victims of the Nazi regime.

The Avalon Project: The Nuremberg War Crimes Trials. http:// www.yale.edu/lawweb/avalon/imt/imt.htm/.

This Web site, located at the Yale Law School, contains full text access to the Nuremberg trial proceedings and transcripts first published by the International Military Tribunal. Many Holocaust-related documents related to the Nuremberg trials also are available on the Web site in full-text format.

Beyond the Pale: The History of Jews in Russia http://www.friends-partners.org/partners/beyond-the-pale/index.html.

This Web site presents in electronic form the contents of an exhibit developed by historians Joke Kniesmeyer and Daniel Cil Brecher, which has toured Russia since 1995, and which was the first major exhibit to present the history of anti-Semitism in Russia. Text, graphics, and both historical and artifact-based photographs are employed. Among the topics included in the exhibit are "Jewish Life in the Middle Ages," "The Development of Modern Anti-Semitism," "Jews in the Russian Empire," "Jews in the Soviet Union," "Nazism and the Holocaust," "Jews in the Soviet Union: 1941-Present," and "Epilogue: Democracy and Human Rights."

The exhibit can be viewed in either Russian or English versions, and an extensive set of credits is provided.

Calvin College. German Propaganda Archive. http://www.calvin.edu/academic/cas/gpa.

Created by Randall Bytwerk, this extensive archive of propaganda created during the Third Reich and in the former German Democratic Republic (East Germany) is a well-organized and comprehensive collection of German propaganda materials in English translation. The site is easy to navigate, and has a very useful set of FAQs (Frequently Asked Questions) that helps the user understand the origins, development, and structure of the site. Actual propaganda documents designed to influence citizens are included, along with documents created for the propaganda designers, which illustrate their strategies at mass persuasion.

Central Archives for Research on the History of the Jews in Germany. http://www.uniheidelberg.de/institute/sonst/aj.

This Web site provides an introduction to one of the most important collections of documentation on Jewish life in Germany. Institutional records, personal papers, documentation of cemeteries, newsletters, and other archival resources are described on this Web site, along with contact information for individuals doing research on the history of the Jews in Germany. The site can be viewed in either German or English.

Claims Conference. http://www.claimscon.org/.

This Web site represents the Conference on Jewish Material Claims against Germany, which includes the Guide to Compensation and Restitution for Holocaust Survivors. Information on the Conference's programs and resources is provided, along with information on the Committee for Jewish Claims in Austria.

Commission for Art Recovery. http://www.wjc-artrecovery.org/.

This project of the World Jewish Congress is affiliated with the World Jewish Restitution Organization, which seeks out works of art stolen by the Nazis. Information on how to file a claim, reports on the current status of the organization's work, and a detailed set of links are provided.

Cybrary of the Holocaust. http://remember.org/.

Organized into two major sections, research and forums, the Cybrary of the Holocaust contains a diverse set of resources and online communication forums about Holocaust content. The Web site contains many photos, first-hand accounts drawn from books and testimonies, a teacher's guide for classroom use, time lines and lesson plans, along with a series of discussion boards, an online Holocaust Quilt for development of remembrance pages, and on online art gallery with student poems and paintings. The Web site contains a search engine, an online bookstore, and a set of links to Holocaust-related Web sites.

Czech Republic: The Holocaust Phenomenon. http://www.hrad.cz/kpr/holocaust/index-uk.html/.

This Web site contains information on the items held by various archives in the Czech Republic, as well as a list of individuals whose property was confiscated by the Nazis. A summary of the Holocaust Phenomen Conference, held in Terezin and Prague in 1999, is provided along with substantive articles on the history of the Holocaust in the Czech Republic and the oppression of Czech Gypsies under Nazi rule.

Forced Labor Camps: Hagen Region. http://www.hco.hagen.de/zwangsarbeit/index2.html.

This Web site of the Historical Center of Hagen tells the story of forced and slave labor projects in the Hagen region. The Web site includes photos, archival sources, and contact information, as well as a list of businesses that utilized forced labor.

Forced Labor Camps: Koln City. http://www.museenkoeln.de/museenkoeln.de/ns-dok/.

This Web site includes resources on the camps and businesses that used forced or slave labor during World War II. Users can search the site for camps and businesses involved in forced/slave labor activities. The site is available only in German.

The Forgotten Camps. http://www.jewishgen.org/ForgottenCamps/.

Hosted by JewishGen, this is a comprehensive listing of camps, organized by type. The Web site is searchable and an important feature is the focus on the less well-known subcamps. A glossary of camp terms and a listing of companies that employed camp inmates for slave labor are provided.

Freedom, Democracy, Peace; Power, Democide, and War. http://www.hawaii.edu/powerkills.

This Web site presents the research and scholarship of R.J. Rummel, professor emeritus of political science at the University of Hawaii. The extensive contents present data, statistics, selections from books and articles regarding major pre-twentieth-century episodes of democide (genocide and mass murder), and all twentieth-century cases of democide from 1900 through 1987. An extensive series of links is provided, and a search engine is available to locate specific site content.

The Ghetto Fighters House: Holocaust and Jewish Resistance Heritage Museum. http://www.gfh.org.il/.

Containing over 20,000 images (photos and artwork), the Ghetto Fighters House (Lochamei Hagetaot) Web site includes information on its programs (conferences, seminars, online sharing projects) as well as online exhibitions.

Holocaust Educational Foundation. http://www2.dsu.nodak.edu/users/dmeier/hef.hef.html.

This Web site contains information on the development of Holocaust studies programs at the collegiate level. Program descriptions, financial support for scholarship, and a listing of related Holocaust Web sites are provided.

Holocaust History Project. http://www.holocaust-history.org/.

This Web site seeks to refute Holocaust denial and revisionism through the presentation of documents, photos, audio files, essays, and links to related Web sites.

Holocaust Literature Research Project. http://www.arts.uwo.ca/HLRI.

This Web site serves as a resource center for professors and students at the University of Western Ontario regarding Holocaust studies, and in the future will provide an online annotated bibliography of more than 2,000 survivor narratives currently housed at the University.

The Holocaust Remembrance Project. http://www.hklaw.com/holocaust/.

This Web site contains information about the educational activities of the Holland and Knight Charitable Foundation, Inc., whose annual writing contest for high school students addresses Holocaust content. Transcripts of winning entries, photos of the winners, and other resources (bibliographies, Web site links) are contained on the site.

Holocaust Survivors. http://www.holocaustsurvivors.org.

This Web site, initially developed as a photography exhibit, is directed by John Menszer with support by the Louisiana Endowment for the Humanities and the Jewish Community Center of New Orleans. The site's contents emphasize the personal dimension of Holocaust history, particularly in the survivor stories, which are supplemented by a photo gallery and audio gallery. An historical introduction, an online encyclopedia, some primary documents and scholarly articles, a bibliography, and a set of links to related Web sites also are provided. A discussion forum exists for ongoing communication with site users.

Holocaust Teacher Resource Center. http://www.Holocaust-trc.org/.

This Web site contains resources, lesson plans, and links for Holocaust educators at the kingergarten through collegiate levels. A number of the resources on the site are drawn from the educational materials of the U.S. Holocaust Memorial Museum. This Web site is linked to the Holocaust Listserver, a moderated electronic discussion forum concerning Holocaust education.

HopeSite. http://www.hopesite.ca/.

This Web site contains many resources for Holocaust study and education, including over 1,000 pages of news clippings from 1938 and 1939, organized by topic and date; poems and essays written by students and adults on Holocaust topics; quotes from student work about the Holocaust; and extensive links to related Holocaust Web sites. The site is sponsored by the Victoria Holocaust Remembrance and Education Committee in British Columbia, Canada.

I*EARN Holocaust/Genocide Project Web Site. http://www.iearn.org/hgp.

This Web site provides access to an international telecommunications project emphasizing study of the Holocaust and other genocides. Its purpose is to foster education and awareness using electronic discussions between students ages twelve through seventeen, as well as their teachers. The moderators of the project are listed on the Web site, along with the online student magazine developed as part of the project. Online resources are available to project participants, including the Web site, a gopher server, bibliographies, survivor testimonies, and access to electronic conferences, e-mail discussions, and UseNet newsgroups.

International Commission on Holocaust-Era Insurance Claims. http://www.icheic.org/.

This is a searchable list of insurance policies that were in force from 1920 to 1945. Life, education, and dowry insurance policies are included. (Available in 24 languages.)

The Israel Diaspora Museum. http://www.bh.org.il/.

The Nahum Goldmann Museum of the Jewish Diaspora (Beth Hatefutsoth) presents the history of the Jewish people from the ancient world to the present. Using resources on this Web site, individuals can pursue research on both Jewish communities and families, drawing upon the extensive databases located at the Museum.

Issues of the Holocaust: A Curriculum Guide for Secondary School Educators Based on the Nuremberg Trial Files of Senator Thomas Dodd. http://www.lib.uconn.edu/DoddCenter/ASC/Nuremberg/introduction.htm.

This Web site contains a curriculum guide regarding the issues raised at the Nuremberg Trials, where former U.S. senator from Connecticut Thomas J. Dodd served as executive trial counsel for the U.S. prosecution team. An historical introduction, photographs, and translations of key trial documents are among the varied aspects of the curriculum guide on the Web site.

Italian Life under Fascism. http://www.library.wisc.edu/libraries/dpf/Fascism/Home.html.

This online exhibition presents digital reproductions of primary source documents with descriptive captions regarding varied dimensions of Italian Fascism. With specific reference to the Holocaust, one section of the online exhibition examines

Italy's racial laws promulgated in the late 1930s, while another addresses the anti-fascist resistance.

Jewish-Christian Relations. http://www.jcrelations.net/index.htm.

This Web site is maintained by the International Council of Christians and Jews, and contains content in English, German, Portuguese, and Spanish. The contents include an extensive list of articles and papers on Jewish-Christian relations (both historical and contemporary), links to Councils of Christians and Jews, links to journals on Jewish-Christian relations, information about institutes and meetings, an archive of statements made by organizations about Jewish-Christian relations, and a set of "other resources" that includes considerable material about the Holocaust (such as bibliographies, glossaries, and other items).

JewishGen: The Home of Jewish Genealogy. http://www.jewishgen.org/.

This extensive Web site contains many resources for study of Jewish genealogy, including searchable databases, a comprehensive set of guidelines for pursuing genealogical research, and many links to related Web sites.

Jewish Museum of Rhodes. http://www.rhodesjewishmuseum.org/index.htm.

The online exhibits of the Jewish Museum of Rhodes include photographs and audio files of survivor testimony regarding the history of Jews on Rhodes during Italian rule and later as victims of Nazism during World War II. Other exhibits about the history and contemporary life of Jews from Rhodes are provided, along with links to related Web sites.

The Kindertransport Association. http://cartan.cas.suffolk.edu/~kta/.

This Web site presents an introduction to the history of the Kindertransport program, which provided 10,000 Jewish children with refuge in Great Britain prior to World War II. In addition to the history of the Kindertransport program, the Web site presents information on reunions of Kindertransport survivors and related programs of their organization.

Labor and the Holocaust: The Jewish Labor Committee and the Anti-Nazi Struggle. http://www.nyu.edu/library/bobst/collections/exhibits/tam/JLC/opener.html.

This Web site presents the history of the Jewish Labor Committee and its activities during the period of the Third Reich. The site is divided into eight sections plus a credits and bibliography page. The eight sections are: "Introduction," "Origins," "Anti-Nazi Activity of the 1930s," "Rescue Efforts 1939–1941," "War, Holocaust and Jewish Response," "Postwar Aid and Reconstruction," "'Child Adoption' Program," and "Post-war Politics." The site's contents is drawn from the Jewish Labor Committee's collection in the Robert F. Wagner Labor Archives, and primarily uses graphic and text materials.

Learning From History: The Nazi Era and the Holocaust in German Education. http://www.history.zkm.de/e/.

This web site contains content regarding how the Holocaust is taught and learned in German classrooms. Drawing upon an earlier CD-ROM produced by the Goethe Institute, the Robert Bosch Foundation, and the Press and Information Office of the Federal Government of Germany regarding the theory and practice of Holocaust education in Germany, the web site includes content on projects done within school classrooms and outside of schools, emphasizing how study of the Holocaust contributes to a deeper understanding of European history and to developing reflective citizens. Textbook recommendations, a summary of how the Holocaust is included within German school curricula, an overview of German history curricula and instruction, and sample lesson materials are provided.

Liberators: 761st. Tank Battalion. http://members.aol.com/dignews/l-promo.htm.

This Web site supplements the documentary film and book *Liberators: Fighting on Two Fronts in World War II*. Helping to tell the story of African-American soldiers who participated in the liberation of concentration camps, the Web site addresses the controversy regarding the film and book. Additional resource links are provided.

A Look Back at Nuremberg. http://www.courttv.com/casefiles/nuremberg/.

Full-text excerpts from the Nuremberg trials, an interview with a member of the U.S. prosecution team, a listing of defendants, the sentences rendered by the International Military Tribunal, and the text of international human rights documents whose origins were informed by the Nuremberg trials are located on this Web site, which was created by Court TV to supplement its televised presentation of segments of the Nuremberg Trials in the 1990s.

March of the Living. http://www.motl.org/.

The March of the Living is a program that engages Jewish teens in studying the lessons of the Holocaust through participation in a retracing of the death march between Auschwitz and Birkenau on Yom Hashoah Day, followed by travel to Israel for further study. The Web site contains excerpts of work produced by March participants, a curriculum guide, photos of recent tours, and a set of links to Holocaust-related Web sites.

Memory of the Camps. http://www.pbs.org/wgbh/pages/frontline/camp/.

This Web site supports the film of the same title, which was broadcast as part of the PBS *Frontline* series. Although created in 1945, the film was not aired until 1985. The Web site contains the transcript of the film, articles from the press about the film, and a set of links to additional resources.

Montreal Institute of Genocide and Human Rights Studies. http://www.migs.concordia.ca.

This Web site describes the programs of the Montreal Institute for Genocide and Human Rights Studies, based at the History and Sociology Departments of Concordia University. The Web site's contents include information about books, articles, and papers related to the work of the Institute, courses offered, a set of links to related Web sites, and a limited number of Holocaust survivor memoirs.

National Archives and Records Administration: Holocaust-Era Assets. http://www.nara.gov/research/assets/.

This research guide to the National Archives provides information about various resources concerning Holocaust-era assets. Finding aids, the proceedings of conferences, research papers, news briefs, and links to other organizations are included.

National Museum Directors' Conference. http://www.nationalmuseums.org.uk/spoliation/spoliation.html.

This project emanates from the United Kingdom, where the National Museum Directors' Conference, an organization of museums, libraries, and related cultural institutions, assists with the hunt for artworks stolen during the Holocaust. Plans of action by member institutions to identify stolen materials in the collections are included, along with contact information for claimants and a set of links to related Web sites.

Nazi Gold. http://www.pbs.org/wgbh/pages/frontline/shows/nazis.

This Web site supplements the PBS *Frontline* documentary that examined the financial relationships between Switzerland and Nazi Germany. A chronology of events, a set of links to related Web sites, and information for claimants are provided.

Nazi War Criminals Records Interagency Working Group. http://www.nara.gov/iwg.

This Web site presents the work of the Interagency Working Group within the National Archives and Records Administration to review and declassify Nazi war criminal records and make them accessible to the public. Research finding aids, bibliographic resources, an inventory of declassified records, and links to related Web sites are included.

Netherlands Slave Laborers—World War II. http://fox.nstn.ca/~avg/.

This Web site contains information on compensation for former slave laborers, and is funded by the government of the Netherlands. It also contains information on the War Graves Foundation of the Netherlands, and has a list of related Web site links. The Web site is operated by the Foundation of Civilian War Victims.

The Nizkor Project. http://www.nizkor.org.

Under the direction of Ken McVay, this very large Web site was developed to refute claims of Holocaust deniers and revisionists. Among the many resources included on the site are many primary sources, detailed discussions of Nazi documents, extensive records of the Nuremberg trials, and comprehensive critiques of claims and assertions by Holocaust deniers and revisionists. This is the best Web site available for individuals seeking to counter denier and revisionist claims.

One Hundred Fourth Infantry Division: Mittelbau-Dora Concentration Camp. http://www.104indiv.org/CONCAMP.HTM/.

The story of the liberation of the Mittelbau-Dora concentration camp complex by the One Hundred Fourth Infantry Division of the U.S. Army is told on this Web site. Photos, firsthand accounts of liberators and survivors, and links to related Web sites are included.

Presidential Advisory Commission on Holocaust Assets in the United States. http://www.pcha.gov/index.htm/.

This Commission's mandate is to locate stolen Holocaust-era assets that are possessed by the U.S. government, and to advise the president on policies, such as restitution. Links to related resources and contact information for other organizations are included on the Web site.

The Remember the Women Institute. http://www.rememberwomen.org/.

This Web site includes information on Institute projects dealing with research on women, focusing on the Holocaust era. Updated information on current projects and a bibliography of works in English are included.

Remembering the Kindertransports. http://home.earthlink.net/~kinderfilm/.

This Web site complements the film entitled *My Knees Were Jumping: Remembering the Kindertransports* by Melissa Hacker. The filmmaker's mother was rescued from Vienna by the Kindertransport program, and the Web site contains a photo album, a set of Web site links, and related resources.

Salvation of Bulgarian Jewry during World War II. http://www.b-info.com/places/Bulgaria/Jewish/.

This Web site includes resources on Bulgarian Jews, the history of the Holocaust in Bulgaria, and how Bulgarian Jews were rescued.

The Seventy-First Came to Gunskirchen Lager. http://www.remember.org/mooney/text.html.

Including an electronic version of the booklet *The Seventy-First Came to Gunskirchen Lager*, originally produced in 1945 by the Seventy-First Army

Infantry, this Web site details the liberation of Gunskirchen, a subcamp of Mauthausen, on May 4, 1945. Photographs and firsthand accounts are included on the site.

Shtetl: A Journey Home. http://www.logtv.com/shtetl/.

This Web site supplements the documentary of a Holocaust survivor's return to the shtetl of his ancestors in Poland. Transcripts, photos, and related articles are provided.

SICSA: The Vidal Sassoon International Center for the Study of Anti-Semitism. http://sicsa.huji.ac.il/.

This Web site contains comprehensive information regarding the study of anti-Semitism, its centerpiece being their searchable online "Bibliography on Anti-Semitism," which includes over 30,000 entries. Other sections of the Web site contain scholarly studies, a thesaurus of anti-Semitism, publication listings, links to related Web sites, updates on research initiatives, and an analysis of contemporary trends in anti-Semitism. The Vidal Sassoon International Center for the Study of Anti-Semitism created the Web site, which is maintained by the Hebrew University of Jerusalem.

Simon Wiesenthal Center. http://www.wiesenthal.com.

The Simon Wiesenthal Center Web site combines information about the broad mission of the Center with a variety of other presentations, including a multimedia online learning center, listings of teacher resources, online exhibitions, updates on efforts to combat and monitor hate and bias content on the Internet, and Center activities to promote tolerance and understanding.

Southern Institute for Education and Research. http://www.tulane.edu/~so-inst/.

This Web site includes content on Holocaust education situated within the broader mission of educating for tolerance. Lesson plans, information about teacher training workshops, transcripts of Holocaust survivor testimony, and links to Web sites on the Holocaust, human rights, and civil rights are provided.

Swiss Bankers Association: Dormant Accounts. http://www. dormantaccounts. ch/.

This Web site contains information about researching dormant accounts with Holocaust-era assets at Swiss banks and initiating claims with the Claims Resolution Tribunal.

Switzerland: Independent Commission of Experts. http://www.uek.ch/.

This commission was established by the Swiss federal assembly and their Web site contains a selection of reports on the issue. Also included are links to Swiss organizations and repositories.

A Teacher's Guide to the Holocaust. http://fcit.coedu.usf.edu/holocaust/.

This very comprehensive Web site includes text, audio, graphic, and motion video resources about the Holocaust. The main divisions of the site are "Timeline," "People," "The Arts," "Teacher Resources," "Student Activities," and "Site Map." An introduction to the site, along with a detailed credits page, also is provided. The site index is especially helpful, given the vast number of resources on the Web site. A very extensive set of links to related Holocaust Web sites is located in the "Teacher Resources" section.

Topography of Terror. http://www.topographie.de/gedenkstaettenforum/uebersicht/e/.

This Web site provides a detailed overview of the major memorial locations about the Holocaust in Germany, published by the Topography of Terror Foundation, directed by Thomas Lutz. Among the sites identified on this Web site are former concentration camps, prisons, euthanasia killing locations, and destroyed synagogues and public buildings. The Web site can be searched by site name or geographic location. Time lines, photographs, and contact information for all the memorial locations included on the Web site are provided.

To Save a Life: Stories of Holocaust Rescue. http://www.humboldt.edu/~rescuers/.

This Web site consists of an online book by Ellen Land-Weber, who teaches in the Art Department at Humboldt State University in California. Based upon interviews the author completed with individuals recognized as Righteous Gentiles by Yad Vashem, the Web site includes the rescuers' narratives, photos, and brief biographies of both survivors and rescuers.

United States Holocaust Memorial Museum. http://ushmm.org.

The very extensive Web site of the U.S. Holocaust Memorial Museum (USHMM) contains an expanding set of materials and resources for Holocaust study and teaching. The Web site of the USHMM includes descriptions of educational activities, materials from the Museum's *Resource Book for Educators* and other publications, an online learning site for students, a series of online exhibitions (electronic versions of temporary exhibitions at the USHMM in Washington, DC), archival research aids (including more than 1,000 public-domain photographs that can be searched and viewed online), bibliographic research aids, and listings of public programs and professional development programs for educators.

United States of America. Department of State: Holocaust Issues. http://www.state.gov/www/regions/eur/holocausthp.html/.

Issues of the Holocaust related to the Department of State are addressed on this Web site, particularly the issue of Holocaust assets. Reports, press releases, and fact sheets are provided on the Web site, along with the complete proceedings of the Washington Conference on Holocaust-Era Assets. Contact information for dormant Swiss accounts is included as well.

Varian Fry. http://www.almondseed.com/vfry/.
This Web site tells the story of Varian Fry, the U.S. journalist who helped to rescue thousands of Jews from Vichy, France prior to the outbreak of war between the United States and Germany in 1941. The Varian Fry Foundation Project/IRC maintains this Web site, which has a bibliography, a national calendar of events concerning Varian Fry, and a detailed set of links to Holocaust resources.

Voice Vision: Holocaust Survivor Oral Histories. http://holocaust.umd. umich.edu/.
This Web site contains information about the oral history project conducted by Dr. Sidney Bolkosky of the University of Michigan-Dearborn, which encompasses over 150 interviews of Holocaust survivors. The Web site contains transcripts and audio excerpts of selected interviews from this collection, as well as information about how to access other interviews from the collection via interlibrary loan.

Women and the Holocaust. http://www.interlog.com/~mighty/.
Created by Holocaust survivor Judy Cohen and a team of contributors, this Web site includes first-person accounts, reviews of relevant books, articles and essays, poetry, and links to additional first-person accounts and other Holocaust resources. The Web site is dedicated to women who perished in the Holocaust and those who survived.

Yad Vashem. http://www.yadvashem.org.il.
The recently revised and expanded Web site of Yad Vashem contains an Internet journal, a series of online exhibitions, documents, and teaching aids, information on the Righteous among the Nations (individuals honored by Yad Vashem for rescuing Jews during the Holocaust), information on educational seminars and programs, and comprehensive information on how to access the Yad Vashem collections (archives, historical museum, art museum, and library).

Yale Center for International and Area Studies: Genocide Studies Program. http://www.yale.edu/gsp/.
This Web site describes the program at Yale University concerning Holocaust and genocide studies. Scholarly papers, reports, and other research findings are available on the Web site, along with a set of links to related resources and information about the Center for International and Area Studies' seminars and workshops.

COLLECTIONS OF LINKS TO WORLD WIDE WEB RESOURCES ON THE HOLOCAUST

About.com: The Holocaust. http://history1900s.about.com/library/ holocaust/blholocaust.htm/. This is part of About.com's twentieth century history site, and includes articles written by About.com's online expert as a guide to the site, maps, a glossary of terms, photographs, a time line and some student projects. The extensive list of links is organized alphabetically, and users can subscribe to an online newsletter regarding twentieth-century history. Links to discussion forums and live chat rooms also are provided.

The Holocaust Ring. http://D.webring.com/hub?ring=shoah&list/.

This listing of thirty-five diverse Web sites provides access to content on many aspects of Holocaust study, including but not limited to: Web sites about individual survivors, Web sites about liberation of the camps, teacher resource Web sites, Web sites about specific camps (Westerbork is one example), Web sites regarding rescue efforts, and Web sites countering Holocaust denial.

Shamash. http://www.shamash.org/holocaust/.

The emphasis of the Shamash collection of Web site resources is on combating Holocaust denial and revisionism. There are links within this collection to historical documents and excerpts of perpetrator testimonies.

shoahBook. http://www.javari.com/shoahbook/.

This set of electronic resources and Web site links is quite extensive, and contains a comprehensive set of links designed to assist educators in Holocaust instruction. Archival materials, books, videos, photos, and bibliographies are among the resources located on this Web site.

Social Studies School Service. http://socialstudies.com/holo.html.

This Web site identifies educational resources (books, posters, and other items) available in the company's Holocaust resources and materials catalogue, along with Internet lesson plans and classroom activities and an annotated list of Holocaust-related Web sites.

Virtual Library: History: German History. http://www.phil.uni-erlangen.de/~p1ges/heidelberg/gh/gh.html/. (In German and English)

As one section of the Virtual Library's History Index, this collection of resources is arranged by format, type, time period, and topic. Links to Jewish history and reference sources are also provided.

Virtual Shtetl. http://metalab.unc.edu/yiddish/roots/html/.

This Web site contains many links to online resources on Yiddish culture. The Holocaust is included among the topics, which also encompass Jews in Eastern Europe.

10

ELECTRONIC RESOURCES: CD-ROMs

OVERVIEW

The rapid development of electronic resources for study and teaching has clearly impacted the field of Holocaust studies, as represented by the CD-ROMs listed in this chapter. During the 1990s, as greater numbers of schools, libraries, and homes obtained access to personal computers, the potential for multimedia presentations of Holocaust content expanded considerably. The CD-ROMs (compact disc–read only memory) presented here all contain some multimedia capabilities, defined as the presentation of Holocaust content using more than a single medium of representation. Photographs, graphics, audio files, text, maps, motion video, and other media forms are contained on most of these CD-ROMs. The level of complexity evident in these multimedia products varies, but all offer the user a greater variety of media representations than was possible prior to the use of CD-ROMs for educational and scholarly use. Only the Internet rivals the CD-ROMs in its capacity for multimedia presentation. For each item listed in this chapter, a discussion of the CD-ROM's contents is provided, along with some discussion of its unique features (navigation, user's manual, forms of media available) and vendor information. Addresses for vendors are included at the conclusion of this chapter.

CD-ROMS

Beth Shalom Holocaust Education Center. *Learning about the Holocaust: The Racial State.* Windows 98/95/NT CD-ROM. Laxton, Newark, Nottinghamshire: Beth Shalom Holocaust Multimedia Productions, n.d. Available from Beth Shalom Holocaust Memorial Centre.

This multimedia CD-ROM is one in a series of four prepared by the Beth Shalom Holocaust Memorial Centre, the others encompassing "The Jewish Tradition," "The Final Solution," and "The Pain of Survival." Utilizing sources from the period between World War I and 1945, the program is divided into four modules: "The Rise to Power," "Racial State," "Gathering Storm" and "Road to War." The modules are stand-alone topical units, but are best studied in their chronological sequence. Video, audio, photographs, and quotes from diverse sources are integral components of the modules, while the main menu encompasses the four topical units, a comprehensive bibliography, and a glossary. Text overviews, hotwords highlighted to help students learn more about terms, and icons for users to pursue more in-depth information on photograph content are provided within the topical modules. A "q and a" section, which has multiple-choice questions, is included to help users check their comprehension of faculty information, while the discussion questions focus on interpretations of events within the topical units. Answers to questions in the discussion section, as well as notes that the user creates while accessing the program, can be saved in a word-processing file.

Brinkmann, Annette, Annegret Ehmann, Sybil Milton, Hans Fred Rathenow, and Regina Wyrwoll, editors. *Learning from History: The Nazi Era and the Holocaust in German Education.* Book and Windows 95/higher and Macintosh System 7.5 or higher CD-ROM. Bonn: ARCult Media Verlag, 2000. ISBN 3–930395–23–1. Published in English and German. Available from Goethe House.

The book is divided into a preface and five sections: "Introduction" (background on the project's development), "Holocaust Education in the USA and Germany," "Education on National Socialism and the Holocaust," "Chronology," and "How to Use the CD-ROM." The multimedia CD-ROM contains text, visuals, documents, maps, and audio/video files primarily emphasizing learning activities and projects about the Holocaust that have been put into practice by teachers and students in Germany. A comprehensive reference section permits the user to find bibliographic materials, a glossary, contact information for project participants, and media and project credits. The CD-ROM can be accessed in English or German at the discretion of the user. The book contains an excellent manual for use of the CD-ROM written in clear, precise language.

Darmont, J.J-M. Drewfus, D. Lewiner-Elalouf, and P. Raiman. *Stories from the Warsaw Ghetto.* Windows 3.1 or higher and Macintosh System 7 or higher CD-ROM. Paris: Montparnasse Multimedia, 1997. ISBN 588530–110101. Available from Montparnasse Multimedia and Social Studies School Service. Technical support: email suptech@itw.fr.

Focusing on the lives of nine members of the Jewish resistance in the Warsaw Ghetto, this multimedia CD-ROM contains both documentary material and animated recreations seeking to reconstruct events for which little visual materials is available. Sections entitled "Destinies," "Tales," "Memories," "Chronology," and "Map" are the main content segments, and each provides opportunities for in-depth study with many subtopics. An index and bibliography are provided to assist the user in locating specific topics, or to facilitate further research about the Warsaw Ghetto, respectively. The "Chronology" permits exploration at both general and detailed levels, focusing on seven key moments in the Ghetto's history, while the "Map" section includes not only a detailed map of the Ghetto, but a three-dimensional, computer-assisted model that creates a virtual reconstruction of the Ghetto in 1942.

Endless, S.A. *Lest We Forget, a History of the Holocaust.* Windows 3.1 or higher and Macintosh System 7 or higher CD-ROM. Oak Harbor, WA: Logos Research Systems, n.d. Available from Social Studies School Service.

This multimedia CD-ROM addresses the time period 1919–1960s, with emphasis on the era of the Third Reich. Three main menu topics ("Hitler's Germany," "The Holocaust," "The Aftermath") are the primary content themes of the CD-ROM, which contains a glossary, biographies, and interactive maps. Over 500 photographs and many documentary film segments are included, along with approximately 250 pages of text. The CD-ROM includes a table of contents, and each main topic has subtopics encouraging in-depth exploration of the three main menu topics.

Khush Multimedia. *The Yellow Star: The Persecution of the Jews in Europe from 1933 to 1945.* CD-ROM. Chicago: Khush Multimedia, 1996. CD-ROM. Macintosh and Windows 95 CD-ROM. Available from Khush Multimedia.

This CD-ROM contains primarily excerpts from the film of the same name and is introduced by Simon Wiesenthal.

Spiegelman, Art. *The Complete MAUS: A Survivor's Tale.* New York: Voyager, 1994. Macintosh System 7 or higher CD-ROM. ISBN 1–559404–53–1. Available from Social Studies School Service or from Learn Technologies Interactive.

This version of Art Spiegelman's memoir of his father's experiences during the Holocaust includes not only the complete texts of both volumes of *MAUS*, but preliminary sketches, alternate drafts, archival photographs, and drawings made by prisoners during the Holocaust. Additionally, audio excerpts from the interviews between Spiegelman and his father that served as the basis for the original books are provided, along with video and audio segments of Spiegelman discussing how he conceptualized and created *MAUS*. The five sections of the main menu are "The Introduction," "Art on Art," "Appendices," "Supplements," and "The Working Transcripts." A search function provides easy access to words, audio, and video on the CD-ROM.

Survivors of the Shoah Visual History Foundation. *Survivors: Testimonies of the Holocaust.* Torrance, CA: Knowledge Adventure, Inc./Simon & Schuster, 1999. Power Macintosh and Windows 98/95 CD-ROM. Available from Social Studies School Service.

This multimedia two-CD-ROM set contains the video testimonies of four survivors, combined with a variety of other features and information that supplement the testimony details. Two males (Germany and Czechoslovakia) and two females (Poland and Austria) comprise the subjects of the testimonies, drawn from the Shoah Foundation's video archives. The interactive features of the CD-ROM include maps (with a zoom feature), a comprehensive time line, an "Overview" section that provides the historical context for the years encompassed by the Holocaust, and links to a related Web page where a study guide, bibliographic resources, updates provided by the publisher, and other research materials are found, along with links to related Holocaust Web sites. Transcripts of the video testimonies and an alphabetic glossary are included as well.

United States Holocaust Memorial Museum. *Historical Atlas of the Holocaust.* CD-ROM. New York: Macmillan, 1996. Windows CD-ROM. Available from U.S. Holocaust Memorial Museum Shop.

This CD-ROM utilizes maps, text files, photographs, a glossary, and comprehensive help/reference screens to tell the history of the Holocaust and relevant content from the immediate post–World War II period (1933–1950). A total of 270 maps, more than 500 photographs, an audio glossary, a comprehensive bibliography, a place name index, and the USHMM "Guidelines for Teaching about the Holocaust" accompany over 75,000 words of text on the CD-ROM. The CD-ROM is easy to navigate and contains a series of thematically organized menus where related maps are identified using a "See Also" submenu. All maps were originally created and produced for the Wexner Learning Center of the USHMM. While the maps and photographs do not print, the text files can be printed.

Wigoder, Geoffrey, editor-in-chief. *Encyclopedia Judaica.* CD-ROM. Danbury, CT: Grolier, Inc., 2000. Windows 3.x or Windows 95. Network version available. Available from Torah Educational Software (www.jewishsoftware.com).

This version of the landmark *Encyclopedia Judaica* includes the original 1972 sixteen-volume text version, plus eight yearbooks and two decennial volumes that updated the original publication between 1972 and 1992. Updates, new articles, and multimedia features have been added to this version, which now has 25,000 articles by more than 2,200 authors. The CD-ROM version has a comprehensive search function that permits subject or text searches, hyperlinks within the text to related articles and definitions in the glossary, hyperlinks from author names to brief author biographies, a multifunction toolbar that lets the user choose related articles, a bibliography for additional sources, bookmarks, as well as copy and print functions. The Media Gallery provides opportunities to explore slide shows, videos, music pictures, maps, tables, and charts, with some topics presented in thematic collections, such as the Holocaust, American Jewry, Israel, and others. Additionally, a time line is provided to help users locate historical events and cultural developments throughout Jewish history. This CD-ROM is easy to use and is an essential resource for the broader study of Jewish culture, history, and society, within which the Holocaust is situated.

Yad Vashem International School for Holocaust Studies. *Return to Life: The Story of Holocaust Survivors*. CD-ROM. Jerusalem: Yad Vashem, 1997. Windows 95 CD-ROM. Available from Yad Vashem Martyrs' and Heroes' Remembrance Authority or Social Studies School Service.

This CD-ROM addresses the efforts by Holocaust survivors to reconstruct their lives during the post–World War II period (1945–1957), primarily in Israel. There are many automated presentations and film testimonies, along with over seventy audio segments from historians and survivors. Hundreds of photographs, documents, and secondary source excerpts are included, along with an extensive glossary, time line, and set of seven interactive maps. Citations to many of the sources employed are provided.

VENDORS AND DISTRIBUTORS OF CD-ROMS

Beth Shalom Holocaust Memorial Centre, Laxton, Newark, Notts NG22 OPA, United Kingdom. Phone: +44 (0)1623 836627 Fax: +44 (0) 1623 836647. www.bethshalom.com

Goethe House/Learning From History. http://holocaust-education.de.

Khush Multimedia, 100 W. Monroe Street, Suite 501, Chicago, IL 60603. Phone: 312-346-2048.

Learn Technologies Interactive, 361 Broadway, Suite 610, New York, NY 10013. Phone: 212-334-2225. http://voyager.learntech.com.

Montparnasse Multimedia. http://www.montparnasse.net/us.

Social Studies School Service, 10200 Jefferson Boulevard, Room 171, PO Box 802, Culver City, CA 90232-0802. Phone: 800-421-4246. http://socialstudies.com.

Torah Educational Software, 455 Route 306, Monsey, NY 10952. Phone: 845-362-6380. http://www.jewishsoftware.com.

U.S. Holocaust Memorial Museum Shop, 100 Raoul Wallenberg Place SW, Washington, DC 20024. Phone: 800-259-9998. http://www.holocaustbooks.org.

Yad Vashem Martyrs' and Heroes' Remembrance Authority, PO Box 3477, Jerusalem 91034, Israel. Phone: (972) 2-654-1334. Fax: (972) 2-643-3511. e-mail: edu@yadvashem.org.il. http://www.yadvashem.org.il.

PART IV

AUDIOVISUAL RESOURCES

11

ART OF THE HOLOCAUST AND ITS LEGACY

OVERVIEW

Representations of Holocaust content and themes in visual art have become increasingly significant as topics of appreciation and study, as the books and other resources in this chapter demonstrate. A decided focus on testimony and remembrance is evident in a broad array of the visual art works discussed in these works, many of which were created by survivors or artists who are second generation children of survivors. The examination of broad historical themes and imagery in Judaism also is prominent, not only in the work of European and Israeli artists, but in those from North America as well. In some cases, the books combine discussion of visual art with analyses of public memorials, where sculpture and other public art is often placed for permanent display. Given the increasing prominence of the Holocaust as subject matter for artistic inspiration, selected catalogues of exhibits from the 1990s have been included to emphasize the public's growing attention and interest in this field. The entries provided here were selected based upon their prominence in discussing major themes and works in Holocaust visual art, as well as their scholarly merit and value as resources for study and teaching this content. A listing of Web sites detailing online presentations of Holocaust art along with a listing of Holocaust art collections is included at the end of this chapter.

BOOKS

Amishai-Maisels, Ziva. *Depiction and Interpretation: The Influence of the Holocaust on the Visual Arts.* Oxford: Pergamon Press, 1993. ISBN 0–08040–656–4. 567 pages. Hardcover.

This is the most comprehensive survey of Holocaust-inspired visual art available. In addition to the thorough discussion of diverse approaches to Holocaust visual art, there are over 140 pages with plates illustrating works discussed in the text. A thorough bibliography is provided, as well as a detailed index.

Baigell, Matthew. *Jewish-American Artists and the Holocaust.* New Brunswick: Rutgers University Press, 1997. ISBN 0–8135–2404–0. 132 pages. Hardcover.

This book by the distinguished American art historian Matthew Baigell focuses on Holocaust art in the United States during the period from the 1970s through the mid-1990s, with the work of Jewish-American artists as the focal point for analysis. Drawing upon the work of dozens of artists who have used Holocaust imagery in their work, Baigell organizes his work chronologically and addresses themes such as how these artists use biblical and mythological imagery, along with their efforts to render the "inexpressible" in artistic form. Extensive notes are provided along with a detailed index.

Bohm-Duchen, Monica, editor. *After Auschwitz: Responses to the Holocaust in Contemporary Art.* London: Northern Centre for Contemporary Art, 1995. ISBN 0–85331–666–X. 162 pages. Hardcover.

This book, developed to accompany the exhibition of the same name, includes essays by art historians, dramatists and essayists, historians, and scholars of Judaic studies on connections between art and the Holocaust. Topics of the essays deal with "The Complexities of Witnessing" (Ziva Amishai-Maisels), "Memory and Counter-Memory: Towards a Social Aesthetic of Holocaust Memorials" (James Young), and "Fifty Years On" (Monica Bohn-Duchen), among others. Statements by the artists whose works were included in the exhibition, as well as a list of the works in the exhibition and a selected bibliography, conclude the book. No index.

Feinstein, Stephen, editor. *Witness & Legacy: Contemporary Art About the Holocaust.* Minneapolis: Lerner Publications Co., 1995. ISBN 0–8225–3148–8. 64 pages. Paperback.

This combined exhibit catalogue and set of essays accompanied an exhibit held at the Minnesota Museum of American Art in 1995. The essay authors attempt to bring the Holocaust into the cultural dialogue of American culture in various ways. Stephen Feinstein discusses the relationship of the artwork to Holocaust history, noting that one-third of the artists represented are survivors, another third are children of survivors, and the final third are not directly connected with the Holocaust. He provides extended descriptions of individual artists and their works, and discusses how each of the three groups' approaches inclusion of the Holocaust in visual art. Yehudit Shendar examines the work of five installation artists, emphasizing the significance of collective memory. By placing a heavy focus on the bond between art works and the real world, the installation artists, according to Shendar, force the viewer to participate in the search for collective memory. Matthew Baigell, distinguished historian of American art at Rutgers University— New Brunswick, discusses the shared qualities of Holocaust imagery in American art—anger, the desire for reconciliation among people, the necessity for remembrance, and the concern for victims of brutality. He also contrasts the more recent artistic trend to use Holocaust imagery to highlight Jewish particularism rather with more long-standing efforts to employ Holocaust imagery in the service of universal themes. Plates are provided of all works in the exhibit in color or black and white. A list of artworks in the exhibition is provided, along with a bibliography. No index.

Feliciano, Hector. *The Lost Museum.* New York: Basic Books, 1997. Updated English edition of original published in French in 1995. ISBN 0–465–04191–4. 280 pages. Paperback.

Hector Feliciano's book presents the story of Nazi art looting during World War II, focusing on how the Nazis systematically accumulated art collections from five Jewish families in France. The author exposes how over 20,000 works of art were stolen by the Nazis for eventual placement in Adolf Hitler's proposed European art museum in Austria, for use by Nazi dignitaries, or for sale in art markets located in France and Switzerland between 1940 and 1945. Greed and self-interest characterized the transactions between the Nazis and French art dealers, while postwar bureaucratic indifference by the French government saw little movement to return the works of art to their rightful owners. Indeed, Feliciano demonstrates that over 2,000 works of art stolen by the Nazis remained as "unclaimed" works in the holdings of French museums for decades after World War II. Chapter notes are provided, along with two appendices: facsimile reproductions of the Schenker papers (a British army report on art looted by the Germans based upon documents found at the close of the war) and an interview with Alain Vernay, the grandson of Adolphe Schloss, whose collection of Dutch masterworks was looted by the Nazis during the occupation of France. Indexed.

Furth, Valerie Jakober. *Cabbages and Geraniums: Memories of the Holocaust.* New York: Columbia University Press, 1989. ISBN 0–88033–962–4. 118 pages. Hardcover.

This account describes the author's upbringing in Czechoslovakia and Hungary, her experiences in Auschwitz, and how she survived the Holocaust. It includes her own paintings and sculptures, which she began creating thirty-six years after her liberation, incorporating sixty photos that accompany the text. Each plate of artwork is associated with a particular element of the story by means of quoted excerpts used as captions. No index.

Olere, David, and Alexander Olere. *Witness: Images of Auschwitz.* Foreword by Serge Klarsfeld. North Richland Hills, TX: West Wind Press, 1998. ISBN 0–94103–769–X. 112 pages. Hardcover.

The drawings in this book by Holocaust survivor David Olere were drawn soon after his liberation and were used as documentation for investigations of the Holocaust after World War II. The originals of the drawings used in the book are located at Yad Vashem and the Ghetto Fighters' House Museum in Israel, while the sculptures and paintings are in private collections or at the Cinematheque (Museum of Cinema) in Paris—Trocadero. Olere was one of the few survivors of the Auschwitz *sonderkommando*, and his drawings are powerful renderings of his experiences. The poetry accompanying the drawings, written by his son Alexander Olere, complements the visual material quite effectively. A brief biography of David Olere and list of works by Alexander Olere are included in the book. No index.

Spiegelman, Art. *Maus I: A Survivor's Tale. My Father Bleeds History.* New York: Pantheon Books, 1986. ISBN 0–394–74723–2. 159 pages. Paperback.

———. *Maus II: A Survivor's Tale. And Here My Troubles Began.* New York: Pantheon Books, 1991. ISBN 0–679–72977–1. 136 pages. Paperback.

Crossing the boundaries of art, memoir, and historical fiction, Art Spiegelman's *Maus I* and *Maus II* render the story of the author's connections to the Holocaust through the relationship with his father and, ultimately, with the twentieth century history of his Jewish family. The cartoon genre employed by Spiegelman draws the reader into the tale, with the visual narrative and dialogue providing a highly effective medium for the presentation of intimate details about how Spiegelman's family experienced the Holocaust and its lifelong impact on family relationships. *Maus* is faithful to the key themes and ideas evident in Holocaust scholarship, but the power of its message remains its compelling use of black and white cartoons to tell a moving, compassionate story of family relationships intertwined with the history of this tragic period. No index.

Toll, Nelly. *When Memory Speaks: The Holocaust in Art.* Westport, CT: Praeger Publishers, 1998. ISBN 0–275–95534–6. 123 pages. Hardcover.

In four thematic chapters, the author provides an overview of Holocaust art through the work of selected artists. Beginning with art completed during the

Holocaust in camps, and continuing with issues placing the issues of artistic control in historical perspective under Nazism, the work then proceeds to address specific responses by artists who have interpreted the Holocaust in retrospect, twenty-seven in all. The last section of the book deals with "Living Memorials and Educational Institutions," focusing on the Musuem of Jewish Heritage in New York (written by David Altshuler), the preservation of the past, and the role of Holocaust museums in the United States. Notes are provided, along with a selected bibliography for further study. Indexed.

Willett, John. *Art and Politics in the Weimar Period: The New Sobriety, 1917–1933.* New York: Da Capo Press, 1996. Reprint of 1978 edition by Thames & Hudson, Ltd. ISBN 0–306–80724–6. 272 pages. Paperback.

This work, which contains extensive illustrations, photos, and visual organizers for its wide-ranging subject matter, explores two key themes: (1) the simultaneously hopeful and desperate character of the civilization established in Germany by 1925 and (2) the pressures that gave art in the Weimar period a sense of urgency and desperation, and which eventually led to the destruction of this art by totalitarian forces. Willett discusses the broadly political purposes of art in the Weimar period and the conscious involvement of artists with the development of a new society. He also clearly shows how the conflict between members of the artistic avant-garde and their lack of political unity contributed to the victory of totalitarian forces in artistic affairs. This book contains a comparative chronology for the Weimar period that chronicles political events and major developments in five areas of the arts discussed in the text. A select bibliography is included, along with a detailed index.

Young, James. *At Memory's Edge: After-images of the Holocaust in Contemporary Art and Architecture.* New Haven: Yale University Press, 2000. ISBN 0–300–08032–8. 248 pages. Hardcover.

James Young presents seven essays in this volume about the relationship between memory and history, as mediated through art and architecture, with greatest emphasis placed on how Germany should confront this issue. Examining a diverse range of topics, including Art Spiegelman's *Maus*, the controversy surrounding the construction of a German national Holocaust memorial, Shimon Attie's "Acts of Remembrance" installations, David Liventhal's photographic work, the design of the Berlin Jewish Museum, and others, Young raises questions about how contemporary artists and architects can create artworks and structures about an event they never experienced directly. Because these artists and architects by definition must deal with what Young calls the "after-images" of the Holocaust, they have a critical role in shaping how future generations understand the Holocaust and its legacy. Not only are they helping to shape the understanding of future generations, but they are augmenting the traditional narrative role of historical inquiry by adding another very important dimension: the analysis of how that history is passed on to the future. Many photographs are included along with illustrations from the artists' works, as well as extensive chapter notes, and a detailed bibliography. Indexed.

WEB SITES: ART COLLECTIONS ON THE HOLOCAUST

The Web sites described here either contain representations of Holocaust art in electronic form and/or provide descriptions and listings of Holocaust art held at museums, memorials, and study centers.

Beit Lohamei Haghetaot—The Ghetto Fighters' House. The Art Collection of the Ghetto Fighters' House Museum. http://www.gfh.org.il/english/exhibit/toc.htm#art.

Over 3,000 works of art comprise the Ghetto Fighters' House collection of Holocaust art. In addition to descriptions of the exhibitions at the Ghetto Fighters' House Museum and Children's Memorial (Yad Layeled), traveling exhibitions are described, including the works of David Olere (*Witness: Images of Auschwitz*), which is referenced in this chapter. The Ghetto Fighters' House Museum is participating in an online international project regarding Holocaust art, using art created in the ghettos and camps of Europe during World War II. This section of the Web site is currently under construction, and will contain information on the works of art, the artists, and the conditions under which the art was created. e-mail: prosenberg@gfh.org.il.

Block Gallery of Northwestern University. http://lastexpression.northwestern.edu.

This Web site contains the virtual exhibition "The Last Expression," where art created in Nazi concentration and death camps is examined, with special emphasis placed on works created at Auschwitz-Birkenau. In addition to textual introductions to the works and electronic versions of the artwork, videotaped interviews with artist-survivors can be accessed by users of the Web site. e-mail: block-museum@northwestern.edu.

Center for Holocaust and Genocide Studies at the University of Minnesota. Virtual Museum of Holocaust Art. http:chgs.hispeed.com/Visual_Artistic_Resources/visual_artistic-resources.html.

This comprehensive Web site, supervised by Stephen Feinstein, contains five sections: a virtual museum, histories, narratives and documents, educational resources and contact information, and a section with links and a bibliography. Presentations of works from prior exhibitions held at the University of Minnesota are displayed on the Web site, and the Web site is regularly updated with new online exhibitions. e-mail: feins001@tc.umn.edu.

Yad Vashem: The Holocaust Martyrs' and Heroes' Remembrance Authority. The Art Museum. http://www.yadvashem.org.il/exhibitions/museums/art_museum/home_art_museum.html.

This section of the Yad Vashem Web site presents selected artworks in the Yad Vashem collection, which is the largest collection of Holocaust artwork in the world. Within the series of online exhibitions on the Yad Vashem Web site, selected works of art from the Yad Vashem art collection are included. e-mail: art.museum@yadvashem.org.il.

12

PHOTOGRAPHS

OVERVIEW

The photographic record of the Holocaust is extensive, and this chapter offers a variety of photographic sources for study and teaching. Photographs play a major role in the documentation of Holocaust history, as well as the presentation of evidence about the pre-war culture of European Jewish life that Nazism sought to eradicate. The listing of photographic archives emphasizes those with major collections on the Holocaust, based upon review of directories of Holocaust institutions and the use of materials from selected archives in works relying on photographic evidence. Interested readers who desire more information on German state archives with Holocaust photograph collections should consult Chapter 17, where German museums, memorials, libraries, and archives with substantial Holocaust content can be found. Each photographic archive listing includes a brief description of its holdings, along with its address, phone, fax, e-mail address, and Web site address (where applicable). The books containing collections of Holocaust photographs are a selective listing; those chosen for inclusion all met the criteria of scholarly merit, while a conscious effort has been made to present varied dimensions of photographic evidence about the Holocaust. A select list of Web sites providing announcements of traveling photographic exhibitions, as well as online exhibitions of Holocaust photographs, is provided at the end of this chapter.

PHOTOGRAPHIC ARCHIVES

Beit Lohamei Hagetaot. Ghetto Fighters' House Holocaust and Jewish Resistance Heritage Museum. Kibbutz Lohamei-Hagetaot D.N., Western Galilee 25220, Israel. Phone: (972) 4-995-8080. FAX: (972) 4-995-8007. e-mail: yshavit@gfh.org.il. http://www.gfh.org.il.

The Ghetto Fighters' House contains a range of photograph collections, including specific collections on Jewish children who emigrated to Israel after World War II, the "Helahutz" archives of photos, and many others related to Holocaust topics.

Institute of Contemporary History and Wiener Library. 4 Devonshire Street, London W1N 2BH, United Kingdom. Phone: (44) 171-636-7247. FAX: (44) 171-436-6428. e-mail: lib@wienerlibrary.co.uk. http://www.wienerlibrary.co.uk.

Among the collections of the Wiener Library in London are photographs dealing with a variety of Holocaust topics, including modern Jewish history, the rise of fascism and Nazism, the Weimar Republic, the policies and practices of the Third Reich, World War II, and anti-Semitism.

The Leo Baeck Institute, Center for Jewish History. 15 West 16th Street, New York, NY 10011. Phone: 212-744-6400. FAX: 212-988-1305. e-mail: lbil@lbi.com. http://www.lbi.org.

The Leo Baeck Institute emphasizes the study of German-speaking Jewry and the preservation of German Jewish culture from its origins to the period of its destruction under Nazism. Among its many collections, the Leo Baeck Institute has a collection of over 12,500 photographs that range across the full range of German Jewish life.

National Archives and Records Administration of the United States of America. Washington, DC. The National Archives and Records Administration has many depositories in the United States. Consult the NARA Web site for their specific locations. e-mail: stillpix@nara.gov http://www.nara.gov.

Among its vast photographic collections of over eight million photographs and graphic images, the Still Picture Unit has extensive collections on World War II, including photos taken by liberators of concentration camps, photos of war crimes trials, and others. Online finding aids are available on the NARA Web site, located at http://www.nara.gov.

State Museum of the KL Auschwitz-Birkenau. ul. Wiezniow Oswiecimia 20, Oswiecim 32-603, Poland. Phone: (48) 33-843-2022. FAX: (48) 33-

843-1934. e-mail: muzeum@auschwitz-muzeum.oswiecim.pl. http://
www.auschwitz.org.pl.

The archives located at the State Museum contain photographs available for
research and study concerning the history of the Auschwitz camp complex.
Among the tens of thousands of photographs in the collections are photographic
negatives of prisoners taken by the camp authorities for the purposes of identifying
prisoners, SS photographs of Jews from Hungary, clandestine photographs taken
by the *sonderkommando* in the vicinity of the gas chambers, and private photographs brought to Auschwitz by deportees from ghettos.

United States Holocaust Memorial Museum. Photo Archives. 100 Raoul
Wallenberg Place SW, Washington, DC 20024. Phone: 202-488-0429.
http://www.ushmm.org./archives/photo.htm.

The U.S. Holocaust Memorial Museum's Photographic Archive holds 65,000
photographs concerning the Holocaust. The range of topics is vast, including
Jewish life before the Holocaust in Europe, the rise of Nazism in Germany and
Austria, Nazi racial science and propaganda, the flight of refugees from Nazi
Germany, the implementation of genocide and mass murder in Europe, the liberation of Europe and revelation of the Nazi concentration camps, war crimes trials,
and others.

Yad Vashem—The Holocaust Martyrs' and Heroes' Remembrance Authority. PO Box 3477, Jerusalem 91034, Israel. Phone: (972) 2-644-3721.
FAX: (972) 2-644-3719. e-mail: archive@yadvashem.org.il. http://
www.yadvashem.org.il.

Containing over 100,000 photographs on the Holocaust and Holocaust-related
topics, Yad Vashem provides both in-person and mail service to research queries.
A master computerized data bank contains information on all photos in the
collection for users.

YIVO Institute for Jewish Research. Archives/Library, 15 West 16th
Street, New York, NY 10011-6301. Phone: 212-294-6142. FAX: 212-292-
1892. e-mail: kfisher@yivo.cjh.org. http://www.yivoinstitute.org/archlib/
archlib_fr.htm.

Among the 150,000 photographs in the archives of the YIVO Institute are approximately 10,000 on Holocaust and Holocaust-related topics. Among the topics
included in this collection are early Nazi persecution of Jews in Germany, Jewish
refugees, Jewish life in ghettos established by the Nazis, deportations and mass
executions of Jews, concentration and death camps, and the Nuremberg Trials,
among others. Related collections in the YIVO archives include Displaced Persons
Camps and Centers and the Territorial Photographic Collection, which contains a

rich record of European Jewish life before World War II. The Holocaust photograph collection has been placed on a computerized database for research access.

PHOTOGRAPHS: PUBLISHED COLLECTIONS

Abels, Chana Byers. *The Children We Remember: Photographs from the Archives of Yad Vashem, the Holocaust Martyrs and Heroes Remembrance Authority, Jerusalem, Israel.* New York: Greenwillow Books, 1986. ISBN 0–688–063721. 42 pages. Hardcover.

This book includes photographs from the Yad Vashem archives with brief introductory sentences that show activities and life experiences of children prior to, during, and after the Holocaust. No introductory essay is provided, nor is there an index, bibliography, or glossary.

Arad, Yitzhak, editor, and Yad Vashem, the Holocaust Martyrs' and Heroes' Remembrance Authority. *The Pictorial History of the Holocaust.* New York: Macmillan, 1990. ISBN 0–02–897011–X. 396 pages. Hardcover.

Relying primarily on the photographic collections of Yad Vashem in Jerusalem, this photographic history of the Holocaust is divided into four key periods: 1933–1939 ("Persecution of Jews in the Third Reich"), 1939–1941 ("Nazi Conquest of Europe, Ghettoization and Slave Labor"), 1941–1945 ("Mass Murder of the Jews and Resistance Efforts"), and 1945–1948 ("Liberation, Surviving Jews and Efforts to Reach Eretz Israel"). Brief text introductions are provided at the outset of the four topical sections, and all photographs are black and white, with captions. The strong emphasis on partisan activities, Jewish resistance, liberation, and emigration to Israel in the post-1945 period makes this photograph anthology a valuable supplement to narrative histories of the Holocaust, particularly those with limited visual sources. No index.

Del Calzo, Nick. *The Triumphant Spirit: Portraits and Stories of Holocaust Survivors . . . Their Messages of Hope and Compassion.* Introduction by Thomas Keneally. Foreword by Jan Karski. Denver: Triumphant Spirit Publishing, 1997. ISBN 0–9655260–1–1. 172 pages. Paperback.

This collection of photographs and biographical sketches of Holocaust survivors illustrates how each individual endured the Holocaust and how each rebuilt his or her life following the end of World War II. The full page black and white photographs stand alone, with the facing pages containing the survivor's name, the camps or ghettos he or she encountered, and a biographical sketch. A quote from each survivor is highlighted on the same page as the biographical sketch. The book has a bibliography of works for further study, a listing of photographic sites used for the book, notes, and an index.

Dobroszycki, Lucjan, and Barbara Kirshenblatt-Gimblett. *Image before My Eyes: A Photographic History of Jewish Life in Poland before the Holocaust.* New York: Schocken Books, 1977. ISBN 0–8052–1026–1. 269 pages. Paperback.

Drawing heavily from the YIVO Institute's collection of historical photographs, the authors have created a book that invites the reader to journey back into a world that was destroyed during the Holocaust—the world of pre–World War II Polish Jewry. The book is divided into four thematic sections: "A History of Jewish Photography in Poland," "The Persistence of the Past," "The Camera as Chronicler," and "Creating a Modern Existence." Within each thematic section, separate chapters are organized with text introductions that establish a context for the captioned photos about topics such as emigration, communal institutions, celebrations, and many others. The black-and-white photographs represent a seventy-five-year span (1864–1939), documenting a culture that was destroyed by the onslaught of Nazi Germany and their occupation of Poland from 1939 to 1945. An appendix of sources consulted for the book is provided, along with tables of statistical data on Polish Jewry prior to World War II. Along with the film based upon this book (see Chapter 13) and Roman Vishniac's photographic documentation of pre–World War II Eastern European Jewish culture, this book is mandatory reading for persons interested in the rich Jewish culture that was lost due to the Holocaust. Indexed.

Grossman, Mendel. *With a Camera in the Ghetto.* Edited by Zvi Szner and Alexander Sened. Kibbutz Lohamei-Haghetaot D. N. Western Galilee Israel: Ghetto Fighters' House, 1970. No ISBN. 112 pages. Hardcover.

This compilation of black-and-white photographs by Mendel Grossman illustrates his documentation of life in the Lodz Ghetto. The ninety-six photos included in this book are among the few by Grossman that survived the end of World War II, and their documentary power illustrating the hardships of ghetto life and the efforts by Jews to survive Nazi persecution has rarely been equaled. Excerpts from *The Chronicle of the Lodz Ghetto* are interspersed with the photographs to provide additional contextual details. An appreciation of Grossman's work by Arieh Ben-Menaam, as well as a complete listing of the ninety-six photos and their subjects, is included. No index or bibliography.

Hamburg Institute for Social Research. *The German Army and Genocide: Crimes against War Prisoners, Jews, and Other Civilians, 1939–1944.* New York: New Press, 1999. ISBN 1–56584–525–0. 223 pages. Paperback.

This book, heavily based upon the original German exhibit "The German Army and Genocide," includes black-and-white-photos and accompanying text about the critical role the Wehrmacht played in supporting the consolidation of Nazi power in Germany between 1933 and 1939, and the implementation of the Nazi Germany's genocidal policies between 1939 and 1945. Introduced with a comprehensive critical essay by historian Omer Bartov, the photos and text examine topics as diverse as the German army's activities in Serbia, the Soviet Union, and Poland. An essay by Jan Philipp Reemstsma on the reception of the exhibition in Germany and Austria details the continuing controversy over the legacy of the German army's involvement in genocide, and its implications for German society today. A glossary of German terms used in the text, a listing of abbreviations used in German documents, a set of recommended sources for further reading, a comprehensive listing of photographic credits, and brief biographies of the contributors to the book are provided. This book makes an important contribution to our understanding of the widespread involvement in genocide of major social institutions in Germany during the Third Reich. No index.

Keller, Ulrich, editor. *The Warsaw Ghetto in Photographs*. New York: Dover Publications, 1984. ISBN 0–486–24665–5. 160 pages. Paperback.

Following an introduction by photohistorian and editor Ulrich Keller, 206 black-and-white photos from the Bundesarchiv in Koblenz, Germany are presented about life in the Warsaw Ghetto and the Lodz ghetto. The photos, organized into fifteen categories (examples include "children," "burials," "internal ghetto police," "street scenes," and others), were most likely taken during 1941 by German visitors to the ghetto. The introduction describes the context of how and by whom the photos were taken, the purposes of their creation, and the relationship of the photos to other depictions of ghetto daily life, such as those provided in written documents. An excerpt from Stanislaw Rozycki's diary of life in the Warsaw Ghetto is included as an appendix. No index.

Krizkova, Marie Rut, Kurt Jiri Kotouc, and Zdenek Ornest. *We Are Children Just the Same. Vedem: The Secret Magazine by the Boys of Terezin*. Translated by R. Elizabeth Novak. Edited by Paul Wilson. Foreword by Vaclav Havel. Philadelphia: The Jewish Publication Society, 1995. ISBN 0–8276–0534–X. 199 pages. Hardcover.

This book, heavily illustrated with documentary photographs and photos of artwork created in the Terezin ghetto and camp, contains selected editions of the boys' magazine *Vedem*. This magazine was secretly published in the Terezin camp by thirteen-to-fifteen-year-old boys from 1942 to 1944. This edition contains selected contents from the *Vedem* magazine, commentaries on the magazine texts, reflections by Terezin survivors, poetry and artwork completed in the Terezin ghetto and camp by children, and historic photos that enrich understanding of the daily life discussed in *Vedem*. Two of the editors of this edition were survivors of Terezin, and worked with Marie Rut Krizkova to bring this edition to fruition. Complementing the moving and powerful children's poetry and artwork collection

I Never Saw Another Butterfly, *Vedem* brings to light another important dimension of how children, under the guidance of enlightened adults in Terezin, used their creativity to confront the daily horrors of camp existence. No index or bibliography.

Schwarberg, Gunther. *In the Ghetto of Warsaw: Heinrich Jost's Photographs*. Gottingen: Steidl Verlag, 2001. ISBN 3–88243–214–4. 137 pages. Hardcover.

Displaying one of the most powerful of all Holocaust photo collections, this book contains the complete set of photos taken by German Wehrmacht sergeant Heinrich Jost during his walk through the Warsaw ghetto on September 19, 1941. The photographs were kept in hiding by Jost for over forty years, and were given to journalist Gunther Schwarberg in November 1982 for publication. Schwarberg asked Jost to describe each photo, and those captions are included in this photographic collection. An introduction describing the origins of the photos, and their eventual publication in Germany's *Stern* magazine, as well as their display in photographic exhibitions in Israel, is included. Selected photos from this collection formed the basis for the film *A Day in the Warsaw Ghetto: A Birthday Trip in Hell*, which is discussed in Chapter 13. No index.

Swiebocka, Teresa, compiler and editor. *Auschwitz: A History in Photographs*. English edition prepared by Jonathan Webber and Connie Wilsach. Bloomington: Indiana University Press, 1993. ISBN 0–2533–5581–8. 395 pages. Hardcover.

This collection of photos, many drawn from the Auschwitz State Museum collection, is a visual presentation of the Auschwitz death camp complex using historical and some contemporary photographs. A series of essays are included in the book, addressing the history of Auschwitz, how Auschwitz is presented in documentary photographs, art inspired by Auschwitz, the role of the Auschwitz-Birkenau State Museum, and personal reflections on Auschwitz. Brief contributor biographies are provided, along with notes about the sources of the principal texts quoted in the work, and a series of supplementary photograph captions. No index.

Weinberg, Jeshajahu, and Rina Elieli. *The Holocaust Museum in Washington, D.C.* Foreword by Chaim Potok. New York: Rizzoli International Publications Inc., 1995. ISBN 0–8478–1906–X. 200 pages. Hardcover.

This book, heavily illustrated with color and black-and-white photographs from the U.S. Holocaust Memorial Museum, tells the story of the development, design, and operation of the Museum. Narrative text takes a back seat to the photos, which are of outstanding quality and which highlight many components of the Museum's permanent exhibition, as well as the Museum's architecture. The text, cowritten by the Museum's founding director Jeshajahu Weinberg and consultant Rina Elieli, details the process by which the Museum and its design were created, how the exhibition(s) were developed, and the overall purposes of the Museum as a comprehensive educational and commemorative institution on the Holocaust. Indexed.

Wiesel, Marion, editor. *To Give Them Light: The Legacy of Roman Vishniac.* Preface by Elie Wiesel. New York: Simon & Schuster, 1993. ISBN 0–671–63872–6. 160 pages. Paperback.

Vishniac's black-and-white photos of Eastern European Jewish culture taken between 1936 and 1939 illustrate with compassion and warmth the daily life of communities in Poland, Carpathia, Ruthenia, Czechoslovakia, and Lithuania. The book is divided into eight sections, each focused on a specific location, such as Vilna (then in Poland, now in Lithuania). The editor introduces each location, and many of the 140 photos (each with a caption) in the book are juxtaposed with excerpts from Vishniac's unpublished diaries from the period. A map of Eastern Europe in the mid-1930s is included, which identifies the locations visited or mentioned by Vishniac, as well as other major population centers. The book concludes with a biographical note by Vishniac's daughter. No index.

PHOTOGRAPHS: EXHIBITIONS

The following Web sites provide information about major Holocaust photographic exhibitions, and in some cases provide access to online exhibitions and collections of photographs.

Anne Frank Center USA. http://www.annefrank.com/site/afexhib/ 1exhibhome/1exhibitions.htm. E-mail contact: exhibitions@annefrank.com.

The Anne Frank Center provides information about the content and scheduling of their traveling exhibitions on this Web site. Links to the current schedule of traveling exhibits, past exhibition venues, exhibition specifications, and exhibition sponsorship resources are provided.

United States Holocaust Memorial Museum. http://ushmm.org/. E-mail contact: cslms@ushmm.org.

This Web site contains online exhibitions of artwork, a searchable database of over 1,000 photographs from the Museum's photo archives, and an international listing of Holocaust exhibitions, conferences, and events. The international calendar listing is located at ushmm.org/assets/taskforce/calendar.

Yad Vashem: The Holocaust Martyrs' and Heroes' Remembrance Authority. http://yadvashem.org.il/exhibitions/homeexhibitions.html. E-mail contact: photo.archive@yadvashem.org.il. This section of the Yad Vashem

Web site contains online exhibitions, primarily of photographs. Among the topics currently available are the "Historical Museum Collection," "Visas for Life," "The Auschwitz Album," "No Child's Play," "Photo Archive Collection—Recent Addition" and others. Photographs presented online are taken from the over 130,000 photographs in Yad Vashem's photo archives.

13

FILM AND VIDEOTAPE

OVERVIEW

It is not an understatement to assert that more individuals have likely encountered aspects of the Holocaust through film than through any other medium. This chapter presents entries on books that discuss major trends in film interpretation of the Holocaust, followed by a topical categorization of entries on films about the Holocaust. The films were selected using the following criteria: (1) they had been identified as works of historical and/or contemporary quality by independent experts, (2) they are available in VHS videotape format, and (3) their content enriches the viewer's understanding of the Holocaust and related topics using the unique attributes of motion pictures. Film entries in this chapter include both documentaries and feature films created in many societies, ranging from Europe to North America to Israel. In some cases, films present stories and topics that are discussed in other chapters of this book, but do so in a way that merits further attention and analysis. A listing of film vendors is provided at the end of this chapter. Dates of publication for films were not readily available in most cases, and can be obtained from the vendors.

BOOKS ON HOLOCAUST FILM

Doneson, Judith E. *The Holocaust in American Film*. Philadelphia: Jewish Publication Society, 1987. ISBN 0–8276–0281–2. 262 pages. Hardcover.

Doneson discusses the role of film in shaping the U.S. response to the Holocaust, particularly in the area of attitudes. Films give "image and shape" to the Holocaust, helping to create and revive memory. The author discusses how the U.S. film industry has brought the Holocaust to the attention of a wider international audience, thus producing an "Americanization" of the Holocaust in the global arena. Because films reveal insights about both the historical context of the topic and contemporary meaning and relationships of the Holocaust, Doneson argues that film is a cultural metaphor that provides a structure for understanding that more often than not teaches lessons to the viewer. Seven key trends in Holocaust film are examined: demystification, democratization, universalization, trivialization, politicization, commercialization, and popularization. These trends are employed as part of the author's interpretive framework, which is applied to the historical development of films on Nazism and the Holocaust, beginning in the 1930s and continuing through the mid-1980s, and including films and miniseries made for television. Doneson's work remains a major contribution to the understanding of Holocaust film, and a new version with an expanded discussion of more recent films would be welcomed. Extensive chapter notes, a thorough bibliography, and a filmography are provided, along with a detailed index.

Gellert, Charles Lawrence. *The Holocaust, Israel and the Jews: Motion Pictures in the National Archives.* Washington, DC: National Archives and Records Administration, 1989. ISBN 0–911333–78–9. 117 pages. Hardcover.

This reference work contains 583 annotated entries, as well as an appendix of film titles organized alphabetically. Each annotated entry includes the title, the creator of the item, its date of creation, its time, whether it was a sound film, in black and white or color, and its cataloguing information for the National Archives system. Indexed.

Insdorf, Annette. *Indelible Shadows: Film and the Holocaust.* New York: Random House, 1983. ISBN 0–394–71464–4. 234 pages. Paperback.

Employing a thematic approach, the author seeks to explore the degree to which films from the United States and Europe retain artistic and moral integrity in depiction of the Holocaust. The book contains four sections: "Finding an Appropriate Language," "Narrative Strategies," "Responses to Nazi Atrocity," and "Shaping Reality." Subtopics within each thematic section address between four and nine films each, while the author emphasizes in her discussion of each film how specific cinematic devices express or evade moral issues about their subject matter. The author recognizes that the scope of Holocaust victims included non-Jews, but the book emphasizes films about the genocide of European Jewry. Overall, Insdorf sees film as a way for humans to encounter actual horrors through images that reproduce their actual appearance; films also serve as a way to commemorate the dead, and to help viewers encounter horrors and address their relationship to contemporary consciousness, particularly if they send warnings against blind obedience to governmental authority and the indifference of humans to suffering. A filmography and bibliography are provided, and still images from many of the films are included in the narrative. This wide-ranging analysis of seventy-five films is a worthy companion to Judith Doneson's work on American film, and a more recent edition reflecting films released since the early 1980s would be a valuable addition to the field. Indexed.

Lewis, Stephen. *Art out of Agony: The Holocaust Theme in Literature, Sculpture and Film*. Toronto: CBC Enterprises, 1984. ISBN 0–88794–121–4. 194 pages. Paperback.

This book contains a series of interviews by Canadian broadcaster Stephen Lewis with ten individuals who have helped bring the Holocaust to public attention. Seven individuals are authors, including two survivors (Aharon Appelfeld and Elie Wiesel); others are artists (sculptor George Segal), filmmakers (Hans Jurgen Syderberg), and film historians/critics (Annette Insdorf). Each chapter includes a biographical sketch of the informant, followed by brief observations on the subject and some of the work, followed by the interview transcript. For the authors included in the book, excerpts from their works discussed in the interview are provided. A selected bibliography is included. No index.

Loshitsky, Yosefa, editor. *Spielberg's Holocaust: Critical Perspectives on* Schindler's List. Bloomington: Indiana University Press, 1997. ISBN 0–253–21098–4. 250 pages. Paperback.

Following an introduction by the work's editor, twelve contributors from the fields of history, literature, film, and other humanities disciplines present essays interpreting the content, form, and international response to Steven Spielberg's film *Schindler's List*. Among the contributors are Barbie Zelizer, Judith Doneson, and Jeffrey Shandler, all of whom have written extensively on film and television representations of the Holocaust. Additionally, the book's inclusion of chapters specifically focused on the French, German, and Israeli responses to *Schindler's List* contributes to the expanding scholarly discussion of how both the expert and lay public respond to issues of Holocaust education and remembrance. Each chapter has extensive scholarly documentation, and a brief set of contributor biographies is included.

COLLECTIONS OF HOLOCAUST FILM AND VIDEOTAPE

Beit Lohamei Haghetaot—The Ghetto Fighters' House. Kibbutz Lohamei-Haghetaot, D.N. Western Galilee 25220, Israel. Phone: (972) 4-995-8029. FAX: (972) 4-995-8007. http://www.gfh.org.il. e-mail: yshavit@gfh.org.il.

The Ghetto Fighters' House contains a large collection of films dealing with twentieth century Jewish life in Europe and Israel, as well as many films about the Holocaust, including a collection of German films.

National Center for Jewish Film. Brandeis University—Lown 102 MS 053, Waltham, MA 02254-9110. Phone: 781-899-7044. http://www.jewishfilm.org. e-mail: ncjf@brandeis.edu.

The National Center for Jewish Film contains an archive, lending library, and study center. It houses the world's largest Yiddish film collection, and its collections include over 7,000 cans of film dealing with many aspects of twentieth-century Jewish life, including the Holocaust. It is also the largest distribution library of films and video materials on Jewish content in the world.

United States Holocaust Memorial Museum. 100 Raoul Wallenberg Place, SW, Washington, DC 20024-2156, United States of America. Phone: 202-488-6113. http://ushmm.org. e-mail: archives@ushmm.org.

The film and video archive of the U.S. Holocaust Memorial Museum contains motion picture materials that are used within the Museum's Permanent Exhibition, as well as approximately 200 hours of motion picture footage from the 1920s to 1948, ranging across topics such as pre-war Jewish and Gypsy life, Nazi propaganda films, deportations of Jews to German ghettos and concentration camps, the liberation of Nazi camps in Europe, and others. Additionally, the collection has 250 or more documentary and feature films on the Holocaust and related topics.

Yad Vashem—The Holocaust Martyrs' and Heroes' Remembrance Authority. PO Box 3477, Jerusalem 91034, Israel. Phone (972) 2-644-3712. FAX (972) 2-643-3511. http://www.yadvashem.org.il. e-mail: photo.archive@yadvashem.org.il.

The Film and Photo Department of the Yad Vashem Archive contains over 3,300 video titles, along with 240 in original roll format, which are also available in videotape. Both documentary and feature films are represented in the collection, in many languages. Most of the collection is accessible for viewing and an online search system is available in the reading room of the archives.

FILM AND VIDEOTAPE BY CATEGORY

The videotapes listed in this chapter are organized into five categories. When the content of some individual videotapes and videotape series span more than one category, the decision to locate the videotape listing in a specific category has been based upon where the preponderance of the videotape's content rests. The total time of each videotape and the type of film (feature film, documentary, instructional film) are noted at the conclusion of each entry. Brief descriptions of each film are provided, and where applicable, notes on the appropriateness of the film content for audiences. Film vendors are listed at the conclusion of each entry.

Jewish Life in Europe and the Rise of Nazism (Pre-1933)

Adolf Hitler.

This brief film charts Adolf Hitler's rise to power and his eventual decline, emphasizing the conditions that contributed to the Nazi triumph in Germany. 12 minutes. VHS videotape. Documentary. Vendor: Films for the Humanities and Sciences, Inc.

The Dybbuk.

This historic film, made in Kazimierz, Poland in 1937, concerns the most widely performed play in Yiddish theater. The film presents a classic Yiddish mystical tale, and features the famed cantor Gerszon Sirota in the liturgical performances. Sirota and his family perished in the Warsaw Ghetto in 1943. English subtitles are provided. 121 minutes. VHS videotape. Feature film. Vendor: Bel Canto Society.

Image before My Eyes.

Based upon the book of the same title, this documentary uses historic films, photographs, interviews, music, and commentary to recreate the rich life of Polish Jews prior to World War II. 90 minutes. See the book of the same title in Chapter 12. VHS videotape. Documentary. Vendor: Zenger Video.

Itzhak Perlman: In the Fiddler's House.

Combining musical performances by contemporary klezmer musicians with discussions between Itzhak Perlman and the few remaining klezmer musicians from pre-war Poland, this film explores the rich musical culture that characterized Eastern European Jewish life prior to World War II. 55 minutes. VHS videotape. Documentary. Vendor: Angel Records.

The Longest Hatred: The History of Anti-Semitism.

Employing interviews with eminent scholars as well as historical film footage, this film details the historical development of anti-Semitism from the ancient world to Nazi Germany, and then to its more recent expressions in areas of Europe, the Middle East, and other areas of the world. See Robert Wistrich's book of the same title in Chapter 2. 180 minutes. VHS videotape. Documentary. Vendor: Films for the Humanities and Sciences, Inc.

The Nazi Assumption of Power and the Exclusion of Jews from German Society (1933–1939)

All Jews Out.

Tracing the life of Holocaust survivor and author Inge Auerbacher, this film follows this German Jewish family's odyssey from the mid-1930s in Goppingen, Germany, through the period of their deportation and internment in Theresienstadt. It includes interviews of people in the family's hometown of Goppingen, Germany. 82 minutes. VHS videotape. Documentary. Vendor: National Center for Jewish Film.

Born in Berlin.

This film traces the lives of three young women who lived in Berlin during the 1930s, and how they were affected by the imposition of Nazi racial laws. The film also deals with their response to World War II and its legacy. 85 minutes. VHS videotape. Documentary. Vendor: National Center for Jewish Film.

The Camera of My Family.

This film describes the history of four generations of a German Jewish family, examining the attitudes and values of German Jews and their response to persecution by the Nazis. 18 minutes. VHS videotape. Documentary. Vendor: Anti-Defamation League.

Charlie Grant's War.

This film presents the story of Charlie Grant, a Canadian diamond vendor in Vienna during the 1930s who works to help 600 Jews leave Europe despite the obstacles and restrictions to Jewish emigration imposed by the Canadian government. 125 minutes. VHS videotape. Documentary/Drama. Vendor: Zenger Media.

The Cross and the Star.

This film explores the origins and development of Christian anti-Semitism, and its relationships to the ideology of Nazism. Historical film footage and interviews with Holocaust survivors, clergy, and other experts are included. 55 minutes. VHS videotape. Documentary. Vendor: First Run Icarus Films.

Degenerate Art.

This film explores the Nazi assault on the visual arts, focusing specifically on how individual modern artists in Germany were affected by the imposition of censorship and ideological restrictions on artistic expression. The focal point of the film is the infamous "entartete arte" exhibition in Munich during the Third Reich, which juxtaposed approved "Aryan" art with what the Nazis claimed was "degenerate" art (expressionism, surrealism, works by Jewish artists, and others). 60 minutes. VHS videotape. Documentary. Vendor: PBS Video.

The Double Crossing: The Voyage of the St. Louis.

Using archival footage as well as many interviews with survivors of the *St. Louis* voyage, this film tells the story of how German Jewish refugees could not find a safe haven in the spring of 1939 when the Cuban, U.S., and other world governments refused them entry. 29 minutes. VHS videotape. Documentary. Vendor: Ergo Media, Inc.

The Eye of the Dictator.

This documentary examines the efforts of Nazi propaganda, primarily through use of films and weekly newsreels, to shape public opinion and reinforce conformity to Nazi ideology during the Third Reich. Historic film footage and expert commentary are utilized throughout the documentary. 55 minutes. VHS videotape. Documentary. Vendor: Films for the Humanities and Sciences, Inc.

A Friendship in Vienna.

This film tells the story of the friendship between two young girls, one Jewish and one Christian, in Vienna following the Anschluss in 1938. Although persecution of Jews intensifies, the friendship between the two girls remains strong and unwavering. 94 minutes. VHS videotape. Feature film. Vendor: Buena Vista Home Video.

Heil Hitler! Confessions of a Hitler Youth.

Based upon the book by former Hitler Youth Alfons Heck, this film explores how close to 8,000,000 German youth became part of the Hitler Youth movement, swearing total allegiance to Adolf Hitler and participating in the development of Nazi programs, while observing the persecution of German Jews. Alfons Heck narrates the film, interspersing his personal reflections and commentary with documentary film footage. 30 minutes. VHS videotape. Documentary. Vendor: Social Studies School Service.

Hitler: The Whole Story. Volume 1: The Early Years. Volume 2: The Rise of the Reich. Volume 3: The War Years.

Based upon Joachim Fest's comprehensive biography of Adolf Hitler, this three-volume videotape set traces Hitler's career from the origins of his political aspirations through his rise to power, the development of Germany into a police state and aggressive military power, and the eventual implementation of genocide, and a tragic war ending in Germany's defeat and ruin. 150 minutes. VHS videotape. Documentary. Vendor: BMG Video.

In the Shadow of the Reich: Nazi Medicine.

This film explores the ideological origins as well as the daily efforts of doctors, scientists, and other members of the medical profession who participated in crimes against civilians such as euthanasia, forced sterilization, and medical experimentation under Nazi rule. It also examines the international support for eugenics that contributed to the development of a "biocracy" during the Third Reich in Germany. 54 minutes. VHS videotape. Documentary. Vendor: First Run Features.

Jehovah's Witnesses Stand Firm against Nazi Assault.

This film demonstrates how Jehovah's Witnesses were persecuted in Germany under the Third Reich, along with their response to Nazism. A study guide accompanies the film. 28 minutes. VHS videotape. Documentary. Vendor: Watch Tower Bible and Tract Society of Pennsylvania.

Kristallnacht: The Journey from 1933–1938.

This film includes personal testimonies and archival film footage about the "Night of Broken Glass" in November 1938, when the Nazi government instigated a nationwide pogrom against German and Austrian Jews. It was created for the commemoration of the fiftieth anniversary of Kristallnacht in 1988. 60 minutes. VHS videotape. Documentary. Vendor: WETA, Washington, DC.

The Lost Children of Berlin.

This film explores the contemporary and historical experiences of Jewish children from a Berlin neighborhood who survived the Holocaust. The film intersperses recollections of their home and school life under Nazi rule with their return to the recently reopened Jewish school they attended in the 1930s. 50 minutes. VHS videotape. Documentary. Vendor: Survivors of the Shoah Visual History Foundation.

The Master Race.

This documentary details how Nazi racial ideology developed and how efforts at "coordination" of German institutions (education, medicine, the legal system, and others) were implemented to achieve the goal of a "racial state" during the Third Reich. 20 minutes. VHS videotape. Documentary. Vendor: Films for the Sciences and Humanities, Inc.

The Music Survives.

Presented as a package with an accompanying compact disc of musical excerpts, this documentary presents the efforts of the Decca record company to bring to light music of composers determined "degenerate" by the Nazi regime. Historical film footage, interviews with musicians, composers, and experts, and excerpts from performances of works by "banned" composers are included. See the compact disc recording of the same title in Chapter 15. 30 minutes. VHS videotape. Documentary. Vendor: Decca Record Company.

The Nazis.

This six-volume documentary series draws upon much recent research and explores how Nazism came to power in Germany, consolidated its control over German society, engaged in aggressive war and policies of genocide, and eventually was defeated by its opponents. Film footage from archives previously closed to researchers in the former Soviet bloc, formerly unpublished documents, as well as interviews with a wide range of informants characterize the video series. 300 minutes. VHS videotape. Documentary. Vendor: New Video Group.

Swing Kids.

Based upon the historical movement of German teenagers who defied Nazi censorship and advocated appreciation of swing and jazz music, this film tells the story of how a group of German teenagers sustained their devotion to "swing" when confronted with the persecution of the Gestapo and the pressure to join the Hitler Youth. 114 minutes. VHS videotape. Feature film. Vendor: Buena Vista Home Video.

Triumph of the Will.

This documentary of the 1934 Sixth Annual Party Congress in Nuremberg is a glorification of Adolf Hitler, the National Socialist Party, and Nazi ideology. The cinematography makes clear how Nazi ideology submerged the individual to the mass, a key element of Nazism. 110 minutes. VHS videotape. Documentary. Vendor: Social Studies School Service.

World War II and Nazi Domination of Europe (1939–1941)

Assignment Rescue.

This film examines how Varian Fry, an American journalist working for the International Rescue Committee in Vichy France, worked to save over 1,500 Jews and political enemies of the Third Reich during the period following the fall of France. 26 minutes. VHS videotape. Documentary. Vendor: Social Studies School Service.

The Exiles.

This film examines the plight of intellectuals, scholars, and artists who suffered from repression under the Nazis, and their experiences in both seeking exile and readjusting to their new homelands. 116 minutes. VHS videotape. Documentary. Vendor: Connoisseur Video Collection.

From Swastika to Jim Crow.

This film explores the interaction between Jewish intellectuals who emigrated to the United States in the 1930s and their students at black colleges and universities in the South. Facing anti-Semitism and distrust of immigrants in higher education, the emigré scholars rose to positions at institutions such as Howard University, Tugalou College, and Hampton Institute, establishing lifelong relationships with their African-American students and making important contributions to their local communities. The efforts of Jewish scholars and African-American scholars to share their dual burdens of oppression and discrimination is a major theme emphasized in the film. 60 minutes. VHS videotape. Documentary. Vendor: The Cinema Guild.

The Garden of the Finzi-Continis.

This film tells the story of how an upper-class Italian Jewish family is gradually destroyed by Mussolini's anti-Semitic campaign, as well as their failure to recognize the implications of such efforts for Italian Jews. 95 minutes. VHS videotape. Feature film. Vendor: Social Studies School Service.

The Visas that Saved Lives.

Relating the story of Japanese consulate Chiune Sugihara, this film tells the story of how Sugihara defied both the Nazis and his own government and issued over 1,600 visas to Jews in Lithuania to help them find refuge from persecution. 115 minutes. VHS videotape. Documentary/Drama. Vendor: Ergo Media, Inc.

Implementation of Mass Murder and World Responses (1941–1945)

Act of Faith.

This is a brief film using first-hand evidence on the rescue of Danish Jews from the Nazis in 1943. 28 minutes. VHS videotape. Documentary. Vendor: Anti-Defamation League.

America and the Holocaust: Deceit and Indifference.

Using the efforts by German emigré Kurt Klein to secure entry for his parents into the United States during the pre-World War II period, this film examines the factors contributing to the U.S. response to the Holocaust, notably the issue of refugee policy and efforts at rescue. 87 minutes. VHS videotape. Documentary. Vendor: PBS Video.

Anne Frank: The Life of a Young Girl.

This segment in the Arts and Entertainment Network's *Biography* series on "Legendary Women" focuses on Anne Frank, drawing upon her diary and other sources to tell the story of her brief life. 50 minutes. VHS videotape. Documentary. Vendor: New Video Group.

Anne Frank: The Missing Chapter.

This video presents findings from the book *Anne Frank [The Biography]* by Melissa Muller, which portrays other aspects of Anne Frank's life that were not highlighted in the famous diary. Included are segments about Anne Frank's concerns regarding the difficulties evident in her parents' marriage, the life of the Frank family in Germany before their emigration to Holland, and investigation of the motives behind the betrayal of the Frank family in Amsterdam, which eventually led to their deportation to the East. See Chapter 8 for the entry on Melissa Muller's biography. 45 minutes. VHS videotape. Documentary. Vendor: Home Vision Entertainment.

Anne Frank Remembered.

This film presents remembrances of Anne Frank's life and family, employing interviews with her contemporaries, documents, and archival photographs. 117 minutes. VHS videotape. Documentary. Vendor: Social Studies School Service.

Art and Remembrance: The Legacy of Felix Nussbaum.

This film details the life and work of Felix Nussbaum, a German Jewish artist who created paintings about European Jews during the Holocaust before he was deported from Belgium and murdered in Auschwitz. 29 minutes. VHS videotape. Documentary. Vendor: First Run/Icarus Films.

As If It Were Yesterday.

This film explores the efforts of Belgian people who acted to save over 4,000 Jewish children by hiding them or helping them evade deportation to death camps. 85 minutes. VHS videotape. Documentary. Vendor: Almi Home Video Corporation.

The Assassination of Reinhard Heydrich.

This film relates the story of how the Czech resistance in 1942 assassinated Reinhard Heydrich, the SS leader designated to oversee implementation of the "final solution" to the Jewish Question. 56 minutes. VHS videotape. Documentary/Drama. Vendor: U.S. Holocaust Memorial Museum.

The Assisi Underground.

This film tells the story of how Catholic priests, Italian partisans, and local residents of the Assisi region rescued Italian Jews during the German occupation of Italy after mid-September 1943. 115 minutes. VHS videotape. Feature film. Vendor: Social Studies School Service.

The Attic.

Based upon the book *Anne Frank Remembered*, this film tells the story of how Miep Gies assisted Anne Frank, her family, and other Dutch Jews in efforts to hide them during the Nazi occupation of the Netherlands. 95 minutes. VHS videotape. Feature film. Vendor: Zenger Media.

Au Revoir les Enfants.

Drawing upon filmmaker Louis Malle's experiences in World War II, this film tells the story of how a friendship between a Catholic schoolboy and his Jewish friend emerged during World War II. The Jewish schoolboy, given refuge by a Catholic priest, eventually is betrayed and sent to Auschwitz with the Catholic priest who had aided him. 103 minutes. VHS videotape. Feature film. Vendor: Social Studies School Service.

Auschwitz and the Allies.

This film details the story of how two men escaped from Auschwitz and shared their stories about the systematic mass murder of Jews and other targeted victims at the largest extermination center in Europe. 113 minutes. VHS videotape. Documentary. Vendor: Films Incorporated.

Bach in Auschwitz.

This film examines the experiences of the musicians who performed in the women's orchestra at Auschwitz-Birkenau, using interviews with survivors as well as documentary sources. 105 minutes. VHS videotape. Documentary. Vendor: FoxLorber.

Bergen-Belsen, United States Congress Tour of Camps in 1945.

This film essay of Bergen-Belsen discusses initial American encounters with the liberated camp of Bergen-Belsen, as discussed by the daughter of the U.S. photographer sent to the camp in 1945 and a U.S. congressman who visited the camp at the invitation of General Eisenhower. 30 minutes. VHS videotape. Documentary. Vendor: Emory University.

Bergen-Belsen, Woebbelin, and Gardelegen Massacres.

This film presents eyewitness accounts of the liberation of the Bergen-Belsen camp and the Woebbelin and Gardelegen massacres of Jews late in the war. 30 minutes. VHS videotape. Documentary. Vendor: Emory University.

The Bielski Brothers.

This film examines the resistance activities of the two brothers who led the largest Jewish partisan unit in Occupied Europe (Byelorussia) during World War II. 53 minutes. VHS videotape. Documentary. Vendor: Films for the Humanities and Sciences, Inc.

Blood Money: Switzerland's Nazi Gold.

This documentary deals with the ongoing controversy concerning Switzerland's economic and financial relationships with Nazi Germany during the period 1939–1945. 100 minutes. VHS videotape. Documentary. Vendor: Ergo Media, Inc.

The Boat Is Full.

This film tells the story of five Jews who escape from Germany and try to avoid deportation from Switzerland by posing as a family that has standing to remain in Switzerland. Eventually betrayed by an innkeeper and her husband, the family is returned to Germany by Swiss bureaucrats. 104 minutes. VHS videotape. Feature Film. Vendor: Social Studies School Service.

Buchenwald.

Three soldiers who encountered Buchenwald as liberators describe their experiences, which are interspersed with historical photographs and archival film footage of the liberation at Buchenwald. 30 minutes. VHS videotape. Documentary. Vendor: Emory University.

Camp of Hope and Despair—Witnesses of Westerbork.

Using eyewitness accounts, historical photos, and film footage from the period, this film examines the daily life in the Westerbork camp, which was used as a concentration/transit camp for the deportations of Dutch Jews to Eastern Europe. 70 minutes. VHS videotape. Documentary. Vendor: Ergo Media, Inc.

The Children from Villa Emma.

This film explores the rescue of a group of Jewish children by Italian peasants and partisans in Northern Italy during the German occupation of Italy following September 1943. Interviews with the survivors, now adults, are included. 50 minutes. VHS videotape. Documentary/Drama. Vendor: Doko Media.

Children in the Holocaust.

This film describes the experience of children during the Holocaust, as related by adult survivors who were children during the Nazi occupation of Europe. 70 minutes. VHS videotape. Documentary. Vendor: Phoenix Films and Video, Inc.

The Children of Izieu.

This film examines the deportation and eventual murder of forty-four Jewish children and their five adult supervisors in 1944 from the orphanage Maison d'Izieu, an act ordered by war criminal Klaus Barbie. Interviews with the remaining eyewitnesses to the SS raid on the orphanage and with Serge and Beate Klarsfeld are included. 28 minutes. VHS videotape. Documentary. Vendor: National Center for Jewish Film.

Choosing One's Way—Resistance in Auschwitz-Birkenau.

This documentary describes the resistance efforts conducted in Auschwitz-Birkenau, focusing primarily on the destruction of Crematorium Four in 1944 by a group of prisoners. Eyewitness accounts by survivors of Auschwitz-Birkenau are included in the film. 30 minutes. VHS videotape. Documentary. Vendor: Ergo Media, Inc.

Courage to Care.

This film explores the actions of individuals who helped to hide, rescue, or provide support for Jews during the Holocaust. Interviews with rescuers and survivors who lived as a result of the efforts by these Righteous Gentiles are combined with contemporary film footage and historical photographs. See the book of the same title in Chapter 3. 28 minutes. VHS videotape. Documentary. Vendor: Anti-Defamation League.

A Day in the Warsaw Ghetto: A Birthday Trip in Hell.

Documentary photographs by a German army sergeant taken illegally in the Warsaw Ghetto are combined with ghetto diary readings, Yiddish songs, and klezmer music to provide an eyewitness perspective on ghetto life in 1941. See the collection of photographs compiled by Gunther Schwarberg in Chapter 12. 30 minutes. VHS videotape. Documentary. Vendor: Filmmakers Library, Inc.

A Debt to Honor.

This film examines the efforts of Italian clergy and laypersons who acted on behalf of Jews by risking their lives to provide refuge and support for Jews during the German occupation of Italy. Interviews with rescuers and survivors are included. 29 minutes. VHS videotape. Documentary. Vendor: Documentaries International.

The Diary of Anne Frank.

Based upon the famous diary, this film was the first feature-length film rendering of the Anne Frank story. See the *Diary* entry in Chapter 8. 151 minutes. VHS videotape. Feature film. Vendor: Social Studies School Service.

Escape from Sobibor.

This film draws upon eyewitness accounts to tell the story of the largest death camp escape during World War II, when over 250 prisoners at the Sobibor extermination camp revolted and escaped in 1943. 120 minutes. VHS videotape. Documentary/Drama. Vendor: Social Studies School Service.

Europa Europa.

This film relates the story of Solomon Perel, a German-Jewish teenager who disguised his identity and survived by living as a Nazi following the German invasion of Poland. 115 minutes. VHS videotape. Feature film. Vendor: Orion Home Video.

Forest of Valor.

Historic film footage obtained from Soviet archives, interviews with surviving Jewish partisans, and contemporary film footage of areas where partisan activities were undertaken are highlighted in this documentary about Jewish partisans in the Rudniki and Nalibuki forests of Eastern Europe. 52 minutes. VHS videotape. Documentary. Vendor: SISU Home Entertainment.

The Führer Gives a City to the Jews.

This historic film, restored although incomplete, is the only film made by Germans inside any operating concentration camp. It was meant to be shown to the International Red Cross on occasion of their 1944 visit to the Theresienstadt camp, and is an elaborately staged movie presenting a false and deceptive impression of camp life. Most of the individuals who were in the film, including the director, were sent to Auschwitz upon its completion. 23 minutes. VHS videotape. Documentary. Vendor: National Center for Jewish Film.

Holocaust: Liberation of Auschwitz.

This film documents the liberation of Auschwitz by Soviet forces on January 27, 1945 and offers commentary about the atrocities carried out by the Nazis on camp inmates. 19 minutes. VHS videotape. Documentary. Vendor: Social Studies School Service. *Graphic content.*

Holocaust: Parts 1, 2, and 3.

Divided into three parts, this film explores the history of the Nazi period through the lives of two families who take different paths in response to the rise of Nazism. 7 hours and 30 minutes. Documentary/Drama. VHS videotape. Vendor: Social Studies School Service.

The Holocaust: A Teenager's Experience.

This instructional video and accompanying teacher's guide and learning materials relate the story of David Bergman, who survived the Holocaust as a teenager. The film integrates historical photos with artwork by David Bergman reflecting his experiences in Poland, Germany, and Austria. 30 minutes. VHS videotape. Instructional video with teacher's guide and learning materials. Vendor: United Learning.

The Holocaust: Through Our Own Eyes.

This film tells the story of the Holocaust by relying upon first-hand accounts by survivors, non-Jewish citizens of Occupied Europe, refugees, individuals in hiding, and liberators. Combined with archival footage and historical photos, the eyewitness excerpts begin with the end of World War I and continue through to the liberation of the camps in 1945. 58 minutes. VHS videotape. Documentary. Vendor: Midwest Center for Holocaust Education.

It Was Nothing . . . It Was Everything.

Exploring the experiences of Greek Jews who were rescued and helped by Christian Greeks, this film uses archival photographs and film footage as well as interviews with rescuers and survivors to tell this story of moral heroism. 28 minutes. VHS videotape. Documentary. Vendor: Ergo Media, Inc.

Jakob the Liar.

Based upon the novel by Jurek Becker, this feature film stars Robin Williams as Jacob Heym, who lives in a Polish ghetto. Overhearing a clandestine newscast relating the story of a German defeat at the hands of Soviet forces, Heym gains access to a radio and spreads rumors of Allied advances to raise the hopes and spirits of the ghetto inhabitants. Later, the Germans find out about his efforts, eventually locate him, and deport ghetto inhabitants to a death camp. See the entry on the fictional novel in Chapter 4. 120 minutes. VHS videotape. Feature film. Vendor: U.S. Holocaust Memorial Museum.

The Janowska Camp at Lvov.

Detailing the fate of the over 200,00 Jews from Galicia who were deported to the Janowska camp, this film interviews survivors and others, including Simon Wiesenthal, to shed light on the horrors of the Janowska camp. Of the over 200,000 who were deported to Janowska, only 300 survived. 52 minutes. VHS videotape. Documentary. Vendor: Ergo Media, Inc.

The Journey of the Butterfly.

Integrating music, art, poetry, and history, this film relates the story of children imprisoned in the Terezin ghetto between 1941 and 1945. 62 minutes. VHS videotape. Documentary. Vendor: U.S. Holocaust Memorial Museum.

Korczak.

Relating the true story of Janusz Korczak, the internationally recognized children's rights advocate and orphanage director, this film traces his life during the period from the late 1930s through the German occupation of Poland. Despite opportunities for escape, Korczak refused to abandon his children at the orphanage and supported them until the entire orphanage, as well as Korczak, were deported in 1942 to be murdered at Treblinka. 118 minutes. VHS videotape. Feature film. Vendor: Social Studies School Service.

Kovno Ghetto: A Buried History.

Drawing upon the hidden diaries, photos, and recollections of eighteen Kovno survivors, this documentary reconstructs life in the Kovno ghetto, where the effort to prepare records of the ghetto experience in both written and photographic records survived the ghetto's destruction and the passage of decades following liberation by Soviet forces. 100 minutes. VHS videotape. Documentary. Vendor: New Video Group.

The Last Days.

Detailing the lives of five Hungarian survivors of the Holocaust, this film examines the last major deportations and mass killings of the Holocaust, which followed the Nazi occupation of Hungary in 1944. Archival footage as well as interviews are interspersed with returns of the survivors to their hometowns and the sites of the persecution. Vendor: 87 minutes. VHS videotape. Documentary. Vendor: Survivors of the Shoah Visual History Foundation.

The Last Seven Days of Anne Frank.

Relying upon interviews with eight women who were with Anne Frank and her family in the Westerbork, Auschwitz-Birkenau, and Bergen-Belsen camps, this film examines what the Frank family experienced, particularly what occurred after the final diary entry. 75 minutes. VHS videotape. Documentary. Vendor: Simon Wiesenthal Center.

Liberation 1945: Testimony.

This film, originally used as part of an exhibit at the U.S. Holocaust Memorial Museum about the liberation of the camps, contains thematic segments incorporating survivor and liberator testimony, interspersed with unifying commentary. Some archival footage is employed in addition to the interview excerpts. 60

minutes. VHS videotape. Documentary. Vendor: U.S. Holocaust Memorial Museum.

The Liberation of Auschwitz.

This documentary includes previously unreleased film footage of the liberation by Soviet forces on January 27, 1945, as well as an interview with an eyewitness Soviet cameraman. Film footage taken between January 27 and February 28, 1945 clearly documents the evidence of Nazi crimes at the Auschwitz death camp. 55 minutes. VHS videotape. Documentary. Vendor: National Center for Jewish Film.

Liberators: Fighting on Two Fronts in World War II.

Examining the African-American members of the 761st Tank Battalion who participated in the liberation of the Buchenwald, Dachau, and Lambach concentration camps, this film addresses not only the astonishment of the soldiers upon encountering Nazi atrocities, but also the discrimination and violence faced by those soldiers in the segregated U.S. army of World War II. 55 minutes. VHS videotape. Documentary. Vendor: Direct Cinema Limited.

Life Is Beautiful.

This film explores the response of a Jewish family to persecution of Jews in Italy during World War II, as well as to the deportation of the father and son to a German concentration camp. 118 minutes. VHS videotape. Feature film. Vendor: Social Studies School Service.

Lodz Ghetto.

Based upon the secret diaries of individuals in the Lodz ghetto, this documentary integrates the actual words of ghetto inhabitants with historical photos taken in the ghetto and contemporary footage to relate the story of how 200,000 persons struggled to survive under Nazi occupation. 118 minutes. VHS videotape. Documentary. Vendor: Social Studies School Service.

Memory of the Camps.

Brought to light after four decades of residing in a vault at the British Imperial War Museum, this film includes the record of British and American film crews that encountered Nazi concentration camps in 1945. Scenes of gas chambers, crematoria, medical experimentation labs, and survivors in Dachau, Auschwitz, and Buchenwald along with other camps are presented. 60 minutes. VHS Videotape. Documentary. Vendor: PBS Video. *Graphic content.*

Nazi War Crimes: Babi Yar.

This documentary presents the story of the mass murder of Jews at Babi Yar in the Ukraine. Historical film footage and documentary photos are combined with interviews with survivors. 50 minutes. VHS videotape. Documentary. Vendor: MPI Home Video.

Night and Fog.

Combining historical black-and-white footage of the camps with color scenes of the same locations ten years after the Holocaust, this film attempts to depict the world of the camps. It contains explicit scenes of Nazi atrocities. 31 minutes. VHS videotape. Documentary. Vendor: Social Studies School Service. *Graphic content.*

Not Like Sheep to the Slaughter: The Story of the Bialystok Ghetto.

This film examines the resistance movement in the Bialystok ghetto, where resistance fighters led by twenty-four-year-old Mordechai Tenenbaum attempted to block the Nazi plan to liquidate the ghetto. Interviews with survivors and witnesses are heavily employed in the film. 150 minutes. VHS videotape. Documentary. Vendor: Ergo Media, Inc.

One Survivor Remembers.

Gerda Weissman Klein relates the story of her life as a Holocaust survivor, combining historical photographs, contemporary film footage, and personal recollections. 39 minutes. VHS videotape. Documentary. Vendor: Direct Cinema Limited.

The Only Way.

This film focuses on one Jewish family in Denmark, emphasizing how Danes from many walks of life assisted Jews to rescue them from Nazi deportation. 86 minutes. VHS videotape. Feature film. Vendor: Social Studies School Service.

Opening the Gates of Hell: American Liberators of the Nazi Concentration Camps.

This film presents interviews with American soldiers who were present at the liberation of the Buchenwald, Dachau, Nordhausen, Landsberg, Orhdruf, and Mauthausen camps. Interspersed with the interview content is archival footage filmed in the camps at liberation and soon thereafter. 45 minutes. VHS videotape. Documentary. Vendor: Ergo Media, Inc.

The Other Side of Faith.

This film explores the words and feelings of two individuals: one a Jew seeking refuge and the other a Polish Gentile who acted heroically to save the Jew from Nazi oppression. 27 minutes. VHS videotape. Documentary. Vendor: Documentaries International.

Partisans of Vilna.

Using interviews with surviving partisans and rare archival footage from the period 1939–1944, this documentary tells the story of partisan resistance by Jews in the Vilna ghetto and the forests of Lithuania and Poland. 130 minutes. VHS videotape. Documentary. Vendor: Social Studies School Service.

The Power of Conscience: The Danish Resistance and the Rescue of the Jews.

Employing extensive material from interviews with rescuers and the rescued, this film recounts the story of how Danes saved over ninety percent of the Danish Jews from Nazi persecution in 1943. 55 minutes. VHS videotape. Documentary. Vendor: Direct Cinema Limited.

Purple Triangles.

This documentary, focusing on the history of the Kusserow family in Germany, details the persecution of Jehovah's Witnesses at the hands of the Third Reich. 25 minutes. VHS videotape. Documentary. Vendor: Watch Tower Bible and Tract Society of Pennsylvania.

Raoul Wallenberg: Between the Lines.

Utilizing interviews with colleagues and survivors, archival footage, and newsreel excerpts, this film details the efforts by Raoul Wallenberg to provide a safe haven for Jews in Budapest during the Nazi deportations from Hungary in 1944. 85 minutes. VHS Videotape. Documentary. Vendor: Facets Multimedia, Inc.

Rescue in October.

This brief film tells the story of the rescue of Danish Jews from Nazi persecution in October 1943. 15 minutes. VHS videotape. Documentary. Vendor: Anti-Defamation League.

Rescue in Scandinavia.

This film relates how Jews in Norway, Denmark, Sweden, and Finland were helped and given refuge during the Holocaust. Narrated by Liv Ullmann, the film uses interviews with survivors and rescuers, as well as archival photographs and film footage to explain how Jews were rescued. 55 minutes. VHS videotape. Documentary. Vendor: Ergo Media, Inc.

Rescuers: Stories of Courage. Two Couples.

Based upon true stories from the book *Rescuers: Portraits of Moral Courage in the Holocaust* by Gay Block and Malka Drucker, this film tells the story of two couples who risked their lives to hide Jewish refugees during World War II. 109 minutes. VHS videotape. Feature film. Vendor: Paramount Pictures.

Rescuers: Stories of Courage. Two Families.

Based upon true stories from the book *Rescuers: Portraits of Moral Courage in the Holocaust* by Gay Block and Malka Drucker, this film tells the story of two families who assisted Jews during the Holocaust. One family provides the help required for a Jewish refugee and others to escape from a Nazi prison camp, while the other hides a Jewish family in their traveling circus. 105 minutes. VHS videotape. Feature film. Vendor: Paramount Pictures.

Rescuers: Stories of Courage. Two Women.

Based upon true stories from the book *Rescuers: Portraits of Moral Courage in the Holocaust* by Gay Block and Malka Drucker, this film tells the story of two women who risked their lives to assist Jews during the Holocaust, one in Poland and the other in France. 107 minutes. VHS videotape. Feature film. Vendor: Paramount Pictures.

The Restless Conscience.

Using historical film footage, interviews with participants in the resistance movement, and commentary by scholars, this film examines the anti-Nazi resistance movement within Germany between 1933 and 1945. 113 minutes. VHS videotape. Documentary. Vendor: Direct Cinema Limited.

The Righteous Enemy.

This documentary presents the story of how the Italian diplomatic corps and military refused to turn over Jews in occupied areas of Europe to German officials for deportation. Combining historical film footage, archival photographs, and interviews with both survivors and experts, the film presents the Italian rescue efforts in a comprehensive, yet personal manner. 84 minutes. VHS videotape. Documentary. Vendor: National Center for Jewish Film.

The Road to Wannsee: Eleven Million Sentenced to Death.

Combining rare archival footage with commentary and interviews by scholars, this film traces Hitler's rise to power, his political goals, and his genocidal project of annihilating the Jews of Europe. 50 minutes. VHS videotape. Documentary. Vendor: Ergo Media, Inc.

Schindler.

This documentary tells the story of Oskar Schindler, the German businessman who changed from war profiteer to rescuer of over 1,100 Jews during the Holocaust. Interviews with Schindler's widow, Emilie, survivors rescued by Schindler, and individuals who worked with Schindler are combined with archival film and historical photos to relate this complex story. 82 minutes. VHS videotape. Documentary. Vendor: HBO Video.

Schindler's List.

The most widely viewed Holocaust film in history, *Schindler's List* by Steven Spielberg is the story of Oskar Schindler, who despite his Nazi affiliations emerged as the rescuer of over 1,100 Jews during the Holocaust. 197 minutes. VHS videotape. Feature film. Vendor: Social Studies School Service.

Theresienstadt: Gateway to Auschwitz.

This film explores the daily life of the 15,000 children who were imprisoned in the "model" ghetto and camp of Theresienstadt. Emphasizing the use of cultural activities to retain the dignity and humanity of the children, the film uses interviews with child survivors and other sources to tell its tragic story. 57 minutes. VHS videotape. Documentary. Vendor: Ergo Media, Inc.

They Risked Their Lives: Rescuers of the Holocaust.

Based upon the book by Gay Block and Malka Drucker, this film explores the motivations and behaviors of individuals who risked their lives to rescue Jews, primarily drawing upon interviews with the rescuers themselves. 54 minutes. VHS videotape. Documentary. Vendor: Ergo Media, Inc.

Tsvi Nussbaum: A Boy from Warsaw.

The famous photograph of a boy holding his hands in the air as the Nazis liquidate the Warsaw Ghetto does not reveal the boy's name, but this video does by exploring the life of Dr. Tsvi C. Nussbaum, the subject of that famous photograph. 50 minutes. VHS videotape. Documentary. Vendor: Ergo Media, Inc.

The Wannsee Conference.

Utilizing actual notes from the January 20, 1942 meeting at the Wannsee Villa outside of Berlin, as well as letters of Hermann Goering and Adolf Eichmann and testimony by Eichmann at his 1961 trial in Israel, the filmmakers have reconstructed the meeting where details of the "final solution to the Jewish question" were systematically discussed and planned. 85 minutes. VHS videotape. Documentary/Drama. Vendor: Films Incorporated.

The Warsaw Ghetto.

This film draws heavily upon a compilation of Nazi photographs, depicting the life in the ghetto as well as how Jews struggled to stay alive in the most difficult of circumstances. 51 minutes. VHS videotape. Documentary. Vendor: Social Studies School Service.

The Warsaw Ghetto: Holocaust and Resistance, a Documentary.

Narrated by Theodore Bikel and including the voice of Jewish underground fighter Vladka Meed, this film presents the story of the Warsaw Ghetto uprising, highlighting the courage of the resistance movement to Nazi persecution. 30 minutes. VHS videotape. Filmstrip converted to videotape with teacher's guide. Vendor: Jewish Labor Committee.

We Were Marked with a Big "A."

This film relates the story of three homosexuals who suffered oppression at the hands of Nazi Germany. 44 minutes. VHS videotape. Documentary. Vendor: U.S. Holocaust Memorial Museum.

We Were There: Jewish Liberators of the Nazi Concentration Camps.

This film examines the special relationships that developed between Jewish members of the American military who participated in the liberation of concentration camps and the survivors of those camps. 35 minutes. VHS videotape. Documentary. Vendor: U.S. Holocaust Memorial Museum.

Weapons of the Spirit.

This film tells the story of Le Chambon, a small village inhabited by French Protestants who managed to save 5,000 Jews during the Holocaust. Interviews with rescuers are an important element of this documentary film, which is based upon a longer film of ninety minutes' duration made by Pierre Sauvage, who was born in Le Chambon to Jewish parents who had been hidden by the villagers. 30 minutes. VHS videotape. Documentary. Vendor: Anti-Defamation League.

The White Rose.

Telling the story of the small group of German students and their professor who opposed the Nazi regime, this film accurately renders the experiences of how the White Rose group distributed anti-Nazi leaflets until they were exposed and prosecuted for their activities by the Nazi government in 1943. 108 minutes. VHS videotape. Feature film. Vendor: National Center for Jewish Film.

Who Shall Live and Who Shall Die?

This film examines the response to the Holocaust by American Jews and the U.S. government during the period of the Third Reich. 90 minutes. VHS videotape. Documentary. Vendor: Zenger Video.

Witness: Voices from the Holocaust.

This documentary, drawn primarily from the archives of the Fortunoff Video Archive for Holocaust Testimonies at Yale University, presents testimonies and rare archival footage regarding the breadth of the Nazi era. Included are testimony excerpts from a Hitler Youth, clergy, resistance fighters, survivors of death camps, American POWs, and liberators. See the book of the same name in Chapter 7. 90 minutes. VHS videotape. Documentary. Vendor: Joshua M. Greene Productions.

The World at War. Volume 20: Genocide, 1941–1945.

This film presents, in precise detail, the implementation of Nazi Germany's genocidal project against European Jews. Interviews with survivors, concentration camp guards, and others are interspersed with powerful archival photographs and film footage to tell the story. 52 minutes. VHS videotape. Documentary. Vendor: HBO Video.

The World of Anne Frank.

This film intersperses recreations of Anne Frank's diary with historical film footage, archival photographs, and interviews with Anne Frank's father and others to present a picture of the world in which Anne Frank lived and tragically died as a teenager. 28 minutes. VHS Videotape. Documentary/Drama. Vendor: Ergo Media, Inc.

Zegota: A Time to Remember.

This film relates the story of the Zegota organization, comprised of Polish Jewish Christians who aided Polish Jews during the Holocaust. Interviews with Christian rescuers and Jewish survivors are a compelling aspect of this documentary. 52 minutes. VHS videotape. Documentary. Vendor: Documentaries International.

Post-war Trials and the Legacy of the Holocaust for Contemporary Society (1945–present)

About the Holocaust.

The daughter of a death camp survivor discusses her search for understanding about the Holocaust. Included are personal accounts of survivors and some documentary film segments. 26 minutes. VHS videotape. Documentary. Vendor: Anti-Defamation League.

Anne Frank in Maine.

Describing one junior high school's study of the Holocaust, this film describes how classroom instruction on the topic eventually mobilizes the entire town to become involved in Holocaust study, with the *Diary of Anne Frank* as the entry point. 30 minutes. VHS videotape. Documentary. Vendor: Anti-Defamation League.

Anschluss + 50 Years.

This film examines the post-war interpretation of Austria's support of Nazism during and following the Anschluss of 1938, with particular attention to the controversy surrounding Austrian President Kurt Waldheim's role in World War II. 14 minutes. VHS videotape. Documentary. Vendor: Films for the Humanities and Sciences, Inc.

Auschwitz: If You Cried, You Died.

This film relates the return of two Holocaust survivors to the Auschwitz camp complex and their response during that experience. 28 minutes. VHS videotape. Documentary. Vendor: Impact America Foundation.

The Avenue of the Just.

This film details the efforts by individuals in Europe to save Jews during the Holocaust, with emphasis placed on those righteous gentiles honored at Yad Vashem in Jerusalem. 58 minutes. VHS videotape. Documentary. Vendor: Anti-Defamation League.

Beate Klarsfeld: Bringing Nazi War Criminals to Justice.

This film describes the work of Beate Klarsfeld, who brought Klaus Barbie, the "Butcher of Lyons," and other Nazi war criminals to justice. 30 minutes. VHS videotape. Documentary. Vendor: Films for the Humanities and Sciences, Inc.

Bent.

Based upon Martin Sherman's play, this film portrays the persecution of homosexuals in Nazi Germany. Although *Bent* had been produced in the late 1960s for the stage, the screen version was not produced until 1996. Included in the film version is the song "The Streets of Berlin" by American composer Philip Glass, written in collaboration with playwright Martin Sherman. 104 minutes. VHS videotape. Feature film. Vendor: MGM Home Entertainment.

Breaking the Silence.

This film examines how children of survivors have come to terms with the survivor experiences of their parents. Interviews and discussion sessions with survivors and second-generation members are included, along with explanations by experts. 60 minutes. VHS videotape. Documentary. Vendor: PBS Video.

Child of Two Worlds.

This film examines the lives of five hidden children who survived the war by being raised in Christian families. The film examines their individual stories of survival and how they returned to their Jewish roots in adult life. 60 minutes. VHS videotape. Documentary. Vendor: Ergo Media, Inc.

The Demjanjuk Trial.

This documentary examines the complexities of the trial in Israel of John Demjanjuk, accused as "Ivan the Terrible" for his alleged cruelties as a guard at the Treblinka death camp. The courtroom proceedings and issues that surrounded the trial are addressed in detail in the film. 50 minutes. VHS videotape. Documentary. Vendor: Ergo Media, Inc.

The Devil's Arithmetic.

This film, based upon the novel of the same title, relates the story of a contemporary American Jewish teenager who is transported back in time to a concentration camp where she comes to the realization of what European Jews endured during the Holocaust. See the book of the same title in Chapter 5. 97 minutes. Feature film. Vendor: Social Studies School Service.

The Eighty-First Blow.

Composed of testimonies gathered at the Eichmann trial in 1961, this documentary was produced by the Ghetto Fighters' House of Lochamei Hagetaot in Israel. Archival photos and film footage are employed with the testimonies to give a first-hand account of the Holocaust from the survivors' perspectives. 115 minutes. VHS videotape. Documentary. Vendor: Ergo Media, Inc.

Father's Return to Auschwitz.

Detailing the story of Jan Drabek, a Christian who joined the Czech resistance in World War II, this film describes how Drabek was captured, interned in Auschwitz, and decades later returned to Auschwitz with his son, who filmed the documentary. 20 minutes. VHS videotape. Documentary. Vendor: Anti-Defamation League.

For the Living: The Story of the United States Holocaust Memorial Museum.

This documentary examines the origins, development, and completion of the U.S. Holocaust Memorial Museum in Washington, DC. 57 minutes. Documentary. Vendor: WETA, Washington, DC.

Holocaust on Trial.

This film explores the phenomenon of Holocaust denial using the David Irving libel trial in London as a springboard. Utilizing footage from the trial proceedings, as well as interviews with noted Holocaust scholars such as Raul Hilberg, Robert Jan Van Pelt, David Cesarani, and Richard Breitman, the documentary exposes the flawed reasoning and unsupportable claims of Holocaust deniers. 60 minutes. Documentary. Vendor: PBS Video.

Hotel Terminus: The Life and Times of Klaus Barbie.

This film examines the life and forty-year effort to locate and bring to trial Klaus Barbie, known as the "Butcher of Lyons" for his SS activities in France during World War II. 267 minutes. VHS videotape. Documentary. Vendor: U.S. Holocaust Memorial Museum.

Judgment at Nuremberg.

This feature film examines the post-war trials of German judges who upheld Nazi law while in the process facilitating the violation of fundamental human rights in Germany during the Nazi period. 187 minutes. VHS videotape. Feature film. Vendor: Social Studies School Service.

Kitty: A Return to Auschwitz.

Returning to Auschwitz many decades later, survivor Kitty Hart relates the story of her experiences at Auschwitz during the ages of 16–18. 82 minutes. VHS videotape. Documentary. Vendor: Social Studies School Service.

The Last Sea.

This documentary examines the journey of survivors from Europe to Israel after the end of World War II, with emphasis placed on the difficulties survivors faced in emigrating to Israel and their determination to achieve their goal. 90 minutes. VHS videotape. Documentary. Vendor: Ergo Media, Inc.

Lessons for Life: Learning About the Holocaust.

This film examines the development of Holocaust education in New Jersey, utilizing excerpts from classroom instruction, interviews with students and teachers, footage of seminars and study tours to Europe and Israel, and expert commentary to explore how young people learn about the Holocaust and its legacy for contemporary society. 60 minutes. VHS videotape. Documentary. Vendor: New Jersey Public Television.

The Long Way Home.

This film explores the problems and obstacles faced by Holocaust survivors as they sought to emigrate to Israel between 1945 and 1948. 116 minutes. VHS videotape. Documentary. Vendor: Museum of Tolerance.

Murderers Among Us: The Simon Wiesenthal Story.

This film tells the story of the career of Nazi hunter Simon Wiesenthal through the mid-1980s. 160 minutes. VHS videotape. Documentary/Drama. Vendor: Social Studies School Service.

The Music Box.

This film presents the story of a lawyer whose father, a Hungarian emigré, is accused of war crimes during World War II by the U.S. Justice Department. Although not based upon a specific individual's story, the film explores the complexities of locating and prosecuting war criminals many years after the end of World War II. 126 minutes. VHS videotape. Feature film. Vendor: Jewish Heritage Video Collection.

Nazi War Crimes Trials.

This set of five newsreels, a theatrical trailer, and a documentary from the Soviet Union present segments of the Nuremberg Trials. 67 minutes. VHS videotape. Documentary. Vendor: Facets Multimedia., Inc.

Nuremberg: Tyranny on Trial.

This documentary employs commentary, historical film footage, and interviews with participants to examine the trial of the twenty-two major war criminals at Nuremberg following the end of World War II. 50 minutes. VHS videotape. Documentary. Vendor: Social Studies School Service.

The Pawnbroker.

Based upon the novel by American Jewish author Edward Lewis Wallant, this film was one of the first American films to penetrate the psychological world of the death camps. Telling the story of Sol Nazerman, a Holocaust survivor, the film relates how Nazerman gradually comes to recognize human suffering around him based upon a dramatic turn of events in his neighborhood. 120 minutes. VHS videotape. Feature film. Vendor: Jewish Heritage Video Collection.

Persecuted and Forgotten: The Gypsies of Auschwitz.

Following a group of Gypsies from Germany as they return to Auschwitz, this documentary relies on interviews to reveal the oppression suffered by Gypsies at the hands of the Nazis, as well as contemporary patterns of discrimination faced by Gypsies. 54 minutes. VHS videotape. Documentary. Vendor: EBS Productions.

A Portrait of Elie Wiesel.

This interview with Elie Wiesel examines Wiesel's life, his writings, and his legacy as a survivor whose life's work has been recognized with the Nobel Prize, among other awards. 58 minutes. VHS videotape. Documentary. Vendor: PBS Video.

The Quarrel.

This film, based upon a short story by Yiddish writer Chaim Grade, explores an encounter between two Holocaust survivors who share their common past as well as their conflicting views of religious faith after the Holocaust. 88 minutes. VHS videotape. Feature film. Vendor: National Center for Jewish Film.

Robert Clary: A Memoir of Liberation.

This filmed memoir presents actor Robert Clary's story as a Holocaust survivor. Clary's personal testimony is interspersed with contemporary footage of Paris and the Buchenwald concentration camp. 60 minutes. VHS videotape. Documentary. Vendor: Simon Wiesenthal Center.

Shoah.

Using interviews with survivors, Nazi SS members, and local residents who observed the processes of destruction first-hand, director Claude Lanzmann combines these interviews with contemporary footage of the locations where the Holocaust occurred in an epic film that lasts over nine hours. 570 minutes. VHS videotape. Documentary. Vendor: Paramount Pictures.

The Shop on Main Street.

This film is rendered in the form of a fable, relating the story of a Czech peasant (Tano) who is appointed the "controller" of a show run by an elderly, half-deaf Jewish woman (Mrs. Lautmann). While attempting to prevent the elderly woman from deportation, Tano accidentally kills her and then kills himself in remorse. The film depicts the moral compromises of bystanders in Occupied Europe that facilitated the Holocaust. 128 minutes. VHS videotape. Feature film. Vendor: Jewish Heritage Video Collection.

Shtetl.

Seeking to uncover the history of the Jewish community of Bransk Poland, a shtetl liquidated by the Nazis in November 1942, the filmmaker Marian Marzynski journeys to the United States, Israel, and Poland to gather evidence from survivors, archival sources, and experts. In the process, the film reveals much about contemporary attitudes of Poles and Jews regarding their past. 180 minutes. VHS videotape. Documentary. Vendor: PBS Video.

Simon Wiesenthal: Freedom Is Not a Gift from Heaven.

Wiesenthal discusses his life story, beginning with his early life in the Ukraine, his experiences of deportation and survival in several camps, and his liberation by American soldiers in 1945. The documentary also discusses Wiesenthal's work as a Nazi hunter, with emphasis on his activities in the mid-1980s and early 1990s. 60 minutes. VHS videotape. Documentary. Vendor: Ergo Media, Inc.

Sorrow: The Nazi Legacy.

Six Swedish teenagers (two of them Jewish) journey to Auschwitz to seek understanding of what has been termed "incomprehensible." Following a preliminary visit to the Wannsee villa in Berlin, they continue to Auschwitz for an emotional encounter at the death camp, where they meet with Ruth Elias, an Auschwitz survivor. Their journey comes full circle when they return to Stockholm for a meeting with the son of Hans Frank, the former Nazi governor-general of Nazi-occupied Poland. 33 minutes. VHS videotape. Documentary. Vendor: Ergo Media, Inc.

Survivors of the Holocaust.

This documentary illustrates the origin, processes, and results of Steven Spielberg's Survivors of the Shoah Visual History Foundation, which focuses on collecting and documenting the testimony of Holocaust survivors. 70 minutes. VHS videotape. Documentary. Vendor: Social Studies School Service.

A Time to Gather Stones Together.

This film examines how a group of Jewish genealogists and Holocaust survivors returned to Galicia (Poland and Ukraine) to search for ancestral documents and to visit towns of family origin or places from where they had escaped the Holocaust. 29 minutes. VHS videotape. Documentary with viewer's guide. Vendor: Documentaries International.

The Trial of Adolf Eichmann.

This film, part of the series "Witnesses to the Holocaust," presents the testimony and evidence (including many eyewitness accounts) that eventually convicted Eichmann, who was held responsible as a key leader in the planning and implementation of the "final solution to the Jewish question." 90 minutes. VHS video-tape. Documentary. Vendor: Lorimar Home Video.

The Trial of Adolf Eichmann.

This film presents actual trial footage of the Eichmann trial in Jerusalem during 1961. Eyewitness accounts by survivors along with recollections by trial witnesses and other key participants are major elements of this comprehensive documentary film. 120 minutes. VHS videotape. Documentary. Vendor: PBS Video.

The Triumph of Memory.

This film examines the experiences of four non-Jewish resistance fighters in World War II. Each of them relates his individual story, and in the process reveals how the patterns of Nazi persecution impacted Jews and non-Jews alike in camps such as Mauthausen, Auschwitz-Birkenau, and Buchenwald. 30 minutes. VHS videotape. Documentary. Vendor: PBS Video.

War Crimes.

This film from Arts and Entertainment channel's *American Justice* series examines the Nuremberg Trials in 1946 and their impact on two later trials: the trial of Lieutenant William Calley for the My Lai Massacre during the Vietnam War, and the trial of concentration camp guard John Demjanjuk. 50 minutes. VHS video-tape. Documentary. Vendor: New Video Group.

VENDORS AND DISTRIBUTORS

Almi Home Video. Almi Pictures, 1900 Broadway, New York, NY 10023. Phone: 212-769-6400.

Angel Records, c/o Capitol/Angel. 304 Park Avenue South, New York, NY 10010. Phone: 212-253-3200.

Anti-Defamation League of B'nai B'rith. 22-D Hollywood Avenue, Ho-Ho-Kus, NJ 07423. Phone: 800-343-5540.

Bel Canto Society. 11 Riverside Drive, New York, NY 10023. Phone: 800-347-5056 or 212-877-5813.

BMG Video c/o BMG Direct. 1540 Broadway, 32nd Floor, New York, NY 10036. Phone: 212-930-4241.

Buena Vista Home Video. 350 South Buena Vista Street, Burbank, CA 91512. Phone: 818-562-3705.

The Cinema Guild. 130 Madison Avenue, 2nd Floor, New York, NY 10016-7038. Phone: 212-685-6242.

Connoisseur Video Collection. Connoisseur/Meridian Films Inc., 23532-A-Calabasas Road, Calabasas, CA 91302. Phone: 310-231-1350.

Decca Record Company, c/o Universal Music Group. 825 8th Avenue, New York, NY 10019. Phone: 212-333-8000.

Direct Cinema Limited. PO Box 10003, Santa Monica, CA 90410. Phone: 310-636-8200.

Documentaries International Film and Video Foundation. 1800 K Street NW, Suite 1120, Washington, DC 20006. Phone: 202-429-9320.

DoKo Media Ltd. 7 Ha'Amai Street, PO Box 611, OrYehuda 60371, Israel. Phone: (972) 3-634-4776.

EBS Productions. 330 Ritch Street, San Francisco, CA 94107. Phone: 415-495-2327.

Emory University. Fred Roberts Crawford Witness to the Holocaust Project. Atlanta, GA 30322. Phone: 404-329-6428.

Ergo Media, Inc. PO Box 2037, Teaneck, NJ 07666-1437. Phone: 201-692-0404.

Facets Multimedia, Inc. 1517 West Fullerton Avenue, Chicago, IL 60614. Phone: 773-257-5126.

Filmmakers Library, Inc. 124 East 40th Street, Suite 901, New York, NY 10016. Phone: 212-808-4980.

Films for the Humanities and Sciences, Inc. PO Box 2053, Princeton, NJ 08543-2053. Phone: 800-257-5126.

Films Incorporated. 5547 North Ravenswood Avenue, Chicago, IL 60640. Phone: 800-323-4222.

First Run Features/Icarus Films. 153 Waverly Place, 6th Floor, New York, NY 10014. Phone: 212-727-1711.

FoxLorber. 419 Park Avenue South, New York, NY 10016. 212-686-6777.

HBO Video. 1100 Avenue of the Americas, New York, NY 10019. Phone: 212-512-7400.

Home Vision Entertainment. 4411 North Ravenswood Avenue, Third Floor, Chicago, IL 60640-5802. Phone: None provided.

Impact America Foundation. 9100 Keystone at the Crossing, Indianapolis, IN 46240. Phone: 317-848-5134.

Jewish Heritage Video Collection. A Project of the Jewish Media Fund, c/o Charles H. Revson Foundation. 444 Madison Avenue, 30th Floor, New York, NY 10022. Phone: None provided.

Jewish Labor Committee. Atran Center for Jewish Culture. 25 East 21st Street, New York, NY 10010. Phone: 212-477-0707.

Joshua M. Greene Productions. PO Box 311, Old Westbury, NY. Phone: 516-334-0909.

MGM Home Entertainment. 2500 Broadway, Santa Monica, CA 90404-3061. Phone: 310-449-3000.

Midwest Center for Holocaust Education, Inc. 5801 West 115th Street, Suite 106, Overland Park, KS 66211-1800. Phone: 913-327-8190.

MPI Home Video. 1601 S. 108th Avenue, Orland Park, IL 60467. Phone: 708-460-0555.

Museum of Tolerance Bookstore. 9786 Simon Wiesenthal Plaza, West Pico Boulevard, Los Angeles, CA 90035. Phone: 800-553-4474.

National Center for Jewish Film. Brandeis University, Lown 102, MS053, Waltham, MA 02254-9110. Phone: 718-899-7044.

New Jersey Public Television. PO Box 777, Trenton, NJ 08625-0777. Phone: 609-777-5000.

New Video Group. 126 Fifth Avenue, New York, NY 10011. Phone: 212-206-8600.

Orion-Nelson Entertainment. 5547 North Ravenswood Avenue, Chicago, IL 60640-9979. Phone: 312-878-2600.

Paramount Pictures. c/o Viacom Consumer Products/Paramount Pictures, 5555 Melrose Avenue, Hollywood, CA 90038. Phone: 323-956-5583.

PBS Video. 1320 Braddock Place, Alexandria, VA 22314-1698. Phone: 800-344-3337.

Phoenix Films and Video, Inc. 2349 Chaffe Place, St. Louis, MO 63146. Phone: 314-569-0211.

Simon Wiesenthal Center Media Department. 9760 West Pico Boulevard, Los Angeles, CA 90035. Phone: 310-553-9036.

Sisu Home Entertainment, Inc. 18 West 27th Street, 10th Floor, New York, NY 10001. Phone: 212-779-1559.

Social Studies School Service. 10200 Jefferson Boulevard, Room 171, PO Box 802, Culver City, CA 90232-0802. Phone: 800-421-4246. http://socialstudies.com.

Suncoast Media, Inc. 200 Avenue E, Venice, FL 34284. Phone: 941-483-5800.

Survivors of the Shoah Visual History Foundation. PO Box 3168, Los Angeles, CA 90078-3168. Phone: 818-777-4673.

SVE/Churchill Media. 6677 North Northwest Highway, Chicago, IL 60631-1304. Phone: 800-829-1900.

United Learning. 6633 West Howard Street, Niles, IL 60648. Phone: 800-424-0362.

U.S. Holocaust Memorial Museum Shop. 100 Raoul Wallenberg Place SW, Washington, DC 20024. Phone: 800-259-9998. http://www.holocaustbooks.org.

Watch Tower Bible and Tract Society of Pennsylvania. Public Affairs Office, 25 Columbia Heights, Brooklyn, NY 11201-2483. Phone: 718-560-5600.

Zenger Media. 10200 Jefferson Boulevard, Room VC511, Culver City, CA 91021. Phone: 800-421-4246.

14

AUDIOBOOKS ABOUT
THE HOLOCAUST

OVERVIEW

The audiobook entries in this chapter present major works about the Holocaust through the medium of the spoken word. In some cases, the works are shortened versions of the original print publications, but in others they are unabridged. Selections included here represent a variety of styles and genres in works about the Holocaust: historical studies, first-person accounts, and historical fiction. A listing of audiobook vendors is provided at the end of the chapter.

AUDIOBOOKS

Auerbacher, Inge. *I Am A Star: Child of the Holocaust*. Read by Tovah Feldshuh. Two cassettes. Cassette one: 40 minutes, 5 seconds. Cassette two: 59 minutes, 17 seconds. Pinellas Park, FL: Spoken Arts, 1990. ISBN 0–8045–3050–5.

Inge Auerbacher's memoir of her Holocaust experiences begins in Kippenheim, Germany where she discusses her early life as part of the Jewish community in a small German town. This memoir details the gradual intensification of oppression against her family and other Jews in Germany, and their eventual deportation to Terezin. She is one of the very few children to have survived internment in

Terezin, and following liberation by the Soviet army in 1945, she returned to Germany and emigrated to the United States in 1946.

Brecher, Elinor J. *Schindler's Legacy*. Read by Steve Post and actual survivors. Abridged version of original. One cassette. 90 minutes. East Rutherford, NJ: Penguin Putnam, Inc., 1994. ISBN 0–4530–0902–6 . http://www.penguinputnam.com.

This abridged version of *Schindler's Legacy* contains segments of the original anthology of life stories collected by author Elinor Brecher from survivors saved through the efforts of Oskar Schindler. In addition to the readings by Steve Post, this version contains segments read by a selection of the over thirty survivors whose lives are discussed by Elinor Brecher in the complete book version.

Cornwell, John. *Hitler's Pope*. Read by David Case. 12 cassettes. 1,070 minutes. Costa Mesa, CA: Books on Tape, 1999. ISBN 0–7366–4818–6. http://www.booksontape.com.

This controversial work suggests that Pope Pius XII was well informed about the oppression of Jews instituted by Nazi Germany, and did not act effectively to provide support or take efforts to shield Jews during the enactment of the "final solution."

Epstein, Leslie. *King of the Jews*. Read by Noah Waterman. 8 cassettes. 720 minutes. Ashland, OR: Blackstone Audiobooks, 1997. ISBN 0–7861–1178–X. http://www.blackstoneaudio.com.

Drawing upon the history of the Holocaust, this novel relates how one man, orphanage director J.C. Trumpleman, becomes the "king" of the Jews in a Polish ghetto. As the leading figure in the struggle for survival, the main character makes choices that can lead to life or death for the Jewish population. The author effectively describes the overwhelming obstacles and difficult choices faced by Jews suffering in the ghetto, and the tragic consequences of decisions made by ghetto leaders.

Frank, Anne. *The Diary of a Young Girl*. Read by Julie Harris. 2 cassettes. 100 minutes. Auburn, CA: Audio Editions, 1992. ISBN 0–945353–73–1. Excerpted. http://www.audioeditions.com.

This edition of Anne Frank's diary represents the first, somewhat shorter version prepared by her father Otto Frank and published in the 1950s. The reading on this audiotape is an excerpted version of the edition that garnered its author posthumous worldwide acclaim.

————. *The Diary of a Young Girl*. The Definitive Edition. Read by Winona Rider. 4 cassettes. 360 minutes. New York: Bantam Doubleday Dell, 1995. ISBN 0–553–47347–6. Abridged. http://www. randomhouse.com.

From June 12, 1942 to August 1, 1944, Anne Frank, a young Jewish girl living in the Netherlands, wrote diary entries that survived World War II through the efforts of her friend Miep Gies, who placed the diary in safekeeping following the Frank family's deportation to Westerbork, and ultimately to Auschwitz in 1944. The shortened version of the full diary, edited and published by Otto Frank, Anne's father, in the 1950s, became one of the most widely read works on the Holocaust. This edition draws upon the entire set of original diary entries, providing up to thirty percent more text and revealing a more multifaceted view of Anne Frank than was apparent in the first published edition.

Frankl, Viktor. *Man's Search for Meaning*. Read by Simon Vance. 4 cassettes. 360 minutes. Ashland, OR: Blackstone Audiobooks, 1999. ISBN 0–7861–13871. http://www.blackstoneaudio.com.

Written in nine days during 1945, Viktor Frankl's account of how he found the "will to meaning" as a concentration camp inmate served as the basis for his development of the psychiatric approach labeled "logotherapy." Frankl's account of his camp experiences stresses the individual's freedom to "choose one's attitude in a given set of circumstances." Reflecting key elements of existentialist philosophy, Frankl interprets his survival as resting on the individual's acceptance of the need to define a personal reason for living. Once this responsibility is accepted, individuals can rise above their fate and find meaning in their suffering. The tone of the narrative is uplifting, based upon Frankl's core conviction that there is meaning in life itself no matter how difficult the circumstances an individual encounters.

Gilbert, Martin. *Auschwitz and the Allies*. Read by David Case. 12 cassettes. 1,350 minutes. Unabridged. Costa Mesa, CA: Books on Tape, Inc., 1996. ISBN 0–7366–3098–8. http://www.booksontape.com.

Gilbert's study reveals that Allied leaders in Great Britain and the United States were far more concerned with winning World War II in Europe than in saving Jews from destruction by the Third Reich. Focusing primarily on Great Britain, the author documents how Allied leaders minimized the significance of reports about mass extermination and only took action late in the war to provide relief and rescue for Jews. Winston Churchill emerges as a man of compassion and concern for the Jews, but his efforts to assist Jews were stymied by bureaucratic obstacles and British resistance to helping Jews relocate to Palestine. Despite their earlier failures to support havens for refugees, the United States and Great Britain still had opportunities to intervene on behalf of Jews in 1944, notably when the debate over the bombing of Auschwitz arose. Gilbert argues that their unwillingness to support bombing of the rail lines, when thousands of Jews were still being killed at Europe's largest extermination center and when the camp was easily within reach of Allied bombers, was another black mark against the Allies and their approach to helping European Jews during World War II.

————. *The Holocaust*. Read by David Case. Part A: 12 cassettes. Part B: 12 cassettes. Part A: 1,070 minutes. Part B: 1,070 minutes. Unabridged. Costa Mesa, CA: Books on Tape, Inc., 1995. ISBN: Part A: 0–7366–3172–0. Part B: 0–7366–3173–9. http://www.booksontape.com.

Gilbert's work draws heavily upon first-hand accounts to develop a comprehensive history of the Jews in Europe during World War II. The book initially focuses on historical oppression of Jews in Europe, the rise of Nazism, and the development of Nazi policies of oppression in Germany and selected areas of Central Europe prior to the outbreak of World War II in September 1939. With the exception of Chapter 41 and the epilogue, the remainder of the text details the Jewish response to Nazi policies. Chapter 16, "Eyewitness to Mass Murder," contains the notes of a Jew who had witnessed mass murder in the Chelmno death camp, prefaced by a brief introduction and a short concluding section that links eyewitness excerpts to efforts to inform Jews in Polish ghettos such as Lodz about the reality of the "final solution." The author incorporates many eyewitness accounts throughout the text, making it primarily a study of Jewish responses to genocide.

Gutman, Israel. *Resistance: The Warsaw Ghetto Uprising*. Read by Michael Prichard. 8 cassettes. 720 minutes. Unabridged. Costa Mesa, CA: Books on Tape, Inc., 1995. ISBN 0–7366–3107–0. http://www.booksontape.com.

Written by a distinguished historian who himself was a survivor of the Warsaw Ghetto uprising, this work describes the uprising in detail and places it within the broader context of Jewish resistance to Nazism within Occupied Europe during World War II. The work includes many excerpts from memoirs, stories, letters, and other primary sources to tell the story of the heroic uprising against Nazi tyranny.

Johnson, Eric A. *Nazi Terror*. Read by Edward Lewis. 13 cassettes. 1,170 minutes. Ashland, OR: Blackstone Audiobooks, 2000. ISBN 0–7861–1859–8. http://www.blackstoneaudio.com.

Eric Johnson spent five years researching how the Nazi terror apparatus worked, focusing primarily on three German communities in the Rhineland: Cologne, Krefeld, and Bergheim. Using documentary sources from the Gestapo and special court files, along with survey data and interviews with perpetrators, Jewish victims, and bystanders, Johnson concludes that the Nazi terror apparatus relied for its effectiveness on the local population's cooperation and support. Relying heavily on first-hand accounts of how the selective use of terror functioned in the Nazi state, the author discusses how a range of groups—Jews, Communists, Jehovah's Witnesses, clergy, the disabled, and others–suffered while most Germans neither intervened nor protested. Johnson also concludes that it was apparent that substantial numbers of ordinary Germans knew about various aspects of the Nazi mass murder campaign against the Jews, and yet most ordinary Germans did not act on the victims' behalf.

Keneally, Thomas. *Schindler's List*. Read by Walter Zimmerman. 12 cassettes. 1080 minutes. Costa Mesa, CA: Books on Tape, Inc., 1990. ISBN 0–7366–1837–6. http://www.booksontape.com.

Thomas Keneally's book of historical fiction is based upon extensive research in documentary sources and with survivors who were saved through the efforts of Oskar Schindler. Originally a Nazi party member who sought to maximize his financial standing as a war profiteer, Oskar Schindler became a savior for over 1,100 Jews who worked in his factories, first in Poland and later in Czechoslovakia. Keneally's story necessarily focuses on the dominant figure of Schindler, but the listener receives a detailed picture of the sadistic commandant of the Plaszow concentration camp, Amon Goeth, as well as indelible portraits of prisoners who worked closely with Schindler or whose lives illustrated the key elements of survival as part of Schindler's workforce.

——. *Schindler's List*. Read by Ben Kingsley. 4 cassettes. New York: Simon & Schuster, 1993. ISBN 0–6718–8228–7. http://www.SimonSays. com.

This is an abridged version of Keneally's *Schindler's List*, as read by Ben Kingsley, who played the role of accountant Itzhak Stern in the Steven Spielberg film *Schindler's List*.

Nyiszli, Dr. Miklos. *Auschwitz: A Doctor's Eyewitness Account*. Read by Noah Waterman. 5 cassettes. 450 minutes. Unabridged. Ashland, OR: Blackstone Audiobooks, 1995. ISBN 0–7861–0757–X. http:// www.blackstoneaudio.com.

This is an audio version of the celebrated eyewitness account of Auschwitz, originally written in 1946, authored by Jewish medical doctor Miklos Nyiszli. Upon arrival at Auschwitz from Hungary he was named Dr. Josef Mengele's personal research pathologist. His descriptions of daily activities in Auschwitz, most notably the work of the *sonderkommando*, are detailed and unforgettable.

Opdyke, Irene Gut, with Jennifer Armstrong. *In My Hands: Memories of a Holocaust Rescuer*. Read by Hope Davis. 4 cassettes. 360 minutes. New York: Bantam Doubleday Dell, 1999. ISBN 0–553–52658–8. http://www.bdd.com.

Irene Gut Opdyke was a young Polish woman who worked as a waitress and housekeeper for German officers during World War II. At the same time, she relayed information about Nazi plans to Jews in a nearby ghetto, and later hid twelve Jews in the basement of her German army major's home. Her determination and compassion contributed to the survival of the Jews hidden in the major's home. This memoir relates not only how she acted on behalf of others, but how her efforts in World War II became the defining experience of her life.

Ten Boom, Corrie. *The Hiding Place*. Read by Nadia May. 6 cassettes. 540 minutes. Unabridged. Ashland, OR: Blackstone Audiobooks, 1994. ISBN 0–7861–0647–6. http://www.blackstoneaudio.com.

This unabridged version of Corrie Ten Boom's memoir relates how the author and her family worked to hide Jews in Haarlem, the Netherlands during the German occupation in World War II. Eventually discovered and interned by the occupation forces, Corrie and her sister Betsie were deported to Ravensbruck concentration camp, a camp for female prisoners. Despite the loss of her sister and other members of her family during the Holocaust, Corrie Ten Boom did not lose faith and she survived. Following the war, she participated in Christian missionary work and authored this memoir in collaboration with John and Elizabeth Sherrill.

Toland, John. *Adolf Hitler*. Read by John MacDonald. Part A: 12 cassettes. Part B: 15 cassettes. Part A: 1,080 minutes. Part B: 1,350 minutes. Unabridged. Costa Mesa, CA: Books on Tape, Inc., 1992. ISBN: Part A: 0–7366–2132–6. Part B: 0–7366–2133–4. http://www.booksontape.com.

John Toland's biography of Adolf Hitler draws upon extensive interviews with individuals who worked closely with Hitler, as well as in-depth archival research. The work traces Hitler's rise to power from obscurity, placing his political career within the context of a Germany that had suffered a military collapse in 1918, and which was experimenting with its first truly democratic government, the Weimar Republic. Toland details how Hitler's early military successes in World War II did not deter him from reckless and ultimately disastrous strategic decisions later in the war, particularly during the invasion of the Soviet Union. The author argues that the "final solution" for European Jews was always a high priority for Hitler, and that he was firmly in control of the process, not a detached or uninterested observer of the extermination of millions. Ultimately, the vision of Nazism died with Hitler, according to Toland, because so much of its appeal rested on Hitler's own personal authority, which exposed the bankruptcy of its ideology.

Velmans, Edith. *Edith's Story*. Read by Miriam Margolyes, with a newly recorded introduction and epilogue by the author. 6 cassettes. Unabridged. 505 minutes. Auburn, CA: Audio Partners Publishing Group, 2000. ISBN 1–57270–177–3. http://audiopartners.com.

Edith Van Hessen was a young girl in the Netherlands when World War II began, and as a fourteen-year-old she kept a diary with details of a teenager's life. Hidden by a Christian family and forced to deny her Jewish identity, Edith experienced the deportation of her family to the Westerbork transit camp, from which her mother and grandmother were deported to Sobibor and murdered in 1943. The book integrates Edith [Van Hessen] Velmans' memoirs with excerpts from her wartime diaries and selected letters received from her family when she was being hidden. Surviving the war, Edith Velmans eventually emigrated to the United States and became a psychologist. Tine Zur Kleinsmede, the wife in the Christian family who hid Edith from the Nazis, was recognized as a righteous gentile by Yad Vashem in 1983 on her nineteenth birthday, and Edith Velmans accompanied her to the ceremony in Jerusalem.

PRODUCERS AND VENDORS OF AUDIOBOOKS

Audio Editions. PO Box 6930, Auburn, CA 95604-6930. Phone: 800-231-4261. http://www.audioeditions.com.

Audio Partners Publishing Group. 1133 High Street, Auburn, CA 95603. Phone: 800-231-4261. http://audiopartners.com.

Bantam DoubleDay Dell. 1540 Broadway, New York, NY 10036-4094. Phone: 212-782-8394. http://www.randomhouse.com.

Blackstone Audiobooks. Box 969, Ashland, OR 97520. Phone: 800-729-2665. http://www.blackstoneaudio.com.

Books on Tape, Inc. 729 Farad Street, Costa Mesa, CA 92627. Phone: 949-548-5525. http://www.booksontape.com.

Penguin Putnam, Inc. 375 Hudson Street, New York, NY 11014. Phone: 212-366 2000. http://www.penguinputnam.com.

Random House. 1540 Broadway, New York, NY 10036. Phone: 212-782-9000. http://www.randomhouse.com

Simon & Schuster Trade, A Division of Simon & Schuster, Inc., a Viacom Co. 1230 Avenue of the Americas, New York, NY 10020. Phone: 212-698-7000. http://www.SimonSays.com.

15

MUSIC: ARCHIVES AND COLLECTIONS, BOOKS, COMPOSITIONS, AND SOUND RECORDINGS

OVERVIEW

Music is a powerful artistic medium that amplifies understanding of the Holocaust. Whether it be works of Jewish musicians and composers in pre–World War II Europe, the songs of the ghettos and partisans, or the wide variety of Holocaust-inspired compositions evident in this chapter's sound recording entries, music invites an emotional encounter with the Holocaust by engaging the listener's imagination through the use of vocal, instrumental, and other combinations of musical resources. Archives with collections of Holocaust musical compositions, books about music of the Holocaust, and selected musical compositions are included along with an extensive listing of compact disc recordings, organized by category. The reader will note that film music has not been included in this chapter, since the creation of film music is meant to supplement or underline the visual presentation of images on the screen. The recordings included in this chapter are those that were created specifically to address content about the

Holocaust or, as in the case of composers from Terezin and others who were forced to emigrate from Europe, were written by individuals whose careers were directly affected by or ended owing to Nazi oppression. A listing of vendors for both musical compositions and sound recordings is included at the end of the chapter.

ARCHIVES CONTAINING COLLECTIONS OF MUSIC ABOUT THE HOLOCAUST

United States Holocaust Memorial Museum. 100 Raoul Wallenberg Place SW, Washington, DC 20024-2156. http://ushmm.org. e-mail: archives@ ushmm.org.

The major music collection of the U.S. Holocaust Memorial Museum is the Alexander Kulisiewicz collection (1939–1945). This is an archive of music, poetry, literature, sound recordings, and related documents that were collected by Sachsenhausen survivor Alexander Kulisiewicz from former camp inmates and other camp survivors. Kulisiewicz had intended to publish an anthology of concentration camp music and poetry, but this was not accomplished before his death. A composer of over fifty songs while a camp inmate, Kulisiewicz continued to compose music after liberation and both performed and published music, lyrics, and poetry of the camps until the late 1970s. The U.S. Holocaust Memorial Museum acquired this collection, which is chiefly in Polish and German, but also in selected other languages, in the early 1990s. The Museum's Web site contains audio excerpts and background information on selected recordings and compositions regarding the Holocaust.

YIVO Institute for Jewish Research. 15 West 16th Street, New York, NY 10011-6301. Phone: 212-246-6080, extension 6119. FAX: 212-292-1892. http://www.yivoinstitute.org. e-mail: yivomail@yivo.cjh.org.

The YIVO Institute Archives and Library has an extensive music collection that contains published and unpublished works in the genres of art, folk, popular, and theater music, along with Holocaust songs, liturgical music, and choral and instrumental compositions. Musical works about the Holocaust but composed following the end of World War II also are represented, along with a wide range of programs, clippings, photographs, and related documents dealing with Jewish music. A highlight of the collection is the selection of works by the folk poet and songwriter Mordecai Gebirtig, who perished in the Krakow Ghetto in 1942.

BOOKS ON MUSIC IN THE THIRD REICH

Goldsmith, Martin. *The Inextinguishable Symphony: A True Story of Music and Love in Nazi Germany.* New York: John Wiley & Sons, 2000. ISBN 0–471–35097–4. 346 pages. Hardcover.

This book relates the story of flutist Gunter Goldschmidt and violist Rosemarie Gumpert, two musicians who fell in love during the Nazi period while working as orchestral musicians under the auspices of the Jewish Kulturbund. Exploring the impact of Nazi oppression from a cultural perspective, the author describes how his parents (Gunter and Rosemarie) survived, eventually emigrating to the United States through Spain and continuing their musical careers in America. At the same time, the story relates how others of his family were not able to find refuge, and were later murdered by the Nazis. The details of the Kulturbund's activities are presented using both documentary sources and first-person accounts, offering a detailed picture of the Jewish response to Nazi policies of discrimination and segregation in the musical field. Indexed.

Kater, Michael. *The Twisted Muse: Musicians and Their Music in the Third Reich.* New York: Oxford University Press, 1997. ISBN 0–19–509620–7. 327 pages. Hardcover.

This authoritative study of the relationship between politics and music in the Third Reich draws heavily from archival research by the author in North America and Europe. Untangling the complex web of competing interests that placed many musicians in difficult positions during the Third Reich, Kater paints a detailed picture of how Nazi policies, at times rational and at other times arbitrary and based upon personal association, forced many musicians into compromised positions in German society. Among the famous musicians and composers discussed are Elisabeth Schwarzkopf, Herbert Von Karajan, Wilhelm Furtwangler, Richard Strauss, and Karl Amadeus Hartmann. The "de-Judaizing" of musical life in Nazi Germany is thoroughly examined, and the negative impact of Nazism on German musical life in both the short and long term is analyzed. While very thoroughly documented, the work does not employ photographs or musical examples. Indexed.

Levi, Erik. *Music in the Third Reich.* New York: St. Martin's Press, 1994. ISBN 0–312–12948–3. 303 pages. Paperback.

This book is a comprehensive survey of Nazi policies regarding the musical arts, the effects of those policies, and their legacy for musical culture in Germany. The author traces the origins of Nazi musical policies to their roots in conservative musical criticism and responses to the musical avant-garde during the Weimar Republic, when Germany was the center of musical experimentation in post–World War I Europe. Levi discusses the role of anti-Semitism in Nazi musical policy and the expulsion of Jews from German musical life, as well as the emigration of many major figures in German music due to Nazi repression. Thorough notes are included, along with a glossary, a detailed chronology of events concerning Nazi musical policies, and a very comprehensive bibliography of music periodicals, journals, books, and articles. Indexed.

Newman, Richard, with Karen Kirtley. *Alma Rose: Vienna to Auschwitz*. Portland, OR: Amadeus Press, 2000. ISBN 1–57467–051–4. 407 pages. Hardcover.

This biography of Alma Rose, distinguished concert violinist and leader of the women's orchestra at Auschwitz, is a model of scholarship based upon sixteen years of research. Detailing her upbringing in the highly cultural Viennese society where her father was concertmaster of the Vienna Philharmonic and leader of the world-famous Rose String Quartet, the authors tell the story of Alma's rise to prominence as a concert musician, her capture in Holland in 1942, and her deportation and eventual arrival in Auschwitz where she became leader of the women's orchestra in Auschwitz-Birkenau. Working to make the orchestra a quality ensemble under the most difficult of conditions, Rose saved many women prisoners' lives by insisting their involvement in the orchestra was essential for its continuity. The book provides a unique perspective on the camp experience, viewing it through a biographical perspective, in this case the life story of a talented musician whose art and compassion brought glimmers of light into one of the darkest episodes of human history. Extensive notes, a selection of photos showing Alma Rose and her family, and an extensive bibliography are included. Indexed.

BOOKS ABOUT MUSIC IN THE CAMPS

Bor, Josef. *The Terezin Requiem*. Translated from the Czech by Edith Pargeter. New York: Alfred A. Knopf, 1963. No ISBN. 112 pages. Hardcover.

As the only one of his family to survive, the Czech Jew Josef Bor endured internment in Terezin, Auschwitz, and Buchenwald. This book relates the story of how the conductor Raphael Schlachter led a performance of Verdi's *Requiem* mass with a cast of 500 inmates for the SS leadership in Terezin. The performance occurred in 1944, and was intended by Schlachter to signify how a great work of music representing a high point of human creativity could be prepared and performed by a diverse group of artists, irrespective of their ethnic, religious, or cultural backgrounds. The author details how the performance was prepared, the response to the performance, and ultimately the deportation to their deaths of the entire performance company. No index.

Fenelon, Fania, with Marcelle Routier. *Playing for Time*. Translated from the French by Judith Landry. Syracuse: Syracuse University Press, 1997. ISBN 0–8156–0494–7. 262 pages. Paperback.

Originally published in France in 1976, this memoir by Fania Fenelon recounts her experiences as a member of the women's orchestra in Auschwitz-Birkenau. A cabaret singer in Paris, Fenelon worked for the French resistance and was a French

Jew. Following her capture by the Nazis, she was deported to Auschwitz, where she became part of the women's orchestra in Auschwitz under the direction of Alma Rose. Fenelon's memoir relates both the difficulties of survival at the hands of the SS and camp *kapos*, which depended upon the success of the orchestra in pleasing the camp leadership. She also describes the intrigues, love, hate, and political rivalries that existed in the camp, and in the daily operations of the women's orchestra. Eventually deported to Bergen-Belsen, Fania Fenelon was liberated by the British army in 1945. No index.

Flam, Gila. *Singing for Survival: Songs of the Lodz Ghetto, 1940–45.* Urbana: University of Illinois Press, 1992. ISBN 0–252–01817–6. 207 pages. Hardcover.

This ethnomusicological study examines the songs composed and performed in the Lodz ghetto, relying primarily on survivor accounts. Integrating the life histories of the singers with interpretations of the song texts and the conditions under which they were performed, the book includes street songs, domestic songs, songs performed in theaters, in youth organizations, and in the workplace. The author also addresses the role of ghetto songs as commemorative works, notably as representations of collective memory. Song texts are provided throughout the book, along with extended interview excerpts. The book includes a glossary, a selected bibliography, a general index, and an index of song titles.

Karas, Joza. *Music in Terezin, 1941–1945.* New York: Beaufort Books Publishers, 1985. ISBN 0–8253–0287–0. 223 pages. Hardcover.

This comprehensive study is the single best source on the musical world of Terezin. Czech musician Joza Karas ranges across all the musical activities of the Terezin complex, including choral music, opera, chamber music, and orchestral performances. Specific composers receive substantial attention regarding their work in Terezin: Gideon Klein, Pavel Haas, Hans Krasa, and Viktor Ullmann. The vitality of the musical culture in Terezin is well represented, not only in the author's text but in numerous photographs and reproductions of drawings made in Terezin of musicians and performing venues. The book also discusses the impact of deportations on the musical culture, and concludes with an evaluation of the musical life in Terezin, placed in the context of music's role in camps and ghettos during the Holocaust. Biographical sketches of musicians and composers are provided, along with an extensive bibliography and a name index.

Laks, Szymon. *Music of Another World.* Translated from the Polish by Chester A. Kissel. Evanston IL: Northwestern University Press, 1999. Originally published in Polish in 1979. ISBN 0–8101–1802–5. 136 pages. Paperback.

This memoir by the kapellmeister of the Auschwitz orchestra describes how the author and his fellow musicians endured camp life by performing for the SS guards and inmate kapos. Although Polish by birth, the author was interned in France and deported to Auschwitz. The orchestra was often forced to perform on demand, and the author's descriptions of the responses of the SS and *kapos* reveal how unpredictable and dangerous life was in the camp complex. This edition includes an appendix with three Warsaw polonaises that were performed by the Auschwitz orchestra. No index.

MUSICAL COMPOSITIONS: COLLECTIONS

Bluestein, Gene (translator), and Frank Metis (arranger). *Yiddish Song Favorites*. New York: Amsco Publications, 1994. ISBN 0–8256–1419–8. 175 pages. Paperback.

This anthology contains thirty Yiddish songs with complete original Yiddish lyrics and singable English translations, as well as piano/vocal arrangements with guitar chords. Songs composed in Europe and by Jewish immigrants to the United States are included. No index.

Mlotek, Eleanor, and Malike Gottlieb, compilers. *We Are Here: Songs of the Holocaust*. Foreword by Elie Wiesel. New York: Education Department of the Workmen's Circle, 1983. ISBN 0–686–40805–5. 104 pages. Paperback.

This anthology of Holocaust songs contains forty songs organized thematically, using these descriptive section titles: "Our Town Is Burning" (six songs about destruction of Jewish life in Europe), "Ghetto, in My Memory: You'll Never Die" (twelve songs about ghetto experiences), "The Lonely Child" (ten songs about children), "Ani Mamin—I Believe" (four songs on the power of faith), and "We Are Here!" (eight songs of resistance). Each song contains Yiddish and English lyrics, transliterations, translations, guitar chords, and a brief synopsis of the song's origins and use during the Holocaust. A brief bibliography is provided in English and a Yiddish version of notes about the songs in the anthology is included as well. A transliteration guide concludes the book. No index.

Mlotek, Eleanor Gordon, and Joseph Mlotek, compilers. *Pearls of Yiddish Song: Favorite Folk, Art and Theatre Songs*. New York: Education Department of the Workmen's Circle, 1988. No ISBN provided. 286 pages. Paperback.

This anthology of 115 songs is organized thematically and contains some songs that were sung during the Holocaust, although originally composed for other purposes. The detailed introduction explains the origins of the anthology, the thematic organization of the songs, the sources from which the songs were compiled, how composers such as Ravel, Shostakovich, and Prokofiev have used Yiddish songs in their classical compositions, and the foundations of the recent revival of interest in Yiddish music. Each song contains the Yiddish text and music, transliterations, translations, a brief historical background synopsis, and guitar chords. A selected bibliography, index of titles and first lines, author and composer list, and Yiddish translation of the introduction are included. The contents of the first volume in the series of Yiddish song published by the compilers of this volume, *Mir Trogn a Gesang,* also is provided.

————. *Songs of Generations: New Pearls of Yiddish Song.* Preface by Elie Wiesel. Foreword by Doy Noy. New York: The Workmen's Circle, n.d. ISBN 1-877909-65-3. 303 pages. Paperback.

This anthology of Yiddish song contains 126 Yiddish songs organized thematically, including six songs of the Holocaust. Each song contains the Yiddish text and music, transliterations, translations, a brief historical background synopsis, and guitar chords. A selected bibliography, index of titles and first lines, author and composer list, and Yiddish translations of the introduction, foreword, and preface are included. This is one of three books in a series published by the compilers on Yiddish song, and a combined index of the contents for all three volumes is provided.

Readers interested in locating specific works by composers discussed in this chapter are encouraged to investigate the holdings of music publishers provided in the "Vendors of Musical Resources" section.

COMPACT DISC RECORDINGS (CDs)

Jewish Religious and Secular Music

These recordings include both religious compositions and secular works that were commonplace in Central and Eastern European Jewish culture during the period 1880–1939.

Beregovsky's Khasene—Beregovski's Wedding. Forgotten Instrumental Treasures from the Ukraine. Welt Musik CD SM 1614–2 281 614–2. Performed by the Joel Rubin Jewish Music Ensemble. Mainz: Schott Wergo Media GmbH, 1997. TT: 74:07.

Using the research of the Ukrainian-Jewish ethnomusicologist Moyshe Beregovski (1892–1961), the performers on this compact disc recreate the musical traditions of late nineteenth and early twentieth-century Jewish music in the Ukraine. Beregovski did his research on Jewish instrumental folk music prior to World War II, and collected thousands of pieces, which were deposited in the Ukrainian

Academy of Sciences in Kiev. Following his exile to Siberia in 1951–1955 and his death in 1961, his work had been given up for lost, but a large portion of it was rediscovered in Kiev in 1994. The works on this recording reflect the compiler's deep understanding of klezmer music as part of the broader range of Jewish musical traditions in Central and Eastern Europe before the Holocaust.

Es Wird Nicht Untergehen. Jewish Liturgical Singing in Berlin. Historic Recordings from 1909–1937. Performed by notable Cantors and Synagogue Choirs from Berlin. BARBArossa CD EdBa 01317–2. Berlin: Edition Barbarossa, 1996. TT: 68:39.

This compact disc contains historic recordings by cantors and quartets of Jewish liturgical music sung in German synagogues prior to World War II. The accompanying booklet (in German only) contains background information on the performers, the origins of each recording, and texts for the works heard on this recording.

Folklore Yiddish D'Europe Centrale. Performed by the Budapester Klezmer Band. Harmonia Mundi France CD 1903070. Arles: Harmonia Mundi S.A., 1994. TT: 64:49.

This recording was prepared by the Budapest Klezmer Band, which was formed in 1990 to revive the music of Central and Eastern European Jewish communities that had largely been lost due to the Holocaust. The works on this recording reflect the vibrancy of Yiddish culture and include works typically performed at weddings, bar mitzvahs, celebrations such as Purim, and others. Included among the works here are traditional songs such as "Havah Nagilah" and "Mitzva-tants," as well as those by well-known Yiddish composers, such as J. Yellen Polack's "A yiddishe mame" and some of the last remaining klezmers (Dave Tarras' "A gleyzele vayn").

Klezmer Music: A Marriage of Heaven and Earth. Performed by various artists. Ellipsis Arts . . . CD 4090. Roslyn NY: Ellipsis Arts..., 1996. TT: 58:05.

This compact disc contains a very extensive booklet that details the origins of the Klezmer tradition in Europe, along with interviews with Frank London of the Klezmatics and leading klezmer musician Andy Statman. Historical photos of Klezmer performances and rural Jewish life in Europe before the Holocaust are interspersed within the booklet, and the performers represent a cross-section of contemporary klezmer bands, ranging from the Klezmatics to Flying Bulgar Klezmer Band, Alice Svigals, and Budowitz, among others. The organizing principle of the recording emphasizes the performance of klezmer music at a shtetl wedding, hence the subtitle "a marriage of heaven and earth," which also refers to the dual tradition of klezmer music—as an extroverted representation of Jewish celebration and an introspective reflection of Hassidic tradition.

Kol Nidre: Sacred Music of the Synagogue. Leo Roth, tenor, Gloria Selpelt, alto, Rudolf Wiebel, baritone, Harry Foss, organ, Werner Buschnakowski, organ, and the Chor der Judischen Gemeinde Berlin, Leipziger Synagogal-Chor, and Mitglieder des Rundfulk-Sinfonie-Orchesters Leipzig. EMI Classics CD 7243–5–65457–2–4. Cologne: EMI Electrola GmbH, 1995. TT: 75:20.

This compact disc contains eighteen selections of Jewish liturgical music, beginning with "Hashklvenu" (Let Us Respose) and continuing through works for the Friday evening service, the day of Sabbath, a variety of prayers, the "Kol Nidrei," and "El Malei Racahmim" (God Full of Mercy). The "El Malei Racahmim" included on this recording makes direct reference to the victims of the Nazi death camps in Poland by including in its text the names of Auschwitz, Majdanek, and Treblinka.

Mamaloshen. Performed by Mandy Patinkin with orchestra and the Zalmen Mlotek Yiddish Chorale conducted by Eric Stern. Song texts provided. Nonesuch CD 79459-2. New York: Nonesuch Records, 1998. TT: 52:34.

This collection of Yiddish songs sung by American singing actor Mandy Patinkin includes the Holocaust song "Under Your White Stars," which was written by the Israeli poet Abraham Sutzkever in collaboration with Abraham Brudno. All lyrics are sung in Yiddish and the booklet includes an essay about the origin of the recording and complete bilingual Yiddish-English texts.

Mother Tongue: Music of the 19th Century Klezmorim on Original Instruments. Koch Schwann CD 3–1261–2 H 1. Performed by Ensemble Budowitz. Port Washington, NY: Koch International, 1997. TT: 58:44.

This compact disc contains twenty-three traditional Klezmer tunes performed on reproductions of nineteenth-century instruments used in Klezmer bands. The musical selections are drawn from the research of the Ukrainian ethnomusicologist Moyshe Beregovski, as well as historical publications and recordings of Klezmer music from the period 1900–1930. In the English-German dual-language booklet, extensive notes about each work are provided, along with an interview with the performers that discusses the genesis of their historic performance practices. This recording provides an entry point into the daily life and celebrations of Eastern and Central European Jews by illuminating a musical tradition that was almost completely destroyed during the Holocaust.

Netania Davrath: Russian, Israeli and Yiddish Folk Songs. Netania Davrath, soprano, with orchestras conducted by Robert DeCormier and Josef Leo Gruber. Song texts provided. Vanguard Classics 2 CD Set OVC 8058/59.

New York: Omega Record Group, Inc., 1995. TT: CD 1, 70:02. CD 2, 66:08.

This two-disc set includes three collections of folk songs: Yiddish songs from Europe, and songs from Russia and Israel. The soprano Netania Davrath is the soloist on all the selections, and is accompanied by orchestras conducted by Robert DeCormier and Joseph Le Gruber. The Yiddish songs include works from the Hassidic movements of the eighteenth century, as well as the cultural renaissance of Jewish life in late nineteenth and early twentieth-century Europe, which fomented resistance against ghetto life and the violence perpetrated on Jewish communities in pogroms. The famous song "Es Brent" (The Town Is Burning) by Mordecai Gebirtig was written in 1936 in response to a Polish pogrom against Jews in the small town of Pryztyk, and was later applied to the suffering of Jews in the Holocaust. Although texts are not supplied, concise summaries of each song's meaning are included.

Pearls of Yiddish Song. Various artists under the direction of Zalmen Mlotek. Workmen's Circle CD. New York: The Workmen's Circle, 1998. TT: 60:33.

This compact disc contains performances of twenty Yiddish songs that are published in the anthology of the same title (see "Musical Compositions" in this chapter). No texts are provided, although the listing of songs does cross-reference the pages in the anthology where each song is located.

Works by German and Austrian Composers Censored in the Third Reich

Among the composers included here are Hanns Eisler, Karl Amadeus Hartmann, and Kurt Weill, all of whom authored musical compositions that ran afoul of Nazi ideology and were censored during the Third Reich. A number of these composers emigrated to the United States or other European countries to escape Nazi persecution and continued composing in the countries that granted them refuge. This section includes works by these composers that were created following their refugee emigration, but which are connected in content and form to historical circumstances of the period 1919–1945.

Eisler, Hanns. *Deutsche Symphonie, Opus 50 for Soloists, Speaking Voices, Chorus, and Orchestra.* Text by Bertolt Brecht and anonymous authors. Performed by soloists and the Choir and Symphony Orchestra of the Leipzig Radio conducted by Adolf Fritz Guhl. Berlin Classics CD 0030662BC. Berlin: Edel Records, 1998. TT: 62:44.

Hanns Eisler was born in Leipzig in 1898. As a Jew and a communist, he was a marked man in Nazi Germany and in 1933 he left Germany, eventually settling in the United States. He became a noted film composer, residing in Hollywood, California, but following the end of World War II, with the rise of anti-communism during the Cold War he returned to Europe, settling in the German Democratic Republic, where he taught composition in East Berlin. The *Deutsche Symphonie* contains eleven sections, beginning with a prelude that quotes the "Internationale" and a song dedicated to the memory of concentration camp victims. The second movement, a passacaglia, is a lament that condemns the Nazi concentration camp system and its use of terror. The fifth section, an orchestral funeral procession, emphasizes the suffering of the victims in the camps and is based on Bertoldt Brecht's poem "Sonnenburg." Other movements address issues of class conflict and the pain that emerged owing to Germany's aggression in World War II, again drawing upon works by Brecht. While most of the *Deutsche Symphonie* was written between 1935 and 1937, it was not completed until 1959, when it had its premiere in Berlin.

———. *Hollywood Song-book: Lieder of the Exile.* Dietrich Fischer-Dieskau, baritone, and Albert Reimann, piano. Teldec CD 4509–97459–2. Hamburg: Teldec Classics International GMBH, 1994. TT: 44:50.

This collection of songs by German emigré composer Hanns Eisler was largely composed during his exile years in the United States, when he lived in California. Many of the works were the product of a collaboration with Bertholdt Brecht, whom Eisler had known in Europe and who moved to California in 1941, where he worked closely with Eisler for the next five years. Included among the songs are references to the tragedy of war, verses that reflect Brecht and Eisler's commitment to Marxist ideology, and others created in remembrance of other German composers and writers, such as Schumann and Eichendorff. Complete texts are provided in German, English, and French, along with an essay (again in three languages) about Eisler's development as a lied composer in the German tradition.

———. *Works for Orchestra I.* Max Pommer conducts the Chamber Music Group of the Gewandhaus Orchestra of Leipzig (*Suite No. 1, Suite No. 2, Suite No. 3, Theme with Variations on "Der Lange Marsch,"* and *Chamber Symphony*) and Heinz Roger conducts the Berlin Radio Symphony Orchestra (*Suite No. 4*). Berlin Classics CD 0092282BC. Berlin: Edel Records, 1998. TT: 65:44.

Hanns Eisler was active in the composition of film music throughout much of his career. Prior to the appointment of Hitler as chancellor in January 1933, Eisler had prepared film scores for a number of films that emphasized socialist themes, notably advocating the revolutionary labor movement. In *Suites 1, 2, 3,* and *4,* Eisler's political awareness is represented in musical terms through the use of parody, satire, and inclusion of songs representing the collective interests of workers fighting against bourgeois capitalists in Germany and the Soviet Union. He also employs folk songs, as in *Suite 2*, where he creates a "Capriccio on Jewish Folk Songs" by reworking familiar tunes in an unconventional manner. The *Chamber Symphony* contains material originally developed for a documentary film on the Arctic, when Eisler was living in the United States. The constantly shifting, short pieces included in this work reflect Eisler's belief that modern music should be used to influence large groups of people to social action. He rejected the use of large-scale symphonic development, as was practiced in most Hollywood film music of the time, and developed his ideas about film music in a work he co-authored with the philosopher Theodore Adorno in 1947. The *Theme and Variations* emerged from film music that Eisler wrote for a documentary entitled "China 400 Millions." The content of the film deals with the struggles between the "Whites" (Chiang Kai-shek's followers) and the "Reds" (followers of Mao Tse-tung), and is another example of how Eisler's political awareness was translated into musical works.

Goldschmidt, Berthold. *Overture—The Comedy of Errors and Greek Suite*. Also contains Erwin Schulhoff, *Ogelala*. Michail Jurowski conducts the Staatsphilharmonie Rheinland-Pfalz. CPO CD 999–232–2. Georgsmarienhutte: CPO Recordings, 1995. TT: 57:12.

Born in Berlin in 1903, Berthold Goldschmidt was a rising star in Germany's musical world during the 1920s and early 1930s. He achieved a great success with his overture *The Comedy of Errors*, premiered at Oldenburg in 1928, which has a loose connection to the comedy by Shakespeare of the same name. Combining both grace and a dose of the grotesque, Goldschmidt's overture is characteristic of his great potential as a young German Jewish composer in the Weimar Republic. The *Greek Suite*, composed in 1940–1941, was prepared in response to a commission from the publisher Max Hinrichsen for a suite of Greek folk melodies. At the time, Goldschmidt and Hinrichsen were both emigrés from Germany who had fled the Hitler regime, and the inspiration of the commission was the attack on Greece by Italy in 1940. Containing eight short movements, the work is based upon a collection of Greek folk melodies published in Paris in 1876. Erwin Schulhoff, one of the leading young Czech composers of the early twentieth century, composed his ballet score *Ogelala* between 1922 and 1925. The ballet was premiered in Dessau in 1925, and although the music was well received, the choreography for the ballet was not. Drawing its inspiration from ancient Mexican Indian life, the ballet has similarities in its use of ostinato rhythms and sensual orchestration to Stravinsky's *Rite of Spring* and Prokofiev's *Scythian Suite*. Schulhoff died in the Wulzburg Concentration Camp in August 1942.

The Goldschmidt Album. Works by Berthold Goldschmidt. Performed by various artists. London Entartete Musik CD 452 599–2. London: The Decca Record Company Limited, 1996. TT: 66:29.

This compact disc presents a sampling of the compositions of Bertold Goldschmidt, who was one of the leading composers in Germany during the first half of the twentieth century. As a Jew, Goldschmidt was unable to remain in Germany and left for exile in Britain during the 1930s, where he lived the remainder of his life. Beginning with his *Opus 4 Passacaglia* (1925), this recording includes works composed by Goldschmidt in the 1920s and 1930s, as well as works he wrote in the 1990s, when a rebirth of interest in his compositions emerged. As part of the recording project *Entartete Musik*, the notes accompanying this compact disc include a lengthy interview with the composer where he discusses all the works included in the recording. Three of the works receive their world premiere recordings on this compact disc: the 1925 *Passacaglia* for orchestra, the 1994 *Les Petits Adieux* for solo baritone and orchestra, and the 1995 *Rondeau* for solo violin and orchestra.

Hartmann, Karl Amadeus. *Concerto Funebre.* Paul Hindemith. *Violin Concerto. Cello Concerto.* Karel Ancerl conducting the Czech Philharmonic Orchestra with Andre Gertler, violin, and Paul Tortelier, cello. Supraphon CD 11 1955-2 011. Prague: Supraphon, 1993. TT: 75:32.

This compact disc contains works by two composers whose compositions were suppressed during the Third Reich: Karl Amadeus Hartmann and Paul Hindemith. Hartmann's *Concerto Funebre* was composed in 1939 and revised in 1959. As a protest against Nazi oppression, the work begins with the Hussite chorale "Ye Who Are God's Warriors," while the fourth movement quotes the Russian funeral march "For the Fallen Revolutionaries." The two Hindemith concertos included here, one for violin (1939) and other for cello (1940), were composed while the composer was living in exile in the United States. Hindemith's works, notably his opera *Mathis der Maler*, had been attacked in Germany and later suppressed by Nazi officials. In the late 1930s, he emigrated to the United States, where he became a teacher of composition and continued composing.

————. *Symphony No. 1, Symphony No. 6, and Miserae—Symphonic Poem for Orchestra.* Performed by the London Philharmonic Orchestra and Jard van Nes, mezzo-soprano, conducted by Leon Botstein. Telarc CD CD–80528. Cleveland: Telarc, 1999. TT: 67:54.

Karl Amadeus Hartmann was born in 1905 and remained in Germany throughout the Third Reich. He was successful in removing himself from public life late in the 1930s, while continuing to compose works whose content and inspiration were directly opposed to Nazism. Two of the three works on this compact disc, the tone poem *Miserae* of 1933 and his *Symphony No. 1* of 1937 (revised in 1950), reflect

Hartmann's opposition to Nazism and his sympathy for the victims of Nazi persecution. *Miserae* includes a dedication "To my friends who had to die by the hundreds, now sleeping for eternity—we will not forget you (Dachau, 1933–1934)." It was premiered at the International Society for New Music in Prague under Hermann Scherchen's direction in 1935, and was known throughout Germany despite its anti-Nazi inspiration. The *Symphony No. 1*, drawing upon a Walt Whitman poem, blurs the lines between symphony, orchestral song, and cantata by its inclusion of text for a mezzo-soprano and its use of a theme and variations structure for the third movement. The spirit of the work is epitomized in the subtitles of the fourth and fifth movements, "Tranen" (Tears) and "Epilog: Bitte" (Epilogue: Plea), respectively. The *Symphony No. 6*, composed in 1951–1953, completes this recording.

————. *Symphony No. 2 Adagio. Gesangsszene to words from Jean Giraudoux' "Sodom and Gomorrha." Sinfonia Tragica.* Siegmund Nimsgern, baritone, and the Bamberg Symphony conducted by Karl Anton Rickenbacher. Koch Schwann CD 3–1295–2. Port Washington: Koch International, 1993. TT: 63:50.

The three Hartmann works on this compact disc reflect his deep concern with political issues, focused specifically on the tragedy of Nazism and Germany's aggression during World War II (*Symphony No. 2, Sinfonia Tragica*) or on global concerns that emerged after 1945, such as nuclear confrontation and environmental degradation (*Sodom and Gomorrha*). The *Sinfonia Tragica*, composed between 1940 and 1943, directly quotes from works of composers banned by the Nazis, including Mahler, Berg, Webern, Hindemith, Bartok, and Stravinsky. Hartmann's commitment to an "aesthetics of resistance" permeated his compositions during the Nazi period, and his *Symphony No. 2* (Adagio) includes veiled quotations of the socialist anthem the "Internationale" as well as Jewish melodic themes. Although subtitled "Adagio," the work contains one long movement that is subdivided into a slow-fast-slow structure, reflecting Hartmann's central concern that his compositions could serve as "music of confrontation" to bring a more focused awareness to political and social concerns through artistic means. The remaining work, *Sodom and Gomorrha*, based upon the drama of Jean Giraudoux, was Hartmann's final, unfinished work and utilizes a baritone soloist and orchestra to communicate the composer's deep concerns about global problems in the context of a musical fable.

————. *Symphony No. 3. With Charles Ives, Robert Browning Overture.* Performed by the Bamberger Symphoniker, conducted by Ingo Metzmacher. EMI Classics CD 7243 5 55254. Koln: Emi Electrola Gmbh, 1995. TT: 51:59.

This compact disc contains a complete performance of Hartmann's *Symphony No. 3*, which consists of movements from works that he had composed between 1933 and 1945, specifically the *Klagegesang Symphony* (1944) and the *Sinfonia Tragica* (1940). Hartmann reworked sections of the earlier works extensively when composing the *Symphony No. 3*, and by concluding the work with an adagio movement, he continues in the long tradition of German symphonic composers such as Anton Bruckner and Gustav Mahler. The *Symphony No. 3* was premiered in 1948. The remaining work on this recording is Charles Ives' *Robert Browning Overture* (1908–1912), which, like the works of Hartmann, reflects a personal, iconoclastic approach to composition that has gradually brought the composer posthumous acclaim.

Hindemith, Paul. *Mathis der Maler, Nobilissima Visione, and Symphonic Metamorphosis on a Theme by Weber.* Yoel Levi conducting the Atlanta Symphony Orchestra. Telarc CD-80195. Cleveland: Telarc International, 1989. TT: 76:46.

This recording includes three of Hindemith's most famous works, and the one that contributed most directly to his eventual exile from Germany during the period of the Third Reich. The symphony *Mathis der Maler* is based upon the opera of the same title by Hindemith, which draws its subject matter from the life of the sixteenth-century German painter Mathias Grunwald and the creation of his masterpiece, the altarpiece in the Church of St. Anthony in Isenheim, Alsace. Despite the success of the symphony's premiere in 1934 under the baton of Wilhelm Furtwangler with the Berlin Philharmonic, Hindemith's position became increasingly difficult in Germany when Nazi cultural leaders viewed his work as threatening, and the premiere of the opera *Mathis der Maler* was indefinitely postponed (the work was not performed in Germany until after World War II ended). Hindemith left Germany for Switzerland in 1938 and eventually moved to the United States, where his compositional output and influence as a teacher were substantial. The remaining two works on this recording were composed by Hindemith between 1937 and 1943. *Nobilissima Visione* was written as a ballet score based upon the life and works of St. Francis of Assisi, while the *Symphonic Metamorphosis on a Theme by Weber* emerged from an aborted dance project, and has retained its place in the orchestral repertoire based upon its brilliant orchestration of themes from four short works by the German romantic composer Carl Maria von Weber.

Krenek, Ernst. *Jonny Spielt Auf. Opera in Two Parts, Op. 45. (abridged).* Soloists, the Vienna Academy Choir, and the Vienna State Orchestra conducted by Heinrich Hollreiser. Libretto provided. Vanguard Classics OVC 8048. New York: Omega Record Group, Inc., 1993. TT: 50:18.

First performed in Leipzig in February 1927, Ernst Krenek's *Jonny Spielt Auf* became a landmark work of the Weimar period in German cultural history.

Combining jazz, traditional operatic writing, and compositional ideas influenced by music-hall revues and burlesque idioms, Krenek's work was enormously popular, leading to its translation into eighteen languages and performances in many opera houses, such as the Metropolitan Opera in New York (1928). It was also a work reviled by Nazism because it veered significantly from "traditional" operatic subject matter by positing a romance between a black jazz musician and a white woman, it used jazz substantially as part of its musical language, and it satirizes social institutions such as law enforcement. Nazism's racist ideology and opposition to experimentation in the arts doomed Krenek's work in Germany, thus leading to Krenek's emigration to the United States after the 1938 anschluss that brought Austria into the Third Reich. Although one of Austria's leading modern composers, Krenek could not remain in his native land and later taught composition in the United States, where he also wrote scores for film, among other works. This performance uses Krenek's English translation of the libretto, which he authored at age seventy-five. A complete libretto and essay on the work accompany the compact disc.

The Music Survives: Degenerate Music. Music Suppressed by the Third Reich. Performed by various artists. London Entartete Musik CD 452 664-2. London: The Decca Record Company Limited, 1993–1996. Accompanying VHS videocassette. TT: 76:12.

Containing excerpts from the works of eight composers whose works were deemed "degenerate" (unacceptable) by the Nazi regime, this compact disc accompanies the videotape of the same title (see Chapter 13 on film and videotape) and presents an overview of music banned by the Nazis. Included among the selections are opera (*Flammen* by Erwin Schulhoff; *Die Vogel* by Walter Braunfels; *Das Wunder der Heliane* by Erich Wolfgang Korngold; *Jonny Spielt Auf* by Ernst Krenek; *Der Kaiser von Atlantis* by Viktor Ullmann; and *Der Gewaltige Hahnrei* by Berthold Goldschmidt), chamber music (*String Quartet No. 2* by Pavel Haas), and orchestral works by Korngold and Hanns Eisler (the präludium from his *Deutsche Symphonie*). The accompanying booklet provides background on each composer as well as an introduction to the content of the accompanying videotape.

Waxman, Franz. *The Song of Terezin.* Eric Zeisl. *Hebrew Requiem.* Lawrence Foster conducting soloists, the Berlin Radio Symphony Orchestra, and the choir and children's choir of the Berlin Radio Symphony Orchestra. London Entartete Musik CD 289 460 211-2. London: The Decca Record Company Limited, 1998. TT: 57.07.

This compact disc includes two memorial compositions for Jews murdered in the Holocaust, with specific focus on the Terezin ghetto and camp. Franz Waxman, himself a refugee from Nazism, had emigrated to the United States 1935. His career in the United States took two paths: the well-known one being as a composer of 144 film scores such as *A Place in the Sun* and *Sunset Boulevard*, for which he won Oscars. His other creative path involved composition of classical works, of which the *Terezin Requiem* was among his finest. The work was commissioned by the Cincinnati May Festival in 1964, and Waxman employed texts from the poetry of children in Terezin as the sources for his song cycle with orchestra. The work was premiered in Cincinnati on May 22, 1965 and reflects an eclectic mixture of compositional influences drawing from the twelve-tone system of Arnold Schoenberg and the late romantic styles of Richard Strauss and Alexander Zemlinsky. Eric Zeisl's *Requiem Ebraico* was the outgrowth of an earlier work that included settings of music for a synagogue service, but whose design and content were transformed by the news that Zeisl's father and relatives had been murdered by the Nazis. Zeisl's father had initially been interned in Terezin before being transported to a death camp (most likely Treblinka). Using as his source the Ninety-Second Psalm, Zeisl prepared a work for soloists, choir, and orchestra that is musically based upon a single folk-like melody that is varied throughout the work's sections, culminating in a final fugue. Stylistically, Zeisl's *Requiem Ebraico* contains elements of late romanticism and twentieth-century music, echoing Mahler and Bartok. Like Waxman, the Austrian Zeisl was a refugee from Nazism who rebuilt his career in the United States, basing his teaching and composition in California from the early 1940s onward. Texts provided.

Weill, Kurt. *Die Dreigroschenoper (The Threepenny Opera).* Soloists, Handel Collegium Koln and the Konig Ensemble conducted by Jan Latham-Konig. Capriccio CD 60–058–1. Libretto provided. Konigsdorf: Capriccio, 1997. TT: 64:30.

Originally produced in 1928, Bertold Brecht and Kurt Weill's "Play with Music in a Prologue and Eight Scenes" has held the stage for over seventy years, having been produced in France and the United States as well as in German-speaking countries. Based upon the model of John Gay and Johan Christopher Pepusch's *The Beggar's Opera* (1728), the work is employed by Brecht and Weill as a vehicle for social criticism of the abuses of modern capitalism, which were particularly telling in Weimar Germany. Whereas Brecht's text has roots in Lutheran German and biblical language as well as political cliches, Weill's musical score parodies the conventions of opera while retaining a directness that he linked to the original intentions of opera in the Baroque period. By contrasting music that was singularly unrealistic in its form and design with Brecht's very realistic libretto, Weill was able to integrate modern dance patterns (foxtrot, tango) and jazz with ballads and street songs. Combining these elements with Weill's gift for telling melodies, the *Threepenny Opera* has remained an audience favorite since its premiere. However, the same elements that made the work accessible and popular also led to its censorship by the Nazis. Not only were Brecht and Weill politically on the left, but Weill was Jewish, and once Hitler gained power their works were unacceptable to Nazi ideology. Additionally, the satirical focus of *The Threepenny Opera* and its inclusion of jazz musical elements made it anathema to a government whose cultural politics was anti-experimental and racist. A German-only libretto is included with this performance.

———. *Kleine Dreigroschenmusic. Concerto for Violin and Wind Orchestra, Opus 12. Mahagonny Songspiel.* Soloists and the London Sinfonietta conducted by David Atherton. Deutsche Grammophon 20th Century Classics CD 423 255–2. Hamburg: Polydor International GmbH, 1976. TT: 71:24.

This compact disc contains three works by Kurt Weill, two of which he prepared in collaboration with Bertold Brecht: *The Threepenny Opera* (1928) and *The Rise and Fall of the House of Mahagonny* (1927). The *Mahagonny* "songspiel," otherwise known as "The Little Mahagonny," was premiered in Baden-Baden. The work blends modern American dance music and popular song forms with texts drawn from Brecht's Mahagonny poems, which are satirical of modern capitalism and social inequalities. Linking the vocal segments of the work are instrumental interludes that contrast with the popular song design of the vocal segments. This original "songspiel" served as the inspiration for the full-scale opera, *The Rise and Fall of the House of Mahagonny,* which Brecht and Weill premiered in Leipzig in 1930. The remaining work, the *Concerto for Violin and Wind Orchestra,* was composed in 1924.

———. *The Rise and Fall of the City of Mahagonny. Opera in Three Acts.* Text by Bertolt Brecht. Jan Latham-Konig conducting soloists, the "Pro Musica" Vocal Ensemble of the Staatlichen Hochschule for Music in Koln, and the Koln Radio Symphony Orchestra. Capriccio 2-CD set 10 160/61. Frechen-Konigsdorf: Capriccio, 1988. Libretto provided. TT: 141:00.

Following the critical success of their Mahagonny "songspiel" in 1927, Brecht and Weill developed a full-scale opera on the subject. Focusing on the moral and political decline of a "universal" city, the work satirizes modern industrial capitalism, painting a picture of greed, crime, and corruption as endemic in the city of Mahagonny. Following its Leipzig premiere, the work faced a stormy reception in other German cities, particularly due to Nazi opposition and protests. In 1931, the work was premiered in Berlin, where it ran for fifty consecutive performances, an exceptional run for a contemporary opera. Following the ascendancy of the Nazi party and Hitler's assumption of the chancellorship in January 1933, Weill fled Germany and further performances of the work in Germany were not permitted by Nazi officials. The dual-language libretto accompanying this performance is in German and English, and the libretto booklet contains a detailed chronology of the work's development and performance history.

———. *Speak Low: Songs by Kurt Weill and The Seven Deadly Sins.* Anne Sofie Von Otter, mezzo-soprano, with assisting vocal artists, and Bengt

Forsberg, piano. John Eliot Gardiner conducts the NDR-Sinfonieorchester in *The Seven Deadly Sins*. Deutsche Grammophon CD 439 894–2. Hamburg: Deutsche Grammophon GmbH, 1994. TT: 78:09.

This recording includes a broad representation of Weill's writing for voice. The major work is the high voice (soprano) version of the song cycle *The Seven Deadly Sins*, which Weill composed in collaboration with Bertold Brecht in 1933 following his emigration from Germany. The work's seven sections are full of social and moral satire on middle-class values, employing a mixed-voice quartet that comments on the seven sins committed by Anna, the soprano and primary vocalist in the cycle. Originally conceived as a hybrid work of song and dance, two Annas were to perform: Anna I as the vocalist and Anna II as the dancer. The sins (sloth, pride, anger, gluttony, lust, avarice, and envy) are adapted from religious references and made into secular symbols about the hypocrisy of middle-class life. Also included on the compact disc are three songs from the Brecht-Weill work *Happy End* (1929), two songs from the Weill–Moss Hart–Ira Gershwin work *Lady in the Dark* (1941), three songs from the Weill–Ogden Nash work *One Touch of Venus* (1943), and five other songs, two of which ("Buddy on the Nightshift" and "Schickelgruber") were composed in support of the Allied war effort. "Schickelgruber" is a parody on Hitler's early life and predicts his ultimate demise against the Allies, while "Buddy on the Nightshift" is a song dedicated to supporting the round-the-clock efforts by industrial workers to win the war. A dual German-English set of song texts is provided.

———. *Symphonies 1 and 2. Ferruccio Busoni. Berceuse Elegiaque, Opus 42. Arnold Schoenberg. Chamber Symphony No. 2, Opus 38.* Frederik Prausnitz conducting the New Philharmonia Orchestra. EMI Classics CD 7243 5 65869 2 5. London: EMI Records Ltd., 1996. TT: 79:19.

This compact disc contains two instrumental works of Kurt Weill, reflecting his interest in extramusical forms of inspiration (*Symphony No. 1*) and the influence of changing political landscapes (*Symphony No. 2*). The *Symphony No. 1*'s impetus was a play by Johannes Becher, "Workers, Peasants and Soldier's—A People's Awakening," for which Weill was asked to author incidental music. While the incidental music did not come forth, the symphony did. It has one movement, beginning with an allegro, followed by andante religioso, and concluding with a chorale fantasy. The *Symphony No. 2*, premiered in New York and Amsterdam in 1934, is a product of Weill's emigré years. A dark, somber tone is reflected in the first two movements of the work, illustrating the composer's response to the rise of fascism, notably in Germany. The remaining two works are by contemporaries of Weill, Ferruccio Busoni (*Berceuse Elegiaque*) and Arnold Schoenberg (*Chamber Symphony No. 2*).

Works Inspired by the Holocaust and Its Legacy

Included in this category are musical compositions developed in response to the events of the Holocaust, the plight and persecution of Jews, and as forms of Holocaust commemoration and remembrance.

Amram, David. The Final Ingredient: An Opera of the Holocaust in One Act. Music composed by David Amram. Libretto by Arnold Weinstein. Soloists and orchestra conducted by David Amram. Libretto provided. Premier Recordings PRCD 1056. New York: Premier Recordings, 1996. TT: 56:14.

Premiered in 1965 as an opera for television, David Amram's *The Final Ingredient* relates the story of how Jews in Nazi camps sought to maintain the spiritual tradition of Passover despite the daily suffering and oppression they encountered. The opera is based upon a play by Reginald Rose, and is further informed by the composer's discussions with Holocaust survivors. The setting is the Bergen-Belsen concentration camp, and the structure of the work includes arias and duets, choral segments, spoken dialogue, and an orchestral prologue. Although first performed in the 1960s, this compact disc represents the first audio recording of the opera. A complete libretto is provided along with explanatory notes about the origins and development of the opera.

Fiser, Lubos. *Sonata for Solo Violin "In memoriam Terezin."* Also includes works for violin and piano by Ludwig Van Beethoven, Karol Szymanowski, and Henryk Wieniawski. Performed by Viktor Kuna, violin, and Yuri Smirnov, piano. Multisonic CD 31 0213–2. Prague: Multisonic, 1994. TT: 58:41.

This compact disc contains a recording of the contemporary Czech composer Lubos Fiser's sonata for solo violin *In memoriam Terezin.* Composed in 1981, the work challenged the official indifference in cultural circles of communist Czechoslovakia to the victims of the Holocaust, with particular reference to those who suffered and died at the Terezin ghetto/camp complex outside of Prague. The very intense composition moves through frequent mood changes and shifts of tempo to emphasize the expressive nature of the violin in evoking memories of those who perished at the hands of Nazism.

Heritage: The Symphonic Music of the Museum of Jewish Heritage, a Living Memorial to the Holocaust. Michael Isaacson conducting members of the Israel Philharmonic Orchestra. CD ECM 1500. New York: Museum of Jewish Heritage, 1997. TT: 73:58.

This compact disc contains music composed by Michael Isaacson for the exhibits and films of the Museum of Jewish Heritage. Drawing upon a wide range of sources (Ladino, Yiddish, Hebrew, and German), the composer has adapted and integrated liturgical and secular melodies and songs in this work for symphony orchestra. The recording has seven major sections, corresponding to major themes in the Museum's exhibitions: *Fanfare and Belief, Shabbat, Sukkot, Weddings, Synagogues, Occupations, Childhood,* and *Remembrance Suite.* The *Remembrance Suite* has the most direct connection to the Holocaust, containing arrangements of songs such as "Shtiler, Shtiler" (Quiet, Quiet), "Unzer Shtet'l Brent" (As Our Village Burns), "Eli Eli" (My God, My God), "Zog Nit Kein Mol" (Never Say You've Reached Journey's End), and "Ani Maamin" (I Believe). The accompanying booklet includes lyric translations and background information on the recording of the work, as well as information about the development of the Museum of Jewish Heritage.

Holocaust Cantata: Songs from the Camps. Arranged by Donald McCullough. Also includes Seymon Laks' *Passacaille for Cello and Piano* and songs based upon Holocaust texts by Michael Horvit and Donald McCullough. Performed by the Master Chorale of Washington Chamber Singers conducted by Donald McCullough, Robert Lamar Sims, pianist and Mirian Bolkosky, cellist. Texts provided. Albany Records CD TROY 352. Albany: Albany Records, 1999. TT: 67:34.

Drawing upon the vast collection of Holocaust songs held at the United States Holocaust Memorial Museum and collected by the Polish survivor Alexander Kulisiewicz during World War II and afterward, Donald McCullough, music director of the Master Chorale of Washington, fashioned the Holocaust cantata for soloists, chorus, and selected instrumentalists. Divided into twenty sections, the *Holocaust Cantata* presents images of selected camps, individuals, and experiences based upon the songs collected by Kulisiewicz, but structured as a continuous work with readings interspersed between them that speak of life in the camps. While the original songs were in European languages, McCullough arranged for translations of the songs into English for the purposes of the *Cantata.* The *Holocaust Cantata* was premiered on March 17, 1998 at the John F. Kennedy Center for the Performing Arts in Washington, DC. The accompanying booklet includes an essay about the origins and development of the *Cantata,* as well as vocal texts and background information about the Alexander Kuliesiewicz music collection.

Holocaust Requiem. Kaddish for Terezin. A Liturgical Oratorio by Ronald Senator based on poems and diaries of children who died in Theresienstadt. Also includes Bedrich Smetana, *The Moldau.* Performed by the Moscow Philharmonic, Municipal Boys Choir of the Mussorgsky State Conservatory, Yekaterinburg Yurloff State Chorus, narrator, and soloists, conducted by Stanislav D. Gusev. Texts provided. Delos CD DE 1032. Hollywood: Delos International, Inc., 1994. TT: 60:50.

This compact disc preserves the live performance of Ronald Senator's *Holocaust Requiem: Kaddish for Terezin* that was performed in the Great Hall of the Moscow Conservatory in 1992. The work is largely based upon the experiences of children in the Terezin ghetto and camp complex, as represented in their poetry and diaries. The composer also utilized elements of Hebrew liturgy and quotations from poetry by Nelly Sachs and Paul Celan in the *Requiem*. Consisting of four movements (Kyrie, Kadosh, The Transports, and Mourner's Kaddish), the *Holocaust Requiem* intersperses narration, segments for children's chorus and adult chorus, baritone and soprano soloists, and orchestra. The text combines both Hebrew and English selections. The accompanying booklet describes the genesis of the *Holocaust Requiem*, and contains reflections on the first performance by narrator Bel Kaufman, as well as full texts of the work and background information on the Terezin complex.

I Am Anne Frank. Performed by Andrea Marcovicci, Stephen Bogardus, and members of the American Symphony Orchestra, arranged and conducted by Glenn Mehrbach. No CD no. provided. New York: Anne Frank Center USA, 1996. TT: NA.

This work for vocal soloists and symphony orchestra is a dramatic presentation of diary excerpts and musical theater pieces based upon the Anne Frank story.

Innocent Voices: The Verse of Terezin's Children. Musical realization by John Federico. Composed and conducted by John Federico. Performed by soloists, children's choir, and instrumental accompanists. No CD no. provided. Jefferson Valley, NY: Lost Planet Records, 1996. TT: 46:00+.

This compact disc includes twelve selections drawn from songs, prose, and poetry created in the Terezin camp, arranged by John Federico. Texts and introductions to each selection are provided in the accompanying booklet.

Isolamenti 1938–1945. Piano works by Viktor Ullmann (Sonata No. 7), Karl Amadeus Hartmann (Sonata "27 aprile 1945") and Luigi Nono (Rocorda cosa ti hanno fatto in Auschwitz, cori da "Die Ermittlung" of P. Weiss for magnetic tape). Performed by Aldo Orvieto, piano. Stefano Bassanesse, sound manager. Fonit Cetra CD NFCD 2034. Milan: Fonit Cetra, 1996. TT: 51:00.

The three works on this compact disc all reflect differing responses to the Holocaust and Nazi oppression. Viktor Ullmann's *Sonata No. 7* for solo piano was composed while he was interned in Terezin, and consists in large part of a series of variations on a Hebrew folk song. Ironically, while interned in Terezin, Ullmann became more and more interested in his own Jewish heritage, and composed works such as this and his arrangements of Hebrew and Jewish songs while a prisoner of the Nazis. Karl Amadeus Hartmann's *Sonata 27 April 1945* was inspired by the composer's encounter with prisoners from Dachau, who passed his home on Lake Starnberg on April 27 and 28, 1945. Deeply moved by this encounter, Hartmann's three-movement piano sonata integrates echoes of synagogue hymns (first movement), a funeral march, and popular revolutionary songs (second movement), later concluding the work with a percussive and furious finale. Luigi Nono's work for magnetic tape based upon Peter Weiss' play *The Investigation* draws upon the content of the Holocaust as well as his encounter with Hartmann, who was a champion of new music following World War II as leader of the Musica Viva movement in Munich.

Kahn, Erich Itor. *Nenia Judaeis qui Hac Aetate Perierunt (1940–41) (In Memory of the Jews who Perished in the Holocaust).* John Sessions, violoncello, and Thomas Gunther, piano. Plus other compositions for piano, voice and piano and violin and piano by Erich Itor Kahn. CRI CD 563. New York: Composers Recordings Incorporated, 1988. TT: 70:38.

Erich Itor Kahn (1905–1956) was strongly influenced by the serial composer Arnold Schoenberg, but developed his own original musical language during a period of intense cultural conflict, notably when Nazism and fascism were on the rise. He emigrated from Germany in 1933 to France, and when France fell in 1940, he was interned in a concentration camp. He eventually was able to emigrate to the United States, where he was a pianist and teacher until his death in 1956. The work *Nenia Judaeis qui Hac Aetate Perierunt* (In Memory of the Jews who Perished in the Holocaust) is in two movements for cello and piano, and was composed over a period of three years, beginning in 1940 in the French concentration camp of Les Milles and completed in New York City in 1943.

Lees, Benjamin. *Symphony No. 4, "Memorial Candles."* Kimball Wheeler, mezzo-soprano, James Buswell, violin, and the National Symphony Orchestra of Ukraine, conducted by Theodore Kuchar. Naxos American Classics CD 8.559002. Franklin, TN: Naxos of America, 1998. TT: 61:42.

Composed in 1985, Benjamin Lees' *Symphony No. 4* in three movements, subtitled "Memorial Candles," combines texts from poems by Holocaust survivor Nelly Sachs with the use of the orchestra and a solo violinist to create a memorial homage to the victims of the Holocaust. The mezzo-soprano sings three texts from Nelly Sachs' poetry: "Someone Blew the Shofar," "Footsteps," and "But who Emptied Your Shoes of Sand?" The first two vocal texts are included in movement two of the symphony, while the final text is incorporated in the third and final movement. Violin solos and obbligato passages are included throughout the work, with the solo violinist representing the "soul" instrument of Central and Eastern Europe, and at times playing melodies drawn from Jewish folk music. Throughout the work, the orchestra is used to represent many intense emotions: fear, terror, anger, and resignation, among others. The work was begun in 1983 and completed in 1985, to coincide with the fortieth anniversary of the end of the Holocaust. Vocal texts and program notes are included with this recording.

Martinu, Bohuslav. *Memorial to Lidice. Field Mass. Symphony No. 4.* Jiri Belohlavek conducting the Czech Philharmonic Orchestra and the Czech Philharmonic Choir; Lubomir Matl, choirmaster. Texts provided. Chandos CD CHAN 9138. Colchester: Chandos Records, Ltd., 1993. TT: 65:27.

Czech composer Bohuslav Martinu, living in exile in the United States during World War II, composed the *Memorial to Lidice* in response to the annihilation of the Czech villages of Lidice and Lezaky by German forces in 1942. The assassination by Czech partisans of high SS official Reinhard Heydrich (designated by Himmler to oversee the "final solution of the Jewish question" in Europe) in May 1942 produced the Nazi reprisal against the Czech villages, which inspired worldwide indignation at Nazi brutality. Martinu's response to the destruction of the villages and their populace was *Memorial to Lidice*, a work in one movement, but with three distinct sections. An opening adagio is followed by a shorter andante moderato, and the work concludes with a return to the adagio. Martinu quotes the St. Wenceslas chorale, a famous Czech hymn, as well as the four notes of the opening motif of Beethoven's Symphony No. 5, which was well-known as a call to resistance by the Allies to Nazi oppression during World War II. The work was premiered in New York by the New York Philharmonic under Artur Rodzinski on October 28, 1943, and received its first performance in Czechoslovakia with Rafael Kubelik leading the Czech Philharmonic on March 14, 1946. The two remaining works on this recording also were composed during the period of World War II: the *Field Mass* in 1939 and the *Symphony No. 4* in 1945.

Music from Six Continents: 1992 Series. Includes Arnold Schoenberg, A Survivor from Warsaw, Opus 46; Nancy Van De Vate, Katyn and Krakow Concerto; and Krzysztof Penderecki, Dies Irae. Performed by soloists and the Polish Radio and TV Symphony Orchestra and Chorus of Krakow, conducted by Szymon Kawalla. Texts provided. Vienna Modern Masters CD VMM 3015. Vienna: Vienna Modern Masters, 1992. TT: 70:55.

This compact disc contains four works inspired by the suffering of World War II, with particular focus on Poland. Arnold Schoenberg's *A Survivor from Warsaw* was directly influenced by the Warsaw Ghetto uprising, and Schoenberg's deep emotional reaction to the murder of European Jewry. Originally a Jew who had forsaken his religion and converted to Catholicism, Schoenberg returned to his original faith following his emigration to the United States from Germany. The work is written in the twelve-tone idiom, and has a powerful emotional impact, combining the violence of Nazi oppression with the faith of the Jewish victims, who sing "Shema Yisroel" as the Nazis shout they will send the Jews to the gas chamber. The work is scored for orchestra, narrator, and chorus. Krystof Penderecki's *Dies Irae* was composed in memory of the victims of Auschwitz, and was premiered in 1967. The occasion of its composition was the unveiling of an international monument in memory of the victims of fascism at the Auschwitz-Birkenau death camp. Penderecki utilizes texts from Biblical sources, Greek tragedy, and contemporary Polish and French poetry rather than the traditional liturgy of the Latin mass. The texts, although drawn from varied sources, were then translated into Latin, with the exception of the Aeschylus passage, which is sung in Greek. Divided into three parts, Lamentatio, Apocalypsis, and Apotheosis, the work is atonal and dissonant, as well as highly intense and emotional in impact. The remaining two works were composed by American composer Nancy Van De Vate. *Katyn* is an orchestral work in memory of the thousands of Polish officers murdered by the Soviet Union in the Katyn forest following the partition of Poland in 1939, and *Krakow Concerto* is a work dedicated to the city of Krakow, which has symbolized the continuity of Polish culture and nationalism since the thirteenth century. The *Krakow Concerto* and *Katyn* were featured in a 1988 concert broadcast throughout Poland dedicated to the memory of the victims of World War II; this same concert also featured Schoenberg's *A Survivor from Warsaw* and Penderecki's *Dies Irae.*

Music on Hebrew Themes: Shostakovich, Bloch and Prokofiev. Includes From Jewish Folk Poetry, Song Cycle by Dmitri Shostakovich; 5 works by Ernest Bloch; and the Jewish Overture. Opus 34 by Sergey Prokofiev. Performed by Nadia Pelle, soprano, Mary Ann Hart, mezzo-soprano, Rodney Nolan, tenor, and I Musici de Montreal, conducted by Yuli Turovsky. CHANDOS CD CHAN 8800. Colchester: Chandos Records, Ltd., 1990. TT: 58:36.

Containing three major works inspired by Jewish cultural themes, the central work on this compact disc is Dmitri Shostakovich's song cycle *From Jewish Folk Poetry*. Composed in 1948 during the last anti-Semitic purge of Stalin, the work includes eleven songs that draw from the long tradition of Jewish folk music. Shostakovich had already utilized Jewish themes in earlier works, such as his *Piano Trio No. 2*, and was to return again to the issue of anti-Semitism in his *Symphony No. 13*, subtitled "Babi Yar." The eleven texts alternate laughter and despair, and contain veiled references to the continuing oppression of Jews in the Soviet Union. In this performance, three soloists are employed: a soprano, a mezzo-soprano, and a tenor, who share the soloist responsibilities. The other works on this recording are by Ernest Bloch, born in Switzerland, but who resided for most of his adult life in the United States, and Sergei Prokofiev, the famed Soviet composer and contemporary of Shostakovich. Bloch employed Jewish themes in many of his works (all five of those on this recording were written between 1923 and 1934) whereas Prokofiev's *Overture on Hebrew Themes* was composed in 1920 while he was on tour in the United States and orchestrated in 1934.

Ran, Shulamit. *Mirage: Chamber Music for Flute*. Includes 6 works for flute and chamber ensemble, among them *O the Chimneys* (1969), a suite for voice, ensemble, and tape. Mary Stolper, flute, Lucy Shelton soprano, and the Instrumental ensemble conducted by Cliff Colnot. ERATO CD 0630–12787–2. Paris: Erato Disques S. A., 1996. TT: 60:46.

This compact disc contains six chamber works by Pulitzer Prize–winning composer Shulamit Ran. Her work *O the Chimneys*, a setting of five poems by Nelly Sachs, is composed for female voice, flute, clarinet/bass clarinet, cello, piano, electronic tape, and percussion. The work is structured to present poems about the tearing away of a child from his mother at the outset ("A Dead Child Speaks" and "Already Embraced by the Arm of Heavenly Solace"), continuing with two more-reserved poems ("Fleeing" and "Someone Comes"), and concluding with an apocalyptic final poem ("Hell Is Naked"). The contrast of the dark and violent outer poems with the more introspective two inner poems is maximized by the use of different tonal ranges and instrumental colors. *O the Chimneys* was premiered at the Metropolitan Museum of Art in January 1970.

Reich, Steve. *Different Trains. Electronic Counterpoint*. Kronos Quartet. Pat Metheny, guitar. Elektra/Nonesuch CD 9 79176–2. New York: Warner Communications, Inc., 1989. TT: 42:31.

Using recorded excerpts of Holocaust survivors from the Fortunoff Video Archive for Holocaust Testimonies at Yale University and from the American Jewish Committee's William E. Wiener Oral History Library, composer Steve Reich integrates taped speech with the sounds of trains from the 1930s and 1940s in Europe and the United States, as well as the performance of the Kronos String Quartet, to create a work that portrays the different voyages taken by Jews in the United States and Europe resulting from the Holocaust. Using trains as the linking motif, the work includes three movements: America—Before the War, Europe—During the War, and After the War. This composition, scored for tape and string quartet (1988), presents, in Reich's words, "both a documentary and a musical reality." The Holocaust content is based upon three survivor accounts from Holland and Hungary, specifically referring to the arrival of Germans as occupying forces to deportations, camp experiences, and liberation. Also included on this compact disc is a performance of Reich's *Electronic Counterpoint* by guitarist Pat Metheny. The accompanying booklet includes a diagram of how the content of *Different Trains* is organized and structured in each movement.

Requiem of Reconciliation: In Memory of the Victims of the Second World War. A Joint Composition by 15 Contemporary Composers. Helmut Rilling conducting the Gachinger Kantorei Stuttgart, the Krakauer Kammerchor, and the Israel Philharmonic Orchestra. Texts provided. Hanssler Classics

CD 98.931 (2 CD set). Stuttgart: Hanssler-Verlag, 1995. TT: CD 1 47:53. CD 2 59:14.

This composite work, reflecting the contributions of fifteen major contemporary composers, was written "in memory of the victims of the Second World War." Premiered in 1995 as a commission from the International Bach Academy and the European Music Festival in Stuttgart, Germany, the Requiem of Reconciliation utilizes the structure of the Latin requiem mass while incorporating a wide range of creative responses to the work's memorial focus. The conscious use by Luciano Berio of Paul Celan's poetry in the opening Prolog makes direct reference to the long history of Judaism and the tragedy of the Holocaust, and his notation in the score of the Hebrew word "shofar" makes explicit the significance of Judaism in this memorial work. The other composers who contributed to this work include representatives from the former Soviet Union, Hungary, the United States, Japan, Germany France, Poland, Great Britain, Norway, France, and Czechoslovakia. Complete texts are provided along with extensive background notes about the work and biographical information about the composers and performers.

Shostakovich, Dmitri. *From Jewish Folk Poetry, Op. 79.* Yuri Shaporin. *Songs.* Mikhail Ippolitov-Ivanov. *Four Poems of Rabindranath Tagore.* Dmitri Kabalevsky. *Six Joyful Songs.* Dmitri Shostakovich, piano, and Zara Dolukhanova, mezzo-soprano, Nina Dorliak, soprano, and Alexander Maslennikov, tenor (Shostakovich). Zara Dolukhanova, mezzo-soprano, and Berta Kozel, piano (Shaporin). Zara Dolukhanova, mezzo-soprano, Eduard Grach, violin, and Berta Kozel, piano (Ippolitov-Ivanov). Zara Dolukhanova, mezzo-soprano, and Nina Svetlanov, piano (Kabalevsky). Russian Disc CD 15 015. Russian Disc, 1994. TT: 57:33.

This compact disc documents a performance of the song cycle *From Jewish Folk Poetry* in 1956 by the composer and the three vocalists who gave its public premiere in 1955: Zara Dolukhanova, Nina Dorliak, and Alexander Maslennikov. Inspired by a collection of Jewish poems entitled *Jewish Folk Songs* that he had purchased in a train station, Shostakovich wrote eleven songs based upon the poems in the collection. He organized them thematically, with the first three addressing childhood, the next three focusing on love and its misfortunes, the next two about poverty, and the final three about the joy and happiness of rural life. Throughout the cycle, Shostakovich displays his command of the dance rhythms and laments of Jewish folk music, although the melodies are entirely his own. The remaining works on this recording reflect the rich tradition of Russian and Soviet vocal music, ranging from Ippolitov-Ivanov's works based upon Indian texts to Kabalevsky's works based upon English children's folk songs. Dual-language Russian-English texts are provided.

————. *From Jewish Folk Poetry, Op. 79a.* Also contains Shostakovich's completion of Benjamin Fleischmann's opera *Rothschild's Violin.* Sergei Leiferkus, Konstantin Pluzhnikov, Ilya Levinsky, and Marina Shaguch, vocal soloists, with the Rotterdam Philharmonic Orchestra conducted by Gennady Rozhdestvensky. Sergei Leferkus (baritone) is the soloist in *From Jewish Folk Poetry.* RCA Red Seal CD 09026–68434–2. RCA Red Seal, 1996. TT: 66:01.

Following the death of his student Benjamin Fleischmann during the siege of Leningrad, Shostakovich determined to complete his student's opera *Rothschild's Violin,* based upon a story by Anton Chekhov. Set in a shtetl, the opera brings to life a world that was already being destroyed by the genocidal policies of Nazi Germany during their occupation of Central and Eastern Europe. Shostakovich's long-standing interest in Jewish culture and his absolute opposition to anti-Semitism are reflected in his use of Jewish themes and content in a number of his major works, including the *Trio No. 2 for Violin, Cello, and Piano* (1944), the song cycle *From Jewish Folk Poetry* (1948), and the *Symphony No. 13,* "Babi Yar" (1962). This compact disc also contains the version of *From Jewish Folk Poetry* for low voice, here performed by the baritone Sergei Leferkus. Although initially written to help Shostakovich rehabilitate himself in the eyes of the party power structure by using accessible folk materials to create "accessible" music for the masses, *From Jewish Folk Poetry* also contains content that reflects the alternately humorous and sad dimensions of Jewish life in Russia. The song cycle was not publicly performed until 1955, two years after Stalin's death, owing to the intense anti-Semitic climate of Stalin's final five years (1948–1953), which included the notorious "Doctors Trial." *Rothschild's Violin* was not performed until 1968, when a performance led by Shostakovich's son took place. This work too faced official condemnation, and was banned after one performance. Dual-language Russian-English texts are provided for both works.

————. *Symphony No. 13, "Babi Yar," Opus 113.* Kurt Masur conducting the New York Philharmonic, with Sergei Leiferkus, bass, and the Men of the New York Choral Artists, Joseph Flummerfelt, director. Includes Yevgeny Yevtushenko reading his poems "Babi Yar" and "The Loss." Texts provided. Teldec CD 4509–90848–2. Hamburg: Teldec Classsics International GMBH, 1994. TT: 67:15.

This performance of the Shostakovich *Symphony No. 13* also includes a reading by Yevgeny Yevtushenko in Russian of two of his poems: "Babi Yar" and "The Loss." The text of the symphony's vocal portions and the poems by Yevtushenko are provided in Russian and English in the accompanying booklet.

————. *Symphony No. 13, "Babi Yar," Opus 113.* Sir Georg Solti conducting the Chicago Symphony Orchestra, with Sergei Aleksashin, bass, and the Men of the Chicago Symphony Chorus, Duain Wolfe, chorus master. Includes Sir Anthony Hopkins reading poems by Yevgeny Yevtushenko in English. Texts provided. London CD 444 791–2. London: The Decca Record Company, Limited, 1995. TT: 72:40.

This recording of Shostakovich's *Symphony No. 13* also includes readings in English translation by Sir Anthony Hopkins of Yevtushenko poems utilized in the Symphony's five movements by Shostakovich. The accompanying booklet contains a dual-language set of texts in English and Russian of the vocal texts used in the symphony, as well as the poems read by Sir Anthony Hopkins.

————. *Symphony No. 13, "Babi Yar," Opus 113.* Kiril Kondrashin conducting the Moscow Philharmonic Orchestra, Vitaly Gromadsky, bass, and the State Academic Choir and Yurlov Russian Choir. Texts provided. Russian Disc CD RD CD 11 191. Russian Disc, 1993. TT: 56:35.

Premiered on December 18, 1962, Shostakovich's *Symphony No. 13*, subtitled "Babi Yar," was born in controversy owing to its use of Yevtushenko's indictment of Soviet anti-Semitism, the poem "Babi Yar." The power of the opening movement, where Shostakovich employs the orchestra with chorus and baritone soloist to create an unsparing picture of the indifference of the Soviet regime to the oppression of Jews in the USSR, is overwhelming. This performance is taken from the opening-night concert, and uses the unchanged texts of the premiere, which had proceeded despite heavy government pressure to cancel the performance. Following the premiere and a subsequent performance in Moscow, the government demanded that Yevtushenko make changes in the text of the Babi Yar movement to reflect that Russians and Ukrainians had also died at Babi Yar along with Jews. Yevtushenko reluctantly made the changes, and subsequent performances in the Soviet Union, with a few exceptions, used the altered text. Shostakovich refused to alter any aspects of the musical score, however.

————. *Trio No. 2 for Violin, Cello, and Piano, Opus 67.* With *Sonata for Cello and Piano*, Opus 40. Isaac Stern, Violin, Yo-Yo Ma, cello, and Emanuel Ax, piano. Columbia Masterworks CD MK 44664. New York: CBS Records, 1988. TT: 58:49.

Shostakovich composed the *Trio No. 2 for Violin, Cello, and Piano* in 1944, prior to the full revelations of the Holocaust. He had a lifelong affinity for Jewish culture, with a particular interest in Jewish music, as demonstrated in his completion of the opera *Rothschild's Violin* (1944) by his student Benjamin Fleischmann, and later works such as his song cycle *From Jewish Folk Poetry* (1948) and his *Symphony No. 13*, "Babi Yar" (1962). The work contains Jewish themes, with a prominent Jewish tune in the final movement. The other work on this recording is the composer's four-movement *Sonata for Cello and Piano* of 1934, which reflects Shostakovich's ability to combine an almost symphonic structure with elements of sarcasm and despair.

Stoppelenburg, Willem. *Westerbork Symphony (1992)*. National Philharmonic Orchestra of the Netherlands conducted by the composer. Eurosound Digital CD ES 47.086. Herveld Holland: Eurosound Studio, 1992. TT: 36:47.

This seven-part symphony was composed for the special day of remembrance in 1992 when the Westerbork camp was reopened as a museum center by Princess Margriet of the Netherlands. The work is a blend of traditional symphonic forms and the suite, utilizing two thematic songs as key unifying elements: "The Train" by Westerbork survivor Louis de Wijze and the traditional Yiddish song "The Goodbye." Feelings of nostalgia, anxiety, pain, and resignation pervade the work, blending sadness at the loss of over 100,000 deportees from Westerbork with the need for commemoration and homage to those people who perished between 1942 and 1945. The work is scored for a symphony orchestra. Available from Eurosound Digital, Dijkstraat 5 6674 AG Herveld Holland.

Tippett, Michael. *A Child of Our Time*. Performed by the Royal Philharmonic Orchestra, Brighton Festival Chorus, and soloists Sheila Armstrong, Philip Langridge, Felicity Palmer, and John Shirley Quirk, under the direction of Andre Previn. Texts provided. IMP Classics PCD 6702052. United Kingdom: IMP Classics, 1998. TT: 70:00.

First performed on March 19, 1944, Sir Michael Tippett's oratorio *A Child of Our Time* was inspired by the efforts by Herschel Grynspan, a young Polish Jew, to protest the increasing persecution of Jews in Germany by the Third Reich. The libretto and music were both written by Tippett, and the structure of the work draws upon Handel's *Messiah* and the *Passions* of J. S. Bach. It is organized into three sections: Part I presents the general state of the world, Part II introduces the "Child of our Time" and how he grapples with his personal fate and the major social forces of his world, and Part III discusses the significance of the story and how man can pursue paths of healing in a time of darkness. While incorporating the musical language of the twentieth century, Tippett also utilizes traditional Negro spirituals, which he used to convey universal messages and which served as the modern equivalents of the well-known chorales of Bach and his contemporaries. Although the immediate impetus for the work was the murder by Grynspan of German diplomatic attache in Paris Ernst vom Rath and the subsequent Kristallnacht pogrom in Germany, the work more generally is an indictment of man's inhumanity to his fellow man.

Musical Works Created and Performed during the Holocaust

Songs performed in camps and ghettos, along with those performed by partisans comprise this section. Included here are songs that existed prior to the onset of World War II and the Nazi occupation of Europe, but whose lyrics were modified to reflect the unfolding tragedy of European Jews between 1939 and 1945.

Ghetto Tango: Wartime Yiddish Theater. Performed by Adrienne Cooper, voice, and Zalmen Mlotek, piano. Texts provided. Traditional Crossroads CD 4297. New York: Traditional Crossroads, 2000. TT: 53:27.

The performances on this compact disc represent musical theater compositions written and later adapted for performance in Polish and Lithuanian ghettos in Nazi-occupied Europe during World War II. Informed by popular Yiddish songs, Jewish folk and liturgical compositions, ragtime, film music, dance music (tangos, for example), and European opera and operetta styles, the works were performed in the ghettos in formal concert settings, as cabaret entertainments, and as street songs. Among the ghettos represented are Krakow, Lodz, Warsaw, Vilna, Kovno, and Sosnow. Additionally, the famed anti-fascist resistance song "Song of the Peat-Bog Soldiers" is included, which was originally composed in the Borgermoor (Germany) concentration camp in 1933. The topics encompassed in the collection are diverse, ranging from adaptations of works for the classic Yiddish theater such as "Raisins and Almonds" and lullabies ("Close Your Eyes") to works specifically composed for the anti-Nazi cause (Weill and Brecht's "Song of the Nazi Soldier's Wife"). The accompanying booklet includes an historical essay on the development of the compositions, photographs of selected composers and performers, and full texts in Yiddish and English translation.

Hear Our Voices—Songs of the Ghettos and the Camps. Joshua Jacobson, conductor, the Zamir Chorale of Boston, Karen Harvey, piano, and soloists Cantor Charles Osborne, Betty Silberman, Scott Sokol, and Catherine Thorpe. Texts provided. Hazamir CD HZ–909. Newton, MA: Hazamir Recordings, 1995. TT: 70:31.

This recording includes songs performed in the ghettos and camps in Nazi-occupied Europe during World War II. Works created by composers interned in Terezin (Gideon Klein, Pavel Haas, Viktor Ullmann) are complemented by works of Mordecai Gebirtig and other composers of Jewish secular music, as well as traditional Jewish songs such as "Ani Maamin." Conductor Joshua Jacobson provides spoken introductions to the different segments of the recording to provide an historical context for the performances. English texts only are provided.

Kahan, Bente. *Voices from Theresienstadt.* Ilse Weber & Cabaret Songs. Dybbuk CD DP 1818. Oslo: Dybbuk Promotion, 1997. Performed by

Bente Kahan, vocal and guitar, and accompanying artists. Available from www.bentekahan.no. TT: 44:37.

This compact disc contains readings and songs from the monodrama *Voices of Theresienstadt*, which was co-authored by singer Bente Kahan with Ellen Floyn Bruun. Also included on this recording are selected poems and ballads by the Czech Jewish author Ilse Weber, who was interned in Terezin and later was deported to her death in Auschwitz. The accompanying booklet contains historical essays on the Terezin cabaret, musical creativity and activities in Terezin, and Ilse Weber's career, along with complete English texts of the songs.

Krakow Ghetto Notebook: Mordecai Gebirtig. Performed by Daniel Kempin, voice and guitar, with Dimitry Reznik, violin. Koch International Classics CD 3–7295–2H1. Produced in association with the United States Holocaust Memorial Museum. Port Washington, NY: Koch International, 1994. TT: 67:00.

Included on this compact disc are nineteen songs by the Polish musician and composer Mordecai Gebirtig (1877–1942), most of which he composed during the period 1939–1942, when he was suffering with his family under the Nazi occupation. Between 1940 and 1942, Gebirtig and his family were first exiled to the Polish village of Kagiewniki, and were then transferred to the Krakow ghetto, where he and his family were murdered by the Nazis in 1942. The first four songs on the recording illustrate Gebirtig's ability to illuminate the daily aspects of Jewish life prior to the war, while the remaining songs were composed during the Nazi occupation. The final three songs were created while Gebirtig and his family lived in the Krakow ghetto, and reflect the fear and sense of impending doom faced by Jews in the ghetto. With the exception of the four pre-war songs, the remaining compositions on this recording were published in the *Krakow Ghetto Notebook*, which was prepared by Gebirtig during his time in the ghetto, preserved by friends of the composer, and eventually found its way to the archives of the YIVO Institute in New York City. The accompanying booklet contains an historical essay on Gebirtig's life and creative development, summaries of the songs, complete Yiddish and English song texts, biographies of the performers, and source credits.

Our Town Is Burning: Cries from the Holocaust. Leon Lishner, bass, with various artists. Texts provided. Centaur CD 2223. Baton Rouge, LA: Centaur Records, Inc., 1994. TT: 77:37.

This collection of twenty-seven songs from the Holocaust includes songs created and performed in ghettos (Warsaw and Vilna) and camps (Terezin) , songs by well-known composers such as Mordecai Gebirtig and Pavel Haas, partisan songs such as "Zog Nit Keynmol Az Du Geyst Dem Letztn Veg" (Never Say that You Are Going on the Last Road), and works composed after the Holocaust such as "Unter Di Poylishe Grininke Beynmelekh" (Under the Little Green Polish Trees). English texts are provided, along with brief summaries of the origins of each composition and the names of lyricists and composers. A brief introductory essay also is included in the accompanying booklet.

Partisans of Vilna. Flying Fish CD FF 70450. Chicago: Flying Fish Records, Inc., 1989. TT: Not provided.

This compact disc includes twelve songs originally heard in the documentary film *Partisans of Vilna*, performed by assorted instrumentalists and vocalists. Texts of the songs are provided as well as brief notes about each composition.

Paul Robeson: Live Concert from Tchaikovsky Hall in Moscow. Recorded June 14, 1949. Includes performance in Yiddish of the "Song of the Warsaw Ghetto Rebellion" (Zog Nit Keynmol). Song texts provided. Fenix CD PR 7000. Burbank: Fenix Entertainment, 1995. TT: 53:40.

This compact disc preserves the live performance recorded in Moscow on June 14, 1949, of a concert given by the distinguished American bass-baritone Paul Robeson. The concert included an eclectic set of art songs, folk songs, spirituals, labor songs, and other compositions drawn from sources in the United States, Europe, and Asia. As a determined opponent of fascism, Paul Robeson had been a strong advocate of the war effort in the United States, and was a longtime supporter of promoting international understanding through the arts. His visit to the Soviet Union in 1949 was one of many he made throughout his career, and this concert performance is notable for his inclusion of "Zog Nit Keynmol," the song of the Warsaw Ghetto Rebellion. Upon arrival in the Soviet Union, Robeson could not fail to recognize the increasingly virulent anti-Semitism evident in the press, but he insisted on seeing his Jewish friends Solomon Mikhoels and Itzik Feffer. During his brief meeting with Feffer, who had been removed from the Lubyanka prison under guard specifically for this purpose, Feffer communicated to Robeson that Mikhoels had been murdered on orders of Josef Stalin and that a widespread purge was underway of Jewish intellectuals, along with selected other communists in the Soviet Union. Following the conclusion of his scheduled program during the concert, Robeson announced a single encore—the "Song of the Warsaw Ghetto Rebellion," which he was dedicating to the memory of his friend Solomon Mikhoels. Robeson introduced the song in Russian and then sang it in Yiddish. After the performance, as heard on this recording, a single voice begins to applaud, followed by the entire audience. The Soviet censors then cut out the remaining response by the audience, which was overwhelming. This single performance, an eloquent protest against anti-Semitism, bridges the suffering of the Holocaust and the oppression faced by Soviet Jews during the final era of Stalin's rule. An extended essay by Paul Robeson, Jr. about his father and the historic nature of the concert is included in the accompanying booklet, but no song texts are provided.

Remember the Children: Songs for and by Children of the Holocaust. Various performers. Song texts provided. U.S. Holocaust Memorial Museum CD HMCD 1901. Washington, DC: U.S. Holocaust Memorial Museum, n.d. TT: 54:55.

This collection of nineteen songs created and performed in the ghettos of Eastern Europe during the Nazi occupation have as their common theme the topic of children. A number of the works on this compact disc receive their first recording, and the range of ghettos reflected in the works spans not only the more well-known locations (Warsaw, Lodz, Vilna, Kovno) but also Shavli, Lublin, Bochnia, and Oshmen. Summaries of the songs are provided, along with complete Yiddish and English texts.

Rise Up and Fight! Songs of Jewish Partisans. Theodore Bikel and Frieda Enoch, soloists, with the Noble Voices conducted by Robert DeCormier. Song texts provided. U.S. Holocaust Memorial Museum CD USHMM-02. Washington, DC: U.S. Holocaust Memorial Museum, 1996. TT: 51:36.

This compact disc includes eighteen songs sung by Jewish partisans during World War II. Many of these songs were collected and published by Shmerke Kaczerginski, who was a poet and songwriter before World War II, and who also served as a partisan during World War II. Not only did Kaczerginski collect folklore and songs from ghettos camps and partisans, he also composed works while living in the Vilna ghetto, a number of which were translations of Russian wartime songs that were sung in partisan units. Each song is introduced with a brief background summary, and those drawn from Kaczerginski's publications also contain descriptive excerpts authored by him. Complete Yiddish and English texts are provided, along with a comprehensive essay about the history of Jewish partisans and partisan songs by the survivor and historian Dov Levin, and detailed source credits.

U.S. Holocaust Memorial Museum. *Hidden History: Songs of the Kovno Ghetto.* Performers include vocalists Adrienne Cooper, David Stapanovskiy, Dianne Cypkin; pianist/arranger Zalmen Mlotek; and the choral ensemble Noble Voices, conducted by Robert DeCormier. CD USHMM–03. Washington, DC: U.S. Holocaust Memorial Museum, 1997. TT: 61:08.

This compact disc includes performances of seventeen songs written and sung in the Kovno ghetto. An introductory essay, dual-language texts (Yiddish and English), song summaries, and complete source credits are provided in the accompanying booklet.

Musical Works by Composers in the Terezin Ghetto and Camp Complex

A number of notable composers were deported to the Terezin ghetto and camp during the period 1939–1945. These composers represented various compositional styles in twentieth-century European music, but all were highly talented and had their careers ended as a result of their internment.

Al S'fod: Do Not Lament. Hebrew and Jewish Instrumental and Vocal Works. The Terezin Music Anthology, Volume IV. Works by David Grunfeld, Pavel Haas, Gideon Klein, Jugo Lowenthal, Zikmund Schul, Carlo S. Taube, Viktor Ullmann, and Vilem Zrzavy. Performed by the Prague Philharmonic Choir, Jaroslav Brych, conductor; the Bambini di Praga, Bohumil Kulinsky, conductor; and members of the Group for New Music. Koch International Classics CD 3–7173–2H1. Port Washington, NY: Koch International Classics, 1998. TT: 68:51.

This compact disc contains works created and in most cases, performed in the Terezin ghetto/camp complex between 1941 and 1944. The works range from chamber music to works for solo voice and accompaniment, to choral works. In addition to well-known composers such as Viktor Ullmann, Pavel Haas, and Gideon Klein, many other composers are included in this anthology, notably those who wrote works based upon Jewish liturgical themes. The accompanying booklet contains an extensive set of notes and essays about the composers and the Terezin musical environment, as well as a dual-language set of texts (English and either German or Hebrew).

Composers from Theresienstadt 1941–1945. Pavel Haas, Karel Berman. Pavel Haas, Four Songs to the Text of Chinese Poetry. Karel Berman, Four Songs for Bass and Piano and Suite for Piano Solo, 1939–1945. Performed by Karel Berman, bass, Alfred Holocek, piano, and Premsyl Charvat piano. Channel Classics CD CCS–3191. Englewood, NJ: Channel Classics Records, 1991. TT: 48:20.

Containing the works of two composers who were interned in the Terezin camp, this compact disc has a special distinction: Karel Berman, the bass who performs the vocal works, was the artist who premiered the Haas works in Terezin in 1944. The genesis of this recording involved efforts by author Joza Karas to engage Karel Berman and have him record the works on this compact disc in 1985 in Prague, some four decades after their premiere. Berman's own works, the song cycle *Puopata* (Buds) and the *Suite for Piano Solo, 1939–1945* were originally composed while Berman was in Terezin and later in Auschwitz. Following the end of World War II, Berman added some sections to the piano suite, but did not bring that work to its final form until 1984. He also added a final song to the *Poupata* song cycle, "Pred Usnutim" (Before Falling Asleep). The original *Suite Terezin* became the *Suite for Piano Solo, 1939–1945* by inclusion of new names for the segments (the first section, "Terezin," became "March 15, 1939–Occupation"; the second part, "Horror," became "Auschwitz-Corpse Factory," and so forth). Only the original final section ("Alone") retained its original name, but a new section was written that became the last movement of suite, entitled "New Life." While Berman survived the war despite being in Terezin, Auschwitz, and two camps in Germany, Pavel Haas, who arrived in Terezin in 1942 and wrote his *Four Songs to the Text of Chinese Poetry* in 1944, died in Auschwitz in October 1944. These songs were premiered by Karel Berman on June 22, 1944 and were highly praised by another composer interned in Terezin, Viktor Ullmann, not only for their sophisticated design but for their ability to express the mood of the Terezin community.

Haas, Pavel. *Sarlatan, Opera in 3 Acts.* Soloists, the Prague Philharmonic Choir, and Prague State Opera Orchestra conducted by Israel Yinon. Libretto provided. London Entartete Musik 2 CD Set 460 042–2. London: Decca Record Company Limited, 1998. TT: 125.06.

Drawing his inspiration from the legendary story of the German Dr. Eisenbart, as well as traditional Czech plays about musical quack doctors, Pavel Haas (1899–1944) composed this opera in 1935–1936. As the librettist and composer, Haas consciously created a tragicomic work that drew heavily from the novel written by the German author Josef Winckler about a doctor who is a surgeon and well-known miracle worker. The opera's main character, Doktor Pustrpalk, wanders from fair to fair performing his miracles, and the libretto details various adventures of the Doktor and his troupe during the turn of the seventeenth and eighteenth centuries. The opera was premiered to great acclaim in Brno in 1938, having a run of six performances during that spring season. With the darkening political situation and the occupation of Czechoslovakia by Germany in 1939, however, Haas's future as a Jewish composer in his native land dimmed and the work was not performed again. Although Haas died in Auschwitz in 1944, the performing parts of the work survived his death and this recording was prepared under the auspices of the Decca series *Entartete Musik* (Degenerate Music), with the goal of bringing to new audiences the neglected works of composers banned by the Third Reich. A full libretto and two essays about the work and the composer accompany the compact discs.

———. *Scherzo Triste, Op. 5. Suite from the Opera Charlatan, Opus 14. Symphony (unfinished), 1940–41.* Israel Yinon conducting the Brno State Philharmonic. Koch Schwann CD 3–1521–2 H1. Koch International, 1996. TT: 63:49.

The Czech composer Pavel Haas was born in 1899, and died in Auschwitz in 1944. As a major pupil of the esteemed Czech composer Leos Janacek, Haas was critically influenced by the music of Bohemia and Moravia, Hebrew melodies, jazz, and motor rhythms. This compact disc contains a suite from Haas' opera *Sarlatan* (The Charlatan), which was premiered in 1936. The suite contains six movements and reflects the tragicomic style of this dramatic work. The *Scherzo*

Triste is a tone poem composed by Haas when he was studying with Janacek, reflecting the influences of his teacher in its lyricism. The major work on this recording is Haas's *Symphony* (unfinished), the orchestration of which was prepared from sketches that survived the composer's death by the Czech composer Zdenek Zouhar. The first performance of the three-movement work occurred following its completion in 1994, although the first movement had been premiered directly after the war in 1946 by Bretislav Bakala, a fellow pupil of Janacek and a friend of Haas. This work utilizes references to Czech nationalism by quoting the St. Wenzel chorale and a Hussite chorale, while parodying the Nazi "Horst Wessel Lied." Originally composed in 1940–1941, Haas' *Symphony* clearly demonstrates his patriotism while expressing opposition to the Nazi occupation of Czechoslovakia.

————. *Wind Quintet, Opus 10. Suite for Piano, Opus 13. Suite fur Oboe and Piano, Opus 17. Vyvolena, Opus 8.* Performed by tenor Jorg Durmuller, pianist Dennis Russell Davies, violinist Monika Holszky-Wiedemann, and the Stuttgart Wind Quintet. Texts provided. Orfeo CD C 386 961 A. Munich: Orfeo International Music, GmbH, 1996. TT: 55:33.

This compact disc contains works composed by Pavel Haas (1899–1944) during the period 1927–1939, when he was considered one of the most important young Czech composers. Incorporating jazz elements, Moravian folk songs, and traditional Czech national hymns and songs, Haas composed in a wide range of genres, as illustrated in the works performed here: piano solo, wind quintet, suite for oboe and piano, and chamber music for tenor voice and small ensemble. The *Suite for Oboe and Piano* (1939), prepared from the manuscript sketches, includes quotes from the St. Wenzel hymn and a Hussite chorale, reflecting Haas's dedication to Czech nationalism and his opposition to the German occupation, which had already occurred by the time of its composition. Careful listening to this compact disc reveals the gradual development of Haas's compositional style and musical career, which was tragically ended with his murder in Auschwitz in 1944.

Isolamenti, 1938–1945: Volume 3. Orchestral and Choral Music of Hans Krasa, Pavel Haas, Gideon Klein, and Viktor Ullmann. Includes a complete performance of Krasa's children's opera *Brundibar.* Performed by the Orchestra di Padova e del Veneto and the Coro Mladinski Zbor RTV Slovenija under the direction of Mada Matose Vic. Libretto and texts provided. Fonit Cetra CD NJCD 2035. Milan: Fonit Centra, 1996. TT: 66:17.

This compact disc contains works by four composers who were interned in Terezin and who died in Auschwitz: Hans Krasa (1899–1944), Pavel Haas (1899–1944), Gideon Klein (1919–1945), and Viktor Ullmann (1898–1944). The works heard on this recording were all composed or revised in Terezin and (with the exception of Krasa's *Little Overture*) first performed there, many under the direction of Karel Ancerl, the distinguished Czech conductor who survived the war and later led the Czech Philharmonic and the Toronto Symphony orchestras. In addition to the *Little Overture*, Krasa's children's opera *Brundibar* is included, a work that has had a number of performances since the mid-1980s owing to the increasing interest in works of composers interned at Terezin. Gideon Klein is represented by his *Partita for Strings* (1944), a transcription for chamber orchestra of an earlier trio by Klein. Pavel Haas' *Study for String Orchestra* is one of the three works by this composer authored by him in Terezin, while Ullmann's *Three Choruses on Hebrew Texts* receives its first compact disc recording here. The efforts of these highly talented composers to sustain cultural life while living in the difficult world of a Nazi camp illustrate that despite extreme oppression, Nazi terror could not destroy the legacy of Central European Jewish life as represented in the works prepared for this recording. A complete libretto for *Brundibar* is included.

Krasa, Hans. *Brundibar: Children's Opera in Two Acts*. With Frantisec Domazlicky, *Czech Songs for Children's Chorus with a String Quartet Accompaniment*. Disman Radio Children's Ensemble conducted by Joza Karas. Libretto provided. Channel Classics Composers from Theresienstadt CD CCS 5193. Amsterdam: Channel Classics, 1993. TT: 41:45.

Hans Krasa's *Brundibar* was presented over fifty times in Terezin during the years 1943–1944, and became a major cultural event for the Terezin internees. Although originally written to Adolf Hoffmeister's libretto in 1938 for a competition of the Czech Ministry of Education and Culture, the work did not receive a performance until 1941 at the Jewish orphanage for boys in the Vinohrady district of Prague. When the boys from the Prague orphanage were transported to Terezin in 1943, *Brundibar* was then performed in Terezin beginning on September 23, 1943. Its simple story about the triumph of good (two young children, Aninka and Pepicek) over evil (the organ grinder Brundibar) became an allegory of the triumph of justice (the oppressed people of Europe) over evil (Nazism), with *Brundibar* representing the personification of evil, or Hitler. The final song's text was changed in Terezin to represent a joyous triumph over *Brundibar*, with the organ grinder's defeat representing a victorious anthem. Also included on this recording are Terezin survivor Frantisec Domazlicky's *Eight Songs for Children's Chorus with String Quartet Accompaniment*, composed in Terezin and premiered in 1955.

————. *Brundibar: A Children's Opera in Two Acts*. Also includes Hebrew and Yiddish Folk Songs. Arabesque CD Z6680. New York: Arabesque Recordings, 1996. Conducted by Robert DeCormier, and performed by Members of the Vermont Symphony Orchestra and Chorus, with the Essex Children's Choir, Constance J. Price, director. A libretto is provided for the opera, but texts are not provided for the Hebrew and Yiddish songs. TT: 45:28.

————. *The Terezin Music Anthology, Volume III. Contains Songs, Chamber Works, Overture for Small Orchestra and the Terezin Version of Brundibar, a Children's Opera.* Libretto and song texts provided. Various performers and conductors. Koch International Classics CD 3–7151–2 H1. Port Washington, NY: Koch International USA, 1996. ISBN 99923–71512. TT: 62:08.

This anthology of works by Hans Krasa (1899–1944) represents not only works he composed in Terezin, but three works that predated his internment there: the song "Je to smich nebo plac? My vime" for soprano, children's chorus, and piano (1935); the *Theme and Variations* for chamber ensemble (1935); and the children's opera *Brundibar* (1938), which was originally written in 1938 but which received the bulk of its early performances in Terezin during 1943 and 1944. The remainder of the works on this compact disc were all composed during Krasa's internment in Terezin from 1941–1944. Krasa's music reflects influences of Arnold Schoenberg as well as his teacher Alexander Zemlinsky, and the works on this recording reflect his mastery of writing for chamber music groups, which flourished in the artistic life of the Terezin ghetto and camp. This recording contains extensive notes and a background essay on Krasa's works and Terezin's musical life.

The Martyred Musicians of the Holocaust. Rudolf Karel, *Theme et Variations,* Opus 13. Pavel Haas, *Suite,* Opus 13. Gideon Klein, *Sonate Pour Piano.* Viktor Ullman, *Sonate Pour Piano No. 6,* Opus 44. Performed by Francesco Lotoro, piano. Arion CD ARN 68339. France: Arion Recordings, 1995. TT: 65:17.

This compact disc features piano works by composers interned at Terezin. Rudolf Karel (1880–1945) studied with Antonin Dvorak and other teachers at the Prague Conservatory, and composed and taught at the Prague Conservatory until 1941, when he was dismissed from his post by the Nazi occupation authorities. Captured for his resistance efforts in 1943, he composed some works while in the Pangkrac prison, and was transferred to Terezin in 1945, where he died. His work *Theme and Variations* (1910) is represented on this recording. Pavel Haas (1899–1944), Gideon Klein (1919–1945), and Viktor Ullmann (1898–1944) all were interned in Terezin and later were transported to Auschwitz, where Haas and Ullmann died. Klein was transferred to the Furstengrube camp in Silesia, where he died in 1945. Haas' 1935 *Suite for Piano* is included here, along with two works composed in the Terezin complex: Klein's *Sonata for Piano* (1943) and Ullmann's *Sonata No. 6 for Piano* (1943).

Schulhoff, Erwin. *String Quartets 1 and 2.* Also contains *Five Pieces for String Quartet.* Capriccio CD 10 463. Performed by the Petersen Quartett. Konigsdorf: Capriccio, 1993. TT: 46:41.

This compact disc contains three works by Erwin Schulhoff (1894–1942) composed in the mid-1920s, when his compositional style began to combine his interest in jazz rhythms and related avant-garde musical languages with a renewed commitment to representing Central European folklore in his music, particularly following his introduction to the works of the Czech master Leos Janáček. The *Five Pieces for String Quartet* constitute a suite of dances with inspiration drawn from the structure of Baroque musical suites, while the *String Quartets 1 and 2* are composed more strictly in the cycle of sonata movements. Schulhoff died in the Wulzburg Concentration Camp in 1942.

————. *Symphony No. 1, Suite for Chamber Orchestra and Overture.* Czech State Philharmonic Orchestra of Brno conducted by Israel Yinon. Koch Schwann CD 3–1437–2. Port Washington, NY: Koch International, 1995. TT: 55:53.

As a member of the European avant-garde, Erwin Schulhoff was a leading Czech composer of the pre–World War II period. This compact disc contains three of his major orchestral works, the *Suite for Chamber Orchestra* of 1921, his *First Symphony* of 1925, and the *Festive Prelude* (Overture) of 1932. The *Suite for Chamber Orchestra* is decidedly influenced by Schulhoff's interest in jazz rhythms and the influence of Dadaism on his aesthetic philosophy. Combining elements of jazz, Dada, and symphonic structure in a six-movement suite, the work's strength is its stark contrasts, alternating movements based upon ragtime, dance rhythms drawn from the tango and waltz, and grotesque parodies of a military march. The *Symphony No. 1* also relies heavily on contrast, but within a more traditional symphonic structure. Schulhoff's debts to Stravinsky and Debussy are clear in this work, as is the influence of Janáček. The *Festival Prelude* (Overture) began as an overture to the second act of his opera *Flammen*, and was premiered in May 1932.

————. *Symphony No. 2.* Gideon Klein, *Partita for Strings.* Pavel Haas, *Study for String Orchestra.* Viktor Ullmann, *Symphony No. 2.* Performed by the Czech Philharmonic conducted by Gerd Albrecht. Orfeo CD C 337 941 A. Munich: Orfeo International Music Gmbh, 1994. TT: 62:13.

This recording includes works by four composers who died at the hands of the Nazis during World War II. Erwin Schulhoff, represented here by his *Symphony No. 2*, had achieved substantial success in Germany during the 1920s as a member of the compositional avant-garde, and his *Symphony No. 2* (1932) reflects his deep interest in jazz and the possibilities of composing for modern media, since this work was premiered in 1935 for radio broadcast. Pavel Haas (1899–1944), a pupil of Leos Janáček, composed his *Study for String Orchestra* while interned in Terezin, where it was premiered by the Terezin orchestra led by the distinguished Czech conductor Karel Ancerl. Haas was deported to Auschwitz in 1944, where he was gassed. Gideon Klein's (1919–1945) *Partita for Orchestra* was composed as a string trio in Terezin, and was later rearranged by Vojtech Saudek as a string orchestra work. The optimism of the work's finale can be interpreted as an act of resistance to the daily suffering and death that surrounded the Terezin population, most of whom would be deported to their deaths before the end of 1944. Viktor Ullmann (1898–1944) was a student of Arnold Schoenberg in Vienna, and while interned in Terezin he composed a minimum of twenty-five works that could meet the limited resources available to the performers in the ghetto/camp complex. The work performed here is his *Symphony No. 2*, as reconstructed by Bernard Wulff, who also completed the instrumentation of the *Symphony* following indications by Ullmann in his manuscripts. Direct quotations of a famed Czech Hussite hymn, stated against a Bach chorale theme, provide a clear indication of Ullmann's nationalist intent in the final movement of the work. The work was dedicated to his children, and was completed on August 22, 1944, two months before his deportation to Auschwitz.

————. *Symphony No. 2, Symphony No. 3, and Concerto for String Quartet and Winds.* Kyncl Quartet and the Czech Philharmonic Orchestra of Brno conducted by Israel Yinon. Koch Schwann CD 3–1543–2. Port Washington, NY: Koch International, 1995. TT: 61:45.

This compact disc includes three works by Erwin Schulhoff from the 1930s, only two of which he heard performed. The *Concerto for String Quartet and Winds* reflects the composer's interest in writing a work for radio broadcast, and its colorful instrumentation reflects his interest in writing works that would be interesting and accessible to the listener. It was premiered in 1932. Schulhoff's *Symphony No. 2* was composed during the period of the preparation for the premiere of the *Concerto for String Quartet and Winds*, and reflects his changing ideological commitments, which culminated in his enthusiastic support of communism from the early 1930s to the end of his life. This four-movement symphony contains elements of nineteenth-century romanticism, jazz (the third movement is entitled "Scherzo alla Jazz"), and baroque forms. Premiered on April 24, 1935, the work was the last of his compositions to be publicly performed. The final work on this recording, Schulhoff's *Symphony No. 3*, clearly reflects his growing commitment to socialist realism as an artistic ethos. His 1933 trip to Moscow as part of the Czech Communist Party delegation had a strong influence on his compositions after that date, and the finale of this three-movement work contains a repetitive march theme that suggests a "new beginning," or the replacement of the old world order with a new socialist vision. Although he became a Soviet citizen in April 1941, Schulhoff was unable to emigrate to the USSR before the German army occupied Prague in June 1941, and he was interned. He died in the Wulzburg camp in 1942.

————. *Symphonies Nos. 3 and 5.* Vladimir Valek conducting the Prague Radio Symphony Orchestra. Supraphon CD 11 2151–2 031. Prague: Supraphon, 1995. TT: 52:41.

In 1938 and 1939, with German occupation a reality in Czechoslovakia, Erwin Schulhoff had been dismissed from his positions owing to his Jewish origin. He continued to compose however, and he completed his *Symphony No. 5* on May 30, 1939. The work was never performed in Schulhoff's lifetime, and was premiered on March 5, 1965. It consists of four movements, with a deeply felt slow movement and a furious scherzo sandwiched by a first movement characterized by an ostinato figure and a finale that is organized around a series of variations. The other work on this recording is Schulhoff's *Symphony No. 3*, completed in 1935, but first performed in 1950.

————. *Symphonies Nos. 4 and 6*. Roman Janal, baritone, Kuhn Mixed Choir, and the Prague Radio Symphony Orchestra conducted by Vladimir Valek. Supraphon CD 11 2162–2 031. Prague: Supraphon, 1997. TT: 65:00.

Inspired by the Spanish Civil War, Erwin Schulhoff's *Symphony No. 4* was composed in 1937, when the composer had moved from Prague to Moravska Ostrava and held a post as a pianist at the local branch of Prague Radio. Schulhoff includes in this work a baritone vocal solo, the text of which is taken from a poem by Ondra Lysohorsky entitled "Dying in Madrid," written in the Lachian dialect. The five-movement work begins with a march, continues with an elegiac setting of the poem, and concludes with a scherzo, andante, and a march-like finale. The clash of ideas represented by the symphony's contrasts is modeled to some extent on Beethoven's works. The *Symphony No. 6* was Schulhoff's final work in this genre, and it is subtitled "Freedom Symphony," again with reference to Beethoven, in this case his *Symphony No. 9*, "Choral."

Because Schulhoff by this time was seeking to eke out a subsistence living through completion of commissions, given that he could no longer be regularly employed under the Nazi occupation owing to his Jewish background, the work was begun in May 1940 but not completed until February 1941. Opening with a brief and festive march, the work continues with a somber funeral march adagio. The third movement harks back to folkloric elements employed in Schulhoff's works of the 1920s, and the finale introduces the chorus, which sings the "Freedom Song" modeled on Adalbert von Chamisso's poem "Slaves." Closely aligned with the structure of Beethoven's *Symphony No. 9*, the work also contains elements of socialist realism that were popular during World War II and after the war's end in communist countries. The work was first performed in 1946. The multilingual booklet accompanying the compact disc does not include vocal texts.

Silenced Voices: Victims of the Holocaust. Music by Erwin Schulhoff, Vitezslava Kapralova, and Gideon Klein. Includes Erwin Schulhoff, *String Quartet No. 1, Concertino for Flute, Viola and Bass*, and *Sonata for Flute and Piano*; Vitezslava Kapralova, *Dubnova Preludia Suite for Solo Piano*, Opus 13; and Gideon Klein, *Duo for Violin and Cello*. Performed by the

Hawthorne String Quartet and Guest Artists. Northeastern CD NR 248-CD. Boston: Northeastern Records and the Terezin Chamber Music Foundation, 1992. TT: 61:49.

The five works on this compact disc were composed by individuals who died as a result of Nazi persecution during World War II. The Schulhoff works were composed in the 1920s, while Gideon Klein's *Duo for Violin and Cello* was composed in Terezin prior to Klein's deportation to Auschwitz. Klein's work ends abruptly in the second movement, a poignant reminder of the difficulties faced by the artists in the Terezin transit camp. Vitezslava Kapralova's *Dubnova Preludia Suite* for solo piano was dedicated to the eminent Czech pianist Rudolf Firkusny, and was composed prior to her attempts to flee Nazi persecution. While on her way to the United States, Kapralova contracted military tuberculosis and died in Montpellier, France in 1940. The Gideon Klein work receives its world premier recording on this compact disc.

Ullmann, Viktor. *Cornet, Don Quixote Tanzt Fandango and Klavierkonzert.* Erika Pluhar, narrator, and Igor Ardasev, piano, with the Czech Philharmonic conducted by Gerd Albrecht. Orfeo CD C 366 951 A. Munich: Orfeo International Music Gmbh, 1995. TT: 53:34.

As one of the most esteemed young Central European composers of the early twentieth century, Viktor Ullmann's studies with Arnold Schoenberg in Vienna and the pianist Edward Steurmann marked him as a talent with great potential. This compact disc contains a work that Ullmann completed prior to World War II, his *Piano Concerto*, as well as two other works that he composed but did not complete in their final form while interned in Terezin: the *Don Quixote Dances a Fandango* overture for orchestra and *The Way of the Life and Death of Cornet Christoph Rilke* for speaker and orchestra. The latter two works were reconstructed from manuscripts prepared by Ullmann, although in the case of the Rilke work, it was performed in Terezin a few times prior to October 1944 in a version for piano and speaker. The accompanying booklet contains texts in German, English, and French of the twelve poems recit by the speaker in the Rilke work.

————. *The Emperor of Atlantis or Death Abdicates*. Members of the Vermont Symphony Orchestra and Chorus conducted by Robert DeCormier. Arabesque CD Z6681. New York: Arabesque Recordings, 1996. ISBN 26724–6681–2. TT: 51:53.

Composed by Viktor Ullmann in Terezin, The *Emperor of Atlantis or Death Abdicates* is an allegory on the life of a young artist and writer, Peter Kien, an inmate in Terezin who died in Auschwitz. The work sends the message that everyone must hold respect for the joy of life, as well as the pain we endure in our existence. Death cannot be viewed lightly, as we all will face it at some point.

Ullmann employs a number of musical quotations in the work, such as the four note motto from Josef Suk's *Asrael* symphony, a German lullaby, a mocking parody of the German national anthem "Deutschland Uber Alles," an aria from Mendelssohn's *Elijah,* and Martin Luther's hymn "A Mighty Fortress Is Our God." Ullmann's use of the Luther hymn is pointed, as it is utilized by the composer as the final hymn to death in the opera. Although prepared and rehearsed in 1944 by members of the Terezin community, the work was never performed there as Ullmann and most of the performers were deported to Auschwitz in October 1944 before the scheduled premiere. The work was first performed in Amsterdam 1975 following reconstruction of the manuscript by the British conductor Kerry Woodward. This recording includes an English libretto and essays about Ullmann and the origins of the work.

————. *Piano Sonatas Nos. 5, 6, and 7. String Quartet No. 3, Op. 46. The Terezin Music Anthology, Volume I.* Performed by Robert Kolben, and Edith Kraus, pianists, and members of the Group for New Music. Koch International Classics CD 3–7109–2 H1. Port Washington, NY: Koch International USA, 1991. ISBN 99923–71092. TT: 66:14.

Composing approximately twenty-five works while interned in Terezin, as well as being an important author, lecturer, and critic in Terezin's vibrant cultural life, Viktor Ullmann maintained his interest in the piano as his central instrument for composition until his death in 1944. The three piano sonatas on this compact disc were all composed in Terezin, and reflect the composer's use of classical and romantic pianistic structures, including sonata-allegro form, the use of scherzi and trios, and movements with themes and variations. The other work on this recording, the *String Quartet No. 3,* is his only remaining work in that genre, the other two earlier works having been lost. It is in one integrated movement, and has echoes of Debussy and Zemlinsky, although it juxtaposes lyricism, dance-like figures, and heroic themes in Ullmann's own style. Composed in 1943, it was dedicated to Ullmann's friend and fellow Terezin inmate Dr. Emil Utitz.

VENDORS OF MUSICAL RESOURCES

Music Publishers

Jewish Book Center of the Workmen's Circle. 45 East 33rd Street, New York, NY 10016. Phone: 212-889-6800, ext. 285. http://www.circle.org.

Jewish Music WebCenter. http://www.jmwc.org. This well-designed Web site contains extensive listings of web resources on Jewish Music, with links divided into "Web Resources" and "Academic" categories. The webmaster, Judith Shira Pinnolis, can be contacted at pinnolis@jmwc.org.

G. Schirmer Inc. and Associated Music Publishers, Inc. 257 Park Avenue South, 20th Floor, New York, NY 10010. Phone: 212-254-2100. http://www.schirmer.com.

Tara Publications. 8 Music Fair Road, Suite I, Owings Mills, MD 21117. Phone: 410-654-0880. http://www.tara.com.

Terezin Chamber Music Foundation. Astor Station, PO Box 206, Boston, MA 02123. PH: 617-730-8998. FAX: 617-738-1212. http://www.terezinmusic.org.

Transcontinental Music Publications/New Jewish Music Press. 633 Third Avenue, New York, NY 10017-6778. Phone: 800-455-5223. http://uahc.org/transmp/.

The following Web sites contain extensive listings of music publishers for further investigation.

Music Publishers Association. Directory of Music Publishers. http://www.mpa.org/agency/pal.html.

This very comprehensive listing of music publishers can be downloaded and is periodically updated.

William and Gayle Cook Music Library of the Indiana University School of Music.

Worldwide Internet Music Resources. http://music.indiana.edu/music_resources/industry.html.

This extensive listing of music publisher links is international in scope, and resides at one of the most distinguished music schools in the United States, the Indiana University School of Music in Bloomington, Indiana.

Compact Disc Recordings (CDs)

Albany Music Distributors. 915 Broadway, Albany, NY 12207. Phone: 800-752-1951. http://www.zarex.com/AlbanyMusicDist.html.

Angel/EMI Records, c/o Capitol/Angel. 304 Park Avenue, South, New York, NY 10010. Phone: 212-253-3200. http://www.angelrecords.com.

Anne Frank Center USA. 584 Broadway, Suite 408, New York, NY 10012. Phone: 212-431-7993. http://www.annefrank.com.

Arabesque Recordings. 32 West 39th Street, New York, NY 10018. Phone: 800-966-1416. http://www.arabesquerecords.com.

Berlin Classics. Wichmannstrasse 4, 22607 Hamburg, Germany. Phone: 040 890 85600. Distributed by Koch International USA. http://www.kochentertainment.com.

Capriccio Recordings. Delta Music, GmbH D-5, 0216 Frechen, Germany. Phone: (USA) 310-268-1205. http://www.deltamusic.com.

CBS Records, c/o SonyClassical. 550 Madison Avenue, New York, NY 10022-3211. Phone: 212-833-8000. http://www.sonyclassical.com.

Centaur Records, Inc. 136 St. Joseph Street, Baton Rouge, LA 70802. Phone: 225-336-4877. http://www.centaurrecords.com.

Chandos Records Ltd. Chandos House, Commerce Way, Colchester, Essex CO2 8HQ, United Kingdom. Phone: 44 (0) 1206 225225. http://www.chandos.net.

Channel Classics Records. Waaldijk 76, 4171 CG Herwijnen, The Netherlands. Phone: 31 418-581800. http://www.channelclassics.com.

Composers Recordings, Inc. 73 Spring Street, Suite 506, New York, NY 10012. Phone: 212-941-9673. http://www.composersrecordings.com.

CPO Recordings, c/o Naxos of America. 416 Mary Lindsey Polk Drive, Franklin, TN 37067. Phone: 1-615-771-9393. http://www.naxosusa.com.

Decca Record Company, c/o Universal Music Group. 825 8th Avenue, New York, NY 10019. Phone: 212-333-8000. http://www.universalclassics.com.

Delos International. 1645 North Vine St., #340, Hollywood, CA 90028. Phone: 800-364-0645 or 323-962-3636. http://delosmus.com.

Deutsche Grammophon. Deutsche Grammophon GmbH Glockengiesserwall 3, 20095 Hamburg, Germany. Phone: 49 40 44 181-0. http://www.universalclassics.com

Edition Barbarossa. Lehndorffstrasse 16, D-10318 Berlin, Germany.

Ellipsis Arts. 20 Lumber Road, Roslyn, New York 11576-9894. Phone: 800-788-6670. http://www.gaiam.com.

Erato Recordings. http://www.warner-classics.com.

Fenix Entertainment. PO Box 10069, Burbank, CA 91510. Phone: 818-566-4300.

Hanssler Classic, c/o Collegium Records. 12606 South 70th Street, PO Box 31366, Omaha, NE 68133. Phone: 800-367-9059 or 402-597-1240. http://www.collegiumusa.com.

Harmonia Mundi. 2037 Granville Avenue, Los Angeles, CA 90025. Phone: 310-478-1311. http://harmoniamundi.com.

Hazamir. PO Box 590126, Newton, MA 02459. Phone: 866-926-4720 or 603-434-9635. http://www.zamir.org.

IMP Classics, c/o Allegro Corporation. 14136 NE Airport Way, Portland, OR 97230-3443. Phone: 800-288-2007. http://www.allegro-music.com.

Koch International Classics. 2 Tri-Harbor Court, Port Washington, NY 11050. Phone: 800-688-3482. http://www.kochentertainment.com.

Multisonic Records. Lirovnicka 2389, 10600 Prague, Czech Republic. Phone: 02/72760409. http://www.multisonic.cz.

Museum of Jewish Heritage: A Living Memorial to the Holocaust. 18 First Place, Battery Park City, New York, NY 10004-1484. Phone: 212-968-1800 or 212-509-6130. http://www.mjhnyc.org.

Naxos Recordings. 416 Mary Lindsey Polk Drive, Franklin, TN 37067. Phone: 615-771-9393. http://www.naxosusa.com.

Nonesuch Recordings. http://www.warner-classics.com.

Northeastern Records, c/o Koch International USA. 2 Tri-Harbor Court, Port Washington, NY 11050. Phone: 800-688-3482. http://www.kochentertainment.com.

Nuova Fonit Cetra. Corso Sempione 27, palazzo Rai, 20145 Milano, Italy. Phone: 02.34562206.

Orfeo International Music Gmbh. Distributed by Qualiton Imports Ltd., 24-02 40th Avenue, Long Island City, NY 11101. Phone: 718-937-8515. http://www.qualiton.com.

Premier Recordings. PO Box 1214, Gracie Station, New York, NY 10028-0048.

RCA Red Seal. c/o BMG Classics, 1540 Broadway, New York, NY 10036-4098. Phone: 212-930-4941. http://www.getmusic.com/classical/bmg/.

Schott Wergo. Wergo Music and Media, Postfach 36 40, D-55026 Mainz, Germany.

Supraphon. Distributed by Qualiton Imports Ltd., 24-02 40th Avenue, Long Island City, NY 11101. Phone: 718-937-8515. http://www.qualiton.com.

Telarc Recordings. 23307 Commerce Park Road, Cleveland, OH 44122. Phone: 800-801-5810. http://www.telarc.com.

Teldec Recordings. Teldec Classics International GmbH, Schubertstrasse 5-9, 22083 Hamburg, Germany. http://www.warner-classics.com.

Traditional Crossroads. PO Box 20320, Greeley Square, New York, NY 10023. Phone: 800-422-6282. http://www.rootsworld.com.

U.S. Holocaust Memorial Museum Shop. 100 Raoul Wallenberg Place SW, Washington, DC 20024. Phone: 800-259-9998. http://www.holocaustbooks.org.

Vanguard Classics. Omega Record Group, Inc., 27 West 72nd Street, New York, NY 10023. Phone: 212-769-3060. http://www.omegarecords.com.

Vienna Modern Masters Recordings. Margaretenstrasse 125/15, A-1051 Vienna, Austria. Distributed by CdeMusic, 116 North Lake Avenue, Albany, NY 12206. Phone: (USA) 518-434-4110. http://www.xs4all.nl/~gdv/vmm/.

Workmen's Circle. 45 East 33rd Street, New York, NY 10016. Phone: 212-889-6800, ext. 285. http://www.circle.org.

PART V

EDUCATIONAL AND TEACHING MATERIALS

16

PRINT AND ELECTRONIC EDUCATIONAL AND TEACHING MATERIALS

OVERVIEW

The growing prominence of study and teaching about the Holocaust in elementary grades through university level education has generated substantial resources in the form of books and curriculum packets, poster sets, slide sets, instructional videotapes, scholarly works on study and teaching of the Holocaust, curriculum guides, organizations, and teaching training programs dealing with Holocaust education. This chapter introduces the reader to selected resources in those categories, with the hope that individuals and institutions will pursue in-depth study of the Holocaust in a comprehensive but reflective manner. The curriculum guides selected for this chapter represent a range of curricular rationales and designs, and are not meant to be exhaustive in their scope. Rather, they illustrate the range of curricula available for use about the Holocaust in U.S. public schools, as well as the diversity of instructional approaches embodied in their contents. The works on Holocaust study and teaching and teacher training programs also highlight the diversity evident in Holocaust education, which is strikingly evident in the varied emphases of teacher training programs. The variety of selected instructional materials whets the appetite of readers for a closer examination of the rapidly expanding number of resources for students in elementary through collegiate levels about Holocaust study and related topics. Vendor information is provided at the end of the chapter for instructional materials, while curriculum guide contact information is included in specific entries.

INSTRUCTIONAL MATERIALS

Books and Curriculum Packets

Choices for the Twenty-First Century Education Project. *Crisis, Conscience and Choices: Weimar Germany and the Rise of Hitler. Public Policy Debate in the Classroom.* Third edition. Providence, RI: Choices for the 21st Century Education Project, 1994. ISBN 1–891306–31–6. Paperback. Student activity book and teacher's resource book.

This unit presents the competing political perspectives available in Weimar Germany during the period when the Nazi Party gained support and eventually rose to power in 1933. Organized thematically with emphasis on active student learning and public policy analysis, the unit contains overview readings, source materials, optional readings, and resources for more in-depth study, a selected bibliography about the topic, a chronology of German history from 1914 to 1939, and detailed teacher implementation instructions (in the teacher's guide). The teacher's guide also contains suggested activities for interpretation and analysis of student readings, a detailed set of instructions for assessment of student performance, and an overview of the pedagogical design for the unit and suggestions for lesson extensions. This very high quality unit can be used with secondary level students, but is appropriate for college and university level study as well.

Gagnon, Kathleen, and Dianne Ruxton. *Holocaust Literature: Study Guides to Twelve Stories of Courage.* Portland, ME: J. Weston Walch, 1997. ISBN 0–8251–3271–1. 195 pages. Paperback.

This set of lesson plans for teachers helps them design lessons and activities for twelve different works about the Holocaust, including memoirs, fiction, and works of art (Spiegelman's *Maus I* and *Maus II*). Included also is a study guide for *Farewell to Manzanar* by Jeanne Wakatsuki Houston and James D. Houston, a memoir of Japanese internment in the United States during World War II. Each unit includes an introduction for the student, a unit outline for the teacher, activity sheets, and a summative grading sheet where activity grades for the unit can be recorded. The appendix includes summative activities that are generic in design, as well as answer sheets for selected activities included in specific units. An evaluation form for unit study of Holocaust literature also is included. Recommended for use in middle and secondary grades. No index.

Gilbert, Martin. *The Holocaust: Maps and Photographs*. Third edition. New York: Braun Holocaust Institute of the Anti-Defamation League, 1994. ISBN 0–88464–141–4. 59 pages. Paperback.

This much briefer version of the author's *Atlas of the Holocaust* is designed for student use, and is appropriate for use in middle grades through high school. It includes a reading list for further study. Middle and secondary grades.

Globe Fearon. *Historical Case Studies: The Holocaust*. Upper Saddle River, NJ: Globe Fearon Educational Publisher, 1997. ISBN 0–835–91826.2. 128 pages. Paperback.

This book provides a useful supplement to more detailed histories of the Holocaust. Its clear and straightforward use of language is augmented by the use of graphics, photographs, selections from first-person accounts, and maps. Each chapter contains discussion questions, a list of core vocabulary, recommendations for further study of selected topics, and a "case study" that examines one source or theme in detail using critical thinking activities, many of which are designed to establish parallels with contemporary life. In contrast to many other works of this type, this book contains a section on the issue of Holocaust remembrance in contemporary society. A glossary and index are included. Recommended for middle and secondary school use.

Highsmith, Inc. *The Way We Saw It: The Holocaust in Illustration and Art. A Teacher's Resource Booklet*. Fort Atkinson, WI: Highsmith, Inc., 1998. ISBN 1–57596–059–1. 18 pages plus pack of 12 visuals (photographs, graphics, and one cartoon). Paperback.

This teacher's guide and accompanying pack of twelve visuals represent a series of four lessons on the Holocaust designed to help young people learn historical content while improving their visual literacy skills. Visuals are drawn from holdings of the National Archives, Library of Congress, and U.S. Holocaust Memorial Museum, organized into four thematic groupings: "The Rise of Hitler," "The Anti-Semitic Mentality," "From Segregation to 'the Final Solution,'" and "The Aftermath." Each lesson contains objectives, background information on the visual sources, specific questions for interpretation and analysis of each visual, and suggested follow-up activities. A key with answers to factual questions in the teacher's guide is provided as well. This learning packet is recommended for use with middle grades and higher.

Isaacson, Clara. *Pathways through the Holocaust. An Oral History by Eye-Witnesses*. Hoboken, NJ: Ktav Publishing House, 1988. ISBN 0–88125–258–1. 109 pages. Paperback.

Following the opening two chapters, which are brief histories of Jews in Europe and the rise of Nazism, the remaining nine chapters are based upon eyewitness accounts of the Holocaust by survivors and one liberator, Dr. Leon Bass. The edited first-person accounts are followed by suggestions for discussion and further study, relating the content of the first-person account to Jewish tradition and educational themes. No index. Recommended for middle and secondary grades.

Knowledge Unlimited. *Crimes against Humanity: A Holocaust Resource Book*. Madison, WI: Knowledge Unlimited, 1999. ISBN 1–55933–279–4. 164 pages. Paperback.

This spiral-bound resource book is organized into "history pages," which are narrative historical summaries of key content, beginning with the history of Judaism and anti-Semitism, and continuing through the post-liberation period; reproducible activity sheets; suggestions for discussion, research, and writing; and guidelines for use of the primary sources included in each section. A time line, glossary, and comprehensive bibliography are provided, along with a selection of relevant Web sites for investigation. In contrast to many other Holocaust resource guides, this book places substantial emphasis on the study of genocide and war crimes, particularly the efforts to hold perpetrators accountable. Recommended for middle and secondary grades. No index.

Meinbach, Anita Meyer, and Miriam Klein Kassenoff. *Memories of the Night: A Study of the Holocaust*. Photographs by Sharon Gurman Socol. Torrance, CA: Frank Schaffer Publications, 1994. ISBN 0–86734–777–5. 148 pages. Paperback.

This study guide to the Holocaust is divided into three sections: "Historical Perspectives," "The Literature of the Holocaust," and "The Holocaust: Lessons for Today." The authors provide an introduction that offers a rationale for Holocaust education, followed by an overview of the work's contents. Each section of the book contains key content themes, activities to help students deepen their under-standing of content and extensions, primarily sets of interdisciplinary activities and research-based investigations. The book also includes a time line, glossary of relevant terms, and comprehensive set of resources for further study of the Holocaust, along with a list of vendors and Holocaust organizations. The literature section provides guidance about the appropriate level for study of each literary work discussed in the book. The photographs interspersed throughout the book can serve both as illustrations of key Holocaust themes and as sources for analysis. Recommended for use by teachers in grades kindergarten through high school, although the majority of the activities and resources are appropriate for middle school and higher grades. No index.

Merti, Betty. *Understanding the Holocaust*. Portland, ME: J. Weston Walch, 1995. ISBN 0–8251–27084. 273 pages. Paperback.

This book is a simplified account of the history of the Holocaust, designed for use with middle and secondary school students. Included within each chapter of the historical narrative are discussion questions, and many chapters include selections from first-person accounts. Following each chapter are review exercises, resources for more in-depth investigation about the chapter's contents, and suggested activities that range across multiple intelligence realms. A list of selected audiovisual aid distributors for films mentioned in the book, a selected bibliography, and an index conclude the work. Recommended for middle and secondary school use.

————. *The World of Anne Frank: A Complete Resource Guide*. Portland, ME: J. Weston Walch, 1998. ISBN 0–8251–3736–5. 146 pages. Paperback.

Organized thematically, this study guide to *The Diary of Anne Frank* incorporates interpretive essays that address content in *The Diary of Anne Frank* and relate it to major historical themes about the Holocaust. The activities for each chapter include reading comprehension quizzes, discussion and essay activities, topics for research reports, and vocabulary exercises. Cooperative learning activities and a list of supplementary resources for instruction, as well as a comprehensive bibliography about Anne Frank, are included. The book concludes with a collection of nine photos concerning the Anne Frank story. Recommended for middle and secondary grades. Not indexed.

Miller, Marcia K. *The Holocaust: A Scholastic Curriculum Guide*. Jefferson City, MO: Scholastic, 1998. ISBN 0–590–37942–9. 48 pages. Paperback.

Part of Scholastic's *Professional Books* series, this slim book contains many teaching suggestions and selected classroom handout materials designed for upper elementary and middle grades study of the Holocaust. Organized to facilitate thematic study of Holocaust history and literature, the book contains assessment suggestions, a selected bibliography of supplementary materials, graphic organizers, and a range of individual and group activities for use with works published by Scholastic about the kindertransport, Anne Frank, and Jewish refugees. This book is available as a package with three other Scholastic publications: Ian Serraillier's *Escape from Warsaw*, Olga Levy Drucker's *Kindertransport,* and Ruud van der Rool and Rian Verhoeven's *Anne Frank: Beyond the Diary*. Recommended for use in upper elementary and middle grades.

Perfection Learning Corporation. *Voices of the Holocaust: Student Reader and Anthology*. Logan, IA: Perfection Learning, 2000. ISBN 0–7891–5050–6. 144 pages. Paperback.

This is a thematically organized anthology that includes poetry, short stories, speeches, letters, excerpts from autobiographies and historical accounts, essays, and diaries. The five clusters (themes) are: "How Could the Holocaust Happen?," "How Were Victims Oppressed?," "Was There Resistance?," "Why Should We Remember?," and "Thinking on Your Own." Specific cognitive skills are linked to each theme, emphasizing analyzing, comparing and contrasting, generalizing, and synthesizing. Historical photographs and artwork about the Holocaust are integrated throughout the anthology. Recommended for middle and high school use. No index.

————. *Voices of the Holocaust: Teacher's Guide.* Logan, IA: Perfection Learning, 2000. ISBN 0–7891–5053–0. 68 pages. Paperback.

This teacher's guide to the *Voices of the Holocaust* anthology contains activities, teaching suggestions, answer keys to vocabulary tests, assessment rubrics, topics for research, writing, and discussion, and suggestions for further reading, all correlated to the thematic clusters in the student anthology. The instructions for teachers are concise and well written, providing specific guidance for the use of learning activities and specifying the skills and content themes to be learned in each section of the student anthology. Recommended for middle and high school use.

Pressler, Mirjam. *Anne Frank: A Hidden Life.* New York: Dutton Children's Books, 2000. ISBN 0–525–46330–5. 176 pages. Hardcover.

This companion to *The Diary of Anne Frank* includes a foreword by Rabbi Hugo Gryn, as well as an introductory note by Eva Schloss, an Auschwitz survivor and the daughter of Otto Frank's second wife. The book places the story of the Frank family and the famous diary in an historical context, combining biographical descriptions of the family with commentary on *The Diary of Anne Frank.* Chapters are devoted to main characters in Anne Frank's diary, such as Mr. and Mrs. Frank, Mr. and Mrs. Van Pels, and others, as well as chapters about Anne herself, including her development as a writer and her self-image. A brief chronology, selected bibliography, chapter notes, and an index are included. Recommended for use by middle and high school students.

Readings on Anne Frank: The Diary of a Young Girl. San Diego: Greenhaven Press, 1998. ISBN 1–56510–660–1. 144 pages. Paperback.

This literary anthology about *The Diary of Anne Frank* contains an introduction and three coordinated sections: "Important Themes," "A Critical Assessment," and "Legacy." Each section includes between four and six contributions related to the section theme, each beginning with contextual introductions. The book's Introduction describes the content organization of the work, presents a biography of Anne Frank and the history of her family, summarizes the various editions of the *Diary,* and discusses the literary legacy of *The Diary of Anne Frank.* The contents of the anthology are drawn from previously published journal articles, essays, book chapters, and articles in magazines. A chronology about the diary's origins, publication history, and the history of the Frank family is included, along with recommendations of works for further study and an index. For individuals seeking a useful introduction to the literary commentary on *The Diary of Anne Frank*, this anthology is a fine starting point. Recommended for high school use.

Poster Sets for Middle and Secondary School Use

Anti-Defamation League of B'nai B'rith. *The Holocaust: 1939–1945*. Available from the Anti-Defamation League of B'nai B'rith, International Center for Holocaust Studies.

This set of twenty posters is organized in an exhibition format, beginning with German Jewish life prior to the Third Reich, persecution of Jews in Germany, the deportations and killing of Jews in Europe, Jewish resistance to genocide, survivors, the impact of the Nuremberg trials, and the role of survivors in developing Israel. All photos are 29" by 23" and contain captions.

Documentary Photo Aids. *The Nazi Holocaust: Series I*. Mt. Dora, FL: Documentary Photo Aids. No date. Available from Documentary Photo Aids or Social Studies School Service.

This set of thirty-one photos plus a brief teacher's guide addresses the range of German genocidal practices during the period 1939–1945. Topics included are the Warsaw Ghetto, the role of the German military in genocidal practices, slave labor, and the camp system. All photos are printed on 11" x 14" heavy paper and have captions. A brief teacher's guide is included.

———. *The Nazi Holocaust: Series II*. Mt. Dora, FL: Documentary Photo Aids. No date. Available from Documentary Photo Aids.

This set of forty photos includes content on the camp system, anti-Semitic activities in Germany, ghettos, the broad range of German involvement in the "final solution," and encounters by German civilians with atrocities after Allied liberation of the camps. All photos are printed on 11" x 14" heavy paper and have captions. A brief teacher's guide is included.

———. *The Nazi Holocaust Failed in Denmark*. Mt. Dora, FL: Documentary Photo Aids. No date. Available from Documentary Photo Aids or Social Studies School Service.

This set of fourteen photos accompanied by a brief teacher's guide illustrates the occupation policies of Nazi Germany in Denmark, resistance to Nazi occupation by Danes, the rescue efforts by the Danish population that led to the rescue of ninety percent of the Danish Jews in 1943, and their refuge in neutral Sweden. All photos are printed on 11" x 14" heavy paper and have captions.

————. *The Rise and Fall of Nazi Germany.* Mt. Dora, FL: Documentary Photo Aids. No date. Available from Documentary Photo Aids or Social Studies School Service.

This set of forty photos with a brief teacher's guide illustrates the rise of Hitler to power, issues related to the conduct of World War II, and the defeat of Nazi Germany by the Allies. All photos are printed on 11" x 14" heavy paper and have captions.

Golden Owl Publications. *Historical Photo Set: Holocaust Children.* Amawalk,, NY: Golden Owl Publications, 1999. Available from Golden Owl Publications.

Twelve historical photos and a teacher's guide with a broadsheet essay, Holocaust facts, student photo activities, and a photo analysis worksheet are included in this set. Each photo contains a caption, source citation, and identification code linked to the teacher's guide activities. The large photographs, all drawn from the archives of the U.S. Holocaust Memorial Museum, illustrate children in ghettos and death camps, children awaiting deportation, child refugees, and children wearing the identification labels marking them as "Jews." The student activities in the accompanying teacher's guide provide specific suggestions for classroom use, highlighting the unique historical and photographic information evident in each photo.

————. *Jackdaws: The Coming of War.* Amawalk, NY: Golden Owl Publications, 1999. Available from Golden Owl Publications.

This set of eleven documents and four broadsheets examines the years following World War I and the rise of tensions in Europe between Great Britain and Germany, which would eventually lead to war with Germany's invasion of Poland on September 1, 1939. Maps, documents on Hitler's rise to power, sources detailing the Munich agreement and the response to it, and newspaper accounts from 1938 and 1939 are included. The four broadsheets focus on Hitler's rise to power, the European reaction to Nazism's triumph and consolidation of power, the road to Munich, and the final steps leading to war. A study guide with reproducible masters for students and teaching suggestions is provided.

————. *Jackdaws: The Holocaust.* Amawalk, NY: Golden Owl Publications, 1992. Available from Golden Owl Publications.

This set of five broadsheet essays and twelve reproductions of historical documents includes a chronology of the Holocaust (1933–1945), newspaper accounts of Nazi terror, selections from the Wannsee Protocol, five maps about the "geography of genocide" (1918–1945), a collection of photos on atrocities committed against targeted victim groups, and other perpetrator documents. The broadsheet essays set the documents within an historical context, and include historical background on the origins of anti-Semitism, the rise of Hitler and Nazism, the "final solution," the response of the Allies and neutral nations to the Holocaust, and the Holocaust's legacy for contemporary society. Teaching suggestions are included in the study guide, along with reproducible masters for student use.

U.S. Holocaust Memorial Museum. *Artifact Poster Set and Teacher's Guide.* Available from the U.S. Holocaust Memorial Museum Shop.

This set of nine posters and a comprehensive teacher's guide draws upon the rich resources of the Museum's artifact collection. Thematically organized, each poster presents photographs of artifacts with complete citation information. The teacher's guide is thorough and reflects a commitment to the interpretation and analysis of the artifacts within the broader historical context of the Holocaust and the history of Nazi Germany. Topics included in the posters, which have excellent-quality photography, include technology used to effect discrimination in Nazi Germany, Danish rescue efforts, partisan resistance, identification badges for targeted groups, and the impact of the Holocaust on children, among others.

Yad Vashem Martyrs' and Heroes' Remembrance Authority. *But the Story Didn't End That Way.* Available from Yad Vashem Martyrs' and Heroes' Remembrance Authority.

This poster set, videocassette, and accompanying teacher's guide includes eighteen posters (50 × 70 cm) depicting German-Jewish life in the 1920s through Kristallnacht. The video includes testimonies of Jews who lived through the Kristallnacht nationwide pogrom. The materials are available in Hebrew, English, Spanish, French, and German.

————. *The Legend of the Lodz Ghetto Children.* Available from Yad Vashem Martyrs' and Heroes' Remembrance Authority.

Based upon an album of illustrations of the same title, this unit includes seventeen color posters (50 x 70 cm) depicting the life of children in the Lodz ghetto and a teacher's manual. The illustrations were created by unknown authors who lived in the Lodz Ghetto. The unit is available in Hebrew and English.

————. *Return to Life: The Holocaust Survivors from Liberation to Rehabilitation.* Available from Yad Vashem Martyrs' and Heroes' Remembrance Authority.

This set of 20 black-and-white posters (35 x 50 cm) portrays the return of Jewish refugees to Poland, the Kielce pogrom and life in displaced persons camps, clandestine immigration to Palestine, and large-scale immigration to Israel. A teacher's guide is included. The unit is available in Hebrew, English, and Spanish.

————. *To Bear Witness*. Available from Yad Vashem Martyrs' and Heroes' Remembrance Authority.

This poster set with teacher's manual contains thirty-nine photographic images on twenty 50 x 70 cm posters. Topics include the rise of Nazism, deportation to death camps, life in ghettos, the Warsaw Ghetto uprising, and liberation. The set is available in Hebrew, English, French, Spanish, and Russian.

Slide Sets for Middle and Secondary School Use

Buchenwald Memorial. *Slide Set of 36 Slides with Accompanying Titles in German, English, and French*. Weimar: Stiftung Gedenskatte Buchenwald und Mittelbau-Dora. No date. Available from Gedenkstatte Buchenwald.

These slides display various views of the remains of the Buchenwald Concentration Camp, its surroundings, and memorials erected at the camp site after World War II.

Imperial War Museum. *Nazi Germany: Study Slide Pack*. London: Imperial War Museum, 1986. Available from the Imperial War Museum, Lambeth Road, London SE 1 6HZ, United Kingdom.

This slide set contains twenty-four black-and-white slides with an accompanying sheet of detailed descriptions for each slide. One slide addresses the liberation of Bergen-Belsen concentration camp, while the others focus on the rise of the Nazi regime and the conduct and effects of World War II on Germany. No teaching suggestions are included with the slides and descriptions.

Treblinka State Museum. *Slide Set*. Siedlce: Treblinka State Museum, 1986. 20 slides and accompanying explanation in Polish. Background information and slide listing in Polish. Slide listing by title only in English. Available from Muzeum Okregowe (Treblinka State Museum).

These slides display views of the Treblinka camp memorial, including reconstructed areas symbolizing the entrance gate to the extermination camp, the loading platform for prisoners, and others. Additionally, the monuments and cemeteries within the Treblinka site are included.

Watch Tower Bible and Trace Society of Pennsylvania. *The Spirit and the Sword: Jehovah's Witnesses Expose the Third Reich*. Brooklyn: Watchtower, Office of Public Affairs, no date. Available from Watch Tower Bible and Trace Society of Pennsylvania.

This set of slides with accompanying lecture notes is based upon a presentation made on September 29, 1994 at the U.S. Holocaust Memorial Museum by James

Pellachia, editor of *Awake! Magazine*. It deals with the resistance of Jehovah's Witnesses to Nazi persecution.

Yad Vashem. *Everyday Life in the Warsaw Ghetto—1941. A Study Unit for Junior High School Students*. 28 slides with accompanying student workbook. Jerusalem: Yad Vashem, 1993. ISBN 965–308–024–5. 50 pages. Available from Yad Vashem Martyrs' and Heroes' Remembrance Authority.

This study unit comprises twenty-eight black-and-white slides, coordinated with study questions for students and readings associated with specific slides drawn from eyewitness accounts of the Warsaw Ghetto created in 1941. Reproductions of the slides are printed in the study guide with the accompanying eyewitness account excerpts, which are intended to be read as the slide is displayed. A bibliography of sources consulted for the guide is included.

————. *The Holocaust: An Audio Visual History Based on the Yad Vashem Museum*. Script by Shalmi Barmore. 34 slides with accompanying script on audiocassette. Jerusalem: Yad Vashem, no date. Available from Yad Vashem Martyrs' and Heroes' Remembrance Authority.

The black-and-white slides, beginning with the rise of Nazism in Germany and concluding with the founding of Israel, are to be displayed with the accompanying audiocassette narration. Content of the slides includes Jewish resistance in the Warsaw Ghetto, as well as the patterns of persecution resulting in mass murder that characterized Germany's genocidal policies toward Jews.

————. *The Jew and Nazi Ideology*. Slide set of 28 slides with accompanying teacher's guide. Available from Yad Vashem Martyrs' and Heroes' Remembrance Authority.

This slide set illustrates how Nazism employed historical stereotypes of Jews in Europe, blending them with concepts and images based upon racial anti-Semitism to influence public opinion and socialize Germans to ostracize and eventually destroy European Jews. The accompanying teacher's guide explains how the twenty-eight images in the set reflected a worldview emphasizing biological racism, aggressive nationalism, authoritarian rule, and coordination of social institutions to achieve the utopian vision of a "racial state" envisioned in Nazi ideology. The slide images are drawn from four major Nazi sources: the exhibition entitled "The Eternal Jew" from 1938; the weekly newspaper *Der Sturmer*; and two Nazi children's books. A comprehensive introduction to the content and detailed translations and summaries of visual images and associated captions are provided in the teacher's guide. A diverse selection of excerpts from Hitler's *Mein Kampf* is included to establish the links between Nazi ideology and the slide images.

Teaching Materials for Study of the Holocaust on the Internet

Willis, Aaron, Project Editor, with Paul Barstow, Lois M. Christensen, Betsy Hedberg-Keramidas, Eleanor Kykendall, and Joseph Korn. *Teaching Holocaust Studies with the Internet: Internet Lesson Plans and Classroom Activities*. Culver City, CA: Social Studies School Service and Classroom Connect (http://www.classroom.com), 1999. Classroom Connect, 1999. ISBN 0–932577–62–8. 137 pages. Paperback.

This collection of nineteen lessons and classroom activities provides opportunities for classroom teachers to integrate Internet-based Holocaust resources into Holocaust instruction. A brief introduction advises the user about rationales for Holocaust education, and cautions the user to employ the lessons and activities in the book within a larger curriculum unit or set of lessons where key themes, concepts, and content about the Holocaust are studied. The lessons and activities emphasize analytical and interpretive skills, such as photograph analysis, critical examination of text, and evaluation of the credibility and authenticity of sources. Listings of selected Web sites referenced in the lessons and activities, as well as a brief listing of books, activity collections, and videocassettes, are provided, along with an answer key for specific questions in a number of the lessons. A companion Web site that provides updates to purchasers of the book is available for supplementary investigation. Recommended for use by middle and high school educators. No index.

Videotapes with Curriculum Materials for Middle and Secondary School Use

The Holocaust: A Teenager's Experience. 30 minutes. VHS videotape. Instructional video with teacher's guide and learning materials. Vendor: United Learning.

This instructional video and accompanying teacher's guide and learning materials relate the story of David Bergman, who survived the Holocaust as a teenager. The film integrates historical photos with artwork by David Bergman reflecting his experiences in Poland, Germany, and Austria.

Jehovah's Witnesses Stand Firm against Nazi Assault. 28 minutes. VHS videotape. Documentary. Vendor: Watch Tower Bible and Tract Society of Pennsylvania.

This film demonstrates how Jehovah's Witnesses were persecuted in Germany under the Third Reich, along with their response to Nazism. A study guide accompanies the film.

Live from the Past: The Holocaust—The Death Camps, 1935–1945. 20 minutes. VHS videotape. Instructional video with teacher's guide and related learning materials. Vendor: Social Studies School Service.

This video learning module examines the development, operation, and liberation of the Nazi death camp system. Accompanying facsimiles of *New York Times* articles and related teaching resources complement the content of the video, which provides an overview of the topic using historical film footage, still photos, and commentary by reporters and others.

Live from the Past: The Holocaust—The Trial of Adolf Eichmann, 1961. 16 minutes. VHS videotape. Instructional video with teacher's guide and related learning materials. Vendor: Social Studies School Service.

This video learning module examines the Eichmann trial of 1961, and includes facsimile reproductions of *New York Times* articles on the trial, along with a video that includes historical footage, still photos, and commentary by *New York Times* reporters and other experts.

Publications on Holocaust Study and Teaching

Danks, Carol, and Leatrice Rabinsky, editors. *Teaching for a Tolerant World. Grades 9–12. Essays and Resources.* Urbana, IL: National Council of Teachers of English, 1999. ISBN 0–8141–4296–6. 399 pages. Paperback.

Written by practicing teachers of language arts and English at the kindergarten through secondary and collegiate levels, this anthology of essays is an important resource for educators who teach about the Holocaust, genocide, and intolerance. The twenty-three chapters are divided into three major sections: "Teaching about Issues of Intolerance," "Teaching about Issues of Genocide," and "Resources for Teaching about Issues of Genocide and Intolerance." The introductory essay by Grace M. Caporino and Rose Rudnitski, "General Guidelines for Teaching about Intolerance and Genocide," offers expert guidance to teachers concerning the selection and use of instructional materials, as well as guidance for lesson and unit design in the language arts and English classroom. There are three articles in the "Teaching about Issues of Genocide" section specifically concerning the Holocaust, and the resources section contains a select annotated bibliography of print, electronic, and audiovisual resources, as well as a brief listing of Holocaust-related organizations. Brief contributor biographies are provided. Indexed.

Davies, Ian. *Teaching the Holocaust: Educational Dimensions, Principles and Practices.* New York: Continuum, 2000. ISBN 0–8264–48518. 178 pages. Paperback.

Primarily directed to a British audience, this work contains twelve essays concerning the study of the Holocaust in pre-collegiate settings. Part I, "Understanding the Holocaust," includes essays on the historical roots of anti-Semitism, relationships between Judaism and Christianity, and reflections on both philosophical and curricular issues that arise in preparing for Holocaust study. The second section, "International Overviews," provides concise essays that summarize the current state of Holocaust education in Germany, the United States, and England, along with an essay on the work of the Education Centre at the Auschwitz-Birkenau Memorial and Museum in Poland. The final section, "Case Studies of Teaching and Learning about the Holocaust," consists of four essays on instruction about the Holocaust in religion, English, and history courses, as well as how to study the Holocaust using an educational exhibition (in this case, a visiting exhibition from the Anne Frank Educational Trust in York, England). References are provided at the end of each essay. The international section is particularly useful in providing a current understanding of themes in Holocaust education in selected countries. Indexed.

Garber, Zev, editor, with Alan L. Berger and Richard Libowitz. *Methodology in the Academic Teaching of the Holocaust*. Lanham, MD: University Press of America, 1988. Part of the series Studies in Judaism. ISBN 0–8191–6961–7. 327 pages. Hardcover.

This work primarily focuses on Holocaust teaching at the college and university level. The contributors are diverse, coming from Israel and the North America, and reflecting a broad range of subject fields, including history, philosophy, religious studies, literature, and the arts. Sources cited in each article are provided at the end of each chapter. Indexed.

Haynes, Stephen R. *Holocaust Education and the Church-Related College. Restoring Ruptured Traditions*. Foreword by Franklin H. Littell. Westport, CT: Greenwood Press, 1997. ISBN 0–313–29023–7. 185 pages. Hardcover.

This work addresses the study of the Holocaust in church-related colleges in the United States, examining the relationship of Holocaust education to two critical traditions of church-related colleges in the United States: Christian confession and liberal learning. Haynes argues that given the moral rupture of those traditions during the Holocaust, church-related colleges have an obligation to address the meaning of the Holocaust. Important data for the book was gathered through use of a survey instrument prepared by the author, which is included as an appendix. An extensive bibliography is provided, along with a comprehensive index. This book is part of the series *Contributions to the Study of Religion, Number 49: Christianity and the Holocaust—Core Issues,* Carol Rittner and John Roth, series editors.

Millen, Rochelle L., editor. *New Perspectives on the Holocaust: A Guide for Teachers and Students*. New York: NYU Press, 1996. ISBN 0–8147–5540–2. 382 pages. Paperback.

Originating from an international conference held at Wittenberg University in 1993, this set of twenty-five essays is divided into three sections: "Viewing the Holocaust in Context," "Considering Issues of Teaching and Curriculum," and "Teaching toward Dialogue: Spiritual and Moral Issues." Each of the three sections begins with a brief introduction that describes the context for the essays that follow. Among the topics addressed in the work are the debate concerning the uniqueness and universality of the Holocaust; varied approaches to curriculum design (examples include use of literature, interdisciplinary approaches, study of the Holocaust through landscape study, and others); and continuing efforts at dialogue about the Holocaust and its legacy, such as those encountered in religious settings, medicine, education, and between Israelis and Germans. Each essay concludes with extensive notes and a comprehensive reference list. Indexed.

Schreier, Helmut, and Matthias Heyl, editors. *Never Again! The Holocaust's Challenge for Educators*. Hamburg: Kramer, 1997. ISBN 3–89622–018–7. 214 pages. Hardcover.

This book is an anthology of essays that emerged primarily from a conference held in Hamburg, Germany in 1995 on the occasion of the fiftieth anniversary of the liberation of Auschwitz. The contributors are international, ranging from North America to Europe to Israel, and including university professors, museum directors, teacher trainers, and others who study the nature of Holocaust education in various settings. The anthology includes two sections: "Premises" (issues of rationale and context) and "Approaches" (issues of curriculum design and methodology, and the relationship of memory to education). Extensive notes for each chapter are included, along with brief contributor biographies. No index.

Shimoni, Gideon. *The Holocaust in University Teaching*. New York: Pergamon Press, 1991. ISBN 0–08–040798–6. 278 pages. Hardcover.

This extensive anthology includes two major sections: "Teaching Approaches and Resources" and "Selected Syllabi." The contributors to the "Teaching Approaches and Resources" section examine use of visual arts in Holocaust teaching, interdisciplinary approaches to Holocaust study, the use of film in Holocaust teaching, and issues related to integrating theological analysis into Holocaust courses. The much larger second section, "Selected Syllabi," includes twenty-six essays by individual scholars who describe their specific curricular designs for Holocaust study. Among the subject fields included in this section are history, literature, theology, Judaic studies, sociology, and comparative genocide studies. Also encompassed in this section is a chapter on analysis of children's and young adult literature for Holocaust study. The work includes a bibliography, but is not indexed.

Stephens, Elaine C., Jean E. Brown, and Janet E. Rubin. *Learning about the Holocaust: Literature and Other Resources for Young People*. North Haven, CT: Library Professional Publications, 1995. ISBN 0–208–02408–5. 198 pages. Paperback.

Written as a resource guide for individuals who work with young people, this book is a very useful introduction to books and related resources on the Holocaust. While primarily focusing on book and print materials, the authors have included selected films and videos, listings of curriculum guides, journals, and other educational materials, as well as a list of selected Holocaust organizations and institutions. Each chapter contains a brief introduction to the literature (some examples include fiction, plays, and historical fiction), followed by thematic questions to consider in making choices from the selections included in the chapter, and discussion questions for the classroom. Following the brief reviews of each book, a concluding section provides brief instructional strategies for use with titles reviewed in the chapter. Each title is categorized by its appropriate grade level (primary through secondary) and the reviews offer content summaries and teaching considerations; plus, when applicable, a list of related titles at the same grade level. Two indexes are provided: authors, and titles by chapter and genre, making the book very user-friendly for prospective classroom teachers seeking recommendations for titles to include in curricula.

Supple, Carrie. *From Prejudice to Genocide: Learning about the Holocaust*. Stoke-on-Trent, UK: Trentham Books, 1993. ISBN 0–948080–60–4. 316 pages. Paperback.

Designed as a text for secondary school students in England, this work integrates many sources (photographs, graphics, text) within its narrative structure, along with activities for source interpretation and analysis. The life experiences of four individuals are thematically intertwined throughout the book to personalize the narrative. In the final chapter, entitled "Then and Now," the continuing problem of prejudice and genocide since the conclusion of World War II is addressed, and the author brings the reader up-to-date on the current status of the four individuals whose life experiences are integrated throughout the narrative. A glossary, works cited and consulted list, recommendations for further reading, list of organizations in the United Kingdom dealing with Holocaust studies, and two appendices (factors facilitating the occurrence of the Holocaust and examples of how to integrate the study of the Holocaust into the English national school curriculum) are included. Indexed.

Totten, Samuel, editor. *Teaching Holocaust Literature*. Boston: Allyn & Bacon, 2001. ISBN 0–205–27402–1. 258 pages. Paperback.

This very helpful anthology of essays provides expert advice on how to teach about the Holocaust using literary resources. Samuel Totten's contributions to the anthology include the "Introduction," which discusses critical issues regarding teacher planning and scholarship for Holocaust instruction; "Incorporating Fiction and Poetry into a Study of the Holocaust," a thorough discussion of this topic with a comprehensive annotated bibliography; and three chapters on the use of short stories, poetry, and first-person accounts in Holocaust instruction. He also provides a brief appendix where the controversial issue of simulation use in Holocaust education is analyzed. Essays on the use of novels, poetry, and drama in Holocaust instruction are provided by other contributors, along with essays on guidelines for the teaching of Holocaust literature and why *The Diary of Anne Frank* may not be the most appropriate work for Holocaust study in classrooms. For educators seeking guidance and specific strategies for including Holocaust literature in classroom instruction, this is an essential book. Brief contributor biographies are included. Indexed.

Totten, Samuel, and Stephen Feinberg, editors. *Teaching and Studying the Holocaust*. Boston: Allyn & Bacon, 2001. ISBN 0–205–18495–2. 320 pages. Hardcover.

Thirteen chapters address a multidimensional approach to Holocaust education, beginning with a detailed discussion of rationale building for Holocaust education and continuing with chapters on Holocaust historiography; use of primary source documents; incorporating first-person accounts, film, literature, art, drama, and music; and the integration of technology resources into Holocaust study. A thorough and detailed annotated bibliography is provided, along with notes for each chapter. A strength of the work is the editors' reliance on a varied mixture of classroom practitioners and scholars as contributors to the book. Indexed.

Totten, Samuel, and William S. Parsons. "State Developed Teacher Guides and Curricula on Genocide and/or the Holocaust: A Succinct Review and Critique." *Inquiry in Social Studies: Curriculum, Research, and Instruction. The Journal of the North Carolina Council for the Social Studies*. Vol. 28, No. 1, Spring 1992: 27–47.

This article critiques nine curricula/resource guides for Holocaust and genocide education from New Jersey, New York, North Carolina, Pennsylvania, Florida, California, Ohio, Connecticut, and Virginia. The authors provide critiques and suggestions for continuing improvement of curricula and resource guides, emphasizing strong rationale sections, improved teacher training programs, involvement of classroom teachers in design and writing of curricula/resource guides, and field testing of curricula and instructional materials.

U.S. Holocaust Memorial Museum. *Teacher Guide to the Permanent Exhibition: The Holocaust*. Washington, DC: USHMM, 1999. No ISBN. 36 pages. Paperback. Available from the Education Department, USHMM,

100 Wallenberg Place SW, Washington, DC 20024-2126. Phone: School and Adult Programs, 202-488-0493. Free.

Providing an introduction and teaching suggestions for group visits to the USHMM in Washington, DC, this guide includes historical summaries of key components of the permanent exhibit, plus pre-, during and post-visit activities. It also contains a structural analysis of the exhibition display panels for the museum visitor, information on the use of photo ID cards of individuals affected by the Holocaust (provided to group visitors upon arrival for consultation and use in the permanent exhibit and later), and information on other exhibitions and facilities at the USHMM. Information on obtaining materials from the Education Department, as well as how to schedule a group visit, is provided as well. No index.

————. *Teaching about the Holocaust: A Resource Book for Educators.* Revised edition. Washington, DC: United States Holocaust Memorial Council, 2000. No ISBN provided. 115 pages. Paperback. Available upon request from the Education Department of the U.S. Holocaust Memorial Museum.

Containing an in-depth examination of educational rationales and methodological concerns in the teaching of the Holocaust, this guidebook provides a comprehensive starting point for any educator who chooses to teach about this period of history. Information regarding site visits to the Washington, DC Museum, availability of educational materials, and frequently asked questions about the history of the Holocaust are combined with extensive age-level-appropriate annotated bibliographies and videographies, as well as a detailed chronology of the Holocaust. Additionally, concise historical summaries of the Holocaust and the impact of the Holocaust on children of the era are included. The book is illustrated with historical photos and photos of educational materials and activities prepared by the Museum staff. No index.

Selected State-Level Curriculum Guides (USA) for Grades 7 and Higher

California State Board of Education. *Model Curriculum for Human Rights and Genocide.* Sacramento: California State Department of Education, 1987. ISBN 0–8011–0725–3. 66 pages. Paperback. Available from Bureau of Publications Sales, California State Department of Education, PO Box 271, Sacramento, CA 95802-0271.

This model curriculum includes a listing of curriculum resources and two appendices: "Summary of Human Rights and Genocide in the Curriculum" and "Examples of Violations of Human Rights." Genocides in Armenia and the Ukraine are included as well as continuing problems of totalitarian violations in Argentina, Cambodia, and

South Africa. Specific curricular connections are provided in Appendix A for California teachers. Contact Information: State of California, Bureau of Publications Sales, California State Department of Education, PO Box 271, Sacramento, CA 95802-0271.

Florida Commissioner's Task Force on Holocaust Education. *State of Florida Resource Manual on Holocaust Education*. Tallahassee: Florida State Department of Education, 1996–.

Following the passage and signing of the state of Florida's Holocaust education legislation in 1994, the Commissioner's Task Force on Holocaust Education created a Resource Manual for grades 9–12. This manual includes 8 major units: prejudice and genocide, historical roots of the Holocaust, history of the Nazi party, ghettos, the camp system, resistance, liberation, and lessons for today's world. Each unit includes an introduction, objectives, vocabulary, a content overview, suggested activities, correlations to Florida's content standards for additional activities and readings, photographs, and eyewitness testimonies. Implementation of the guide is assisted by the five resource centers in Florida designated to serve this purpose: the Holocaust Outreach Center of Florida Atlantic University, the Center for Professional Development at Florida State University, the Holocaust Memorial Resource and Education Center of Central Florida, the Holocaust Documentation and Education Center at Florida International University, and the Florida Holocaust Museum in St. Petersburg. Contact Information: Florida Commissioner's Task Force on Holocaust Education, c/o Florida International University, 3000 NE 161st Street, North Miami, FL 33181. Phone: 305-919-5690. FAX: 305-919-5691. http://holocaust.fiu.edu.

New Jersey Commission on Holocaust Education. *The Holocaust: The Betrayal of Mankind. Curriculum Guide Grades 7–12*. Trenton: New Jersey Commission on Holocaust Education, 1995.

Designed for teachers and students in grades 7–12, this curriculum resource guide utilizes historical, psychological, literary, and artistic sources along with first-person accounts to investigate human nature, hatred, and prejudice, with emphasis placed on the study of the Holocaust. Since the initial publication of the guide, units on other genocides have been added, including the genocide of the Armenians in the Ottoman Empire, the forced famine in the Ukraine of 1932–1933, the genocide in Cambodia of the late 1970s, and the Irish famine of the nineteenth century. The guide includes seven major units: "The Nature of Human Behavior," "Views of Prejudice and Genocide," "The Rise of Nazism," "From Persecution to Mass Murder," "Resistance and Intervention," "Genocide," and "Issues of Conscience and Moral Responsibility." Each of the seven major units begins with a brief overview and list of student readings, followed by a chart that identifies performance objectives, teaching/learning strategies, and instructional materials and resources for the unit. No summative assessments are provided for units or for the entire curriculum guide. Contact Information: New Jersey Commission on Holocaust Education, PO Box 500, Trenton, NJ 08625-0500. Phone: 609-292-9274. FAX: 609-292-1211. http://www.state.nj.us/njded/holocaust/.

New York State Department of Education. *Case Studies: Persecution/ Genocide. The Human Rights Series. Volume III.* Albany: University of the State of New York, 1985. No ISBN. 166 pages. Paperback.

Consisting of four units, two on the Ukraine and two on Cambodia, this third and final volume in New York's Human Rights Series places substantial emphasis on the forced famine in the Ukraine under Soviet rule, with a complementary unit on human rights violations in the Ukraine under Soviet rule. The two very brief units on Cambodia, entitled "The Killing of Cambodia" and "Human Rights Violations in Cambodia," contain a total of five learning resources overall, in contrast to the over sixty learning resources provided on the Ukraine. A useful guide to developing case studies is included as Unit 5 in the guide, and the guide concludes with a selected bibliography on genocide and human rights violations in the Ukraine and Cambodia. Contact Information: State of New York, University of the State of New York, State Education Department, Bureau of Curriculum Development, Albany, NY 12234.

————. *Teaching about the Holocaust and Genocide: Introduction. The Human Rights Series. Volume I.* Albany: University of the State of New York, 1985. No ISBN. 68 pages. Paperback.

The first in a three-volume series of teacher's guides intended to educate young people and classroom teachers about the Holocaust, genocide, and human rights, this volume includes a rationale for inclusion of this content in the school curriculum and two units: "The Roots of Intolerance and Persecution" and "Precursors to the Holocaust." In each section of the guide, a statement of purpose, list of learning objectives, and set of learning activities and student materials are provided. Excerpted readings from scholars and others are included, along with a number of facsimile documents as resources for student activities. While genocide and human rights are discussed, the primary content of the guide addresses the history of the Holocaust. Contact Information: State of New York, University of the State of New York, State Education Department, Bureau of Curriculum Development, Albany, NY 12234.

————. *Teaching about the Holocaust and Genocide: The Human Rights Series. Volume II.* Albany: University of the State of New York, 1985. No ISBN. 323 pages. Paperback.

This second volume in New York State's curriculum for teaching the Holocaust, genocide, and human rights is devoted to "The Nazi Holocaust," with a brief second section on "Implications for Our Future." Organized in the same manner as Volume I, the contents draw upon themes as diverse as "Anti-Semitism" (traditional, religious, and racial), "Nazi Thought," "The Final Solution," "Responses by Individuals, Institutions, and Nations," and "Judgment, Justice, and Survivors," among others. The unit on future implications addresses the issue of choice by individuals and groups, and posits possible connections between behavior exhibited during the Holocaust and contemporary social life. The volume also includes a select bibliography that addresses the contents of Volumes I and II in the series. Contact Information: State of New York, University of the State of New York, State Education Department, Bureau of Curriculum Development, Albany, NY 12234.

Ohio Council on Holocaust Education. Leatrice B. Rabinsky and Carol Danks, co-editors. *The Holocaust: Prejudice Unleashed.*

This curriculum guide is divided into five major sections: "Foundations of the Holocaust," "The Culture of a People," "The Road to the 'Final Solution,'" "Responses to the Holocaust," and "Meaning of the Holocaust in Today's World." Utilizing historical, literary, and artistic sources, as well as first-person accounts and examples of student writing, each unit of the curriculum contains instructional objectives, instructional materials, procedures, supplementary materials suggestions, and a listing of relevant vocabulary. An introduction for teachers describing the overall curricular goals is provided, and the guide includes a series of suggestions for student activities encompassing writing activities, commemorative activities, research assignments, and conducting interviews with survivors. A comprehensive annotated list of resources concludes the curriculum guide, which also contains a curriculum evaluation instrument for students. Contact Information: Ohio Council on Holocaust Education. 314 Satterfield Hall, Kent State University, Kent, OH 44242. Phone: 330-672-2389. FAX: 330-672-4009.

State of Washington. *Human Rights: A Case Study through the Holocaust.* Olympia: State Superintendent of Public Instruction, 1994. Available from State Superintendent of Public Instruction, Old Capitol Building, PO Box 47200, Olympia, WA 98504-7200.

This guide includes five lessons: "Introduction to the Holocaust," "History/Maps/ Uniqueness of the Holocaust," "Perpetrators, Victims and Bystanders," "Rescuers and Resistance," and "Applying Universal Lessons of the Holocaust." A bibliography with brief annotations is geared to high school teaching. Lessons are organized with title, grades, time required, objectives, purpose, materials, and teacher notes (brief suggestions). No methodology section or assessment suggestions are included. Materials are provided with lessons. Contact Information: State of Washington, State Superintendent of Public Instruction, Old Capitol Building, PO Box 47200, Olympia, WA 98504-7200.

Curricula Produced by Organizations

Center for the Study of the Child. Sidney Bolkosky, Betty Rotberg Elias, and David Harris. *A Holocaust Curriculum: Life Unworthy of Life*. Farmington Hills, MI: The Center for the Study of the Child, 1987. ISBN 0–961–9288–0–8.

This curriculum guide contains eighteen lessons, and includes a videotape with survivor and documentary film excerpts. The curriculum guide is organized as a multimedia resource package, with a common organizing framework for each of the eighteen lessons: lesson objectives, a listing of key glossary terms, instructional materials, and instructional methodology. The learning goals in the curriculum address knowledge, skills, and values, all of which are summarized in the guide's "Introduction for Teachers." The topics addressed in the eighteen lessons are "The Destruction of Families and the Question of Personal Responsibility," "The Aftermath of World War I," "Germans, Jews and Anti-Semitism," "Hitler and the Nazi Party," "Toward the Final Solution," "Planet Auschwitz," "Rescuers," "Resistance and Survival," "Sounds of Silence: World Responses," and "Aftermath: Consequences and Implications." Also included in the guide are appendixes that comprise a glossary, chronology of the Holocaust, the text of the accompanying video, a summary of Nazi leaders and departments, a unit test addressing the curriculum's knowledge goals, and a select, annotated bibliography. Contact Information: Center for the Study of the Child, 914 Lincoln Avenue, Ann Arbor, MI 4801-3508. Phone: 313-761-6440. FAX: 313-761-5629.

PROGRAMS FOR TEACHER TRAINING

Organizations

Facing History and Ourselves.

As a national educational and professional development organization, Facing History and Ourselves addresses issues of racism, prejudice, and anti-Semitism to further development of a more humane and informed citizenry. Study of the Holocaust and other examples of collective violence provides the opportunity for students to establish connections between history and contemporary moral and ethical choices. The organization has extensive teacher training programs, including two-day introductory workshops, five-day training institutes, and extensive follow-up support for professional development. With a network of six regional offices, a national office, and a European office, Facing History and Ourselves also produces classroom resources, teacher training materials, and study guides for learning materials produced by other vendors. Contact Information: Facing History and Ourselves National Foundation, Inc., 16 Hurd Road, Brookline, MA 02445. Phone: 617-232-1595. FAX: 617-232-0281. http://www.facing.org.

Florida Commissioner's Task Force on Holocaust Education.

Five task force sites exist in the state of Florida to offer teacher training in Holocaust education, with the Holocaust Documentation and Education Center, Inc. in North Miami, Florida serving as the headquarters of the initiative. College-accredited summer teacher institutes are presented annually, and the Center has produced the *State of Florida Resource Manual on Holocaust Education* for secondary schools (grades 9–12). Resource manuals are currently under development for grades K–3, 4–6 and 7–8. Contact Information: Florida Commissioner's Task Force on Holocaust Education, c/o Florida International University, 3000 NE 161st Street, North Miami, FL 33181. Phone: 305-919-5690. FAX: 305-919-5691. http://holocaust.fiu.edu.

Holocaust and Jewish Resistance Teachers Training Program.

This summer study program in Poland and Israel runs during July and involves approximately forty to fifty teachers per year in an intensive study of the history of the Holocaust and Jewish resistance. Under the direction of Holocaust survivors Vladka and Benjamin Meed, the program begins with a week in Poland, where participants study the history of the Warsaw Ghetto, the Warsaw Ghetto uprising, and visit death camps such as Majdanek and Auschwitz-Birkenau. Following the week in Poland, the seminar participants travel to Israel, where they study at both Yad Vashem and the Ghetto Fighters' House Museum. First-hand accounts by survivors are employed along with presentations by experts and renowned scholars in the field of Holocaust studies. Field trips to other sites in Israel are typically included in the seminar itinerary. Applications are available from the Jewish Labor Committee headquarters in New York, and are due in April. Contact Information: Holocaust and Jewish Resistance Teachers Training Program, Jewish Labor Committee, 25 East 21st Street, New York, NY 10010.

Holocaust Museum Houston.

The Holocaust Museum Houston's Curriculum Trunk Program is a national teacher training program centering on use of the resources provided in the Museum's curriculum trunks, which are designed especially for use by middle school, high school, and college educators to teach about the Holocaust and the related lessons on prejudice awareness and citizenship responsibility. The emphasis in the curriculum trunk materials is on active learning and the development of personal responsibility and moral courage. Training programs for users of the trunks are available from the Holocaust Museum Houston. Contact Information: Holocaust Museum Houston, 5401 Caroline Street, Houston, TX 77004. Phone: 713-942-8000. FAX: 713-942-7953. http://www.hmh.org.

Master of Arts in Holocaust and Genocide Studies. Richard Stockton College of New Jersey.

This program emphasizes the study of the Holocaust and genocide in a comparative context, and is designed to provide educators with the requisite training and background needed to teach effectively about the Holocaust and other genocides. An interdisciplinary faculty enriched by visiting faculty from around the world provides students with multidimensional perspectives as they pursue the core requirements and elective courses for the master's degree. Contact Information: Program Director, Master of Arts in Holocaust and Genocide Studies, Richard Stockton College of New Jersey, PO Box 195, Pomona, NJ 08240-0195. Phone: 609-652-4418.

Teaching the Holocaust: History, Perspectives and Choices.

This program, run by the Jewish Foundation for the Righteous, began in June 2000 with a summer residential institute at Clark University. The publication of the work *Voices and Views: A History of the Holocaust,* written by Dr. Deborah Dwork of Clark University, coincides with the inauguration of the residential program. *Voices and Views* is a ten-chapter edited and annotated collection of scholarly works designed to help teachers learn from eminent scholars in the field. Accompanying the *Voices and Views* anthology is a *Resource for Teachers* and a separate *Student Reader,* both organized according to the thematic design of *Voices and Views.* Focusing on the history of the Holocaust and concentrating on the topic of rescue, the work's focus on moral courage and rescue efforts presents ethical models for teachers to introduce in their classes. Beginning in summer 2001, residential institutes were offered for teachers in the United States and Europe. A complementary goal of this program is the development of a "Holocaust Centers of Excellence" program at sixteen selected Holocaust centers across the United States where the materials and approaches developed in the "Teaching the Holocaust" program will be utilized and evaluated. Interested educators should contact the Education Director for further information concerning summer residential institutes and other details about the "Teaching the Holocaust" program. Contact Information: Teaching the Holocaust: History, Perspectives and Choices, Jewish Foundation for the Righteous, 305 Seventh Avenue, 19th Floor, New York, NY 10001. Phone: 212-727-9955. FAX: 212-727-9956. http://www.jfr.org.

U.S. Holocaust Memorial Museum. Arthur and Rochelle Belfer Conference for Educators and Mandel Teacher Fellowship Program.

These two programs are held at the U.S. Holocaust Memorial Museum in Washington, DC. The Arthur and Rochelle Belfer Conference is geared to educators from middle and high school levels with less than five years of experience in teaching the Holocaust. Museum educators and scholars share rationales, strategies, and approaches for study of the Holocaust, and participants have extensive time to view the Museum's permanent exhibition and other special exhibitions. as well as the interactive learning programs in the Wexner Learning Center. The program is regularly held in July and applications are normally due in March. The Mandel Teacher Fellowship Program is geared to secondary school teachers of the humanities, librarians, and instructional media specialists with an extensive knowledge of Holocaust history, who have taught the Holocaust for at least five years in the United States and who have a demonstrated record of community and professional organization work. A five-day summer program is held at the U.S. Holocaust Memorial Museum with a follow-up program the following May. Each participant has the opportunity to learn from scholars and expert practitioners, explore the many resources of the Museum, and develop outreach programs for use in their home communities. Applications are available from the Museum's Web site at ushmm.org/education/mandel. Contact Information: U.S. Holocaust Memorial Museum, Division of Education, 100 Raoul Wallenberg Place SW, Washington, DC 20024-2136. Belfer Program—Phone: 202-488-6138. FAX: 202-314-7888. Mandel Program—Phone: 202-488-0456. FAX: 202-314-7888. http://ushmm.org.

Yad Vashem. International School for Holocaust Studies. Program run in conjunction with the Vidal Sassoon International Center for the Study of Anti-Semitism of the Hebrew University of Jerusalem.

Both summer and winter institutes are conducted at Yad Vashem in Jerusalem for Israeli educators and educators from around the world. The institutes last twenty-four days and address content ranging from historical anti-Semitism to the content of the Holocaust, artistic responses to the Holocaust, theological responses, the unique and universal aspects of the Holocaust, the legacy of the Holocaust for survivors and their children, pedagogic theory and practice, and related topics. The full resources of Yad Vashem, including the archives, pedagogical center, museum, and memorials, are used in the Institutes. Field trips to other sites in Israel, such as the Ghetto Fighters' House Museum and the Museum of the Diaspora are included, along with meetings with survivors. Participants cannot be undergraduates, but can be educators, community leaders, and/or clergy. Applications for the summer seminar in July should be submitted by the end of April, and for the winter seminar in January by the end of October. Contact Information: Yad Vashem International School for Holocaust Studies. For applicants in the United States and Canada: Contact Dr. Marlene Warshawski Yahalom, Ph.D., American Society for Yad Vashem, Educational Director, 500 Fifth Avenue, Suite 1600, New York, NY 10016-1699. Phone: 212-220-4304. FAX: 212-220-4308. e-mail: marleneyv@aol.com. For applicants outside of the United States and Canada: Contact Ephraim Kaye, Course Director, Seminars for Educators from Abroad, International School for Holocaust Studies, Yad Vashem, PO Box 3477, Jerusalem 91034, Israel. Phone: (972) 2-654-1334. FAX: (972) 2-643-3511. e-mail: ekaye@yadvashem.org.il. http://www.yadvashem.org.il.

DISTRIBUTORS AND VENDORS OF EDUCATIONAL AND TEACHING MATERIALS

Anti-Defamation League of B'Nai B'rith. International Center for Holocaust Studies, 823 United Nations Plaza, New York, NY 10017. Phone: 212-490-2525. http://www.adl.org.

Documentary Photo Aids. PO Box 956, Mount Dora, FL 32757.

Gedenkstatte Buchenwald. D-99427, Weimar-Buchenwald, Federal Republic of Germany. Phone: (49) 3643-430-0. FAX: (49) 3643-430-100. http://www.buchenwald.de.

Golden Owl Publications. PO Box 503, Amawalk, NY, 10501. Phone: 914-962-6911. Fax: 914-962-0344. http: www.jackdaw.com.

Imperial War Museum. Lambeth Road, London SE 1 6HZ, United Kingdom. Phone: (44) 020-741-65204 FAX: (44) 020-741-65285. e-mail: sbardgett@iwm.org.uk. http://www.iwm.org.uk.

Social Studies School Service. 10200 Jefferson Boulevard, Room 171, PO Box 802, Culver City, CA 90232-0802. Phone: 800-421-4246. http://socialstudies.com.

Muzeum Okregowe (Treblinka State Museum). W Siedlcach UL, Swierczewskiego 1, Siedlce, Poland.

U.S. Holocaust Memorial Museum Shop. 100 Raoul Wallenberg Place SW, Washington, DC 20024. Phone: 800-259-9998. http://www.holocaustbooks.org.

Watch Tower Bible and Tract Society of Pennsylvania. Public Affairs Office, 25 Columbia Heights, Brooklyn, NY 11201-2483. Phone: 718-560-5600.

Yad Vashem Martyrs' and Heroes' Remembrance Authority. PO Box 3477, Jerusalem 91034, Israel. Phone: (972) 2-644-3626. FAX: (972) 2-644-3623. e-mail: edu@yadvashem.org.il. http://www.yadvashem.org.il.

PART VI

INSTITUTIONS AND ORGANIZATIONS ABOUT THE HOLOCAUST

17

MUSEUMS, MEMORIALS, AND ORGANIZATIONS FOR STUDY AND REMEMBRANCE OF THE HOLOCAUST

OVERVIEW: MUSEUMS AND MEMORIALS

The continued expansion of museums and memorials about the Holocaust has characterized the post–World War II period, with many of the major Holocaust museums and memorials having been created during the period 1975–2000. In this chapter, a selection of important books about museums and memorials is presented, followed by a listing of major Holocaust museums and memorials organized by country. The address, phone, fax, and Web site address (where applicable) for each museum and memorial are provided, along with a brief description of their content focus and programs. The title of each museum or memorial is provided, and where needed, the English translation of the museum or memorial also is given. The selection process for the museums and memorials included in this chapter involved review of major directories of Holocaust institutions, and those chosen for inclusion met the criteria of (1) having the Holocaust as their major content focus and (2) including services and programs that educate the public about the Holocaust and its legacy.

MUSEUMS AND MEMORIALS: BOOKS

Milton, Sybil. *In Fitting Memory: The Art and Politics of Holocaust Memorials.* Photographs by Ira Nowinski. Detroit: Wayne University Press, 1991. ISBN 0–8143–2066–X. 341 pages. Hardcover.

This book is a comprehensive study of Holocaust memorials, examining both their artistic elements and the politics surrounding their creation. The book attempts to analyze the tangled relationships between historical sites, various representations of history, and the political and ideological forces that shape the response to memorials and monuments about the Holocaust. Research and photographic work was done in seven European countries (Austria, Federal Republic of Germany, the former German Democratic Republic, France, Italy, the Netherlands, and Poland) with other data drawn from the Soviet Union, Israel, Canada, the United States of America, South Africa, and Japan. The book contains many photographic plates of the memorial and monument sites discussed in the text, along with a selected list of Holocaust memorial sites, which contain brief descriptions of the sites as well as their locations. An annotated bibliography is provided as a spur to additional research and study. Indexed.

Young, James, editor. *The Art of Memory: Holocaust Memorials in History.* New York: Prestel-Verlag, 1994. ISBN 3–7913–1322–3. 194 pages. Hardcover.

Originating from an exhibit at the Jewish Museum in New York, this collection of essays includes contributions by art historians, artists, historians of the Holocaust, and survivors (including Primo Levi), all focused on the issue of Holocaust memorials. Divided into three sections ("The Artist as Monument Maker," "The Holocaust in National Memorial Traditions," and "Return to Memory"), the work juxtaposes the creators of memorials such as George Segal and Nathan Rappoport and architects such as James Ingo Freed (architect of the U.S. Holocaust Memorial Museum) with historians who analyze the meaning of memorials in national traditions, such as Claudia Koonz on Germany's Buchenwald and Saul Friedlander on the memory of the Shoah in Israel. Concluding the work is a list of Holocaust memorials and monuments, brief contributor biographies, and a selected bibliography, which is very useful for further study of this complex topic. No index.

———. *The Texture of Memory: Holocaust Memorials and Meaning.* New Haven: Yale University Press, 1993. ISBN 0–300–05991–4. 398 pages. Paperback.

Examining Holocaust memorials and monuments in Germany, Poland, Israel, and the United States of America, James Young discusses the often complex struggle to define the relationship between collective memory, national identity and self-interest. The introduction, entitled "The Texture of Memory," establishes the work's focus, which is concerned with how memorials and monuments, often created under the auspices of the state, function as representations of shared memory. This is a problematic issue, since the content and meaning of both memorials and monuments have the potential to perpetuate illusions of common memory, as well as historical myths. Young includes introductions to each section of the book where he provides an historical overview of the development of memorials and monuments about the Holocaust in that country. Integrated in the chapters devoted to specific memorials and monuments are many photographs that complement the textual analysis. Extensive chapter notes, a detailed bibliography, and an index conclude this important work, which argues convincingly for the study of Holocaust memorials and monuments as an important element of Holocaust scholarship.

MUSEUMS AND MEMORIALS: COUNTRY LISTINGS

Argentina

Fundacion Memoria Del Holocausto (Memory of Holocaust Foundation). Montevideo 919, Buenos Aires CP 1019, Argentina. Phone (54) 11-481-13588. FAX (54) 11-481-13537. e-mail: fumemhol@einstein.com.ar.

Provides educational seminars, organizes conferences, and will house a museum, currently under construction. Publications include both magazines and newsletters. (MUSEUM)

Australia

Jewish Holocaust Museum and Research Centre of Melbourne, Australia. 13 Selwyn Street, Elsternwick, Melbourne, VIC 3185 Australia. Phone (61) 3-952-81985. FAX (61) 3-952-83758. http://www.arts.monash.edu.au/affiliates/hlc.

Provides educational services both at the Museum and via outreach programs, seminars and courses for educators and the general public. The Museum houses a permanent photo exhibition, as well as an archives and library. Publications include a newsletter issued three times annually. (MUSEUM)

Sydney Jewish Museum. 146 Darlinghurst Road, Darlinghurst, NSW 2010 Australia. Phone (61) 2-936-07999. FAX (61) 2-933-14245. http://www.join.org.au/sydjmus/. e-mail: sydjmus@tmx.mhs.oz.au.

Permanent exhibit focuses on the Holocaust and history of the Australian Jewish community. Houses a resource center and contains a speakers bureau. Publishes a newsletter. (MUSEUM)

Austria

Judisches Museum der Stadt Wien (City of Vienna Jewish Museum). Dorotheergasse, 11 Wien, A-1010, Austria. Office address: Trattnerhof 2/ 106, Wien A-1010, Austria. Phone (43) 1-535-04-31. FAX (43) 1-535-04-24. http://www.jmw.at. e-mail: info@jmw.at.

Permanent exhibit houses an historical exhibition of Austrian-Jewish relations, as well as temporary exhibits on varied themes related to Jewish literature, visual arts, and architecture. Contains a library and archives, and holds events and conferences as well. (MUSEUM)

Mauthausen Memorial. Errinerungstrasse 1 A-4310 Mauthausen Austria. Phone (43) 7238-2269. FAX: (43) 7238-4889. http://www.mauthausen-memorial.gv.at/engl/einstieg.html. e-mail: mauthausen-memorial@mail. bmi.gv.at.

Located on the site of the Mauthausen Concentration Camp, this combined museum and memorial includes a permanent exhibition on the Mauthausen concentration camp and its satellite camps, as well as archives and a library. (MUSEUM and MEMORIAL)

Osterreichisches Judisches Museum in Eisenstadt (Austrian Jewish Museum of Eisenstadt). Unterbergstrasse 6, PO Box 67, Eisenstadt A-7000, Austria. Phone (43) 2-682-65-145. FAX (43) 2-682-65-14-54. http:// www.oejudmus.or.at. e-mail: info@oejudmus.or.at.

The permanent exhibit includes a tour through the Jewish year and festivals, with emphasis placed on religious-cultural objects and the history of the Jewish Quarter. Includes the private synagogue of Samson Wertheimer. Publications include books and epitaphs. (MUSEUM)

Belarus

Minsk Museum of the Great Patriotic War. 25A F. Skorina Avenue, Minsk 220600, Belarus.

Contains exhibits on the history of the Soviet Army during the period 1941–1945, as well as a library of over 12,000 volumes. Phone (375) 227-635. (MUSEUM)

Belgium

Joods Museum van Belgie (Jewish Museum of Belgium). 74 Stalingrad Avenue, Brussels B-1000, Belgium. Phone (32) 2-512-1963. FAX (32) 2-513-4859. http://www.mjbjmb.org. e-mail: info@mjb-jmb.org.

Contains archives regarding history of the Jews of Belgium and an extensive library. Publications include a quarterly newsletter and catalogues. (MUSEUM)

Joods Museum Van Deportatie en Verzet-Pro Museo Judaico (Jewish Museum of Deportation and Resistance). C.I.C.B.-Goswin de Stassartstraat 153, Mechelen B-2800, Belgium. Phone (32) 015-29-0660. FAX (32) 015-29-0876. http://www.cicb.be. e-mail: infos@cicb.be.

This government-supported museum contains exhibitions and its staff provides research consultations on the history of the Shoah in Belgium. The Museum also serves as a documentation center regarding the issues of deportation and resistance. Publications include museum guides published in four languages and topical folders. (MUSEUM)

Memorial National du Fort de Breendonk. Fort Breendonk, Willebroek B-2830, Belgium. Phone (32) 3-886-62-09. FAX (32) 3-866-53-91. http://www.breendonk.be. e-mail: info@breendonk.be.

Serving as a fortress (1914–1940), concentration camp (September 1940-August 1944), and national memorial and museum (1947–present), this memorial organization publishes folders in twelve languages and booklets in French, Dutch, and English. It has also recorded eyewitness testimonies and contains a film library for educators. (MEMORIAL and MUSEUM)

Canada

Holocaust Education and Memorial Centre of Toronto. 4600 Bathurst Street, Toronto, Ontario M2R 3V2, Canada. Phone 416-635-2883, ext. 153. FAX 416-635-0925. http://www.feduja.org. e-mail: jinfo@ujafed.org.

Containing a museum, resource center, and library, this center provides programs for commemorations, child survivors and second-generation families, teacher training, a speakers bureau, and special services to the Jewish Family and Child Service, along with others focused on Christian outreach. Publications include a newsletter and resource book. (MUSEUM)

The Montreal Holocaust Memorial Center. 1 Carre Cummings Square, Montreal, Quebec H3W 1M6, Canada. Phone 514-345-2605. FAX 514-344-2651. e-mail: natashal@fedcjamtl.org.

This museum, archives, and resource center includes a permanent exhibit on Jewish life prior to the Holocaust and the impact of the Shoah on Jewish culture, an extensive archive with over 90,000 items, an active oral history program, and outreach activities encompassing traveling exhibits, conferences, seminars, curriculum development projects, and a speakers bureau. Publications include a newsletter published three times annually. (MUSEUM)

Czech Republic

Jewish Museum in Prague. U Stare Skoly 1 110 00 Prague 1, Czech Republic. Phone (420) 2-248-194-56. FAX (420) 2-24-81-94-58. e-mail: office@jewishmuseum.cz.

This historic museum, established in 1906, has a permanent exhibition on Jewish life in Czechoslovakia. Publications include a newsletter. (MUSEUM)

Pamatnik Terezin (Museum of the Terezin Ghetto). Principova alej 304, Terezin CZ-411 55, Czech Republic. Phone (420) 416-782-225. FAX (420) 416-782-245. http://www.pamatnik-terezin.cz. e-mail: pamatnik@pamatnik-terezin.cz.

Located at the site of the former Terezin ghetto and camp, this memorial museum has a permanent exhibition, library, archives, and meeting center. Art exhibitions are frequently mounted as well as educational programs. Publications include the *Terezinske Listy* (year book) and an annual report. (MUSEUM and MEMORIAL)

Denmark

Frihedsmuseet (Danish Resistance Museum 1940–1945). Churchillparken, Copenhagen K DK-1263, Denmark. Phone (45) 33-137714. FAX (45) 33-140314. http://www.natmus.dk. e-mail: frihedsmuseet@natmus.dk.

The permanent exhibition addresses Danish resistance to Nazi occupation during World War II. (MUSEUM)

France

Fraternite Edmond Michelet. 4 rue Champanatier, Brive F-19100, France.

Functioning as a museum, archive, and research center, the emphasis is on research and study concerning resistance to the deportations of Jews during World War II. In addition to the permament exhibition, commemoration activities, seminars, and outreach services for schools are undertaken. Publications include proceedings of colloquia sponsored by the institution. (MUSEUM)

Musee de la Resistance et de la Deportation (Museum of the Resistance and Deportation). La Citadelle, Besancon F-25000, France. Phone (33) 03-81-87-83-12. FAX (33) 03-81-87-83-13. http://www.besancon.com. e-mail: elizabeth.pastwa@besancon.com.

This combined museum and archives/documentation center provides services to educators and researchers, including an extensive study center containing comprehensive multimedia resources. Publications include books about drawings, paintings, and sculptures. (MUSEUM)

Germany

Alte Synagoge Essen (The Old Synagogue Essen). Steeler Strasse 29, Essen D-45127, Germany. Phone (49) 201-884-5218. FAX (49) 201-884-5225. http://www.essen.de/kultur/synagoge/index.htm. e-mail: info@alte-synagoge.essen.de.

This combination memorial site and museum contains a permanent exhibition, archive, memorial book, and teacher training program. Publications are frequent and varied. (MEMORIAL and MUSEUM)

Begegnungsstatte Alte Synagoge Wuppertal (Old Synagogue Wuppertal Encounter Center). Genugsamkeitstrasse, Wuppertal D-42105, Germany. Phone (49) 020-256-32843. FAX (49) 20-256-32843. http://www.wuppertal.de.

Memorial site regarding Jewish life and culture in Wuppertal. (MEMORIAL)

Brandenburgische Landeszentrale fur Politische Bildung (Brandenburg State Council Office for Political Education). Heinrich-Mann-Allee 107/Haus 17, Potsdam D-14473, Germany. Phone (49)331-866-3540. http://www.brandenburg.de/netpol. e-mail: netpol.blzpb@mpjs.brandenburg.de.

Memorial site dealing with the local and regional history of Germany during the period 1933–1945. (MEMORIAL)

Deutsches Hygiene Museum Dresden. Lingnerplatz 1, Dresden D-01069, Germany. Phone (49) 351-484-60. FAX (49) 351-495-5162. http://www.dhmd.de. e-mail: service@dhmd.de.

This combination museum, convention center, and media center includes both permanent and temporary exhibits, and sponsors events as well as educational programs. Publications concern the role of science in the German hygiene museum. (MUSEUM)

Dokumentations-und Gedenkstatte Sandbostel E.V. (Sandbostel Documentation and Memorial Museum). c/o Dr. Klaus Volland. Frans-Hals-Strasse 1, Bremervorde D-27432, Germany. Phone (49) 0476-13267. FAX

(49) 0476-170-396. http://www.dokumentationsstaette-sandbostel.de. e-mail: info@dokumentationsstaette-sandbostel.de.

Combining a museum, archive, and resource center, this memorial/museum prepares exhibits, commemorative events, and lecture series. Publications are frequent and varied. (MEMORIAL and MUSEUM)

Dokumentations-und Informationszentrum (DIZ) Stadtallendorf (Stadtallendorf Documentation and Information Centre). Aufbauplatz 4, Stadtallendorf D-35260, Germany. Phone (49) 06428-70762. FAX (49) 06428-4111.

This memorial site addresses the local and regional history of Germany during the period 1933–1945. (MEMORIAL)

Dokumentations-und Informationszentrum (DIZ) Torgau (Torgau Documentation and Information Center). Rosa-Luxemburg-Platz 16, Torgau D-04860, Germany. Phone (49) 03421-713468. FAX (49) 03421-713468. http://www.stsg.de. e-mail: diz.info@diz-torgau.de.

This memorial site addresses the local and regional history of Germany during the period 1933-1945. (MEMORIAL)

Dokumentations-und Informationszentrum Emslandlager (DIZ) (The Emsland Camps Documentation and Information Center). Postfach 1132, Papenburg D-26851, Germany. Phone (49) 04961-916306. FAX (40) 04961-916308. http://www.diz-emslandlager.de. e-mail: mail@diz-emslandlager.de.

Encompassing not only a memorial site but also a museum and documentation center, the services provided include a permament exhibition, photo and document archive, oral history program, seminars, and other public programs, teacher training activities, and outreach programs. Publications include educational materials. (MUSEUM and MEMORIAL)

Dokumentationsstatte "Gelsenkirchen im Nationalsozialismus" (Documentation Center of Gelsenkirchen during the National Socialist Period). Hans-Sachs-Haus Ebertstrasse 15, Gelsenkirchen D-45891, Germany. Phone (49) 02091-69-2823. FAX (49) 02091-69-3518.

This memorial site addresses the local and regional history of Germany during the period 1933–1945. (MEMORIAL)

Dokumentationszentrum Oberer Kulberg Ulm E.V., KZ-Gedenkstatte (Documentation Center and Concentration Camp Memorial Kulberg Ulm).

Postfach 2066, Ulm D-89010, Germany. Phone (49) 0731-21312. FAX (49) 0731-21312. http://www.lpb.bwue.de/gedenk/gedenk21.htm.

Functioning as a memorial site and museum, the permanent exhibition addresses the Nazi period in the Ulm region. Other services include commemorative events, lectures, and the collection and preservation of documentation on the period 1933–1945. (MEMORIAL and MUSEUM)

Forderverein Dokumentationszentrum Stalag 326 (VI K) Senne E.V. Stalag 326 (Documentation Center Sponsor Association). Lippstadter Weg 26 Schloss, Holte-Stukenbrock D-33758, Germany. Phone (49) 05257-3033. FAX (49) 05257-3033.

This memorial site addresses the local and regional history of Germany during the period 1933–1945. (MEMORIAL)

Gedenk-und Dokumentationsstatte KZ Druette (Druette Concentration Camp Memorial and Documentation Center). Wehrstrasse 27 (Alte Feuerwache), Salzgitter D-38226, Germany. Phone (49) 05341-44581.

This memorial site and documentation center addresses the local and regional history of Germany during the period 1933–1945, with special attention to the history of the Druette concentration camp. (MEMORIAL)

Gedenkhalle Schloss Oberhausen (Oberhausen Castle Commemorative Hall). Konrad-Adenauer-Allee 46, Oberhausen D-46042, Germany. Phone (49) 0208-202-452. FAX (49) 0208-856-990.

This memorial site addresses the local and regional history of Germany during the period 1933–1945. (MEMORIAL)

Gedenkstatte Breitenau (Breitenau Memorial Museum). Bruckenstrasse 12, Guxhagen D-34302, Germany. Phone (49) 05665-3533. FAX (49) 05665-1727. http://www.guxhagen.net/gedenkstaette/index.html. e-mail: gedenkstaette-breitenau@t-online.de.

This memorial site and museum addresses the local and regional history of Germany during the period 1933–1945. (MEMORIAL and MUSEUM)

Gedenkstatte Unter den Eichen. (Memorial Site and Exhibition Under the Oak Trees). Carl-von-Ibell-Weg, Wiesbaden D-65195, Germany. Phone (49) 0611-314-291 and (49) 0611-313-219. FAX (49) 0611-313-977. http://www.dhm.de/ausstellungen/ns_gedenk/d_52.htm.

This memorial site and exhibition addresses the local and regional history of Germany in the Wiesbaden area during the period 1933–1945. (MEMORIAL)

Gedenkstatte Bergen-Belsen (Bergen-Belsen Memorial Museum). Lohheide D-29303, Germany. Phone (49) 05051-475910. FAX (49) 05051-4759-18. http://www.bergenbelsen.de. e-mail: Bergen-Belsen@t-online.de.

This memorial site and museum addresses the local and regional history of Germany during the period 1933–1945, concentrating on the history of the Bergen-Belsen concentration camp. (MEMORIAL and MUSEUM)

Gedenkstatte Buchenwald (Buchenwald Memorial Museum). Gedenkstatte Buchenwald Weimar, Buchenwald D-99427, Germany. Phone (49) 3643-430-0. FAX (49) 3643-430-100. http://www.buchenwald.de.

This memorial site and museum addresses the local and regional history of Germany during the period 1933–1945, concentrating on the history of the Buchenwald concentration camp. It also contains information and exhibits on the use of the Buchenwald camp site by the Soviet Union following the defeat of Germany in World War II. (MEMORIAL and MUSEUM)

Gedenkstatte "Ehemaliges SS-Sonderlager/KZ Hinzert" (Former SS Special Camp/Hinzert Camp Memorial). Landeszentrale fur politische Bildung An der Gedenkstatte, 55421 Hinzert-Polert, Germany. Phone (49) 06131-164660. FAX (49) 06131-162980.

This memorial site addresses the local and regional history of Germany during the period 1933–1945, with particular emphasis on activities of the SS at the Hinzer Camp. (MEMORIAL)

Gedenkstatte fur das KZ Husum-Schwesing Aussenkommando des KZ Neuengamme (Husum-Schwesing Concentration Camp Memorial). Schloss vor Husum, Husum D-25813, Germany. Phone (49) 04841-8973-0. FAX (49) 04841-8973-120. http://www.dhm.de/ausstellungen/ns_gedenk/d_25.htm.

This memorial site and exhibition addresses the local and regional history of Germany in the Husum area during the period 1933–1945, with specific attention given to the history of the Neuengamme Concentration Camp. (MEMORIAL)

Gedenkstatte fur Opfer der NS-"Euthanasie" Bernburg (Memorial Site of the "Euthanasia" Program Site at Bernburg). Olga-Benario-Strasse 16/18, Bernburg D-06406, Germany. Phone (49) 03471-319816. FAX (49) 03471-319816.

This memorial site addresses the history of the "euthanasia" program conducted at the Bernburg hospital/institution during the period 1939–1945. (MEMORIAL)

Gedenkstatte Hadamar (Hadamar Memorial). Monchberg 8, Hadamar D-65589, Germany. Phone (49) 06433-917-0. FAX (49) 06433-917-175.

This memorial site dealing with the use of the Hadamar medical facility as a killing center between 1939 and 1945 contains an exhibition and provides a range of services, including commemorative events, an archive and library, teacher training programs, and publications. (MEMORIAL and MUSEUM)

Gedenkstatte Kopenicker Blutwoche Juni 1933 (Kopenick Bloody Week Memorial Museum). Puchanstrasse 12, Berlin D-12555, Germany. Phone (49) 030-657-1467. FAX (49) 030-658-4409.

This memorial site, archive, and permanent exhibition addresses events of Nazi repression that occurred in Berlin-Kopenick between June 21 and 26, 1933. A publications program is underway. (MEMORIAL)

Gedenkstatte Konzentrationslager und Strafanstalten Fuhlsbuttel 1933–1945 (Fuhlsbuttel Memorial Museum). Suhrenkamp 98, Hamburg D-22335, Germany. Phone (49) 040-723-7403. FAX (49) 040-723-74525. http://www.hamburg.de/Neuengamme/fuhlsbuettel.html. e-mail: pressestellekb@kulturbehoerde.hamburg.de.

This memorial site and museum addresses the history of the Fuhlsbuttel camp during the period 1933–1945. Publications include a memorial book. (MEMORIAL and MUSEUM)

Gedenkstatte Langenstin-Zwieberge Landratsamt (Langenstein-Zwieberge Memorial Museum). Friedrich-Ebert-Strasse 42, Halberstadt D-38820, Germany. Phone (49) 039-413-0248. FAX (49) 039-413-0248.

This memorial site concerns the history of this former Buchenwald satellite camp. The site includes a memorial monument and exhibition buildings, as well as a publications program. (MEMORIAL)

Gedenkstatte Plotzensee (Plotzensee Memorial Museum). Huttigpfad Berlin, D-13627, Germany. Phone (49) 030-344-3226.

This memorial site addresses the local and regional history of Germany during the period 1933–1945. (MEMORIAL)

Gedenkstatte und Museum Sachsenhausen/Stiftung Brandenburgische Gedenkstatten (Sachsenhausen Memorial and Museum). Strasse der Nationen 22 Oranienburg D-16515, Germany. Phone (49) 033-01-200200. FAX (49) 033-01-200201.

This memorial site and museum addresses the local and regional history of Germany during the period 1933–1945, with specific attention to the Sachsenhausen concentration camp. (MEMORIAL and MUSEUM)

Gedenkstatte/Museum Seelower Hohen (Seelower Hohen Memorial Museum). Kustriner Strasse 28a, Seelow D-15306, Germany. Phone (49) 033-46597. FAX (49) 033-46598.

This memorial site addresses the local and regional history of Germany during the period 1933–1945. (MEMORIAL)

Haus der Wannsee-Konferenz (House of the Wannsee Conference Educational and Memorial Museum). Am Grossen Wannsee 56-58, Berlin 14109, Germany. Phone (49) 30-805-0010. FAX (49) 30-805-00127. http://www.ghwk.de. e-mail: info@ghwk.de.

This museum and historical site concerning the 1942 meeting where the planning for the "final solution" was detailed combines educational outreach activities with seminars and a publications program. (MUSEUM)

Initiative Gedenkstatte Eckerwald (Eckerwald [Schorzingen] Memorial Initiative). Schorzinger Strasse 61, Wellendingen D-78669, Germany. Phone (49) 0742-63373.

This memorial site and documentation center addresses the local and regional history of Germany during the period 1933–1945. (MEMORIAL)

Judisches Museum Westfalen (Westphalian Jewish Museum). Postfach 622, Julius Ambrunn-Strasse 1, Dorsten D-46282, Germany. Phone (49) 23-624-5279. FAX (49) 23-624-5386. http://www.pomoerium.com/museum. e-mail: jeudmuseum_westfalen@t-online.de.

This museum serves as a documentation and educational center for Jewish religion and history. (MUSEUM)

Jewish Museum Frankfurt am Main. Untermainkai 14/15, Frankfurt D-60311, Germany. Phone (49) 069-212-35000. FAX (49) 069-212-30705. http://www.juedischesmuseum.de. e-mail: info@juedischmuseum.de.

This museum and archive encompasses the history of the Jewish community in Frankfurt before, during, and after the Holocaust. The museum contains an archive and conducts annual Kristallnacht commemorations. A publications program includes a museum periodical and exhibition catalogues. (MUSEUM)

Judisches Museum Berlin (Jewish Museum of Berlin). Lindenstrasse 9-14, Berlin D-10969, Germany. Phone (49) 30-308785-681. FAX (49) 30-25993-409. http://www.jmberlin.de. e-mail: info@jmberlin.de.

This museum, which opened in September 2001, presents the history of Germany's Jewish community from its origins through the Middle Ages and up to the present day. Section 13 of the permanent exhibition is entitled "Persecution-Resistance-Extermination" and it presents how the German Jewish community was targeted by the Nazi regime for annihilation, as well as the German Jewish community's response to Nazi persecution. A multifaceted program of education, public programs and changing exhibitions is planned, in addition to the permanent exhibition and development of the Museum's archives and collections.

Kreismuseum Wewelsburg (Cult and Terror Site of the SS). Burgwall 19, Buren-Wewelsburg D-33142, Germany. Phone (49) 02955-7622-0. FAX (49) 02955-7622-22. http://www.ns-gedenkstaetten.de/nrw/de/wewelsburg/besucherinfo. e-mail: Kreismuseum.Wewelsburg@t-online.de.

This memorial site includes a documentary exhibition, as well as an archive with extensive holdings (including videotapes). Publications. (MEMORIAL)

KZ-Gedenkstatte Mittelbau-Dora (Mittelbau Dora Concentration Camp Memorial). Kohnsteinweg 20, Nordhausen D-99734, Germany. Phone (49) 03631-4958-0. FAX (49) 03631-4958-13. http://www.dora.de. e-mail: Gedenkstaette.Mittelbau-Dora@t-online.de.

This memorial site contains an archives, films, and a recently opened exhibition (1995). Publications are frequent and varied. (MEMORIAL)

KZ-Gedenkstatte Moringen (Moringen Concentration Camp Memorial Museum). KZ-Gedenkstatte im Torhaus Moringen, Postfach 1131, D-37182, Moringen Germany. Phone (49) 05554-2520. FAX (49) 05554-8807. http://www.gedenkstaette-moringen.de. e-mail: info@gedenkstaette-moringen.de.

This memorial site also contains a museum, archive, and resource center. The publications program includes a catalogue. (MEMORIAL and MUSEUM)

KZ-Gedenkstatte Neuengamme (Neuengamme Concentration Camp Memorial Museum). Jean-Dolidier-Weg 39, Hamburg D-21039, Germany. Phone (49) 40-428-9603. FAX (49) 40-428-96525. http://www.hamburg.de/Neuengamme/. e-mail: mgh@kulturbehoerde.hamburg.de.

This combined memorial and museum includes an archives and memorial center along with a varied publications program. (MEMORIAL and MUSEUM)

KZ-Gedenkstatte Beendorf (Beendord Concentration Camp Memorial). Gemeinde Beendorf Schulplatz 5, Beendorf D-39343, Germany. Phone (40) 039-050-239.

This memorial site and documentation center addresses the local and regional history of Germany during the period 1933–1945, with special attention to the history of the Beendorf Concentration Camp. (MEMORIAL)

KZ-Gedenkstatte Dachau (Dachau Concentration Camp Memorial Museum). Alte Roemerstrasse 75, Dachau D-85221, Germany. Phone (49) 08131-1741. FAX (49) 08131-2235. http://www.infospace.de/gedenkstaette/index.html. e-mail: gedenkstaette.dachau@extern.lrz.muenchen.de.

The memorial site and museum of the Dachau Concentration Camp includes an archive, library, international youth meeting center, and publications program. (MEMORIAL and MUSEUM)

KZ-Gedenkstatte Ladelund (Ladelund Concentration Camp Memorial Museum). Ladelund D-25926, Germany. Phone (49) 04666-449. FAX (49) 04666-989537. http://www.kz-gedenkstaette-ladelund.de/index.html. e-mail: kz-gedenkstaette-ladelund@t-online.de.

This memorial site contains a permament exhibition on the history of the Ladelund concentration camp. (MEMORIAL)

KZ-Gedenkstatte Sandhofen/Aussenkommando KZ Natzweiler-Struthof (Sandhofen Concentration Camp Memorial Museum). Kriegerstrasse 28, Mannheim D-68307, Germany. Phone (49) 0621-338-560. FAX (49) 0621-338-5616.

This memorial site and documentation center addresses the local and regional history of Germany during the period 1933–1945, with emphasis given to the history of the Sandhofen Concentration Camp. (MEMORIAL)

KZ-Grab-und Gedenkstatte Flossenburg (Flossenburg Concentration Camp Memorial and Museum). Gedachtnisallee 7, Flossenburg D-92696, Germany. Phone (49) 09603-921980. FAX (49) 09603-921990. http://www.flossenbuerg.de. e-mail: information@gedenkstaette-flossenbuerg.de.

This memorial site combines a permanent exhibition with an archive, educational activities, and an extensive publications program. (MEMORIAL and MUSEUM)

Mahn-und Gedenkstatte Ahlem (Ahlem Memorial Museum). Postfach 147, Hannover D-30001, Germany. Phone (49) 0511-989-2256. FAX (49) 0511-989-2499.

This memorial site and museum addresses the local and regional history of Germany during the period 1933–1945. (MEMORIAL and MUSEUM)

Mahn-und Gedeknstatte Gardelegen (Gardelegen Memorial Site). Rathausplatz 10, Gardelegen D-39638, Germany. Phone (49) 03907-6519. FAX (49) 03907-6586.

This memorial site addresses the local and regional history of Germany during the period 1933–1945. (MEMORIAL)

Mahn-und Gedenkstatte Lieberose (Lieberose Memorial Museum). Bahnhofstrasse 4, Lieberose D-15868, Germany. Phone (49) 0336-712511. http://www.dhm.de/ausstellungen/ns_gedenk/d_17.htm.

This memorial site includes an exhibition and a small library, as well as audiovisual presentations (slides and videos). This memorial site addresses the local and regional history of Germany during the period 1933–1945. (MEMORIAL)

Mahn-und Gedenkstatte Wernigerode (Wernigerode Memorial Museum). Veckenstedter Weg 43, Wernigerode D-38855, Germany. Phone (49) 03943-632109. FAX (49) 03943-632109.

This memorial site addresses the local and regional history of Germany during the period 1933–1945. (MEMORIAL)

Mahn-und Gedenkstatte zum KZ-Lichtenburg (Lichtenburg Concentration Camp Memorial). Schloss Lichtenburg, Prettin D-06922, Germany. Phone (49) 0353-862-2382. FAX (49) 0353-862-2134.

This memorial site addresses the local and regional history of Germany during the period 1933–1945, with special attention to the history of the Lichtenburg Concentration Camp. (MEMORIAL)

Mahn-und Gedenkstatte Dusseldorf (Dusseldorf Memorial Museum). Muhlenstrasse 29, Dusseldorf D-40200, Germany. Phone (49) 0211-899-6663. FAX (49) 0211-892-9137. http://www.rp-online.de/dusseldorf/mahn-und-gedenkstaette.

This memorial site and museum addresses the local and regional history of Dusseldorf during the period 1933–1945, and contains a memorial site and museum with exhibitions and an extensive publications program. (MEMORIAL and MUSEUM)

Mahn-und Gedenkstatte Ehrenhain Zeithain (Zeithain Memorial Grove). An der Gorlitzer Strasse, Zeithain D-01619, Germany. Phone (49) 03525-760392. FAX (49) 03525-760392. http://www.stsg.de/main/index.htm.

This memorial site and museum addresses the local and regional history of Germany during the period 1933–1945. (MEMORIAL)

Mahn-und Gedenkstatte Munchener Platz Dresden (Munchener Platz National Memorial Site). Georg-Bahr-Strasse 7, Dresden D-01069, Germany. Phone (49) 0351-463-6466. FAX (49) 0351-463-6466. http://stsg.de/main.index.htm.

This memorial site addresses the local and regional history of Germany during the period 1933-1945. (MEMORIAL)

Mahn-und Gedenkstatte Ravensbruck Stiftung Brandenburgische Gedenkstatten (Ravensbruck Concentration Camp Memorial Museum). Strasse der Nationen, Furstenberg D-16798, Germany. Phone (49) 0330-9339241. FAX (49) 0330-933-8397. http://www.ravensbrueck.de.

This memorial site and museum addresses the local and regional history of Germany during the period 1933–1945, emphasizing the history of the Ravensbruck Concentration Camp. (MEMORIAL and MUSEUM)

Mahn-und Gedenkstatte Steinwache Dortmund (Steinwache Memorial Museum Dortmund). Steinstrasse 50, Dortmund D-44147, Germany. Phone (49) 0231-502-5002 and (49) 0231-50-2215. FAX (49) 231-502-6011.

This memorial site and museum houses a permanent exhibition and has a publication program. (MEMORIAL and MUSEUM)

Deutsch-Russisches Museum Berlin (German-Russian Museum of Berlin). Zwiesler Strasse 4, Karlshorst 10318 S3, Karlhorst, Berlin, Germany. Phone (49) 05501-50810. http://www.dhm.de/ausstellungen/ns_gedenk/d_9.htm.

This memorial site of the German surrender on May 8, 1945 contains exhibitions and teacher training programs on German-Soviet relations and Nazi extermination policies in the former Soviet Union. A publications program and series of war veterans meetings also are underway. (MEMORIAL)

Museum "Cap Arcona"/Stadtverwaltung Neustadt i. H. Am Markt 1, Neustadt in Holstein D-23730, Germany. Phone (49) 0456-16190. FAX (49) 0456-161-9328.

This memorial site, archive, and museum includes exhibitions and publications among its services, as well as an annual commemoration on May 3. (MEMORIAL and MUSEUM)

Museum Mahn-und Gedenkstatte Wobbelin. (Wobbelin Museum and Memorial Center). Ludwigsluster Strasse, Wobbelin D-19288, Germany. http://www.m-vp.de/English/3667.htm.

This memorial site, museum, and archive concerns the local and regional history of Germany during the period 1933–1945. (MEMORIAL and MUSEUM)

NS-Dokumentationszentrum und Gedenkstatte Gestapogefangnis im EL-DE-Haus (NS Documentation Center and Memorial Museum Gestapo Prison). Appellhofplatz 23-35, Koln D-50667, Germany. Phone (49) 0221-221-6331. FAX (49) 0221-221-5512.

This memorial site addresses the local and regional history of Germany during the period 1933–1945, with emphasis on the history of the Gestapo as represented in this prison. (MEMORIAL)

NS-Dokumentationszentrum Rheinland-Pfalz/Gedenkstatte KZ Osthofen (Rhineland-Pfalz National Socialist Documentation Center/Osthofen Concentration Camp). Ziegelhuettenweg 38, Osthofen D-67574, Germany. Phone (49) 0631-162-660 or (49) 0631-164-561. FAX (49) 0631-162-980. http://www.projektosthofen-gedenkstaette.de.

This memorial site and documentation center addresses the local and regional history of Germany during the period 1933–1945, with emphasis on the history of the Osthofen Concentration Camp. (MEMORIAL)

Stiftung Neue Synagoge Centrum Judaicum (New Jewish Synagogue and Cultural Center). Oranienburgerstrasse 28-30, Berlin 10117, Germany. Phone (49) 30-280-1250. FAX (49) 30-282-1176. http://www.snafu.de/~cjudaicum. e-mail: cjudaicum@snafu.de.

This memorial and study center promotes Jewish culture in Berlin. (MEMORIAL)

Greece

Jewish Museum of Greece. 39 Nikis Street, Athens 105 58, Greece. Phone (30) 1-322-5582. FAX (30) 1-323-1577. http://www.jewishmuseum.gr. e-mail: jmg@otenet.gr.

This museum has both historical and ethnographical exhibits, and includes a program of lectures, permanent and temporary exhibits, concerts, workshops, and a varied publications program with newsletters, informational books, and pamphlets. (MUSEUM)

Museum of the Jewish Presence in Thessaloniki. Ag. Mina 13, Thessaloniki, Greece. Phone (30) 275-701.

This museum traces the history of the largest Jewish community in Greece prior to World War II, and contains a special exhibit on the Holocaust and its effects on the city's Jewish community.

The Simon Marks Museum of Jewish History in Thessaloniki. 26 Vasileos Irakliou Street, 1st Floor, Thessaloniki 546 24, Greece. Phone (30) 31-273-767. FAX (30) 31-229-063. http://www.energy.gr/jct. e-mail: jct1@compulink.gr.

Museum on the history of Jewish culture in Thessaloniki. (MUSEUM)

Hungary

Hungarian Jewish Museum and Archives. Dohany u.2, Budapest H-1077, Hungary. Phone (36) 1-342-8949. http://www.c3.hu/~bpjewmus/. e-mail: bpjewmus@mail.c3.hu.

This museum and archives includes a library, exhibitions, research and information center, and active publications program that encompasses catalogues and research papers. (MUSEUM)

Israel

Beit Lohamei Haghetaot—The Ghetto Fighters' House. Kibbutz Lohamei-Haghetaot D.N., Western Galilee 25220, Israel. Phone (972) 4-995-8080. FAX (972) 4-995-8007. http://www.gfh.org.il. e-mail: Simstein@gfh.org.il.

A combined museum, archive, library, study center, and children's memorial (Yad Layeled), The Ghetto Fighters' House was the first major museum in Israel dedicated to study of the Holocaust. An extensive series of educational programs and seminars is provided, along with an extensive publications program that includes curriculum materials (print and multimedia). (MEMORIAL and MUSEUM)

Beit Theresienstadt. Kibbutz Givat Hayim-Ihud, Mobile Post Emek Hefer, Givat Hatim-Ihud 38395, Israel. Phone (972) 6-636-9515 and (972) 6-636-9793. FAX (972) 6-636-9611. http://www.bterezin.org.il. e-mail: bterezin@inter.net.il.

Combining a museum, study center, archive, library, and art collection, Beit Theresienstadt's focus is on the history and legacy of the Terezin ghetto and camp in the Czech Republic. Educational programs for students and teachers, documentation activities about the prisoners interned at Terezin, and an extensive publications program including a periodic newsletter, books, and educational materials are provided. (MUSEUM)

International Memorial Holocaust Fund "Drobitzky Yar." PO Box 7055, Bat-Yan 59170, Israel. Phone (972) 3-6570364. FAX (972) 3-5558666. http://www.drob.ya.int.org. e-mail: lyakh@drobya.int.org.

This resource and documentation center also contains an archive, museum, and publishing house. It sponsors annual research conferences, lecture series, traveling exhibits, and educational programs and has a broad-based publications program including a monthly newsletter and books on the genocide of Jews in the Ukraine. (MEMORIAL and MUSEUM)

Moreshet-Mordechai Anielevich Memorial. Youth Movement Campus, Moreshet Instruction Center, Givat Haviva Mobil Post, Menashe 37850, Israel. Phone (972) 06-630-9275. FAX (972) 06-630-9305. http://www.inter.net.il/~givat/moreshet/moreshet.htm. e-mail: meir_yk@inter.net.il.

This combined memorial, library, and study center has educational programs and workshops and publishes a biannual journal. (MEMORIAL)

Yad Vashem—The Holocaust Martyrs' and Heroes' Remembrance Authority. PO Box 3477, Jerusalem 91034, Israel. Phone (972) 2-644-3400. FAX (972) 2-643-3511. http://www.yadvashem.org.il.

Israel's national museum and remembrance authority dealing with the Holocaust, Yad Vashem contains a broad range of departments and services: art and historical museums, memorials and monuments, a research institute and archives, and numerous educational activities, including seminars, conferences, development of pedagogical materials, and teacher training programs. The extensive publications program includes the scholarly journal *Yad Vashem Studies*, books, monographs, diaries, bibliographies, and other journals for educators and the general public. (MUSEUM and MEMORIAL)

Latvia

Latvijas Okupacijas Muzejs (Museum of the Occupation of Latvia, 1940-1941). Strelnieku laukums 1, Riga LV-1050, Latvia. Phone (371) 721-2715. FAX (371) 722-9255. http://www.occupationmuseum.lv. e-mail: omf@latnet.lv.

This museum provides exhibits, teacher seminars, public lectures, and a publications program that includes a newsletter, scholarly journals, and materials for school children. (MUSEUM)

Muzejs un Dokomentacijas Centrs "Ebreji Latvija" (Museum and Documentation Center "Jews in Latvia"). 6 Skolas Street, Riga LV-1322, Latvia. Phone (371) 728-3484. FAX (371) 728-3484.

Run by the organization of the Riga Jewish Community, this museum contains an exhibition and publications program that includes an exhibition guide and research works about the Holocaust in Latvia. (MUSEUM)

Lithuania

Atminties Namai (House of Memory). Klaipedos 6-406, LT-2600 Vilnius, Lithuania. Phone (370) 2-227-183. FAX (370) 2-227-173. e-mail: jmorkus@takas.lt.

This museum develops educational and research programs and commemorations on the Holocaust and Jewish heritage in Lithuania. (MUSEUM)

Kauno IX Forto Muziejus (Kaunas IX Fort Museum). Fiemaiei Pl. 73, LT-3032 Kaunas, Lithuania. Phone (370) 8-27-377-715. FAX (370) 8-27-377-715. http://muziejai.mch.mii.lt/Kaunas/forto_muziejus.htm. e-mail: jmenciun@takas.lt.

This museum contains an exhibition dealing with the Holocaust in Lithuania, with emphasis on what transpired in Kaunas (Kovno) during World War II. Meetings, exhibitions, and publications are part of the museum's annual activities. (MUSEUM)

Vilna Gaon Jewish State Museum of Lithuania. Pamenkalnio 12, LT-2001, Vilnius, Lithuania. Phone (370) 2-620-730. FAX (370) 2-227-083. http://www.litvakai.mch.mii.lt. e-mail: jmuseum@pub.osf.lt.

This museum of Jewish history and culture includes an exhibition on the Holocaust as well as a memorial. Conferences, tours of the former Vilna Ghetto and Jewish Vilnius, research activities, and publications (books and articles, as well as a newsletter) are core programs of the Museum. (MEMORIAL and MUSEUM)

Luxembourg

Musee National De la Resistance (National Museum of Resistance). Place de la Resistance, ancienne Place du Brill, Esch-sur-Alzette L-4002, Luxembourg. Phone (352) 548-472. FAX (352) 542-927.

This museum contains exhibitions about resistance to the Nazi invasion of Luxembourg during World War II. A publications catalogue and media collection are among the Museum's services. (MUSEUM)

Mexico

Museo Historico Judio y del Holocausto "Tuvie Maizel" (Historical Jewish and Holocaust Musem). Acapulco #70—Piso Primero (1st Floor),

Colonia Condesa, Acapulco 06110, Mexico. Phone (52) 11-6908. FAX (52) 11-2839. e-mail: ashkenaz@mail.internet.com.mx.

This museum contains exhibits and a library, organizes conferences, and offers educational services for schools and the general public. (MUSEUM)

The Netherlands

Anne Frank House. Prinsengracht 263, Amsterdam, The Netherlands. Phone (31) 20-556-7100. FAX (31) 20-620-7999. http://www.annefrank.nl. e-mail: info@annefrank.nl.

Combining an historic site and museum, the services of the Anne Frank House include tours and related outreach activities. (MUSEUM)

Herinneringscentrum Kamp Westerbork (Westerbork Camp Memorial). Oosthalen 8, Hooghalen 9414 TG, The Netherlands. Phone (31) 59-359-2600. FAX (31) 59-359-2546. http://www.westerbork.nl. e-mail: hckampw@bart.nl.

Functioning as an historical site, monument, and museum, the Westerbork Camp Museum's activities encompass educational programs, tours, and related projects about the history of the Westerbork Camp during the Nazi occupation of the Netherlands during World War II. (MEMORIAL and MUSEUM)

Joods-Histrorisch Museum (Jewish Historical Museum). Jonas Daniel Meijerplein 2-4, Amsterdam 1001 RH, The Netherlands. Phone (31) 20-626-9945. FAX (31) 20-624-1721. http://www.jhm.nl. e-mail: info@jhm.nl.

This historical museum chronicles the history of Judaism in the Netherlands, utilizing both a permanent exhibition and temporary exhibitions. Mailing address: PO Box 16737, 1001 RE, Amsterdam, The Netherlands. (MUSEUM)

National Monument Kamp Vught (Vught Concentration Camp). PO Box 47, Vught 5260 AA, The Netherlands. Phone (31) 73-656-6764. FAX (31) 73-656-0835. http://www.nmkampvught.nl. e-mail: info@kampvught.nl.

Functioning as an historical site, museum, and monument, services provided include both tours of the former Vught Concentration Camp site and educational programs. (MEMORIAL and MUSEUM)

National Oorlogs—en Verzetmuseum Overloon (Overloon National War and Resistance Museum). Museumpark 1, Overloon 5825 AM, The Netherlands. Phone (31) 47-864-1820. FAX (31) 47-864-2405. http://www.oorlogsmuseum.nl. e-mail: overloon@oorlogsmuseum.nl.

This combined museum and historical site regarding the history of World War II and Dutch resistance to the Nazi occupation includes tours and educational programs among its services. (MUSEUM)

Verzetsmuseum Amsterdam (Museum of the Dutch Resistance). Plantage Kerklaan 61, Amsterdam 1018 CK, The Netherlands. Phone (31) 20-620-2535. FAX (31) 20-620-2960. http://www.verzetsmuseum.nl. e-mail: info@verzetsmuseum.org.

This museum of the Dutch resistance to Nazi occupation during World War II includes a permanent exhibition, tours, and educational programs among its services. (MUSEUM)

Verzetsmuseum Friesland (Friesland Resistance Museum). Turfmarkt 11, Leeuwarden 8911 KS, The Netherlands. Phone (31) 58-212-3001. FAX (31) 58-213-2271. http://www.verzetsmuseum.nl. e-mail: info@verzetzmuseum. nl.

Tours and educational programs are the core services of this museum devoted to detailing the resistance to the Nazi occupation in Friesland during World War II. (MUSEUM)

Norway

Norges Hjemmefrontmuseum (Norway's Resistance Museum). Oslo mil/ Akerhus, Oslo N-0015, Norway. Phone (47) 23-093280. FAX (47) 23-093137. http://www.nhm.mil.no. e-mail: norges.hjemmefront@c2i.net.

This museum presents the history of the persecution of Norwegian Jews during World War II, and includes a publication program among its services. (MUSEUM)

Poland

Muzeum Gross-Rosen (State Museum of KL Gross-Rosen). Skrytka Pocztowa 217, Walbrzych 58-300, Poland. Phone (48) 74-855-9007 and (48) 74-846-4566. FAX (48) 74-842-1580. http://www.region-walbrzych.org/pl/grosrosen. e-mail: pmgr@wb.onet.pl.

Including a permanent exhibition, collection of archival materials and educational activities among its services, this State Museum presents the history of the Gross-Rosen Concentration Camp. (MUSEUM)

Panstwowe Muzeum Auschwitz-Birkenau (State Museum of the KL Auschwitz-Birkenau). ul. Wiezniow Oswiecimia 20, Oswiecim 32-603, Poland. Phone (48) 33-843-2022. FAX (48) 33-843-1934. http://www.auschwitz.org.pl. e-mail: muzeum@auschwitz-muzeum.oswiecim.pl.

This State Museum located at the site of the former Auschwitz camp complex includes tours, seminars, and lectures among its activities, in addition to a permanent exhibition and archives on the history of the Auschwitz camps. The museum also has an extensive publications program including books, posters, cassettes, and other print materials. (MUSEUM)

Panstwowe Muzeum na Majdanek (State Museum at Majdanek). ul. Dr. Méczennikow Majdanka 67, Lublin 20-325, Poland. Phone (48) 81-744-2640. FAX (48) 81-744-0526. http://www.majdanek.pl. e-mail: dyr@majdanek.pl.

The State Museum at Majdanek includes a permament exhibition, tours of the camp site, teacher training, and historical workshops for students and teachers, conferences and seminars, and an extensive publications program. (MUSEUM)

Panstwowe Muzeum Stutthof w Sztutowie (State Museum Stutthof in Sztutowo). Ul. Muzealna 6, Sztutowo 82-110, Poland. Phone (48) 55-247-8353. FAX (48) 55-247-8358. http://www.kki.net.pl/museum/. e-mail: museum@kki.net.pl.

The State Museum of the Stutthof Concentration Camp contains an archives, lecture series, tours of the former camp site, temporary exhibitions, and a publications program. (MUSEUM)

Russia

Museum of Jewish Heritage and Holocaust in the Memorial Synagogue on the Poklonnaya Gora. Poklonnaya Gora, 3, Moscow, Russia. Phone (7) 95-148-1907 and (7) 95-148-0887. FAX (7) 95-148-1907. e-mail: klim@sovintel.ru.

This museum is a branch of the Russian Jewish Congress and includes both permanent and temporary exhibitions, lecture and seminar series, an archive, library, and publications program among its services. (MUSEUM)

Slovak Republic

Muzeum Slovenskeho Narodneho Povstania (Museum of the Slovak National Uprising). Kapitulska 23, Banska Bystrica 975 99, Slovak Republic. Phone (421) 88-412-3258. FAX (421) 88-412-3716. http://www.muzeumsnp.sk. e-mail: MuzeumSNP@isternet.sk.

Part of the Slovak Ministry of Culture, this museum includes exhibitions and tours as well as an extensive publications program. (MUSEUM)

Muzeum Zidovskej Kultury (Museum of Jewish Culture). 17 Zidovska ul. Str. Bratislava 811 01, Slovak Republic. Phone (421) 7-322-985-9. FAX

(421) 7-593-49145. http://nic.savba.sk/blava/muzea-e7html. e-mail: mestan@snm.sk.

In addition to an extensive publications program, this museum includes permanent and temporary exhibitions and lectures among its services. (MUSEUM)

Sweden

Judiska Museet i Stockholm (Jewish Museum in Stockholm). Halsingegatan 2, Box 6299, Stockholm 102 34, Sweden. Phone (46) 8-310-143. FAX (46) 8-318-404. http://www.judiska-museet.a.se. e-mail: info@judiska-museet.a.se.

In addition to exhibitions on the history of Judaism in Sweden, this museum has an extensive publications program. (MUSEUM)

Switzerland

Judisches Museum der Schweiz (Jewish Museum of Switzerland). Kornhausgasse 8, CH-4051 Basel, Switzerland. Phone (41) 61-261-9514. http://www.igb.ch. e-mail: igb@igb.ch.

This museum contains exhibitions on the history of Judaism in Switzerland, as well as a publications program. (MUSEUM)

Ukraine

Ukrainian State Museum of the Great Patriotic War. 44 Yanvarskogo Vosstaniya Street, Kyiv 252015, Ukraine. Phone (380) 44-295-9457. FAX (380) 44-295-9444.

This museum about the history of World War II in the Ukraine contains collections for use by researchers as well as a publications program. (MUSEUM)

United Kingdom

Beth Shalom Holocaust Memorial and Education Centre. Laxton Newark, Notts NG22 OPA, United Kingdom. Phone (44) 0162-383-6627. FAX (44) 0162-383-6647. http://www.bethshalom.com. e-mail: office@bethshalom.com.

Functioning as a museum, educational center, and memorial, Beth Shalom has an extensive roster of educational activities including print and multimedia publications, seminars, a library, and a permanent exhibition dealing with the Holocaust. (MEMORIAL and MUSEUM)

Imperial War Museum. Lambeth Road, London SE1 6HZ, United Kingdom. Phone (44) 020-741-65204 and (44) 020-741-65285. FAX (44) 020-741-65278. http://www.iwm.org.uk. e-mail: mail@iwm.org.uk.

Serving as Britain's national museum of twentieth-century conflict, this museum opened a major permanent exhibition in 2000 dealing with the Holocaust. Educational programs related to the new exhibition on the Holocaust are available, as well as publications (print and multimedia) for the general public and educators. (MUSEUM)

The Jewish Museum, London. The Sternberg Centre, 80 East End Road, London NC 2SY, United Kingdom. Phone (44) 020-8349-1143. FAX (44) 020-8343-2162. http://www.jewmusm.ort.org. e-mail: jml.finchley@lineone.net.

This museum includes a permanent exhibition as well as a gallery devoted to Holocaust education. An educational program, traveling exhibitions, archive, and reference library provide additional services. An extensive publication program includes materials specifically designed for teachers and students on Holocaust topics such as the kindertransport and others. (MUSEUM)

Manchester Jewish Museum. 190 Cheetham Hill Road, Manchester M8 8LW, United Kingdom. Phone (44) 0161-834-8979. FAX (44) 0161-834-9801. http://www.manchesterjewishmuseum.com. e-mail: info@manchesterjewishmuseum.com.

This museum details the social history of Jews in Britain and includes programs for teachers and students as well as research services. (MUSEUM)

United States

Desert Holocaust Memorial. PO Box 2865, Rancho Mirage, CA 92270, USA. Phone: 760-325-7281. http://palmsprings.com/points/holocaust.

Public memorial incorporating bronze figures, bas-reliefs, and a granite base that details the persecution of Jews by Nazi Germany, efforts at resistance to oppression, and the scope of the Holocaust in Europe. (MEMORIAL)

Florida Holocaust Museum. 55 Fifth Street South, St. Petersburg, FL 33701, USA. Phone 727-820-0100. FAX 727-821-8435. http://www.flholocaustmuseum.org. e-mail: smgoldman@flholocaustmuseum.org.

Among the services provided by the Florida Holocaust Museum are permanent and traveling exhibitions, an extensive library with print and multimedia resources, an archive, teacher-training programs, outreach programs for educators, commemorations, author/lecture series, and publications that include a quarterly newsletter. (MUSEUM)

Holocaust Memorial and Educational Center of Nassau County. Welwyn Preserve, 100 Crescent Beach Road, Glen Cove, NY 11542, USA. Phone 516-571-8040. FAX 516-571-8044. http://www.holocaust-nassau.org.

This memorial and educational center includes exhibits, a speakers' bureau, commemorative programs, curriculum development and educational programs, and a lecture series. The publications program includes pamphlets and a videography. (MEMORIAL)

Holocaust Memorial Center. 6602 West Maple Road, West Bloomfield, MI 48322-3005, USA. Phone 248-661-0840. FAX 248-661-4204. http://www.holocaustcenter.org. e-mail: info@holocaustcenter.org.

The extensive services of this Memorial Center include a museum, library-archive, research institute, lecture series, tours, teacher-training programs, commemorative programs, educational outreach activities, and a multifaceted publications program encompassing a newsletter and both print and multimedia works. (MEMORIAL and MUSEUM)

Holocaust Memorial of Miami Beach, Florida. 1933-1945 Meridian Avenue, Miami Beach, FL 33139, USA. Phone 305-538-1663. FAX 305-538-2423. http://www.holocaustmmb.com. e-mail: info@holocaustmmb.org.

As an educational and cultural center, the Memorial's services include commemorations, tours, a lecture series and educational programs, as well as publications. (MEMORIAL)

Holocaust Memorial of San Antonio. 12500 N.W. Military Highway, Suite 200, San Antonio, Texas 78231, USA. Phone 210-302-6807. FAX 210-408-2332. http://www.jfsatx.org/jewish_federation_of_san_antonio.htm. e-mail: cohenm@jfsatx.org.

The Memorial's services include educational outreach to teachers and students, a public library collection, coordination of annual Yom Hashoah activities, and a publications program. (MEMORIAL)

Holocaust Museum Houston. 5401 Caroline Street, Houston, TX 77004-6804, USA. Phone 713-942-8000. FAX 713-942-7953. http://www.hmh.org. e-mail: sllanes@hmh.org.

This combined museum, educational center, and memorial includes a library, teacher resource center, speakers' bureau, teacher training programs, curriculum trunks loan program for schools, both permanent and changing exhibits, annual Yom Hashoah commemoration, and outreach training programs for pre-service teachers and other government agency personnel. (MEMORIAL and MUSEUM)

Los Angeles Holocaust Museum. 6006 Wilshire Boulevard, Los Angeles, CA 90036, USA. Phone 323-761-8170. FAX 323-761-8174. http:// www.remembertoteach.com/museum.htm#. e-mail: kjosephy@earthlink.net.

This museum's services include tours, a resource center and library, speakers bureau, film and lecture series, symposia, and teacher-training workshops. Publications emphasize educational outreach and curriculum materials. (MUSEUM)

Museum of Jewish Heritage: A Living Memorial to the Holocaust. 18 First Place, Battery Park City, New York, NY 10004-1484, USA. Phone 212-968-1800 and 212-509-6130. FAX 212-968-1368. http://www.mjhnyc.org. e-mail: Education@mjhnyc.org.

The Museum of Jewish Heritage addresses the history of Jewish life in Europe and the United States, with specific exhibits focusing on the Holocaust and its legacy. Programs of the Museum of Jewish Heritage include teacher training, a speakers bureau, film and discussion series, and publications. (MUSEUM)

National Museum of American Jewish Military History. 1811 R Street NW, Washington, DC 20009, USA. Phone 202-265-6280. FAX 202-462-3192. http://www.nmajmh.org. e-mail: nmajmh@nmajmh.org.

This historical museum contains exhibitions, archives, and a library, and conducts tours. Publications address exhibitions displayed in the museum. (MUSEUM)

Rhode Island Holocaust Memorial Museum: An Educational Outreach Center. 401 Elmgrove Avenue, Providence, RI 02906, USA. Phone 401-881-8800.

This museum and educational resource center has varied services, including exhibits, commemorations, educational programs for teachers and students, film series, lectures, and a publications program. (MUSEUM)

Rockland Center for Holocaust Studies, Inc. The Holocaust Museum and Study Center, 17 South Madison Avenue, Spring Valley, NY 10877-5525, USA. Phone 845-356-2700. FAX 845-356-1974. http://www. holocauststudies.org. e-mail: rchs@ucs.net.

Functioning as a resource center, museum, library, and archive, this museum includes tours, teacher training, a speakers bureau, and film series among its services. The publications program includes a newsletter. (MUSEUM)

Simon Wiesenthal Center—Museum of Tolerance. Simon Wiesenthal Plaza, 9786 West Pico Boulevard, Los Angeles, California 90035-4792, USA. Phone 310-553-9036. FAX 310-553-4521. http://www. wiesenthal.com. e-mail: information@wiesenthal.com.

Encompassing a museum, library/resource center, archive, and research institute, the Museum of Tolerance engages in an extensive series of teacher-training and commemorative programs, as well as providing lecture and film series and book award programs. The very extensive publications program includes books for educators and the general public, multimedia productions (CD-ROMs and posters), films, journals, and other print publications. (MUSEUM)

U.S. Holocaust Memorial Museum. 100 Raoul Wallenberg Place SW, Washington, DC 20024-2156, USA. http://ushmm.org. e-mail: education@ushmm.org.

As the national institution for documentation, study, and interpretation of Holocaust history in the United States, the Museum's mission is to advance and disseminate knowledge of the Holocaust, to preserve the memory of those who suffered, and to encourage visitors to reflect on the moral and spiritual questions raised by the Holocaust as well as their responsibilities as citizens of a democracy. The extensive services of the Museum include a registry of Holocaust survivors, education resource center, teacher-training programs (for novice and advanced teachers of the Holocaust), permanent, rotating, and traveling exhibitions, archives (film, photo, print, and oral history), concert/lecture/seminar series, the Center for Advanced Holocaust Studies, and a very broad publications program encompassing scholarly publications, educational materials, audio recordings, posters, multimedia (CD-ROMs), and public outreach programs. (MEMORIAL and MUSEUM)

Virginia Holocaust Museum. 213 Roseneath Road, PO Box 14809, Richmond, VA 23221, USA. Phone 804-257-5400. FAX 804-257-4314. http:// www.va-holocaust.com. e-mail: info@va-holocaust.com.

Functioning as a museum, resource center and archives, and center for survivors, the Virginia Holocaust Museum's services include tours, lectures, and multimedia presentations, teacher training, research support, collection of oral histories and artifacts from survivors, and publications. (MUSEUM)

Uruguay

Centro Recordatorio del Holocausto Soc. Amigos de Yad Vashem (Holocaust Memorial Center, Friends of Yad Vashem). Canelones 1084, Piso 3, Montevideo 11100, Uruguay. Phone (598) 2-902-5750, ext. 124. FAX (598) 2-203-1746. e-mail: benvin@redfacil.com.uy.

In addition to its function as a museum on the Holocaust, the Holocaust Memorial Center organizes activities for first- through third-generation survivors, conducts Holocaust commemorations, publishes a bulletin, and participates in the interview project of the Survivors of the Shoah Visual History Foundation. (MUSEUM)

Yugoslavia

Jevrejski Istorijski Muzej, Beograd (Jewish Historical Museum of Belgrade). 71a Kralja Petra St., Belgrade 11000, Yugoslavia. Phone (381) 11-622-634. FAX (381) 11-626-674. http://www.jim-bg.org. e-mail: muzej@jim-bg.org.

Combining a museum and archives, this museum presents information on the history and culture of Jews in the territory of the former Yugoslavia. Publications include a bulletin and exhibition catalogues. (MUSEUM)

OVERVIEW: ORGANIZATIONS

The proliferation of organizations dedicated to education, remembrance, and research about the Holocaust has been an important development of the period 1970–2000. The creation of the Association of Holocaust Organizations and the Task Force for International Cooperation on Holocaust Education, Remembrance, and Research has stimulated the exchange of information and ideas, along with the creation of formal networks of conferences and related initiatives to enhance Holocaust study worldwide. The organizations included in this chapter were selected based upon the following criteria: (1) their primary mission is to educate, commemorate, and/or study the Holocaust, (2) they have staff and resources that indicate they function as permanent entities in their respective countries, and (3) they provide services and programs to the public and other constituencies that relate to their mission. In each case, the organization's title, address, phone, fax, and e-mail and Web site addresses (where applicable) are provided. Descriptions of each organization's programs and activities are not provided for two reasons: (1) lack of available information from many organizations and (2) the constantly changing nature of programs and activities, which makes presentation of accurate information difficult in a book of this type. For further details on a specific organization's mission and programs, readers are encouraged to contact the organization directly, or consult the Association of Holocaust Organizations or the Task Force for International Cooperation on Holocaust Education, Remembrance, and Research, located at http://ntdata.ushmm.org/ad/.

ASSOCIATIONS AND NETWORKS OF HOLOCAUST-RELATED ORGANIZATIONS

The Association of Holocaust Organizations. *Directory*. Published annually by the Association of Holocaust Organizations, c/o Holocaust Resource Center and Archives, Queensborough Community College, City University of New York, 222-05 56th Avenue, Bayside, NY 11364-1497. Phone: 718-225-0378. FAX: 718-631-6306. http://www.ushmm.org/organizations/list.html. e-mail: hrcaho@worldnet.att.net.

The *Directory* of the Association of Holocaust Organizations provides a current listing of its membership, including the member organization's address, director/person in charge, number of staff, year of establishment, a description of the member organization's function and activities, and a listing of the publications and services provided. In some cases, the days and hours the organization is open to the public also are given. International in scope, the *Directory* is organized alphabetically by member organization name, and both alphabetical and geographic indices are provided to assist in locating Association members in the *Directory*. A separate page with Association members who are individuals rather than organizations also is included.

COUNTRY LISTINGS OF HOLOCAUST-RELATED ORGANIZATIONS

Australia

Australian Institute for Holocaust and Genocide Studies. Shalom College, University of New South Wales, Sydney NSW, 2052, Australia. Phone (61) 2-9931-9628. FAX: (61) 2-9313-7145. http://www.aihgs.com. e-mail: aihgs@shalom.edu.au.

Descendants of the Shoah, Inc. Melbourne, VIC, Australia. Phone: (61) 3-952-39575. http://www.dosinc.org.au. e-mail: holocaust@dosinc.org.au.

Holocaust Institute of W.A. Incorporated. 61 Woodrow Avenue, Yokine, WA. 6060, Australia. Phone: (61) 08-927-68730. FAX: (61) 08-927-68330. e-mail: tamara_k@nw.com.au.

Austria

Arbeitskreis fuer Heimat–Denkmal–und Geschichtspflege (KZ Gusen Memorial Committee). PO Box 54, Sankt Georgen an der Gusen A-4222, Austria. Phone (43) 7-237-39-46. FAX: (43) 7-229-76-920. http://linz.orf.at/orf/gusen/pf/ahdg.htm. e-mail: rahd@nextra.at.

Documentationsarchiv des osterreichischen Widerstandes (Archive and Documentation Center Dealing with the Nazi Period in Austria). Wipplingerstrasse 6-8

(Altes Rathaus), A-1010 Wien, Austria. Phone (43) 01-534-3690319. FAX (43) 01-534-369-901771. http://www.doew.at. e-mail: erfassung@doew.at.

Gedenkdienst (Private organization for service in foreign Holocaust memorials as an alternative to Austrian military service). Treitlstrasse 3, A-1040 Wien, Austria. Phone (43) 1-581-04-90. FAX: (43) 1-581-04-90. http://www.gedenkdienst.at. e-mail: gedenkdienst@gedenkdienst.at.

Belarus

Belaruskii Republikanskii Fond (Belarusian Republican Foundation). Ya. Kolas Street 39A, Minsk 220013, Belarus. Phone (375) 17-232-7096. FAX: (375) 17-232-1133. e-mail: brfvp@belsonet.net.

Belgium

Centre d'Etudes et de Documentation Guerre et Societes Contemporaines (Center for Historical Research and Documentation on War and Contemporary Society). Residence Palace Block E, Rue de la Loi 155/Bte 2-1040, Brussels, Belgium. Phone: (32) 02-287-4811. FAX: (32) 02-287-4710. http://www.cegesoma.be/. e-mail: cegesoma@cegesoma.be.

Centre Europeen Juif d'Information (CEJI) (European Center for Jewish Information). 319 Avenue Brugmann, Bruxelles 1180, Belgium. Phone: (32) 2-344-3444. FAX: (32) 2-344-6735.

Foundation Auschwitz (Auschwitz Foundation). 65 Rue Des Tanneurs, Bruxelles B-1000, Belgium. Phone: (32) 02-512-7998. FAX: (32) 02-512-5884. http://www.auschwitz.be. e-mail: foundation@auschwitz.be.

Brazil

Nucleo de Historia Oral—Arquivo Historico Judaico Brasileiro (Oral History Department of the Brazilian Historical Jewish Archive). 30 Rua Prates, 90 Sao Paulo 01121-000, Brasil. Phone: (55) 11-228-8769. FAX: (55) 11-228-8769. http://www.ceveh.com.br. e-mail: ahjb@uol.com.br.

Bulgaria

The Sofia University Center for Jewish Studies. 15 Tzar Osvoboditel, Sofie 1504, Bulgaria. Phone (359) 2-871-046. FAX: (359) 2-943-4447. e-mail: cjs@scig.unisofia.bg.

Canada

Association of Survivors of Nazi Oppression. 5782 Ferncroft Road, Montreal, Quebec H3X 1C7, Canada. Phone: 514-488-3027. FAX: 514-488-3148.

Bronfman Jewish Education Center. 1 Carre Cummings Square, 5th Floor, Montreal, Quebec H3W 1M6, Canada. Phone: 514-345-2610. FAX: 514-735-2175. http:// www.jec.org. e-mail: ninaa@bjec.org.

The David J. Azrieli Holocaust Collection—In the Concordia University Library. Concordia University, 1455 de Maisonneuve Boulevard West, Montreal, Quebec H3G 1M8, Canada. Phone: 514-848-2424. FAX: 514-848-7687. http:// www.concordia.ca/collections/azrieli.html. e-mail: drfrank@alcor.concordia.ca.

Holocaust Literature Research Institute. University College, Room 306, University of Western Ontario, London, Ontario N6A 2K7, Canada. Phone: 519-661-3820. FAX: 519-661-3820. http://www.arts.uwo.ca/HLRI. e-mail: agold@julian.uwo.ca.

Kleinmann Family Foundation. 7881 Decarie Boulevard, Suite 309, Montreal, Quebec H4P 2H2, Canada. Phone: 514-735-3663. FAX: 514-735-9041. e-mail: kff@total.net.

London Remembrance and Education Committee. London Jewish Federation, 536 Huron Street, London, Ontario N5Y 4J5, Canada. Phone: 519-673-3310 and 519-673-1161. e-mail: ljf@info.london.on.ca.

Montreal Institute for Genocide and Human Rights Studies. Concordia University, 1455 de Maisonneuve Boulevard West, Montreal, Quebec H3G 1M8, Canada. Phone: 514-848-2404. FAX: 514-848-4538. http://www.migs.concordia.ca. e-mail: drfrank@alcor.concordia.ca.

Vancouver Holocaust Education Center. #50–950 West 41st Avenue, Vancouver, British Columbia V5Z 2N7, Canada. Phone: 604-264-0499. FAX: 604-264-0497. http://www.vhec.org. e-mail: info@vhec.org.

Croatia

Jewish Community of Zagreb. Palmoticeva 16, Zagreb 41000, Croatia. Phone: (385) 142-5517. FAX: (385) 143-4638.

Czech Republic

Education and Cultural Center of the Jewish Museum. U Stare Skoly 1, Prague 1 110 00, Czech Republic. Phone: (420) 2-2481-9456. FAX: (420) 2-2481-9458. http://www.jewishmuseum.cz. e-mail: office@jewishmuseum.cz.

Institut Terezinske Iniciativy (Terezin Initiative Institute). Jachymova 3, Prague 1 110 00. Czech Republic. Phone: (420) 2-2482-6518. http://www.terezinstudies.cz. e-mail: institute@terezinstudies.cz.

Terezinska Iniciativa (Association of Holocaust Survivors in the Czech Republic). Maiselova 18, Prague 1 110 00, Czech Republic. Phone: (420) 2-2231-0681. FAX:

(420) 2-2231-0681. http://www.terezinstudies.cz. e-mail: terezinskainiciative@
cmail.cz.

Denmark

Danish Center for Holocaust and Genocide Studies. Norre Sogade 35, 5, sal 1370,
Copenhagen. Phone: (45) 33-37-00-70. FAX: (45) 33-37-00-80. http://www.
dchf.dk. e-mail: dchf@dchf.dk.

Estonia

Eesti Juudi Kogukond (Jewish Community of Estonia). Karu, Tallinn 16 10120,
Estonia. Phone: (37) 2-6-662-3034. FAX: (37) 2-662-3034. e-mail: ciljal@icom.ee.

France

ACC Institut (Au Coeur de la Communication). 35 rue Jouffroy d'Abbans, Paris F-
75017, France. Phone: (331) 438-05976. FAX: (331) 476-43909. e-mail:
accintl@compuserve.com.

Au Coeur de la Communication. 35 rue Jouffroy d'Abbans, 75017 Paris, France.
Phone: (331) 43-80-59-76. FAX: (331) 47-64-39-09.

Centre de Documentation sur la Deportation des Enfants Juifs (Documentation
Center of the Deportation of Jewish Children). 9 Avenue Leclerc, Lyon F-69007,
France. Phone: (33) 4-786-95093.

Centre d'Histoire de la Resistance et de la Deportation (History Center of Resistance and Deportation). 14 Avenue Berthelot, Lyon F-69007, France. Phone: (33)
04-787-22311. FAX: (33) 04-727-33298. http://www.mairie-lyon.fr/fr/
cult_musee03.htm. e-mail: chrd@mairie-lyon.fr.

Conservatoire Historique du Camp de Drancy (Drancy Camp Historical Association). 14 Rue Arthur Fontaine, Cite de la Muette, Drancy F-93700, France. Phone:
(33) 1-489-53505. http://www.camp-de-drancy.asso.fr/. e-mail: conserv.
histori.drancy@wanadoo.fr.

Foundation Pour La Memoire de la Deportation (Foundation for Memory of the
Deportations). 71 Rue Saint-Dominque, Paris F-75007, France. Phone: (33) 01-
470-53188. FAX: (33) 01-444-23562. http://www.fmd.asso.fr. e-mail:
contactfmd@fmd.asso.fr.

LICRA—Ligue Internationale Contre le Racisme et l'Antisemitisme (International League against Racism and Anti-semitism). 42 Rue de Louvre, Paris F-
75001, France. Phone: (33) 1-450-80808. FAX: (33) 1-450-81818. http://
www.licra.com/. e-mail: licr@licra.com.

Union des Resistants et des Deportes Juifs de France (Union of Jewish Resistance).
35 Place Saint-Ferdinand, Paris F-75017, France. Phone: (33) 1-440-99377. FAX:
(33) 1-457-21170. http://www.cie.fr/urdf. e-mail: arayski@cie.fr.

Germany

Aktion Suhnezeichen Friedensdienste (Action Reconciliation Service for Peace). Auguststrasse 80, Berlin D-10117, Germany. Phone: (49) 030-283-95184. FAX: (49) 030-283-95135. http://www.ipn.de/asf. e-mail: asf@asf-ev/de.

Arbeitsgemeinschaft ehemaliges KZ Flossenburg (Research and Study Center about the Flossenburg Concentration Camp). Rote Hahengasse 6, Regensburg D-93047, Germany. Phone: (49) 94-158-264. FAX: (49) 94-158-264.

Bayerische Landeszentrale fur Politische Bildungsarbeit (Bayern State Office for Political Education). Brienner Strasse 41, Munchen D-80333, Germany. Phone: (49) 089-2186-0. FAX: (49) 089-2186-2800. http://www.stmukwk.bayern.de/blz/index.html. e-mail: landeszentrale@km.bayern.de.

Bundesverband Information und Beratung fur NS-Verfolgte (Federal Advisory and Information Association for Victims of Nazi Persecution). Kammergasse 1, Koln 50676, Germany. Phone: (49) 42-162-2073. http://www.hagalil.com/bvnsv/index.htm. e-mail: nsberatung@netcologne.de.

Bundeszentrale fur Politische Bildung (Federal Office for Political Education—Center for Political Education). Berliner Freiheit 7, Bonn D-53111, Germany. Phone: (49) 0188-515-0. FAX: (49) 01888-515-113. http://www.bpb.de. e-mail: info@bpb.bund.de.

Dokumentations-und Kulturzentrum Deutscher Sinti und Roma (Documentation and Cultural Center of German Sinti and Roma). Bremeneckgasse 2, Heidelberg 69117, Germany. Phone: (49) 6221-981102. FAX: (49) 6221-981177. http://www.sinti-und-roma.de.

Dokumentationsstelle Brandenburg Stiftung Brandenburgische Gedenkstatten (Brandenburg Documentation Center). Anton-Saefkow-Allee 2, Brandenburg an der Havel D-14772, Germany. Phone: (49) 03381-761506 and (49) 03381-761506.

Forschungs-und Arbeitsstelle (Research and Study Center for Holocaust Education). FAS, Box 52 20 08, Hamburg 22598, Germany. Phone: (49) 40-432-51280. FAX: (49) 40-432-51282. http://www.fasena.de. e-mail: info@fasena.org.

Forschungsstelle Widerstand gegen den Nationalsozialismus im deutschen Sudwesten (Research Center of the Resistance against National Socialism in Southwestern Germany). Universitat Karlsruhe/Institute fur Geschichte Franz-Schnabel-Haus, Postfach 6980, Karlsruhe 76128, Germany. Phone: (49) 721-608-4795. FAX: (49) 721-608-4796.

Fritz Bauer Institute, Studien-und Dokumentationszentrum zur Geschichte und Wirkung des Holocaust (Study and Documentation Center on the History and Impact of the Holocaust). Gruneburgplatz 1, Frankfurt am Main 60323, Germany. Phone: (49) 069-798322-40. FAX: (49) 069-798322-41. http://www.fritz-bauer-institut.de. e-mail: info@fritz-bauer-institut.de.

Georg Eckert Institut fur Internationale Schulbuchforschung (Georg Eckert Institute for International Textbook Research). Celler Strasse 3, Braunschweig D-38114, Germany. Phone: (49) 0531-590-990. FAX: (49) 0531-590-9999. http://www.gei.de. e-mail: GEInst@gei.de.

Germania Judaica. Kolner Bibliothek zur Geschichte des deutschen Judentums (Cologne Library for Research on Judaism in Germany). Josef Haubrich-Hof 1, Koln D-50676, Germany. Phone: (49) 0221-23828. FAX: (49) 0221-22519. http://www.stbib-koeln.de/judaica/index. e-mail: gj@ub.uni-koeln.de.

Hamburger Institut fur Sozialforschung (Hamburg Institute for Social Research). Mittelweg 36, Hamburg 20148, Germany. Phone: (49) 40-414-097-0. FAX: (49) 40-414-09711. http://www.his-online.de. e-mail: Presse@his-online.de.

Hannah-Arendt Institute fur Totalitarismusforschung E.V. (Hannah Arendt Institute for Research on Totalitarianism). Mommenstrasse 13, Dresden 01062, Germany. Phone: (49) 0351-463-2802. FAX: (49) 0351-463-6079. http://www.tu-dresden.de/hait. e-mail: hait@rcs.urz.tu-dresden.de.

Landesinstitut fur Pedagogik und Medien—Landeszentrale fur Politische Bildung Saarland (State Institute for Education Methodology and Media/Saarland Office for Political Education). Beethovenstrasse 26, Pavillon, Saarbrucken D-66125, Germany. Phone: (49) 0689-790-844. FAX: (49) 0689-790-877. http://www.politische-bildung.de/. e-mail: lpb@pegasus.lpm.uni-sb.de.

Landeszentrale fur Politische Bildung Baden-Wurttemberg (Baden-Wurttemberg Center for Political Education). Stafflenbergstrasse 38, Stuttgart D-70184, Germany. Phone: (49) 0711-164099-0. FAX: (49) 711-164099-77. http://www.lpb.bwue.de. e-mail: lpb@lpb.bwue.de.

Landeszentrale fur Politische Bildung Bremen (Bremen Center for Political Education). Osterdeich 6, Bremen D-28203, Germany. Phone: (49) 0421-361-2922. FAX: (49) 0421-361-4453. http://www.lzpb-bremen.de. e-mail: office@lzpb. bremen.de.

Landeszentrale fur Politische Bildung Hamburg (Hamburg Center for Political Education). Grosse Bleichen 23, III Hamburg D-20354, Germany. Phone: (49) 42831-2143. FAX: (49) 42831-2050. http://www.hamburg.de/Behoerden/Landeszentrale. e-mail: politischeBildung@sk.hamburg.de.

Landeszentrale fur Politische Bildung Mecklenburg-Vorpommern (Mecklenburg-Pomeranian State Office for Political Education). Jagerweg 2, Schwerin D-19053, Germany. Phone: (49) 0385-302-0910. FAX: (49) 385-302-0922. http://www.mv-regierung.de/lpb. e-mail: LPBM@t-online.de.

Landeszentrale fur Politische Bildung Nordhrein-Westfalen (State Office for Political Education NRW). Neanderstrasse 6, Dusselford D-40233, Germany.

Phone: (49) 211-679-770. FAX: (49) 211-679-7733. http://www.lzpb.nrw.de/mfrset.htm. e-mail: lzpb@compurserve.com.

Landeszentrale fur Politische Bildung Rheinland-Pfalz (Rheinland-Pfalz Center for Political Education). Am Kronberger Hof 6, Postfach 3028 Mainz D-55020, Germany. Phone: (49) 061-311-62970. FAX: (49) 061-311-62980. http://www.politische-bildung-rip.de. e-mail:lpb.zentrale@politische-bildung-rip.de.

Landeszentrale fur Politische Bildung Sachsen-Anhalt (Sachsen-Anhalt Center for Political Education). Schleinufer 12, Magdeburg D-39104, Germany. Phone: (49) 0391-565-340. FAX: (49) 0391-565-3413. http://www.lpb.sachsen-anhalt.de. e-mail: lpblsa.sekretariat@stk.sachsen-anhalt.de.

Landeszentrale fur Politische Bildung Thuringen (Thuringen Center for Political Education). Bergsrtrasse 4, Erfurt D-99092, Germany. Phone: (49) 0361-379-2701. FAX: (49) 0361-379-2702. http://www.thueringen.de/LZT. e-mail: lzt@thueringen.de.

Roma National Congress. RomNews Network, PO Box 304145, Hamburg 20324, Germany. Phone: (49) 40-319-42-49. FAX: (49) 40-31-04-75. http://www.romnews.com. e-mail: rnn@romnews.com.

Stiftung Topographie des Terrors (Topography of Terror Foundation). International Documentation and Study Center, Budapester Strasse 40, Berlin D-10787, Germany. Phone: (49) 030-254-5090. FAX: (49) 030-261-3002. http://www.topographie.de. e-mail: info@topographie.de.

Zentrum fur Antisemitismusforschung (Center for Research into Antisemitism). Technische Universitat Berlin, Ernst-Reuter Platz 7, Berlin D-10587, Germany. Phone: (49) 30-314-23154. FAX: (49) 30-314-21136. http://www.TU-Berlin.de/~zfa. e-mail: zfa10154@mailszrz.zrz.TU-Berlin.De.

Greece

Jewish Community of Rhodes. 5 Polydorou Street, Rhodes 85 100, Greece. Phone: (30) 241-22364. FAX: (30) 241-73039. http://www.rhodesjewishmuseum.org.

Union of Jewish Holocaust Survivors of Greece. 13 Korkinaki Street, Athens 145 61, Greece. Phone: (30) 19-750-7519433.

Hungary

Raoul Wallenberg Egyesulet (Raoul Wallenberg Association). Baross U. 61, Budapest H-108, Hungary. Phone: (36) 1-313-5439. FAX: (36) 1-313-5439.

Israel

AMCHA: Israeli Centers for Holocaust Survivors and the Second Generation. National Office, PO Box 2930, Jerusalem 91029, Israel. Phone: (972) 2-625-0634. FAX: (972) 2-625-0669. http://www.amcha.org. e-mail: amcha@amcha.org.

Avraham Harman Institute of Contemporary Jewry and the Vidal Sassoon International Center for the Study of Antisemitism. Center for the Study of Antisemitism, Hebrew University of Jerusalem, Mount Scopus, Jerusalem 91905, Israel. Phone: (972) 2-588-2494. FAX: (972) 2-588-1002. http://sicsa.huji.ac.il. e-mail: mshelene@mscc.huji.ac.il.

Beit Lohamei Haghetaot—The Ghetto Fighters' House. Kibbutz Lohamei—Haghetaot, D.N., Western Galilee, 25220 Israel. Phone: (972) 4-995-8080. FAX: (972) 4-995-8007. http://www.gfh.org.il. e-mail: Simstein@gfh.org.il.

Beit Theresienstadt. Kibbutz Givat Chaym—Ichud Mobile Post, Emek Hefer 38935, Israel. Phone: 972-6-636-9515. FAX: 972-6-636-9611. http://www.bterezin.org.il. e-mail: bterezin@inter.net.il.

Gansuch Kiddush Hashem. Kiddush Hashem Archives, 15 Rabbi Melzer Street, PO Box 242, Bnei Brak 51102, Israel. Phone: (972) 3-570-3018 and (972) 3-579-5589. FAX: (972) 3-578-7442. http://www.ganzach.org.il. e-mail: ganzach@netvision.net.il.

Hedva Eibeshitz Institute of Holocaust Studies. 39 Hatichon Street, Neve-Shaanan, Haifa, Israel. Phone: (972) 4-832-5978. FAX: (972) 4-822-6617.

Holocaust Education Center. State Teachers' College Seminar, Hakibbutzim 149 Derech Namir Ramat Aviv, Tel Aviv 62057, Israel. Phone: (972) 3-690-2369. FAX: (972) 3-669-0269.

Institute on the Holocaust and Genocide. PO Box 10311, Jerusalem 91102, Israel. Phone: (972) 2-672-0424. FAX: (972) 2-672-0424.

Keren Zikaron Leyahadut Lita (Lithuanian Jewry Memorial Foundation). PO Box 11456, Jerusalem 91114, Israel. Phone: (972) 2-645-0379. FAX: (972) 2-645-0379. http://www.jewishgen.org/litvak.lithnames. e-mail: litvaks@aol.com.

Massuah-Institute for the Study of the Holocaust. Kibbutz Tel-Yitzhak, Tel Aviv 45803, Israel. Phone: (972) 9-899-9997 and (972) 9-899-9563/6997. FAX: (972) 9-899-7410. http://www.massauh.org/home.htm. e-mail: massuah@netvision.net.il.

World Jewish Congress. 21 Arlozorov Street, PO Box 4293, Jerusalem 91042, Israel. Phone: (972) 2-563-5261. FAX: (972) 2-563-5544. http://www.wjc.org.il. e-mail: wjc@netvision.net.il.

World Jewish Restitution Organization (WJRO). 7 Radak Street, Jerusalem 92301, Israel. Phone: (972) 02-561-2497. FAX: (972) 2-562-2496. http://ja-wzo.org.il/wro/whoweare.html. e-mail: wrjo@netvision.com.

Italy

Fondazione Centro di Documentazione Ebraica Contemporanea (CDEC) (Foundation Center for Contemporary Jewish Documentation). Via Eupili N. 8, Milan I-20145, Italy. Phone: (39) 02-396-092 and (39) 02-316-338. FAX: (39) 02-336-02728. http://www.cdec.it. e-mail: edu@cdec.it.

Japan

Holocaust Education Center Hiroshima. 866 Nakatsuhara Miyuki, Fukuyama-City, Hiroshima Prefecture 720, Japan. Phone: (81) 84-955-8001. FAX: (81) 84-955-8001. http://www.urban.ne.jp/home.hecjpn. e-mail: hecjpn@urban.ne.jp.

Tokyo Holocaust Education Resource Center. 28-105 Daikyo-cho Shinjuku-ku, Tokyo 160-5363, Japan. Phone: (81) 3-536-34808. FAX: (81) 3-536-34809. http://www.ne.jp/asahi/holocaust/tokyo. e-mail: Holocaust@Tokyo.e-mail.ne.jp.

Latvia

Latvijas Okupacijas Muzejs (The Museum of the Occupation of Latvia, 1940–1991). Strelnieku laukums 1, Riga LV-1050, Latvia. Phone (371) 721-2715. FAX: (371) 722-9255. http://www.occupationmuseum.lv. e-mail: omf@latnet.lv.

Lithuania

Pilietiniu Iniciatyvu Centras (Centre for Civic Initiatives). Zemaitijos 13/10, Vilnius 2001, Lithuania. Phone: (370) 2-224-418. FAX: (370) 2-615-606. e-mail: Girvydas@post.omnitel.net.

Luxembourg

Conseil Nationale de la Resistance, Centre de Documentation et de Recherche (National Resistance Council, Center for Documentation and Research). 1 Rue de Bonnevoie, Luxembourg L-1260, Luxembourg. Phone: (352) 478-2280. FAX: (352) 290-039. e-mail: paul.dostert@ci.educ.lu.

The Netherlands

Anne Frank Stichting (Anne Frank Foundation). Keizersgracht 192, Amsterdam 1016 DW, The Netherlands. Phone: (31) 20-556-7100. FAX: (31) 20-620-7999. http://www.annefrank.nl. e-mail: info@annefrank.nl.

Nederlands Instituut voor Oorlogsdocumentatie (NIOD) (Netherlands State Institute for War Documentation). Herengracht 380, Amsterdam 1015 CJ, The Netherlands. Phone: (31) 20-523-3800. FAX: (31) 20-523-3888. http://www.oorlogsdoc.knaw.nl. e-mail: info@oorlogsdoc.knaw.nl.

New Zealand

Holocaust Oral History Group. PO Box 63, Auckland, New Zealand. Phone: (64) 9-521-3526. FAX: (64) 9-521-3526. e-mail: narev@clear.net.nz.

Norway

Jewish Museum. DMT Trondheim, PO Box 2183, Trondheim N-7142, Norway. Phone: (47) 735-22030. http://www.dmt.trondheim.no/museum.html.

Poland

Centralna Rada Romow (Central Roma Council in Poland). Ul. Warszawska 43, Bialystok 15-062, Poland. Phone: (48) 85-732-9607. FAX: (48) 85-732-9607. e-mail: stahiros@polbox.com.pl.

Instytut Pamieci Narodowej—Komisja Scigania Zbrodni Przeciwko Narodowi Polskiemu (Institute of National Memory—Commission for the Prosecution of the Crimes against the Polish Nation). Krakowskie Przedmiescie 25, Warszawa 00-071, Poland. Phone: (48) 22-826-2441. FAX: (48) 22-826-2139. http://www.ipn.gov/pl/eng_commission.html.

Miedzynarodowa Rada Oswiecimska (International Council of the State Museum of Auschwitz-Birkenau). Ul. Wiezniow Oswiecimia 20, Oswiecim 32-603, Poland. Phone: (48) 33-843-2022. FAX: (48) 33-843-1934. http://auschwitz.org.pl.

Panstwowe Archiwum s Rzeszowie/Osrodek Badania Historii Zydow (State Archive in Rzeszow/Research Center on Jewish History). Ul. Boznicza 2, Rzeszow 35-959, Poland. Phone: (48) 017-853-2684. FAX: (48) 017-853-8304. http://rzeszow.ap.gov.pl. e-mail: aprzeszow@pro.net.pl.

Stowarzyszenie Dziece Holocaustu (Association of the Hidden Children of the Holocaust). Ul. Twarda 6, Warszawa 00-104, Poland. Phone: (48) 22-620-8245. http://www.jewish.org.pl/english/foundati/HIDDEN.html. e-mail: chsurv@jewish.org.pl.

Zydowski Instytut Historyczny. Instytut Naukowo-Badawczy (Jewish Historical Research Institute). Ul. Tolmackie 3/5, Warszawa 00-090, Poland. Phone: (48) 22-827-9221. FAX: (48) 22-827-8372. e-mail: secretary@jewishinstitute.org.pl. http://www.jewishinstitute.org.pl/OZIH1E.html.

Russia

International Union of Former Juvenile Prisoners of Fascist Concentration Camps. Ul. Griboedova 4, Moscow 101830, Russia. Phone: (7) 095-923-9168. FAX: (7) 95-135-3097. e-mail: Makhutov@iies.msk.su.

Nauchno-Prosvetitel'ny Tsentr (Scientific Educational and Research Center). Ul. Sadovnicheskaya 52/45, Moscow 113025, Russia. Phone: (7) 95-953-3362. FAX: (7) 95-951-5876. e-mail: i.altman@mtu.net.ru.

Shoah Memorial Center. Nab. Kanala Griboedova 190121, Saint Petersburg, Russia. Phone: (821) 114-4664. FAX: (821) 114-4664.

Slovak Republic

Institut Judaistiky, Univerzita Komenskeho (Institute of Jewish Studies, Comenius University). Paneska 4, Bratislava 811 03, Slovak Republic. Phone: (42) 17-544-16867. FAX: (42) 17-544-16867. http://www.ij.uniba.sk. e-mail: ij@ij.uniba.sk.

South Africa

Cape Town Holocaust Centre. 88 Hatfield Street, Cape Town 8001, South Africa. Phone: (27) 21-462-5553. FAX: (27) 21-462-5554. http://www.museums.org.za/ ctholocaust. e-mail: ctholocaust@mweb.co.za.

Sweden

Foreningen Forintelsens Minne (FFM) (Swedish Holocaust Memorial Association). PO Box 125 23, Stockholm SE-102 29, Sweden. Phone: (46) 8-650-5933. FAX: (46) 8-650-5933. e-mail: romwro@ki.se.

Foreningen Forintelsens Overlevande (Swedish Survivors Association). PO Box 12091, Stockholm S-102 23, Sweden. Phone: (46) 8-640-5599. FAX: (46) 8-640-5599 and (46) 8-645-5218. e-mail: FFO@swipnet.se.

Levande Historia-Information Kring Forintelsen (Living History Project—Information about the Holocaust). Regeringskansliet, Stockholm 103 33, Sweden. Phone: (46) 8-405-1000. FAX: (46) 8-405-4111. http: www.levandehistoria.org. e-mail: levhist@ovrigt@adm.ministry.se.

Swedish Committee against Antisemitism. PO Box 14216, Stockholm S-104 40, Sweden. Phone: (46) 8-667-6090. FAX: (46) 8-663-0102. http://www.skma.se.

Uppsala Programme for Holocaust and Genocide Studies. Uppsala University, Box 514, Uppsala 751-20, Sweden. Phone: (46) 18-471-7196. FAX: (46) 18-471-2363. www.multietn.uu.se/uppsalaprogramme.html. e-mail: ulrika.nissell@ multietn.uu.se.

Switzerland

Comite International de la Croix-Rouge (International Committee of the Red Cross). 19 Avenue de la Paix, Geneva CH-1202, Switzerland. Phone: (41) 22-734-6001. FAX: (41) 22-733-2057. http://www.icrc.org. e-mail: webmaster.gva@ icrc.org.

Fonds Zugensten Bedurttiger Opfer von Holocaust/Shoa (Fund for Needy Victims of the Holocaust/Shoah). Waaghausgasse 18, Bern CH-3003, Switzerland. Phone: (41) 31-323-2295. FAX: (41) 31-323-2300. e-mail: Barbara.Ekwall@efv.admin.ch.

Pink Cross–Schwulenburo Schweiz (Pink Cross–National Gay League of Switzerland). Zinggstrasse 16, PO Box 7512, Berne 3001, Switzerland. Phone: (41) 31-

372-3300. FAX: (41) 31-372-3317. http://www.pinkcross.ch. e-mail: office@ pinkcross.ch.

Ukraine

Babi Yar Information Center of the Association of Jewish Organizations and Committees in Ukraine and the Kiev Jewish History Center. 6 Kurskaya Street, Kiev 252049, Ukraine. Phone: (380) 44-271-7144 and (380) 44-276-7431.

Babi Yar Memorial Fund. 7. Nemanskaya Street, 252103, Kiev 103, Ukraine. Phone: (380) 44-295-0206 and (380) 44-294-9154. FAX: (380) 44-295-0206.

Institute of Judaic Studies. Kurskaya Street 6, 252049 Kiev, Ukraine. Phone: (380) 44-271-35-89. FAX: (380) 44-213-9149. http://www.judaica.kiev.ua/eng/. e-mail: finberg@irf.kiev.ua.

International Union of Former Juvenile Prisoners of Fascist Concentration Camps. Nemanskaya Street 7, Kiev-103 252103, Ukraine. Phone: (380) 44-295-6203.

Ukrainian Association of Jews/Former Prisoners of the Ghetto and Nazi Concentration Camps. 46a Malaya Arnaudskaya Street, Odessa 270023, Ukraine. Phone: (380) 482-24-0022. FAX: (380) 482-246197. e-mail: ghetto@tm.odessa.ua.

United Kingdom

Anne Frank Educational Trust. PO Box 11880, London N6 4LN, United Kingdom. Phone: (44) 208-340-9077. FAX: (44) 208-340-9088. http://www.annefrank.org.uk. e-mail: afet@afet.org.uk.

Association of Jewish Refugees in Great Britain. 1 Hampstead Gate, 1a Frognal, London NW3 6AL, United Kingdom. Phone: (44) 171-431-6161. FAX: (44) 171-431-8454. http://www.ajr.org.uk. e-mail: enquiries@ajr.org.uk.

Beth Shalom Holocaust Memorial and Education Centre. Laxton, Newark, Nottinghamshire NG22 OPA, United Kingdom. Phone (44) 162-383-6627. FAX: (44) 162-383-6647. http://www.bethshalom.com. e-mail: office@BethShalom. com.uk.

Commission for Looted Art in Europe (ECLA). 76 Gloucester Place, London W1U 6HJ, United Kingdom. Phone: (44) 020-748-73401. FAX: (44) 020-748-74211. http://www.lootedart.com. e-mail: info@lootedart.com.

The Holocaust Educational Trust. BCM, Box 7892, London WC1N 3XX, United Kindgom. Phone: (44) 020-7222-6822. FAX: (44) 020-7233-0161. http:// www.het.org.uk. e-mail: hetrust@compuserve.com.

Holocaust Survivors Centre. Corner Church Road and Parson Street, London NW4 1QA, United Kingdom. Phone: (44) 181-202-9844. FAX: (44) 181-202-2404.

Institute of Contemporary History and Wiener Library. 4 Devonshire Street, London W1N 2BH, United Kingdom. Phone: (44) 020-7636-7247. FAX: (44) 020-7436-6428. http://www.wienerlibrary.co.uk. e-mail: info@wienerlibrary.co.uk.

Leo Baeck Institute. 4 Devonshire Street, London W1N 2BH, United Kingdom. Phone: (44) 020-7580-3493. FAX: (44) 020-7436-8634. http://www.leobaeck.co.uk. e-mail: ap@lbilon.demon.co.uk.

Oxford Centre for Hebrew and Jewish Studies. Yarnton Manor, Yarnton, Oxford OX5 1PY, United Kingdom. Phone: (44) 020-7580-3493. FAX: (44) 020-7436-8634. http://ochjs@herald.ox.ac.uk. e-mail: ochjs@herald.ox.ac.uk.

Searchlight Educational Trust. 37B New Cavendish Street, London W1M 8JR, United Kingdom. Phone: (44) 0171-284-4040. FAX: (44) 0171-284-4410. http://searchlightmagazine.com/educationtrust/set1htm. e-mail: SET@s-light.demon.co.uk.

The Shoah Centre. Department of Religions and Theology, University of Manchester, Oxford Road, Manchester M13 9PL, United Kingdom. Phone: (44) 161-275-3614. FAX: (44) 161-275-3613. e-mail: Daniel.Langton@man.ac.uk.

The London Jewish Cultural Center. The Old House, c/o Kings College London, Kinderpore Avenue, London NW3 7SZ, United Kingdom. Phone: (44) 020-7431-0345. FAX: (44) 020-7431-0361. http://www.ljcc.org.uk. e-mail: admin@ljcc.org.uk.

United States

Aktion Suehnezeichen Friedensdienste (Action Reconciliation Service for Peace). PO Box 44151, Philadelphia PA 19144, USA. Phone: 215-844-8404. FAX: 215-849-3755. http://www.asf-ev.de/usa. e-mail: arsp4usa@aol.com.

Alabama Holocaust Commission. PO Box 180096, Mobile, AL 36618, USA. Phone: 334-342-9384. FAX: 334-342-6714. http://www.alabamaholocaust.org. e-mail: pfilben@dibbs.net.

American Friends of the Ghetto Fighters' House. 181 The Plaza, Teaneck, NJ 07666, USA. Phone: 201-833-5040. FAX: 201-833-5043. http://www.friendsofgfh.org. e-mail: info@friendsofgfh.org.

American Gathering of Jewish Holocaust Survivors. Suite 205, 122 West 30th Street, New York, NY 10001, USA. Phone: 212-239-4230. FAX: 212-279-2926. e-mail: mail@americangathering.org.

American Jewish Committee. National Headquarters, Jacob Blaustein Building, 165 East 56th Street, New York, NY 10022, USA. Phone: 212-751-4000. FAX: 212-838-2120. http://www.ajc.org. e-mail: PR@ajc.org.

American Jewish Joint Distribution Committee. 711 Third Avenue, New York, NY 10017, USA. Phone: 212-687-6200. FAX: 212-682-7262. http://www.jdc.org. e-mail: admin@jdcny.org.

American Red Cross Holocaust and War Victims Tracing and Information Center. 4700 Mount Hope Drive, Baltimore, MD 21215-3231, USA. Phone: 410-764-5311. FAX: 410-764-4638. http://www.redcross.org.

American Society for Yad Vashem. 500 Fifth Avenue, Suite 1600, New York, NY 10110-1699, USA. Phone: 212-220-4304. FAX: 212-220-4308. http://www.yadvashem.org. e-mail: YadVashem@aol.com.

Anne Frank Center USA. 584 Broadway, Suite 408, New York, NY 10012, USA. Phone: 212-431-7993. FAX: 212-431-8375. http://www.annefrank.com. e-mail: director@annefrank.com.

Annual Scholars' Conference on the Holocaust and the Churches. PO Box 10, Merion Station, PA 19006, USA. Phone: 610-667-5437. FAX: 610-667-0265. http://www.sju.edu/events/scholars_conference/program.htm. e-mail: scholarsconf@aol.com.

Anti-Defamation League of B'nai B'rith Braun Holocaust Institute. 823 United Nations Plaza, New York, NY 10017, USA. Phone: 212-885-7792. FAX: 212-867-0779. http://www.adl.org. e-mail: webmaster@adl.org.

Arkansas Holocaust Education Committee. PO Box 1371, Springdale, AR 72765-1371, USA. Phone: 501-756-8090, ext. 210. FAX: 501-750-7444. e-mail: gdonoho@jcf.jonesnet.org.

Auschwitz Jewish Center Foundation. 36 West 44th Street, Suite 310 New York, NY 10036, USA. Phone: (212) 575-1050. FAX: (212) 575-105. http://www.ajcf.org. e-mail: info@acjf.org.

Auschwitz Study Foundation, Inc. 7422 Cedar Street, PO Box 2232, Huntington Beach, CA 92647, USA. Phone: (714) 848-1101. FAX: (714) 842-1979.

The Austrian Encounter (TAE). TAE c/o TRT, PO Box 183, Newton Centre, MA 02459-0183, USA.

Bagby Videotape Archives of Early Christian Resisters to the Hitler Regime. 1501 Lakeside Drive, Lynchburg, VA 24501-3199, USA. Phone: 804-544-8441. FAX: 804-544-8499. http://www.loc.gov/rr/main/religious/lyn.html.

Baltimore Jewish Council. 5750 Park Heights Avenue, Baltimore, MD 21215, USA. Phone: 410-542-4850. FAX: 410-542-4834. http://www.baltjc.org. e-mail: info@baltjc.org.

B'nai B'rith International Headquarters. 1640 Rhode Island Avenue NW, Washington, DC 20036-3278, USA. Phone: 202-857-6600. FAX: 202-857-1099. http://www.bbinet.org. e-mail: bbyo@bnaibrith.org.

California Association of Holocaust Child Survivors. PO Box 3952, Chatsworth, CA 91311, USA. Phone: 818-886-1979. FAX: 818-886-7969. http://sites.netscape.net/leonstab/nov.htm. e-mail: stabin@earthlink.net.

Center for Holocaust and Genocide Studies—Ramapo College. Ramapo College Library, 505 Ramapo Valley Road, Mahwah, NJ 07446, USA. Phone: 201-684-7409. FAX: 201-684-7953. http://www.ramapo.edu/content/campus.resources/Holocenter/holocaust.html. e-mail: mriff@ramapo.edu.

Center for Holocaust and Genocide Studies—University of Minnesota. 105 Nolte Hall West, 315 Pillsbury Drive, University of Minnesota, Minneapolis, MN 55455, USA. Phone: 612-626-2235. FAX: 612-626-9169. http://chgs.hispeed.com. e-mail: chgs@tc.umn.edu.

Center for Holocaust Awareness and Information (CHAI). Jewish Community Federation of Greater Rochester, 441 East Avenue, Rochester, New York 14607, USA. Phone: 716-461-0490. FAX: 716-461-0912. e-mail: bappelbaum@jewishrochester.org.

Center for Holocaust, Genocide, and Peace Studies—University of Nevada. University of Nevada-Reno, MS (402) Reno, Nevada 89557, USA. Phone: 775-784-6767. FAX: 775-784-6611. http://www.unr.edu/chgps/blank.htm. e-mail: center@scs.uni.nevada.

Center for Holocaust Studies—Brookdale Community College. 765 Newman Springs Road, Lincroft, NJ 07738, USA. Phone: 732-224-2769 and 732-224-2183. FAX: 732-224-2405. e-mail: Holo-Center@Brookdale.CC.NJ.US.

Center for Holocaust Studies—Clark University. Clark University, 950 Main Street, Worcester, MA 01610-1477, USA. Phone: 508-793-8897. FAX: 508-793-8827. http://www.clarku.edu/center/holocaust. e-mail: chs@clarku.edu.

Center for the Study of the Holocaust, Genocide, and Human Rights. Webster University, 470 East Lockwood, St. Louis, MO 63119, USA. Phone: 314-968-6970. FAX: 314-963-6094. http://www.webster.edu/~woolflm/cshghr.html. e-mail: woolflm@webster.edu.

Chambon Foundation. 8033 Sunset Boulevard, Los Angeles, CA 90046-2471, USA. Phone: 323-650-1774. FAX: 323-654-4689. http://www.chambon.org. e-mail: sauvage@chambon.org.

Children of Auschwitz Nazi Deadly Lab Experiments Survivors (CANDLES). 1532 South Third Street, Terre Haute, IN 47802, USA. Phone: 812-234-7881. FAX: 812-232-6044. http://www.candles-museum.com. e-mail: candles@abcs.com.

College of St. Elizabeth Holocaust Education Resource Center. 2 Convent Road, Morristown, NJ 07960, USA. Phone: 973-290-4351 and 973-290-4337. FAX: 973-290-4375. http://www.st-elizabeth.edu/weoffer/resources/rholocaust.html. e-mail: sepinwall@cse.edu.

Columbus Jewish Historical Society. 1175 College Avenue, Columbus, OH 43209-2890, USA. Phone: 614-238-6977. FAX: 614-237-2221. http://www.gcis.net/cjhs. e-mail: cjhs1@tcjf.org.

Combined Generations of the Holocaust of Greater Cincinnati. 11223 Cornell Park Drive, c/o Jewish Family Service, Cincinnati, OH 45242, USA. Phone: 513-469-1188. FAX: 513-221-0321. http://www.huc.edu/index.html. e-mail: gmermelstein@huc.edu.

Committee of Concerned Christians. 222 North Rose Street, Burbank, CA 91505-3944, USA. Phone: 818-845-6620.

Community Relations Council of the Jewish Federation of San Antonio. 12500 NW Military Highway, Suite 200, San Antonio, TX 78231, USA. Phone: 210-302-6960. FAX: 210-408-2332. http://www.jfsatx.org/jewish_federation_of_san_antonio.htm. e-mail:lackritzj@jfsatx.org.

Conference on Jewish Material Claims Against Germany. 15 East 26th Street, Room 906, New York, NY 10010, USA. Phone: 212-696-4944. FAX: 212-679-2126. http://www.claimscon.org. e-mail: info@claimscon.org.

Dallas Holocaust Center. 7900 Northaven Road, Dallas, TX 75230, USA. Phone: 214-750-4654. FAX: 214-750-4672. e-mail: dmchs@mail.swbell.net.

Dayton Holocaust Resource Center. 100 East Woodbury Drive, Dayton, OH 45415, USA. Phone: 937-278-7444. FAX: 937-832-2121. http://members.tripod.com/~dhrc. e-mail: RENAFRY@aol.com.

Department of Jewish-Christian Studies. Seton Hall University, 400 South Orange Avenue, South Orange, NJ 07079, USA. Phone: 973-761-9751. FAX: 973-761-9596. http://artsci.shu.edu/Graduate/Jewish. e-mail: frizzela@shu.edu.

Drew University Center for Holocaust/Genocide Study. Embury Hall, Madison, NJ 07940, USA. Phone: 973-408-3600. FAX: 973-408-3914. http://www.depts.drew.edu/chs. e-mail: ctrholst@drew.edu.

El Paso Holocaust Museum and Study Center. 401 Wallenberg Drive, El Paso, TX 79912, USA. Phone: 915-833-5656. FAX: 915-833-9523. http://www.txtolerance.org. e-mail: mholocau@elp.rr.com.

Federation of Jewish Child Survivors of the Holocaust. PO Box 741, Conshohocken, PA 19428, USA. Phone: 610-527-1039. FAX: 610-520-9283. http://www.FJCSH.org. e-mail: holocaustchild@aol.com.

Florida Commissioner's Task Force on Holocaust Education. c/o Holocaust Documentation and Education Center, Florida International University, 3000 NE 151st Street, North Miami, FL 33181, USA. Phone: 305-919-5690. FAX: 305-919-5691. http://www.holocaust.fiu.edu. e-mail: xholocau@fiu.edu.

Fred R. Crawford Witness to the Holocaust Project—Emory University. Special Collections Department, Robert W. Woodruff Library, Emory University, Atlanta, GA 30322-2870, USA. Phone: 404-329-6428. http://gtel.gatech.edu/projects/holocaust.

Georgia Commission on the Holocaust. 330 Capitol Avenue SE, Atlanta, GA 30334, USA. Phone: 404-651-9273. FAX: 404-657-9449. http://www.ganet.org/holocaust. e-mail: holocaust@sos.state.ga.us.

Halina Wind Preston Holocaust Education Center. 100 West 10th Street, Suite 301, Wilmington, DE 19801, USA. Phone: 302-427-2100. FAX: 302-427-2438. e-mail: Delawarejfd@jon.cjfny.org.

Hatikvah Holocaust Education and Resource Center. 1160 Dickinson Street, Springfield, MA 01108, USA. Phone: 413-737-4313. FAX: 413-734-0919. http://www.hatikvah-center.org. e-mail: director@hatikvahcenter.org.

The Hidden Child Foundation/ADL. 823 United Nations Plaza, New York, NY 10017, USA. Phone: 212-885-7900. FAX: 212-867-0779. http://www.hiddenchild.org. e-mail: hidden-child@adl.org.

Holocaust Awareness Institute—University of Denver. 2199 South University Boulevard, University of Denver, Denver, CO 80208, USA. Phone: 303-871-3013. FAX: 303-871-3037. http://www.du.edu/cjs/hai. e-mail: mspence@du.edu.

Holocaust Center—Boston North. 82 Main Street, Peabody, MA 01960, USA. Phone: 978-535-8288. http://www.holocaustcenterbn.org. e-mail: webadministrator@holocaustcenterbn.org.

Holocaust Center of Northern California. 639 14th Avenue, San Francisco, CA 94118-3052, USA. Phone: 415-751-6040 and 415-751-6041. FAX: 415-751-6735. http://www.holocaust-sf.org. e-mail: educ@holocaust-sf.org.

Holocaust Center of the United Jewish Federation of Greater Pittsburgh. 5738 Darlington Road, Pittsburgh, PA 15217, USA. Phone: 412-421-1500. FAX: 412-422-1996. http://www.ujf.net. e-mail: information@ujf.net.

Holocaust Child Survivors of Connecticut, Inc. 243 Quarry Road, Stamford, CT 06903, USA. Phone: 203-322-7886. FAX: 203-329-3246. e-mail: hscheraga@aol.com.

Holocaust Commission of the United Federation of Tidewater. UJFT 5029 Corporate Woods Drive, Suite 225, Virginia Beach, VA 23462, USA. Phone: 757-671-1600. FAX: 757-671-7613. http://www.holocaustcommission.org. e-mail: betsyk@ujft.org.

Holocaust Education Center of the Delaware Valley. Goodwin Holocaust Museum, Weinberg Jewish Community Campus, 1301 Springdale Road, Cherry Hill, NJ 08003, USA. Phone: 856-751-9500, ext. 249. FAX: 856-751-1697. http:// mpdn.org/goodwin/holocaust_museum.htm. e-mail: arespler1@aol.com.

Holocaust Education Foundation, Inc. Holocaust Teacher Resource Center, PO Box 6153, Newport News, VA 23606-6153, USA. Phone: 757-930-2124. FAX: 757-930-9555. http://www.Holocaust-trc.org. e-mail: info@Holocaust-trc.org.

Holocaust-Era Assets Records Project. National Archives and Records Administration, 8601 Adelphi Road, Room 2608, College Park, MD 20740-6001, USA. Phone: 301-713-7250, ext. 245. FAX: 301-713-6907. http://www.nara.gov/research/assets. e-mail: james.bradsher@arch2.nara.gov.

Holocaust Genocide Education Center. West Chester University, West Chester, PA 19383, USA. Phone: 610-436-2789. FAX: 610-436-3069. http:// www.wcupa.edu/_academics/holocaust. e-mail: ishur@wcupa.edu.

Holocaust and Genocide Resource Center—William Paterson University. 300 Pompton Road, Wayne, NJ 07470, USA. Phone: 973-720-3429 and 973-720-3456. FAX: 973-725-3522. http://www.wpunj.edu/~library/currmats/holo.htm. e-mail: pstein22@aol.com.

Holocaust-Genocide Studies Project at Monroe Community College. 1000 East Henrietta Road, Rochester, NY 14623, USA. Phone: 716-292-3228. FAX: 716-292-3321. e-mail: sdobkin@monroecc.edu.

Holocaust Human Rights Center of Maine. PO Box 4645, Augusta, ME 04330-1664, USA. Phone: 207-993-2620. FAX: 207-993-2620. http://www.hhrc.org. e-mail: hhrc@juno.com.

Holocaust Memorial and Educational Center of Nassau County. Welwyn Preserve, 100 Crescent Beach Road, Glen Cove, NY 11542, USA. Phone: 516-571-8040. FAX: 516-571-8041. http://holocaust-nassau.org.

Holocaust Memorial Foundation of Illinois. 4255 West Main Street, Skokie, IL 60076-2063, USA. Phone: 847-677-4640. FAX: 847-677-4684. http://skokienet.org/ hrememoril/. e-mail: holmemil@flash.net.

Holocaust Memorial Resource and Education Center of Central Florida. 851 North Maitland Avenue, Maitland, FL 32751, USA. Phone: 407-628-0555. FAX: 407-628-1079. http://www.holocaustedu.org. e-mail: execdir@holocaustedu.org.

Holocaust Museum and Learning Center in Memory of Gloria Goldstein. 12 Millstone Campus Drive, St. Louis, MO 63146, USA. Phone: 314-432-0020. FAX: 314-432-1277. www.beaconsystems.com/BSI/Projects/Museums/Holocaust/ holocaust.html. e-mail: dreich@jfedstl.org.

Holocaust Museum and Resource Center of Scranton-Lackawanna Jewish Federation. 601 Jefferson, Avenue Scranton, PA 18510, USA. Phone: 570-961-2300. FAX: 570-346-6147. http://jfednepa.org/hmrc. e-mail: sljfhrc@epix.net.

Holocaust Outreach Center of Florida Atlantic University. 777 Glades Road, Boca Raton, FL 33431-0991, USA. Phone: 561-297-2929. FAX: 561-297-2925. http://www.fau.edu/divdept/coe/specfac/holocst.htm. e-mail: eheckler@fau.edu.

Holocaust Resource Center—Keene State College. Mason Library, Keene State College, 229 Main Street, Keene, NH 03435-3201, USA. Phone: 603-358-2490. FAX: 603-358-2745. http://www.keene.edu/cchs/default.htm. e-mail: pvincent@keene.edu.

Holocaust Resource Center—The Richard Stockton College of New Jersey. The Richard Stockton College, PO Box 195, Pomona, NJ 08240, USA. Phone: 609-652-4699. FAX: 609-748-5543. http://loki.stockton.edu/~holocaus/hrc.htm. e-mail: iaoprod446@stockton.edu.

Holocaust Resource Center and Archives—Queensborough Community College. 222-05 56th Avenue, Bayside, NY 11364, USA. Phone: 718-225-1617. FAX: 718-631-6306. e-mail: hrcaho@qcc.cuny.edu.

Holocaust Resource Center and West River Teacher Center—Dickinson State University. Dickinson State University, North Campus, 1679 6th Avenue, West Dickinson, ND 58601-4896, USA. Phone: 701-483-2166. FAX: 701-483-2028. http://www.dsu.nodak.edu/WRTC. e-mail: dsunorth@dsu.nodak.edu.

Holocaust Resource Center at the Allen and Joan Bildner Center for the Study of Jewish Life—Rutgers, The State University of New Jersey. Rutgers, The State University of New Jersey, 12 College Avenue, New Brunswick, NJ 08901, USA. Phone: 732-932-2033. FAX: 732-932-3052. http://www.rci.rutgers.edu/~jewishnb/. e-mail: csjl@rci.rutgers.edu.

Holocaust Resource Center of Buffalo. 1050 Maryvale Drive, Cheektowage, NY 14225, USA. Phone: 716-634-9535. FAX: 716-634-9625. http://www.holocaustcenterbuff.com. e-mail: hrcmail@holocaustcenterbuff.com_/_hrcl050@aol.com.

Holocaust Resource Center of the Jewish Federation of Greater Clifton-Passaic. 199 Scoles Avenue, Clifton, NJ 07012, USA. Phone: 201-777-7031. FAX: 201-777-6701.

Holocaust Resource Center of Kean University. Thompson Library, Second Floor, Kean University, Union, NJ 07083, USA. Phone: 908-527-3049. FAX: 908-629-7130. http://www.kean.edu/hrc/. e-mail: keanhrc@turbo.kean.edu.

Holocaust Resource Center of Oklahoma. PO Box 774, Edmond, OK 73083-0774, USA. Phone: 405-359-7987. FAX: 405-971-7625. http: www.hrcok.org. e-mail: HRCOK@aol.com.

Holocaust Survivors and Friends Education Center. 800 New Loudon Road, Suite 400, Latham, NY 12110, USA. Phone: 518-785-0035. FAX: 518-783-1557. http://www.holocausteducation.org. e-mail: hsfec@crisny.org.

HUC–JIR Center for Holocaust and Humanity Education. Hebrew Union College–Jewish Institute of Religion, 3101 Clifton Avenue, Cincinnati, OH 45220, USA. Phone: 513-221-1875, ext. 355. FAX: 513-221-1842. http://huc.edu/chhe. e-mail: chhe@huc.edu.

Institute for Holocaust and Genocide Studies at Raritan Valley Community College. Raritan Valley Community College, PO Box 3300, Somerville, New Jersey 08876-1265. Phone: 908-526-1200, ext. 8820. http://www.raritanval.edu/cce/Holocaust/Programs%20and%20Upcoming%20Events.html e-mail: tliscian@raritanval.edu.

Institute on the Holocaust and the Law. 18 West Caner Street, Huntington, NY 11743, USA. Phone: 631-549-5898. FAX: 631-549-1223. http://www.holocaustinstitute.org.

Interagency Group on Nazi Assets, U.S. Department of State. 2401 E Street NW, Washington, DC 20522, USA. Phone: 202-663-1123 and 301-713-7250. FAX: 202-663-1289. http://www.state.gov/www/regions/holocausthp.html.

International Bonhoeffer Society-English Language Section. c/o Department of Religion, La Salle University, Philadelphia, PA 19141-1199, USA. Phone: 215-951-1335. FAX: 215-951-1665. http: dbonhoeffer.org/ibsinfo.htm. e-mail: Kellyg@lasalle.edu.

March of Remembrance and Hope. c/o Holocaust Resource Center, Queensborough Community College, 222-05 56th Avenue, Bayside, NY 11364, USA. Phone: 718-225-1617. FAX: 718-631-6306. e-mail: hrcaho@qcc.cuny.edu.

International Network of Children of Jewish Holocaust Survivors. Florida International University, North Miami Campus—SC 130 3000 N.E. 151st Street, North Miami, FL 33181, USA. Phone: 305-919-5690. FAX: 305-919-5691. e-mail: xholocau@fiu.edu.

International Raoul Wallenberg Foundation. Rep. Off. 34 East 67th Street, 2nd Floor, New York, NY 10021, USA. Phone: 212-737-3275. FAX: 212-535-6262. http://www.raoul-wallenberg.org.ar. e-mail: Raoulwallenberg@34east67.com.

International Romani Union. PO Box 464, Wildwood, NJ 08260, USA. Phone: 609-522-2542, ext. 19. FAX: 609-729-7768.

International Study of Organized Persecution of Children (Sponsored by Development Research). 30 Soundview Lane, Sands Point, NY 11050, USA. Phone: 516-883-7135. FAX: 516-883-3850. e-mail: cdr@inx.net.

Jewish Foundation for the Righteous. 305 7th Avenue, 19th Floor, New York, NY 10001-6008, USA. Phone: 212-727-9955. FAX: 212-727-9956. http://www.jfr.org. e-mail: jfr@jfr.org.

The Jewish Heritage Project, Coordinating the National Initiative in the Literature of the Holocaust. 150 Franklin Street, #1W, New York, NY 10013, USA. Phone: 212-925-9067. FAX: 212-343-2553. e-mail: jhpffh@jps.net.

Jewish Teacher Resource Center. 3301 West Front Street. Harrisburg, PA 17110, USA. Phone: 717-236-9555. FAX: 717-236-2552. http://www. hbgjewishcommunity.com/beta/jcc/ujc/services/teacher_resources.htm.

Julius and Dorothy Koppelman Holocaust/Genocide Resource Center. Rider University, 2083 Lawrenceville Road, Lawrenceville, NJ 08648, USA. Phone: 609-896-5345. FAX: 609-895-5684. http://www.rider.edu/holctr. e-mail: holctr@rider.edu.

Kindertransport Association. 36 Dean Street, Hicksville, NY 11801, USA. Phone: 516-938-6084. FAX: 516-827-3329. http://www.kindertransport.org. e-mail: margkurt@aol.com.

Leo Baeck Institute—United States. 129 East 73rd Street, New York, NY 10021, USA. Phone: 212-744-6400. FAX: 212-988-1305. http://www.lbi.org/. e-mail: lbaeck@lbi.cjh.org.

Lillian and A.J. Weinberg Center for Holocaust Education of the William Breman Jewish Heritage Museum. Selig Center, 1440 Spring Street, Atlanta, GA 30309, USA. Phone: 404-870-1872. FAX: 404-881-4009. http://www. atlantajewishmuseum.org/holocaust.html. e-mail: csinger@atljf.com.

Midwest Center for Holocaust Education. 5801 West 115th Street, Suite 106, Shawnee Mission, KS 66211-1800, USA. Phone: 913-327-8190. FAX: 913-327-8193. http://www.mchekc.org. e-mail: info@mchekc.org.

National Association of Jewish Holocaust Survivors, Inc. (NAHOS). PO Box 670125, Station C, Main Street, Flushing, NY 11367, USA. Phone: 718-380-5576 and 718-998-4307. FAX: 718-820-0859. e-mail: nahos@hotmail.com.

National Catholic Center for Holocaust Education. Seton Hill Drive, Greensburg, PA 15601, USA. Phone: 724-830-1033. FAX: 724-834-2752. http://www.setonhill.edu/~holocst/. e-mail: ncche@setonhill.edu.

Nazi War Criminal Records Interagency Working Group. National Archives and Records Administration, 8601 Adelphi Road, College Park, MD 20740, USA. Phone: 301-713-7230, ext. 231. FAX: 301-713-6907. http://www.nara.gov/iwg. e-mail: alic@nara.gov.

New York Public Library. Dorot Jewish Division, Fifth Avenue and 42nd Street, Room 84, New York, NY 10018, USA. Phone: 212-930-0601. FAX: 212-642-0141. http://www.nypl.org. e-mail: freidus@nypl.org.

The 1939 Club. 8950 West Olympic Boulevard, #437, Beverly Hills, CA 90211, USA. Phone: 310-491-7802. http://www.1939club.com. e-mail: info@1939club.com.

North American Friends of AMCHA-Israel, Inc. Seven Penn Plaza, Suite 1600, New York, NY 10001, USA. Phone: 800-335-9731 and 212-330-6054. FAX: 212-643-1951. http://www.amcha.org. e-mail: amcha@amcha.org.

North Carolina Council on the Holocaust. Department of Health and Human Services, 201 Blair Drive, Room 141, Raleigh, NC 27603, USA. Phone: 919-733-2173. FAX: 919-733-7447. http://www.dhhs.state.nc.us/holocaustcouncil. e-mail: bennie.hollers@ncmail.net.

Ohio Council on Holocaust Education. 314 Satterfield Hall, Kent State University, Kent, OH 44242, USA. Phone: 330-672-2389. FAX: 330-672-4009.

Oregon Holocaust Resource Center. Pacific University, Warner #25, 2043 College Way, Forest Grove, OR 97116, USA. Phone: 503-359-2930. FAX: 503-359-2246. http://nellie.pacificu.edu/ohrc. e-mail: ohrc@pacificu.edu.

International Gay and Lesbian Human Rights Commission. IGLHRC, 1360 Mission Street, Suite 200, San Francisco, CA 94103, USA. Phone: 415-255-8680. FAX: 415-255-8662. http://www.iglhrc.org. e-mail: iglhrc@iglhrc.org.

Robert F. Wagner Labor Archives. Tamiment Institute Library, New York University, 70 Washington Square South, 10th Floor, New York, NY 10012, USA. Phone: 212-998-2640 and 212-998-2636. http://www.nyu.edu/library/bobst/research/tam/. e-mail: Peter.Filardo@nyu.edu.

Rosenthal Institute for Holocaust Studies—CUNY. Graduate School and University, Center City University of New York, 365 Fifth Avenue, Suite 5209, New York, NY 10016, USA. Phone: 212-642-2183. FAX: 212-642-1988. http://web.gc.cuny.edu/dept/cjstu/rosen.htm. e-mail: rbraham@gc.cuny.edu.

Ruth Sajerman Markowicz Holocaust Center of Greater Toledo. 6465 Sylvania Avenue, Sylvania, OH 43560, USA. Phone: 419-885-4485. FAX: 419-885-3207. e-mail: markow@msn.com.

Safe Haven, Inc. PO Box 846, Oswego, NY 123126, USA. Phone: 315-446-9434. FAX: 917-463-4117. http://www.syracuse.com/features/safehaven. e-mail: hegave@twcny.n.com.

Saint Cloud State University Center for Holocaust Education. Miller Center 235, 720 Fourth Avenue South, Saint Cloud, MN 56301-4498, USA. Phone: 320-255-4205. FAX: 320-255-4097. e-mail: holocaustct@stcloudstate.edu.

Seidman Educational Resource Center of the Auerbach Central Agency. 7607 Old York Road, Melrose Park, PA 19027, USA. Phone: 215-635-8940. FAX: 215-635-8946. http://www.acaje.org. e-mail: info@acaje.org.

Society of Survivors of the Riga Ghetto, Inc. PO Box 1034, Riverdale, NY 10471, USA. Phone: 718-543-2655 and 914-235-6427. FAX: 914-636-3100.

Sonoma State University Holocaust Studies Center. 1801 East Cotati Avenue, Rohnert Park, CA 94928, USA. Phone: 707-664-4076. FAX: 707-664-3920. e-mail: centerh@sonoma.edu.

South Carolina Council on the Holocaust. 1429 Senate Street, 801 Rutledge Building, Columbia, SC 29201, USA. Phone: 803-734-0322. FAX: 803-734-6142. e-mail: mwalden@richland2.org.

Southern Institute for Education and Research at Tulane University. Tulane University MR, Box 1692, 31 McAlister Drive, New Orleans, LA 70118-5555, USA. Phone: 504-865-6100. FAX: 504-862-8957. http://www.tulane.edu/~so-inst. e-mail: lhill@mailhost.tcs.tulane.edu.

State of New Jersey Commission on Holocaust Education. 100 Riverview Place, PO Box 500, Trenton, NJ 08625, USA. 609-292-9274. FAX: 609-292-1211. http://www.state.nj.us/njded/holocaust. e-mail: holocaus@doe.state.nj.us.

The Stuart S. Elenko Collection Holocaust Museum and Studies Center. Bronx High School of Science, 75 West 205th Street, Bronx, NY 10468, USA. Phone: 718-367-5252. FAX: 718-796-2421. http://www.bxscience.edu/organizations/holocaust. e-mail: shoah@bxscience.edu.

Survivors of the Shoah Visual History Foundation. PO Box 3168, Los Angeles, CA 90078-3168, USA. Phone: 888-241-0772 and 818-777-7802. FAX: 818-866-3766. http://www.vhf.org. e-mail: educational resources@vhf.org.

Tennessee Commission on Holocaust Education. 2417 West End Avenue, c/o Vanderbilt University, Nashville, TN 37240, USA. Phone: 615-343-2563 and 615-343-1171. FAX: 615-343-8355. http://www. tennesseeholocaustcommission. org. e-mail: ruth.k.tanner@vanderbilt.edu.

Terezin Chamber Music Foundation. Astor Station, PO Box 206, Boston, MA 02123-0206, USA. Phone: 617-730-8998. FAX: 617-730-8998. http://www.terezinmusic.org. e-mail: info@terezinmusic.org.

Thanks to Scandinavia. 165 East 56th Street, New York, NY 10022, USA. Phone: 212-751-4000, ext. 403. FAX: 212-838-2120. http://www.thankstoscandinavia.org. e-mail: tts@ajc.org.

Warsaw Ghetto Resistance Organization (WAGRO). 122 West 30th Street, New York, NY 10001, USA. Phone: 212-239-4230. FAX: 212-279-2926. e-mail: mail@americangathering.org.

Washington State Holocaust Education Resource Center. 2031 Third Avenue, Seattle, WA 98121, USA. Phone: 206-441-5747. FAX: 206-956-0881. http://www.wsherc.org. e-mail: info@wsherc.org.

Watch Tower Society. Public Affairs Office of Jehovah's Witnesses, 25 Columbia Heights, Brooklyn, NY 11201-2483, USA. Phone: 718-560-5600. FAX: 718-560-5619. http://www.watchtower.org. e-mail: pao@wtbts.org.

Westchester Holocaust Commission. 2900 Purchase Street, Purchase, NY 10577, USA. Phone: 914-696-0738. FAX: 914-696-0843. e-mail: whc@bestweb.net.

West Virginia Holocaust Education Commission. PO Box 1125, Morgantown, WV 26507, USA. Phone: 304-291-3732. FAX: 304-292-0095.

World Federation of Bergen-Belsen Survivors. PO Box 288, Lenox Hill Station, New York, NY 10021, USA. Phone: 212-385-6022. FAX: 212-318-6176.

World Jewish Congress. 501 Madison Avenue–17th Floor, New York, NY 10022, USA. Phone: 212-755-5770. FAX: 212-755-5883. http://www.wjc.org.il. e-mail: wjc@netvision.net.il.

YIVO Institute for Jewish Research. The Center for Jewish History, 15 West 16th Street, New York, NY 10011-6301, USA. Phone: 212-246-6080. FAX: 212-292-1892. http://www.yivoinstitute.org. e-mail: yivomail@yivo.cjh.org.

Uruguay

Centro Recordatorio del Holocaust Sociedad Amigos de Yad Vashem (Holocaust Memorial Center, Friends of Yad Vashem). Canelones 1084, Piso 3, Montevideo 11100, Uruguay. Phone: (598) 2-902-5750, ext. 124. FAX: (598) 2-203-1746. e-mail: benvin@redfacil.com.uy.

Appendix

GENERAL DISTRIBUTORS AND VENDORS

Schoen Books
7 Sugarloaf Street
South Deerfield, MA 01373
Phone: 413-665-0066
http://www.schoenbooks.com.

Social Studies School Service
10200 Jefferson Boulevard
Room 171
P.O. Box 802
Culver City, CA 90232-0802
Phone: 800-421-4246
http://socialstudies.com.

Tara Publications
8 Music Fair Road, Suite I
Owings Mills, MD 21117
Phone: 410-654-0880
http://www.tara.com.

**Transcontinental Music Publications/
New Jewish Music Press**
633 Third Avenue
New York, NY 10017-6778
Phone: 800-455-5223
http://uahc.org.

**U.S. Holocaust Memorial Museum
Shop**
100 Raoul Wallenberg Place SW
Washington, DC 20024
Phone: 800-259-9998
http://www.holocaustbooks.org.

**Yad Vashem Martyrs' and Heroes'
Remembrance Authority**
PO Box 3477
Jerusalem 91034, Israel
Phone: 972 2-654-1334
FAX 972 2-643-3511
e-mail: edu@yadvashem.org.il.
http://www.yadvashem.org.il.

AUTHOR, COMPOSER, AND PERFORMER INDEX

TITLE INDEX

SUBJECT INDEX

About the Author

WILLIAM R. FERNEKES is supervisor of social studies at Hunterdon Central Regional High School. Co-author with Beverly C. Edmonds of *Children's Rights: A Reference Handbook* (1996), he has published widely in the fields of Holocaust and genocide studies, human rights education, and social studies education. He has served as a consultant to the Education Department of the U.S. Holocaust Memorial Museum, the New Jersey Commission on Holocaust Education, and numerous other scholarly institutions.